MONSTERS
OF THE
DEEP

NICK REDFERN

ABOUT THE AUTHOR

 Nick Redfern works full time as an author, lecturer, and journalist. He writes about a wide range of unsolved mysteries, including Bigfoot, UFOs, the Loch Ness Monster, alien encounters, and government conspiracies. His many books include *Control, Assassinations, The Alien Book, The Zombie Book, The Bigfoot Book, The Monster Book, Cover-Ups & Secrets, Area 51, Secret History, Secret Societies, and The New World Order Book*. He writes regularly for *Mysterious Universe*. He has appeared on numerous television shows, including History Channel's *Monster Quest, Ancient Aliens,* and *UFO Hunters*; VH1's *Legend Hunters*; National Geographic Channel's *The Truth about UFOs* and *Paranatural*; the BBC's *Out of this World*; MSNBC's *Countdown*; and SyFy Channel's *Proof Positive*. Nick lives just a few miles from Dallas, Texas' infamous Grassy Knoll and can be contacted at his blog: http://nickredfernfortean.blogspot.com.

MONSTERS
OF THE
DEEP

NICK REDFERN

OTHER VISIBLE INK PRESS BOOKS BY NICK REDFERN

ALSO FROM VISIBLE INK PRESS

Real Monsters, Gruesome Critters, and Beasts from the Darkside
by Brad Steiger and Sherry Hansen Steiger
ISBN: 978-1-57859-220-3

Real Vampires, Night Stalkers, and Creatures from the Darkside
by Brad Steiger
ISBN: 978-1-57859-255-5

Real Zombies, the Living Dead, and Creatures of the Apocalypse
by Brad Steiger
ISBN: 978-1-57859-296-8

The Sci-Fi Movie Guide: The Universe of Film from Alien to Zardoz
by Chris Barsanti
ISBN: 978-1-57859-503-7

The Spirit Book: The Encyclopedia of Clairvoyance, Channeling, and Spirit Communication (ebook)
by Raymond Buckland
ISBN: 978-1-57859-172-5

Supernatural Gods: Spiritual Mysteries, Psychic Experiences, and Scientific Truths
by Jim Willis
ISBN: 978-1-57859-660-7

The UFO Dossier: 100 Years of Government Secrets, Conspiracies, and Cover-Ups
by Kevin D. Randle
ISBN: 978-1-57859-564-8

Unexplained! Strange Sightings, Incredible Occurrences, and Puzzling Physical Phenomena, 3rd edition
by Jerome Clark
ISBN: 978-1-57859-344-6

The Vampire Book: The Encyclopedia of the Undead, 3rd edition
by J. Gordon Melton
ISBN: 978-1-57859-281-4

The Werewolf Book: The Encyclopedia of Shape-Shifting Beings, 2nd edition
by Brad Steiger
ISBN: 978-1-57859-367-5

The Witch Book: The Encyclopedia of Witchcraft, Wicca, and Neo-paganism
by Raymond Buckland
ISBN: 978-1-57859-114-5

"REAL NIGHTMARES" E-BOOKS BY BRAD STEIGER

Book 1: *True and Truly Scary Unexplained Phenomenon*

Book 2: *The Unexplained Phenomena and Tales of the Unknown*

Book 3: *Things That Go Bump in the Night*

Book 4: *Things That Prowl and Growl in the Night*

Book 5: *Fiends That Want Your Blood*

Book 6: *Unexpected Visitors and Unwanted Guests*

Book 7: *Dark and Deadly Demons*

Book 8: *Phantoms, Apparitions, and Ghosts*

Book 9: *Alien Strangers and Foreign Worlds*

Book 10: *Ghastly and Grisly Spooks*

Book 11: *Secret Schemes and Conspiring Cabals*

Book 12: *Freaks, Fiends, and Evil Spirits*

PLEASE VISIT US AT VISIBLEINKPRESS.COM

Acknowledgments

I would like to offer my very sincere thanks to my tireless agent and agent, Lisa Hagan, and to everyone at Visible Ink Press, and particularly Roger Jänecke and Kevin Hile.

MONSTERS OF THE DEEP

Copyright © 2021 by Visible Ink Press®

This publication is a creative work fully protected by all applicable copyright laws, as well as by misappropriation, trade secret, unfair competition, and other applicable laws.

No part of this book may be reproduced in any form without permission in writing from the publisher, except by a reviewer who wishes to quote brief passages in connection with a review written for inclusion in a magazine, newspaper, or website.

All rights to this publication will be vigorously defended.

Visible Ink Press®
43311 Joy Rd., #414
Canton, MI 48187-2075

Visible Ink Press is a registered trademark of Visible Ink Press LLC.

Most Visible Ink Press books are available at special quantity discounts when purchased in bulk by corporations, organizations, or groups. Customized printings, special imprints, messages, and excerpts can be produced to meet your needs. For more information, contact Special Markets Director, Visible Ink Press, www.visibleink.com, or 734-667-3211.

Managing Editor: Kevin S. Hile
Art Director: John Gouin
Typesetting: Marco Divita
Proofreaders: Christa Brelin and Shoshana Hurwitz
Indexer: Larry Baker

Cover images: stock.adobe.com.

ISBN: 978-1-57859-705-5

Cataloging-in-Publication Data is on file at the Library of Congress.

Printed in the United States of America.

10 9 8 7 6 5 4 3 2 1

Contents

OCEAN CREATURES

NESSIE AND NESSIE-LIKE MONSTERS

ROTHER INLAND WATER MONSTERS

DRAGONS AND WURMS

SNAKES AND EELS

CREATURES INHABITING CAVES, TUNNELS, AND SEWERS

WATER GODS, SPIRITS, AND MYTHOLOGICALS

HUMANOIDS OF THE WATER

REPTILIANS AND ALIEN INFLUENCES

THEORIES

PHOTO SOURCES

Abbasi1111: p. 338.

Tim Bertelink: p. 297.

Bibliotekarin (Wikicommons): p. 199.

Cave Junction, USA: p. 288.

Centre for Fortean Zoology: pp. 124, 170.

Chiswick Chap (Wikicommons): p. 48.

Tony Corsini: p. 145.

Emöke Dénes: p. 299.

Drw25 (Wikicommons): p. 273.

Dieter Florian: p. 153.

GerardM (Wikicommons): p. 207.

GeShaFish (Wikicommons): p. 181.

Salvor Gissurardottir: p. 205.

Illustrated London News Ltd./Mary Evans Picture Library: p. 58.

Juhauski72 (Wikicommons): p. 210.

Kallerna (Wikicommons): p. 254.

Lynne Kirton: p. 82.

Frederic A. Lucas: p. 137.

Mary Evans Picture Library: pp. 324, 329.

Rolf Müller: p. 284.

Muséum de Toulouse, France: p. 115.

Museum Kunstpalast, Germany: p. 226.

National Oceanic and Atmospheric Administration: p. 43.

Natural History of Norway (1755): p. 18.

New York Public Library Archives: p. 23.

Nuno Nogueira: p. 293.

Rickard Olsson: p. 177.

Oxford Dictionary of National Biography: p. 9.

The Penny Illustrated Paper and Illustrated Times: p. 29.

Sea Monsters Unmasked (1884): p. 33.

Seth J (Wikicommons): p. 332.

Shutterstock: pp. 3, 6, 36, 41, 51, 53, 55, 69, 71, 77, 80, 85, 88, 89, 93, 94, 96, 105, 111, 113, 121, 130, 133, 139, 141, 142, 146, 148, 150, 164, 168, 192, 196, 202, 215, 219, 229, 232, 235, 238, 241, 242, 256, 260, 267, 269, 276, 280, 281, 290, 292, 307, 315, 318, 334.

William Leo Smith: p. 91.

Aaron Sneddon: p. 66.

Ryan Somma: p. 119.

Tfa4freedom (Freedom Festival; Wikicommons): p. 271.

University of Augsburg, Germany: p. 21.

U.S. Geological Survey: p. 341.

U.S. Government: p. 257.

Yale Peabody Museum of Natural History: p. 31.

Public domain: pp. 5, 11, 13, 15, 25, 39, 62, 73, 84, 102, 103, 109, 160, 174, 175, 179, 185, 188, 217, 245, 248, 252, 263, 300, 304.

Introduction

The word "Zoology" is defined by the *Environmental Science* website as "the study of animals and their behavior. Zoologists may study a particular species or group of species, either in the wild or in captivity. Zoologists study animals and their interactions with ecosystems. They study their physical characteristics, diets, behaviors, and the impacts humans have on them. They study all kinds of animals, both in their natural habitats and in captivity in zoos and aquariums. They may specialize in studying a particular animal or animal group."

Just about all zoologists would fully agree with that statement. The book that you are about to read, however, is focused upon animals that the world of mainstream zoology has very little time for and which are very far removed from the domain of zoology. Indeed, they fall into a totally different category: it goes by the title of cryptozoology. Within its many and varied numbers are the chupacabra, the abominable snowman, and mothman. This book, however, focuses on strange and bizarre creatures that may be significantly different to each other and that science decries, but they all have one important thing in common: they all live in the water at least part of the time.

We are talking about lake monsters (such as the famous Loch Ness monster of Scotland, Ogopogo, and Champ), sea serpents, massive eels, the origins and myths surrounding mermaids, the mighty kraken, giant octopi, and oversized and deadly squids. Real-life equivalents of H. P. Lovecraft's near-legendary creation, Cthulhu; snakes in excess of forty-feet in length; and even man-beasts not at all unlike the deadly monster in the 1954 movie *Creature from the Black Lagoon* are part and parcel of the creepy, eerie equation.

In addition, you will learn that some so-called monsters of the deep may not be modern creatures at all. Rather, they might be surviving relics of animals that were presumed to have gone belly-up millions of years ago—even tens of millions of years ago. In other words, some of them might be survivors from millions of years ago when mosasaurs and plesiosaurs swam Earth's waters. A scenario akin to a real-life *Jurassic Park*? Incredibly, that just might be the case. In our arrogance, we believe that we know just about all there is to know about our world. Wrong. The fact is that we don't know much at all. The beasts that I'm talking about may be swimming through the deeper parts of our seas and oceans right now. Or they just might be in your local lake, watching you through a pair of beady, penetrating eyes.

And on the matter of *Jurassic Park*, let us end this introduction with a story that well and truly sets the scene for what is to come ahead: the discovery of an ancient fish that was assumed to be extinct. Those assumptions were incredibly wrong. Against all of the odds, it survived for millions of years after it was presumed long dead. It's a story that prompts an important question: if one such creature can survive across a periods of tens of millions of years, then how many others could do likewise? The answer could be surprising. Now, let us get to the heart of the story.

The keepers of the Smithsonian's website states: "Coelacanths (seel-a-canths) were once known only from fossils and were thought to have gone extinct approximately 65 million years ago (mya), during the great extinction in which the dinosaurs disappeared. The most recent fossil record dates from about 80 mya but the earliest records date back as far as approximately 360 mya. At one time coelacanths were a large group comprising about 90 valid species that were distributed worldwide in both marine and freshwaters. Today, there are two known living species."

It is very important to note that the coelacanth is not a tiny, blink-and-you'll-miss-it type of fish. Rather, it grows to lengths of six-and-a-half-feet in length. An adult coelacanth can weigh up to 175 pounds. And, yet, for so long they remained completely and utterly undetected. The *Sea and Sky* website provide us this information on this legendary and amazing fish: "Fossils of the coelacanth have been found that date back over 350 million years. But, against all odds, in 1938, a fisherman actually caught a live coelacanth off the coast of South Africa. A second specimen was captured in 1952 off the coast of the Comoros Islands off the eastern coast of Africa near Madagascar. Needless to say, this caused a sensation throughout the scientific community. Since then, live coelacanths have been sighted and photographed many times in the wild."

The U.S. government's National Oceanic and Atmospheric Administration (NOAA) has a deep interest in the coelacanth, stating and stressing these words: "The coelacanth has several unique physical features. Most notably are its paired lobe fins that extend away from the body and move in an alternating pattern. The body of the fish appears iridescent dark blue in film or video footage but under natural light the color is light brown with white blotches throughout that have been used for individual identification. They also have thick, armor-like scales and a unique joint at the back of the skull that allows them to open their upper and lower jaws at the same time. The coelacanth is a slow drift-hunter and eats a variety of benthic and epi-benthic prey, such as cephalopods, eels, cuttlefish, and deep-water fishes."

NOAA continues with its background on the coelacanth: "The Tanzanian distinct population segment of African coelacanth lives among deep, rocky terraces comprised of sedimentary limestone. In this habitat, coelacanths are thought to use submarine cavities and shelves that have eroded out of the limestone composite for shelter between 230 to 460 feet in depth and in temperatures around 68°F. The average lifespan of coelacanths is estimated to be 48 years of age. Female coelacanths reach maturity between 16 and 19 years and give birth to live young after a very lengthy gestation period of 3 years, which is the longest gestation period of any vertebrate species."

NOAA concludes: "Historically, fisheries bycatch has been the most significant threat to the coelacanth. The Tanzanian distinct population segment in particular is subject to bycatch in the Tanzanian shark gillnet fishery, which has been expanding over the last decade. The Tanzanian distinct population segment may experience direct habitat loss due to deep-water port construction, including submarine blasting and channel dredging known to occur in coelacanth habitat."

You may wonder why I focus so much in this introduction on the coelacanth. The answer is important: apart from finding fossilized remains of this still somewhat mysterious fish, no one had ever seen a coelacanth until 1938. No sightings. No photographs. No incredible tales from sailors on the high seas. And, yet, for all that time the fish were living very comfortably off the coast of South Africa. What this shows is that relatively large fish (and in large amounts, too) can exist—privately, even—in our world without being found a very long time. Perhaps the coelacanth is not a solitary case. One day, quite out of the blue, we might very well come across something else that was presumed extinct but that turns out not to be gone after all. And, maybe, it won't be just one case.

The waters of our world are both expansive and deep; they can easily hold amazing secrets. As you will now see....

OCEAN CREATURES

Any mention of monsters of the oceans instills in the mind imagery of giant, long-necked monsters. They are famously known as sea serpents. The nineteenth century was the period when fascination for sea serpents was at its peak—and when sightings were at their peak, too. We should be aware, though, that there were far more than just endless sightings, and it wasn't all about sea serpents. Sailors told of giant octopi—and huge squids—rearing out of the waters and plucking their terrified comrades from the decks of ships and dragging them into the ocean depths. Real-life rivals to H. P. Lovecraft's almost legendary creation Cthulhu are said to swim the lower levels of our oceans. The huge, octopus-like kraken of Scandinavian lore terrified seafarers for centuries. I share the above with you to demonstrate the amazing variety of monsters that will soon be coming your way.

TALES OF NINETEENTH-CENTURY SEA SERPENTS

Sea serpents have been seen in numerous and varied areas of our world. It's rare that they are seen more than once in the same locale, but it's not unheard of. For example, the port of Gloucester, Massachusetts, was the site of repeated encounters with massive, dangerous leviathans in the early seventeenth century. From a man named John Josselyn, recounted in the 1638 work *From an Account of Two Voyages to New England*, we have these words to muse upon: "They told me of a sea serpent, or snake, that lay quoiled [sic] up like a cable upon the rock at Cape Ann; a boat passing by with English on board, and two Indians, they would have shot the serpent, but the Indians dissuaded them, saying that if he were not killed outright, they would all be in danger of their lives."

Obadiah Turner, in the same time frame, stated of the creature in old English style:

> Some being on ye great beache gathering of calms and seaweed wch had been cast thereon by ye mightie storm did spy a most wonderful serpent a shorte way off from ye shore. He was big round in ye thickest part as a wine pipe; and they do affirm that he was fifteen fathoms more in length. A most wonderful tale. But ye witnesses be credible, and it would be of no account to them to tell an untrue tale. Wee have likewise heard yt Cape Ann ye people have seene a monster like unto this, whch did there come out of ye land mch to ye terror of them yt did see him.

It should be stressed that the nineteenth century was a period in which sea serpents were really in their element, we might say. From August 10, 1817, we have the following notable report from Amos Story:

> It was between the hours of twelve and one o'clock when I first saw him, and he continued in sight for an hour and a half. I was setting on the shore, and was about twenty rods from him when he was the nearest to me. His head appeared shaped much like that of the sea turtle, and he carried his head from ten to twelve inches above the surface of the water. His head at that distance appeared larger than the head of any dog I ever saw. From the back of his head to the next part of him that was visible, I should judge to be three or four feet. He moved very rapidly through the water, I should say a mile or two, or at most, in three minutes. I saw no bunches on his back. On this day, I did not see more than ten or twelve feet of his body.

Story's account was followed within the week by that of Solomon Allen III, a shipmaster. He said of the incredible beast he spied: "His head formed something like the head of a rattlesnake, but nearly as large as the head of horse. When he moved on the surface of the water his motion was slow, at times playing in circles, and sometimes moving straight forward."

A particularly detailed account came days later from one Cheever Felch, whose sighting of the Gloucester sea serpent was made when Felch was aboard a U.S. schooner, the *Science*. He said of the monstrous thing:

> His color is dark brown with white under his throat. His size we could not accurately ascertain, but his head is about three feet in circumference, flat and much smaller than his body. We did not

Descriptions of sea monsters from centuries past showed them in all shapes and sizes, all of them terrifying.

see his tail; but from the end of the head to the farthest protuberance was not far from one hundred feet. I speak with a degree of certainty, behind much accustomed to measure and estimate distances and length. I counted fourteen bunches on his back, the first one, say, ten or twelve feet from this head, and the others about seven feet apart. They decreased in size towards the tail. These bunches were sometimes counted with and sometimes without a glass. Mr. Malborne counted thirteen, Mr. Blake thirteen and fourteen, and the boatman the same number.... His motion was partly vertical and partly horizontal, like that of freshwater snakes. I have been much acquainted with snakes in our interior waters. His motion was the same.

And still, the reports kept on coming, as seafarer John Brown noted:

I discovered something about three or four miles distant, about two points on the weather bow, which appeared as a mast, as it rose and sunk in a perpendicular manner, once in about eight or ten minutes. I kept the vessel directly for it, and after look at it with my glass, I observed to my mate that it was a wreck, as I could see timbers sticking up, but as we approached nearer, I found what appeared like timbers to be a number of porpoises and black fish playing and jumping around a large Sea-Serpent, which we had supposed to be the mast.

While there certainly have been sightings of sea serpents in the waters of Gloucester since 1817, none of them—in terms of their frequency, number of witnesses, and credibility—has ever come close to matching those tumultuous, early nineteenth-century days when the people of Gloucester were plagued by a monster.

Then, there is an account that appeared in the *British Literary Gazette* on August 1, 1818. In an article called "The Great American Sea Serpent" from August 8, 2016, at the Library of Congress website, Stephanie Hall recounted that "Captain Joseph Woodward of the schooner *Adamant* reported an encounter off the coast of Cape Ann in May, 1818. He said he shot a cannon at the monster." In response to the shot, he said:

> The serpent shook its head and its tail in an extraordinary manner and advanced toward the ship with open jaws; I had caused the cannon to be reloaded, but he had come so near that all the crew were seized with terror, and we thought only of getting out of his way. He almost touched the vessel and, had I not tacked as I did, he would certainly have come on board. He dived, but in a moment we saw him come up again with his head on one side of the vessel and his tail on the other as if he was going to lift up and upset us. However we did not feel any shock. He remained five hours near us, only going backward and forward.

We'll now take a look at some particularly credible claims of encounters with monsters—cases that amazed and terrified the crews and passengers of ships and boats on the high seas. Notably, a number of such reports have been declassified under the terms of the United Kingdom's Freedom of Information Act of 2000. They demonstrate something remarkable and illuminating: namely, that highly credible sources had seen huge monsters of the oceans and were willing to attest to the truth of the amazing incidents. One such case can be found in the nineteenth-century-era archives of the Admiralty, or British Navy.

The first report that was declassified by government personnel dates back to May 9, 1830. The crew that had the amazing encounter were aboard the *Rob Roy*, a military craft navigating the Atlantic Ocean. Little did the crew know when the day began that they would soon come face-to-face with a terrifying monster of the mysterious depths. We have the captain of the ship,

The sea monster spotted at Cape Ann was originally reported in 1639 (as per this illustration of the sighting). It was also seen in 1818, according to Captain Joseph Woodward.

one James Stockdale, to thank for having the guts to inform senior naval personnel of the incredible creature that had been seen.

I will now share with you the unedited words of Captain Stockdale:

About five P.M. all at once while I was walking on the poop my attention was drawn to the water on the port bow by a scuffling noise. Likewise, all the watch on deck were drawn to it. Judge my amazement when what should stare us all in the face as if not knowing whether to come over the deck or to go around the stern—but the great big sea snake! Now I have heard of the fellow before—and I have killed snakes twenty-four feet long in the straits of Malacca, but they would go in his mouth.

I think he must have been asleep for we were going along very softly two knots an hour, and he seemed as much alarmed as we were—and all taken aback for about fifteen seconds. But he soon was underway and, when fairly off, his head was square with our topsail and his tail was square with the foremast.

My ship is 171 feet long overall—and the foremast is 42 feet from the stern which would make the monster about 129 feet long. If I had not seen it I could not have believed it but there was no mistake or doubt of its length—for the brute was so close I could even smell his nasty fishy smell.

Documents from the *Rob Roy* incident contained testimony from witnesses of an enormous, serpentlike creature with a large head and a kind of ruff or fringe around its neck.

When underway he carried his head about six feet out of water—with a fin between the shoulders about two feet long. I think he was swimming about five miles an hour—for I watched him from the topsail yard till I lost sight of him in about fifty minutes. I hope never to see him more. It is enough to frighten the strong at heart.

The report of Captain Stockdale and his crew was not the only one that ended up in U.K. military files. Another was dated December 13, 1857. Commander George Henry Harrington was so impressed—and worried—by an extraordinary sighting that he quickly put together a full report on the encounter with the giant beast. It reads like this:

While myself and officers were standing on the lee side of the poop—looking toward the island—we were startled by the sight of a huge marine animal which reared its head out of the water within twenty yards of the ship—when it suddenly disappeared for about half a minute and then made a reappearance in the same manner again—showing us its neck and head about ten or twenty feet out of the water.

Its head was shaped like a long buoy—and I should suppose the diameter to have been seven or eight feet in the largest part with a kind of scroll or ruff encircling it about two feet from the top. The water was discolored for several hundred feet from the head, so much so that on its first appearance my impression was that the ship was in broken waters, produced, as I supposed, by some volcanic agency, since I passed the island before.

But the second appearance completely dispelled those fears and assured us that it was a monster of extraordinary length and appeared to be moving slowly towards the land. The ship was going too fast to enable us to reach the masthead in time to form a correct estimate of this extreme length—but from what we saw from the deck we conclude that he must have been over two hundred feet long. The Boatswain and several of the crew, who observed it from the forecastle, state that it was more than double the length of the ship, in which case it must have been five hundred feet.

Captain Harrington signed off: "I am convinced that it belonged to the serpent tribe."

January 18, 1875, was the date on which yet another encounter with a massive monster occurred. The *Pauline* was a ship sailing about twenty miles from Cape São Roque, situated on the northeast side of Brazil. All was well until roughly eleven o'clock A.M. That's when the crew's world was turned upside down—not literally, thankfully! But it could have been exactly that, given the size of the monster. The master of the *Pauline* was George Drevar, someone who knew a monster when he saw it. He quickly wrote down the salient facts concerning what happened on that memorable day when a monster surfaced from the mysterious depths of the wild waters:

All was well until roughly eleven o'clock A.M. That's when the crew's world was turned upside down....

> The weather fine and clear, the wind and sea moderate. Observed some black spots on the water, and a whitish pillar, about thirty-five feet high, above them. At the first glance I took all to be breakers, as the sea was splashing up fountain-like about them, and the pillar, a pinnacle rock bleached with the sun; but the pillar fell with a splash, and a similar one rose. They rose and fell alternately in quick succession, and good glasses showed me it was a monster sea-serpent coiled twice round a large sperm whale.

> The head and tail parts, each about thirty feet long, were acting as levers, twisting itself and victim around with great velocity. They sank out of sight about every two minutes, coming to the surface still revolving, and the struggles of the whale and two other whales that were near, frantic with excitement, made the sea in this vicinity like a boiling cauldron; and a loud and confused noise was distinctly heard.

> This strange occurrence lasted some fifteen minutes, and finished with the tail portion of the whale being elevated straight in the air, then waving backwards and forwards, and lashing the water furiously in the last death-struggle, when the whole body disappeared from our view, going down head-foremost towards the bottom, where, no doubt, it was gorged at the serpent's leisure; and that monster of monsters may have been many months in a state of coma, digesting the huge mouthful.

> Then two of the largest sperm whales that I have ever seen moved slowly thence towards the vessel, their bodies more than usually elevated out of the water, and not spouting or making the least noise, but seeming quite paralyzed with fear; indeed, a cold shiver

went through my own frame on beholding the last agonizing struggle of the poor whale that had seemed as helpless in the coils of the vicious monster as a small bird in the talons of a hawk. Allowing for two coils round the whale, I think the serpent was about one hundred and sixty or one hundred and seventy feet long, and seven or eight in girth. It was in color much like a conger eel, and the head, from the mouth being always open, appeared the largest part of the body. I think Cape San Roque is a landmark for whales leaving the south for the North Atlantic.

> It scarcely needs saying ... that any kind of creature that had the ability and muscle power to coil itself around a sperm whale must have been a formidable and dangerous one.

I wrote thus far, little thinking I would ever see the serpent again; but at 7 A.M., July 13th, in the same latitude, and some eighty miles east of San Roque, I was astonished to see the same or a similar monster. It was throwing its head and about forty feet of its body in a horizontal position out of the water as it passed onwards by the stern of our vessel. I began musing why we were so much favored with such a strange visitor, and concluded that the band of white paint, two feet wide above the copper, might have looked like a fellow-serpent to it, and, no doubt, attracted its attention.

While thus thinking, I was startled by the cry of "There it is again," and a short distance to leeward, elevated some sixty feet in the air, was the great leviathan, grimly looking towards the vessel. As I was not sure it was only our free board it was viewing, we had all our axes ready, and were fully determined, should the brute embrace the *Pauline*, to chop away for its backbone with all our might, and the wretch might have found for once in its life that it had caught a Tartar. This statement is strictly true, and the occurrence was witnessed by my officers, half the crew, and myself; and we are ready, at any time, to testify on oath that it is so, and that we are not in the least mistaken. A vessel, about three years ago, was dragged over by some sea-monster in the Indian Ocean.

It scarcely needs saying (but I will do so anyway) that any kind of creature that had the ability and muscle power to coil itself around a sperm whale must have been a formidable and dangerous one. What, precisely, it was remains unknown. The oceans guard their secrets well.

The nineteenth century thus revealed numerous bizarre tales of the serpent kind. Significantly, a great many cases involved sources and witnesses who were willing to have their testimony revealed publicly. In other words, we are not talking about friend-of-a-friend, campfire types of stories. Rather, we are dealing with credible individuals who were more than happy to share their life-changing encounters. One such source was a Victorian-era naturalist named Philip Henry Gosse (1810–1888). From 1845 to 1846, Gosse, always one for wild adventures in exotic lands, explored much of the Caribbean. In doing so, he uncovered a story of a very strange animal that could maneuver on land as easily as it could in the water surrounding the Caribbean islands. Of the eye-opening story, which Gosse heard from a respected medical man, Gosse said: "He had seen, in 1829, a serpent about four feet in length, but of unwonted thickness, dull ochre in color with well-defined dark spots, having on its head a sort of pyramidal helmet, somewhat lobed at the summit, of a pale red hue. The animal, however, was dead, and decomposition was already setting in. He informed me that the Negroes of the district were well acquainted with it; and that they represented it as making a noise, not unlike the crowing of a cock, and being addicted to preying on poultry."

Gosse had a friend named Richard Hill who had also heard of this very odd beast from a Spanish acquaintance on Hispaniola. Those in the know said that it dwelled in the eastern regions of the island in what is now the Dominican Republic. Gosse said of Hill: "My friend's Spanish informant had seen the serpent with mandibles like a bird, with a cock's nest, with scarlet lobes or wattles; and he described its habits—perhaps from common fame rather than personal observation—as a frequenter of hen-roosts, into which it would thrust its head, and deceive the young chickens by its imitative physiognomy, and its attempts to crow."

Jasper Cargill was another of Gosse's sources. Of his in-person discussion with Cargill, Gosse reported: "When visiting Skibo, in St. George, an estate of [Cargill's] father's, in descending the mountain-road, his attention was drawn to a snake of dark hue that erected itself from some fragments of limestone rock that lay about. It was about four feet long and unusually thick bodied. His surprise was greatly increased on perceiving that it was crested, and that from the far side of its cheeks depended some red colored flaps, like gills or wattles. After gazing at him intently for some time, with its head well erect, it drew itself in, and disappeared among the fragmentary rocks."

Cargill's son succeeded in killing one of the strange animals just a few years later, as Gosse also reported:

British naturalist Phillip Henry Gosse was a noted marine biologist, author of popular books on natural science, and inventor of the saltwater aquarium. He recorded the stories of a number of sea monster witnesses.

Some youngsters of the town came running to tell me of a curious snake, unlike any snake they had ever seen before, which young Cargill had shot, when out for a day's sport in the woodlands of a neighbor. They described it as a serpent in all respects, but with a very curious shaped head, with wattles on each side of its jaws. After taking it in hand and looking at it, they placed it in a hollow tree, intending to return for it when they should be coming home, but they had strolled from the place so far that it was inconvenient to retrace their steps when wearied with rambling.

When the boys came back roughly twenty-four hours later, the weird creature was nowhere to be seen. Fortunately, however, that was not the end of the matter. Gosse came across the testimony of a man named Ulick Ramsay. Of Ramsay's story, Gosse put pen to paper and recorded that Ramsay "had seen in the hand of the barrack-master at the barracks of a Spanish town, a curious snake, which he, too, had shot among the rocks of a little line of eminences near the railway, about two miles out, called Craigallechie. It was a serpent with a curious shaped head, and projections on each side, which he likened to the fins of an eel, but said were close up to the jaws."

Truly, this was one of the strangest of all tales of animals that have a connection to both the oceans and the land. And let us not forget the eerie ability of the creature to mimic chickens! One has to wonder if the animals mimicked the cries of a chicken as a means to lure an unwary person—on the lookout for a tasty chicken dinner—into its domain and then slaughter the poor soul and dine upon him or her. A disturbing scenario, for sure.

We would not have all the data we have on sea serpents in the nineteenth century if it were not for the sterling work of Henry Lee. In the 1800s, Lee was at the forefront of research into the domain of massive serpents. Grace Constantino of the Biodiversity Heritage Library, writing for *Smithsonian* magazine on October 27, 2014, states of the sea creature legends: "Where did the accounts of monsters come from in the first place? Were they simply fairy tales invented to scare curious minds and small children? Henry Lee, who wrote extensively on sea creatures and monsters, emphasized that many classical monsters are not simply pure myth. In his publication *Sea Fables Explained* (1883), he wrote, '… the descriptions by ancient writers of so-called "fabulous creatures" are rather distorted portraits than invented falsehoods, and there is hardly any of the monsters of old which has not its prototype in Nature at the present day.'"

I'll share with you a number of incredible examples that came to Lee's attention and that he then brought to the attention of the media and the public, both eager for sensational tales of fabulous beasts. The first, from his book *Sea Monsters Unmasked*, begins as follows:

Gloucester Harbor in Massachusetts was the setting for an 1817 sighting of a sea serpent, according to testimony from eleven witnesses.

In 1817 a large marine animal, supposed to be a serpent, was seen at Gloucester Harbor, near Cape Ann, Massachusetts, about thirty miles from Boston. The Linnaean Society of New England investigated the matter, and took much trouble to obtain evidence thereon. The depositions of eleven credible witnesses were certified on oath before magistrates, one of whom had himself seen the creature, and who confirmed the statements. All agreed that the animal had the appearance of a serpent, but estimated its length, variously, at from fifty to a hundred feet. Its head was in shape like that of a turtle, or snake, but as large as the head of a horse. There was no appearance of a mane. Its mode of progressing was by vertical undulations; and five of the witnesses described it as having the hunched protuberances mentioned by Captain de Ferry and others. Of this, I can offer no zoological explanation. The testimony given was apparently sincere, but it was received with mistrust; for, as Mr. Gosse says, "owing to a habit prevalent in the United States of supposing that there is somewhat of wit in gross exaggeration or hoaxing invention, we do naturally look with a lurking suspicion on American statements when they describe unusual or disputed phenomena."

There was this account from Lee, too:

On the 15th of May, 1833, a party of British officers, consisting of Captain Sullivan, Lieutenants Maclachlan and Malcolm of the Rifle Brigade, Lieutenant Lister of the Artillery, and Mr. Ince of the Ordnance, whilst crossing [St.] Margaret's Bay in a small yacht, on their way from Halifax to Mahone Bay, "saw, at a distance of a hundred and fifty to two hundred yards, the head and neck of some denizen of the deep, precisely like those of a common snake in the act of swimming, the head so far elevated and thrown forward by the curve of the neck, as to enable them to see the water under and beyond it. The creature rapidly passed, leaving a regular wake, from the commencement of which to the fore part, which was out of water, they judged its length to be about eighty feet." They "set down the head at about six feet in length (considerably larger than that of a horse), and that portion of the neck which they saw at the same." There could be no mistake— no delusion, they say; "and we were all perfectly satisfied that we had been favored with a view of the true and veritable sea-serpent." This account was published in the *Zoologist*, in 1847, and at that date all the officers above named were still living.

Of a Norwegian tale, Lee wrote: "The venerable P. W. Deinbolt, Archdeacon of Molde, gives the following account of an incident that occurred there on the 28th of July, 1845." In Deinbolt's own words:

J. C. Lund, bookseller and printer; G. S. Krogh, merchant; Christian Flang, Lund's apprentice, and John Elgenses, labourer, were out on Romsdal-fjord, fishing. The sea was, after a warm, sunshiny day, quite calm. About seven o'clock in the afternoon, at a little distance from the shore, near the ballast place and Molde Hooe, they saw a long marine animal, which slowly moved itself forward, as it appeared to them, with the help of two fins, on the fore-part of the body nearest the head, which they judged by the boiling of the water on both sides of it.

The visible part of the body appeared to be between forty and fifty feet in length, and moved in undulations, like a snake. The body was round and of a dark color. As they discerned a waving motion in the water behind the animal, they concluded that part of the body was concealed under water. That it was one continuous animal they saw plainly from its movement.

When the animal was about one hundred yards from the boat, they noticed tolerably correctly its fore parts, which ended in a sharp snout; its colossal head raised itself above the water in the form of a semi-circle; the lower part was not visible. The color of the head was dark-brown and the skin smooth; they did not notice the eyes, or any mane or bristles on the throat.

When the serpent came about a musket-shot near, Lund fired at it, and was certain the shots hit it in the head. After the shot it dived but came up immediately. It raised its neck in the air, like a snake preparing to dart on his prey. After he had turned and got his body in a straight line, which he appeared to do with great difficulty, he darted like an arrow against the boat. They reached the shore, and the animal, perceiving it had come into shallow water, dived immediately and disappeared in the deep.

Such is the declaration of these four men, and no one has cause to question their veracity, or imagine that they were so seized with fear that they could not observe what took place so near them. There are not many here, or on other parts of the Norwegian coast, who longer doubt the existence of the sea serpent. The writer of this narrative was a long time skeptical, as he had not been so fortunate as to see this monster of the deep; but after the many accounts he has read, and the relations he has received from credible witnesses, he does not dare longer to doubt the existence of the sea-serpent.

There are also these amazing words from Lee, again from *Sea Monsters Unmasked*:

The next incident of the kind in point of date that we find recorded carries us back to the locality of which Pontoppidan wrote, and in which was seen the animal vouched for by Captain de Ferry. In 1847 there appeared in a London daily paper a long account translated from the Norse journals of fresh appearances of the sea-serpent. The statement made was, that it had recently been frequently seen in the neighborhood of Christiansand and Molde. In the large bight of the sea at Christiansand it had been seen every year, only in the warmest weather, and when the sea was perfectly calm, and the surface of the water unruffled.

Nineteenth-century mariners' accounts of sea monsters vary somewhat in their descriptions, but the creatures typically have long bodies and large heads. Other features, such as color, scales, fringes, limbs, and so on, have varied.

The evidence of three respectable persons was taken, namely, Nils Roe, a workman at Mr. William Knudtzon's, who saw it twice there, John Johnson, merchant, and Lars Johnoen, fisherman at Smolen. The latter said he had frequently seen it, and that one afternoon in the dog-days, as he was sitting in his boat, he saw it twice in the course of two hours, and quite close to him.

Lee had far more to say:

It came, indeed, to within six feet of him [Johnoen], and, becoming alarmed, he commended his soul to God, and lay down in the boat, only holding his head high enough to enable him to observe the monster. It passed him, disappeared, and returned; but, a breeze springing up, it sank, and he saw it no more. He described it as being about six fathoms long, the body (which was as round as a serpent's) two feet across, the head as long as a ten-gallon cask, the eyes large, round, red, sparkling, and about five inches in diameter: close behind the head a mane like a fin commenced along the neck, and spread itself out on both sides, right and left, when swimming.

The mane, as well as the head, was of the color of mahogany. The body was quite smooth, its movements occasionally fast and slow. It was serpent-like, and moved up and down. The few undulations which those parts of the body and tail that were out of water made, were scarcely a fathom in length. These undulations were not so high that he could see between them and the water. In confirmation of this account Mr. Soren Knudtzon, Dr. Hoffmann, surgeon in Molde, Rector Hammer, Mr. Kraft, curate, and several other persons, testified that they had seen in the neighborhood of Christiansand a sea serpent of considerable size.

Henry Lee went on: "In the *Times* of the 9th of October, 1848, appeared a paragraph stating that a sea-serpent had been met with by the *Daedalus* frigate, on her homeward voyage from the East Indies. The Admiralty immediately inquired of her commander, Captain M'Quhae, as to the truth of the report; and his official reply, addressed to Admiral Sir W. H. Gage, G.C.H., Devonport, was printed in the *Times* of the 13th of October, 1848."

Captain M'Quhae's account makes for amazing and jaw-dropping reading.

H.M.S. *Daedalus*, Hamoaze, October 11th, 1848.

Sir,

In reply to your letter of this date, requiring information as to the truth of the statement published in the *Times* newspaper, of a sea-serpent of extraordinary dimensions having been seen from

An engraving of the monster reported by crew of the HMS *Daedalus*. If one disregards the long body, the head appears rather whale- or orca-like.

H.M.S. *Daedalus*, under my command, on her passage from the East Indies, I have the honor to acquaint you, for the information of my Lords Commissioners of the Admiralty, that at 5 o'clock P.M. on the 6th of Aug. last, in lat. 24° 44" S. and long. 9° 22" E., the weather dark and cloudy, wind fresh from the N.W. with a long ocean swell from the W., the ship on the port tack, head being N.E. by N., something very unusual was seen by Mr. Sartoris, midshipman, rapidly approaching the ship from before the beam.

The circumstance was immediately reported by him to the officer of the watch, Lieut. Edgar Drummond, with whom and Mr. Wm. Barrett, the Master, I was at the time walking the quarterdeck. The ship's company were at supper. On our attention being called to the object it was discovered to be an enormous serpent, with head and shoulders kept about four feet constantly above the surface of the sea, and, as nearly as we could approximate by comparing it with the length of what our main topsail yard would show in the water, there was at the very least sixty feet of the animal *à fleur d'eau*, no portion of which was, to our perception, used in propelling it through the water, either by vertical or horizontal undulation.

It passed rapidly, but so close under our lee quarter that had it been a man of my acquaintance I should easily have recognized his features with the naked eye; and it did not, either in approaching the ship or after it had passed our wake, deviate in the slightest degree from its course to the S.W., which it held on at the pace of from twelve to fifteen miles per hour, apparently on some determined purpose.

The diameter of the serpent was about fifteen or sixteen inches behind the head, which was without any doubt that of a snake; and it was never, during the twenty minutes it continued in sight of our glasses, once below the surface of the water; its color dark brown, and yellowish white about the throat. It had no fins, but something like the mane of a horse, or rather a bunch of sea-weed, washed about its back. It was seen by the quartermaster, the boatswain's mate, and the man at the wheel, in addition to myself and the officers above mentioned.

I am having a drawing of the serpent made from a sketch taken immediately after it was seen, which I hope to have ready for transmission to my Lords Commissioners of the Admiralty by to-morrow's Post.

—PETER M'QUHAE, Captain.

The story is not over. Our captain had more to say. This report from Captain M'Quhae appeared in the pages of the *Times* newspaper the following month on November 21, 1848, in response to a query about his experience:

Professor Owen correctly states that I evidently saw a large crea-ture moving rapidly through the water very different from any-thing I had before witnessed, neither a whale, a grampus, a great shark, an alligator, nor any of the larger surface-swimming crea-tures fallen in with in ordinary voyages. I now assert—neither was it a common seal nor a sea-elephant, its great length and its totally differing physiognomy precluding the possibility of its being a "*Phoca*" of any species. The head was flat, and not a "capacious vaulted cranium"; nor had it a stiff, inflexible trunk— a conclusion at which Professor Owen has jumped, most certain-ly not justified by the simple statement, that no portion of the sixty feet seen by us was used in propelling it through the water either by vertical or horizontal undulation.

It is also assumed that the "calculation of its length was made under a strong preconception of the nature of the beast"; another conclusion quite contrary to the fact. It was not until after the great length was developed by its nearest approach to the ship, and until after that most important point had been duly considered and debated, as well as such could be in the brief space of time allowed for so doing, that it was pronounced to be a serpent by all who saw it, and who are too well accustomed to judge of lengths and breadths of objects in the sea to mistake a real substance and an actual living body, coolly and dispassionately contemplated, at so short a distance, too, for the "eddy caused by the action of the deeper immersed fins and tail of a rapidly moving gigantic seal raising its head above the surface of the water," as Professor Owen imagines, in quest of its lost iceberg.

The creative powers of the human mind may be very limited. On this occasion they were not called into requisition; my purpose and desire throughout being to furnish eminent naturalists, such as the learned Professor, with accurate facts, and not with exaggerated representations, nor with what could by any possibility proceed from optical illusion; and I beg to assure him that old Pontoppidan having clothed his sea-serpent with a mane could not have suggested the idea of ornamenting the creature seen from the *Daedalus* with a similar appendage, for the simple reason that I had never seen his account, or even heard of his sea-serpent, until my arrival in London. Some other solution must therefore be found for the very remarkable coincidence between us in that particular, in order to unravel the mystery.

Finally, I deny the existence of excitement or the possibility of optical illusion. I adhere to the statements, as to form, colour, and dimensions, contained in my official report to the Admiralty, and I leave them as data whereupon the learned and scientific may exercise the "pleasures of imagination" until some more fortunate opportunity shall occur of making a closer acquaintance with the "great unknown"—in the present instance most assuredly no ghost.

P. M'Quhae, late Captain of H.M.S. *Daedalus*.

Henry Lee also noted on this incredible affair: "Lieutenant Drummond, the officer of the watch mentioned in Captain M'Quhae's report, published his memorandum of the impression made on his mind by the animal at the time of its appearance. It differs somewhat from the captain's description and is the more cautious of the two." Lieutenant Drummond writes:

I beg to send you the following extract from my journal. H.M.S. *Daedalus*, August 6, 1848, lat. 25° S., long. 9° 37' E., St. Helena 1,015 miles. In the 4 to 6 watch, at about 5 o'clock, we observed

An illustration from *Natural History of Norway* (1755) by Bishop Erik Pontoppidan shows a maned sea serpent.

a most remarkable fish on our lee-quarter, crossing the stern in a S.W. direction.

The appearance of its head, which with the back fin was the only portion of the animal visible, was long, pointed and flattened at the top, perhaps ten feet in length, the upper jaw projecting considerably; the fin was perhaps 20 feet in the rear of the head, and visible occasionally; the captain also asserted that he saw the tail, or another fin, about the same distance behind it; the upper part of the head and shoulders appeared of a dark brown color, and beneath the under-jaw a brownish white.

It pursued a steady undeviating course, keeping its head horizontal with the surface of the water, and in rather a raised position, disappearing occasionally beneath a wave for a very brief interval, and not apparently for purposes of respiration. It was going at the rate of perhaps from twelve to fourteen miles an hour, and when nearest was perhaps one hundred yards distant; in fact it gave one quite the idea of a large snake or eel. No one in the ship has ever seen anything similar; so it is at least extraordinary. It was visible to the naked eye for five minutes, and with a glass for perhaps fifteen more. The weather was dark and squally at the time, with some sea running.

EDGAR DRUMMOND,
Lieut. H.M.S. *Daedalus*; Southampton, Oct. 28, 1848.

From Henry Lee again, the story of a sighting that took place off Cape Vito, Sicily, in 1877: "Lieutenant [Douglas] Haynes writes, under date, 'Royal Yacht *Osborne*, Gibraltar, June 6':

"On the evening of that day, the sea being perfectly smooth, my attention was first called by seeing a ridge of fins above the surface of the water, extending about thirty feet, and varying from five to six feet in height. On inspecting it by means of a telescope, at about one and a-half cables' distance, I distinctly saw a head, two flappers, and about thirty feet of an animal's shoulder. The head, as nearly as I could judge, was about six feet thick, the neck narrower, about four to five feet, the shoulder about fifteen feet across, and the flappers each about fifteen feet in length. The movements of the flappers were those of a turtle, and the animal resembled a huge seal, the resemblance being strongest about the back of the head. I could not see the length of the head, but from its crown or top to just below the shoulder (where it became immersed), I should reckon about fifty feet. The tail end I did not see, being under water, unless the ridge of fins to which my attention was first attracted, and which had disappeared by the time I got a telescope, were really the continuation of the shoulder to the end of the object's body. The animal's head was not always above water, but was thrown upwards, remaining above for a few seconds at a time, and then disappearing. There was an entire absence of "blowing," or "spouting." I herewith beg to enclose a rough sketch, showing the view of the "ridge of fins," and also of the animal in the act of propelling itself by its two fins.

> "Most Japanese dragons are benevolent towards mankind, but if treated with disrespect they can wield godlike power. An angry dragon could cause earthquakes, tsunami, typhoons, floods or droughts."

Monster hunter Richard Freeman, former head curator of reptiles at the Twycross Zoo in England, strongly suspects that some tales of dragons actually arise from sightings of all-too-real sea serpents. He told me: "The Tatsu or Ryu, the Japanese dragon, is the most ancient and powerful of all the yokai, as indeed dragons worldwide are the most ancient and powerful of all monsters. Tatsu are creatures of godlike power. They are intimately associated with water and the sea in particular. Most Japanese dragons are benevolent towards mankind, but if treated with disrespect they can wield godlike power. An angry dragon could cause earthquakes, tsunami, typhoons, floods or droughts. The length of the largest dragons is measured in miles. Asian dragons rarely breathe fire, but their breath condenses and forms rain."

Freeman expanded on his words:

Creatures resembling Tatsu are still reported in the world's oceans and deep lakes today. The seas around Japan are no exception. In 1879 the steamship *Kiushiu-maru*, one of a fleet belonging to the Mitsubishi Company, observed a serpentine monster attacking a whale in the Sea of Japan. Captain David-son stated that he saw a whale leaping from the water with the monster biting into its belly. He observed the whale disappear beneath the surface as its assailant reared up thirty feet before plunging down after it. He said the creature was as thick as a junk's mast.

In 1901 a report of a dragon was recorded in a Japanese nature magazine called *Shizen Shimbun*. The creature was seen by flashes of lighting during a storm at sea. It had horns, sharp teeth, large eyes and a rough hide. The Diet Library confirms the existence of both the magazine and the report. There can be little doubt that some of the creatures we call "sea serpents" are one and the same as Asian dragons.

THE MIGHTY KRAKEN

A massive creature that features heavily in Scandinavian folklore and mythology, the kraken is a terrifying beast, perhaps most reminis-cent of horror writer H. P. Lovecraft's (1890–1937) famous, fictional monster Cthulhu. A beast of the mysterious deep, the kraken is a definitive sea monster, although not a sea serpent of the long-necked and humpbacked variety. In many respects, the kraken sounds like a strange combination of a giant octopus and an utterly gargantuan squid. Certainly, both animals have the ability to grow to significantly large proportions, with the colossal squid reaching overall lengths, including tentacles, of up to forty-six feet. The kraken, however, is said to grow much, much bigger—to the point where, in centuries long gone, it sup-posedly dragged ships under the waves, drowning their crews in the process.

The story of Örvar-Oddr, a Scandinavian hero of old whose adventures were chronicled way back in the 1200s, contains a description of a beast called the hafgufa, which scholars of Scandinavian folklore and history believe, with hindsight, may well have been a kraken. As recounted in the 1888 *Örvar-Odds Saga* by Richard Constant Boer, it states:

> Now I will tell you that there are two sea-monsters. One is called the *hafgufa* (sea-mist), another *lyngbakr* (heather-back). It (the *lyngbakr*) is the largest whale in the world, but the *hafgufa* is the

hugest monster in the sea. It is the nature of this creature to swallow men and ships, and even whales and everything else within reach. It stays submerged for days, then rears its head and nostrils above surface and stays that way at least until the change of tide. Now, that sound we just sailed through was the space between its jaws, and its nostrils and lower jaw were those rocks that appeared in the sea, while the *lyngbakr* was the island we saw sinking down. However, Ogmund Tussock has sent these creatures to you by means of his magic to cause the death of you (Odd) and all your men. He thought more men would have gone the same way as those that had already drowned (i.e. to the *lyngbakr* which wasn't an island, and sank), and he expected that the *hafgufa* would have swallowed us all. Today I sailed through its mouth because I knew that it had recently surfaced.

Then there is the sixteenth-century tome *Konungs skuggsja*, which translates into English as *King's Mirror* and also describes what is believed to have been a kraken:

There is a fish that is still unmentioned, which it is scarcely advisable to speak about on account of its size, because it will seem to most people incredible. There are only a very few who can speak upon it clearly, because it is seldom near land nor appears where it may be seen by fishermen, and I suppose there are not many of this sort of fish in the sea. Most often in our tongue we call it hafgufa.

Nor can I conclusively speak about its length in ells, because the times he has shown before men, he has appeared more like land than like a fish. Neither have I heard that one had been caught or found dead; and it seems to me as though there must be no more than two in the oceans, and I deem that each is unable to reproduce itself, for I believe that they are always the same ones. Then too, neither would it do for other fish if the hafgufa were of such a number

The *hafgufa* is a sea monster from the Icelandic *Örvar-Odds* Saga. Inhabiting the Greenland Sea, it can camouflage itself as a rocky island before attacking unwary sailors.

as other whales, on account of their vastness, and how much subsistence that they need.

It is said to be the nature of these fish that when one shall desire to eat, then it stretches up its neck with a great belching, and following this belching comes forth much food, so that all kinds of fish that are near to hand will come to present location, then will gather together, both small and large, believing they shall obtain there food and good eating; but this great fish lets its mouth stand open the while, and the gap is no less wide than that of a great sound or fjord, and nor may the fish avoid running together there in their great numbers. But as soon as its stomach and mouth is full, then it locks together its jaws and has the fish all caught and enclosed, that before greedily came there looking for food.

In addition, we have the words of a Swedish author, a man named Jacob Wallenberg. In the pages of his 1781 title *Min son på galejan* (which translates as *My Son on the Galley*), we're told the following:

Kraken, also called the Crab-fish, which is not that huge, for heads and tails counted, he is no larger than our Öland is wide [i.e., less than 16 km]. He stays at the sea floor, constantly surrounded by innumerable small fishes, who serve as his food and are fed by him in return: for his meal (if I remember correctly what E. Pontoppidan writes) lasts no longer than three months, and another three are then needed to digest it. His excrements nurture in the following an army of lesser fish, and for this reason, fishermen plumb after his resting place.

Gradually, Kraken ascends to the surface, and when he is at ten to twelve fathoms, the boats had better move out of his vicinity, as he will shortly thereafter burst up, like a floating island, spurting water from his dreadful nostrils and making ring waves around him, which can reach many miles. Could one doubt that this is the Leviathan of Job?

And, finally, we have "The Kraken," an 1830 sonnet from the acclaimed poet laureate of Great Britain and Ireland, Alfred, Lord Tennyson (1809–1892). It reads thus:

Below the thunders of the upper deep,
Far, far beneath in the abysmal sea,
His ancient, dreamless, uninvaded sleep
The Kraken sleepeth: faintest sunlights flee
About his shadowy sides; above him swell
Huge sponges of millennial growth and height;

And far away into the sickly light,
From many a wondrous grot and secret cell
Unnumber'd and enormous polypi
Winnow with giant arms the slumbering green.
There hath he lain for ages, and will lie
Battening upon huge sea worms in his sleep,
Until the latter fire shall heat the deep;
Then once by man and angels to be seen,
In roaring he shall rise and on the surface die.

According to Henry Lee in his 1883 book *Sea Monsters Unmasked*, "the Reverend Mr. Friis, Consistorial Assessor, Minister of Bodoen in Nordland, and Vicar of the college for promoting Christian knowledge" related the following:

> In the year 1680, a Kraken (perhaps a young and foolish one) came into the water that runs between the rocks and cliffs in the parish of Alstaboug, though the general custom of that creature is to keep always several leagues from land, and therefore of course they must die there. It happened that its extended long arms or antennae, which this creature seems to use like the snail in turning about, caught hold of some trees standing near the water, which might easily have been torn up by the roots; but beside this, as it was found afterwards, he entangled himself in some openings or clefts in the rock, and therein stuck so fast, and hung so unfortunately, that he could not work himself out, but perished and putrefied on the spot. The carcass, which was a long while decaying, and filled great part of that narrow channel, made it almost impassable by its intolerable stench.
>
> The Kraken has never been known to do any great harm, except they have taken away the lives of those who consequently could not bring the tidings. I have heard but one instance mentioned, which happened a few years ago, near Fridrich-

British poet laureate Alfred, Lord Tennyson was among the many writers who have mentioned the kraken in their works.

stad, in the diocess of Aggerhuus. They say that two fishermen accidentally, and to their great surprise, fell into such a spot on the water as has been before described, full of a thick slime almost like a morass. They immediately strove to get out of this place, but they had not time to turn quick enough to save themselves from one of the Kraken's horns, which crushed the head of the boat, so that it was with great difficulty they saved their lives on the wreck, though the weather was as calm as possible; for these monsters, like the sea-snake, never appear at other times.

In the same work, Lee also explained: "Eric Pontoppidan, the younger, Bishop of Bergen, and member of the Royal Academy of Sciences at Copenhagen, is generally, but unjustly, regarded as the inventor of the semi-fabulous Kraken, and is constantly misquoted by authors who have never read his work, and who, one after another, have copied from their predecessors erroneous statements concerning him."

Let's see what Pontoppidan had to say about all of this himself:

Amongst the many things ... which are in the ocean, and concealed from our eyes, or only presented to our view for a few minutes, is the Kraken. This creature is the largest and most surprising of all the animal creation, and consequently well deserves such an account as the nature of the thing, according to the Creator's wise ordinances, will admit of. Such I shall give at present, and perhaps much greater light on this subject may be reserved for posterity.

Our fishermen unanimously affirm, and without the least variation in their accounts, that when they row out several miles to sea, particularly in the hot summer days, and by their situation (which they know by taking a view of different points of land) expect to find eighty or a hundred fathoms of water, it often happens that they do not find above twenty or thirty, and sometimes less. At these places they generally find the greatest plenty of fish, especially cod and ling. Their lines, they say, are no sooner out than they may draw them up with the hooks all full of fish. By this they know that the Kraken is at the bottom. They say this creature causes those unnatural shallows mentioned above, and prevents their sounding. These the fishermen are always glad to find, looking upon them as a means of their taking abundance of fish. There are sometimes twenty boats or more got together and throwing out their lines at a moderate distance from each other; and the only thing they then have to observe is whether the depth continues the same, which they know by their lines, or whether it grows shallower, by their seeming to have less water.

The kraken attacks a hapless ship in this 1810 engraving.

If this last be the case they know that the Kraken is raising him-self nearer the surface, and then it is not time for them to stay any longer; they immediately leave off fishing, take to their oars, and get away as fast as they can. When they have reached the usual depth of the place, and find themselves out of danger, they lie upon their oars, and in a few minutes after they see this enor-mous monster come up to the surface of the water; he there shows himself sufficiently, though his whole body does not appear, which, in all likelihood, no human eye ever beheld. Its back or upper part, which seems to be in appearance about an English mile and a half in circumference (some say more, but I chuse the least for greater certainty), looks at first like a number of small islands surrounded with something that floats and fluc-tuates like sea-weeds.

Here and there a larger rising is observed like sand-banks, on which various kinds of small fishes are seen continually leaping about till they roll off into the water from the sides of it; at last several bright points or horns appear, which grow thicker and thicker the higher they rise above the surface of the water, and sometimes they stand up as high and as large as the masts of middle-sized vessels. It seems these are the creature's arms, and it is said if they were to lay hold of the largest man of war they would pull it down to the bottom. After this monster has been on the surface of the water a short time it begins slowly to sink again, and then the danger is as great as before; because the motion of his sinking causes such a swell in the sea, and such an eddy or whirlpool, that it draws everything down with it, like the current of the river Male.

Today, sightings and reports of the kraken are not just rare, they are nonexistent. This suggests one of two possibilities: either the kraken was purely a mythical beast, or it was hunted to extinction in centuries past.

As this enormous sea-animal in all probability may be reckoned of the Polype, or of the Starfish kind, as shall hereafter be more fully proved, it seems that the parts which are seen rising at its pleasure, and are called arms, are properly the tentacula, or feeling instruments, called horns, as well as arms. With these they move themselves, and likewise gather in their food.

Besides these, for this last purpose the great Creator has also given this creature a strong and peculiar scent, which it can emit at certain times, and by means of which it beguiles and draws other fish to come in heaps about it. This animal has another strange property, known by the experience of many old fishermen. They observe that for some months the Kraken or Krabben is continually eating, and in other months he always voids his excrements. During this evacuation the surface of the water is colored with the excrement, and appears quite thick and turbid. This muddiness is said to be so very agreeable to the smell or taste of other fishes, or to both, that they gather together from all parts to it, and keep for that purpose directly over the Kraken; he then opens his arms or horns, seizes and swallows his welcome guests, and converts them after due time, by digestion, into a bait for other fish of the same kind. I relate what is affirmed by many; but I cannot give so certain assurances of this particular, as I can of the existence of this surprising creature; though I do not find anything in it absolutely contrary to Nature. As we can hardly expect to examine this enormous sea-animal alive, I am the more concerned that nobody embraced that opportunity which, according to the following account once did, and perhaps never more may offer, of seeing it entire when dead.

Today, sightings and reports of the kraken are not just rare, they are nonexistent. This suggests one of two possibilities: either the kraken was purely a mythical beast, or it was hunted to extinction in centuries past. Whatever the truth of the matter, while the kraken seemingly no longer endures, its legend most assuredly does.

BEWARE OF THE GIANT SQUID

"**G**iant squid live up to their name: the largest giant squid ever recorded by scientists was almost 43 feet (13 meters) long and may have weighed nearly a ton. You'd think such a huge animal wouldn't be hard to miss. But because the ocean is vast and giant squid live deep underwater, they remain elusive and are rarely seen: most of what we know comes from dead carcasses that floated to the surface and were found by fishermen." Those are the insightful words of the Smithsonian Institution, an organization with a long-standing interest in giant squids, as will very quickly become obvious. The employees of the Smithsonian are not alone in that regard.

A writer at the website *Marine Bio* reports:

In 1965, a Soviet whaler watched a battle between a squid and a 40 ton sperm whale. In the case of this battle, neither was victorious. The strangled whale was found floating in the sea with the squid's tentacles wrapped around the whale's throat. The squid's severed head was found in the whale's stomach. In the 1930's a ship owned by the royal Norwegian Navy called the *Brunswick* was attacked at least three times by the giant squid. In each case the attack was deliberate as the squid would pull along side of the ship, pace it, then suddenly turn, run into the ship and wrap its tentacles around the hull. The encounters were fatal for the squid as its grip on the ship's steel surface would come loose, and the animal slid off and fell into the ship's propellers.

The *Museum of UnNatural Mystery* website has a story to tell, too:

One night during World War II a British Admiralty trawler was lying off the Maldives Islands in the Indian Ocean. One of the crew, A. G. Starkey, was up on deck, alone, late at night fishing, when he saw something in the water. "As I gazed, fascinated, a circle of green light glowed in my area of illumination. This green unwinking orb I suddenly realized was an eye. The surface of the water undulated with some strange disturbance. Gradually

I realized that I was gazing at almost point-blank range at a huge squid." Starkey walked the length of the ship finding the tail at one end and the tentacles at the other. The ship was over one hundred and seventy five feet long.

Now let's look at the insightful research of sea-monster specialist Henry Lee as it relates to the matter of giant, dangerous squid.

As someone who had a deep interest in the field of giant squid, Lee collected a huge body of data on the subject, which led him to believe that there were some true monsters swimming and living deep in the waters of Earth— monsters much bigger than had previously been recorded. In his 1883 work *Sea Monsters Unmasked*, Lee listed various sightings of giant squid near Newfoundland and added:

> In the *American Journal of Science and Arts*, of March 1875, Professor Verrill gives particulars and authenticated testimony of several other examples of great calamaries, varying in total length from 30 feet to 52 feet, which have been taken in the neighbourhood of Newfoundland since the year 1870. One of these was found floating, apparently dead, near the Grand Banks in October 1871, by Captain Campbell, of the schooner *B. D. Hoskins*, of Gloucester, Mass. It was taken on board, and part of it used for bait. The body is stated to have been 15 feet long, and the pedal or shorter arms between 9 feet and 10 feet. The beak was forwarded to the Smithsonian Institution.

Lee had barely begun:

> Another instance given by Professor Verrill is of a great squid found alive in shallow water in Coomb's Cove, Fortune Bay, in the year 1872. Its measurements, taken by the Hon. T. R. Bennett, of English Harbour, Newfoundland, were, length of body 10 feet; length of tentacle 42 feet; length of one of the ordinary arms 6 feet: the cups on the tentacles were serrated. Professor Verrill also mentions a pair of jaws and two suckers in the Smithsonian Institution, as having been received from the Rev. A. Munn, with a statement that they were taken from a calamari which went ashore in Bonavista Bay, and which measured 32 feet in total length.

The following account was given to Lee, written by a correspondent but mistakenly attributed to Lee by his publisher:

> On the 22nd of September, 1877, another gigantic squid was stranded at Catalina, on the north shore of Trinity Bay, Newfoundland, during a heavy equinoctial gale. It was alive when first seen, but died soon after the ebbing of the tide, and was left

high and dry upon the beach. Two fishermen took possession of it, and the whole settlement gathered to gaze in astonishment at the monster. Formerly it would have been converted into manure, or cut up as food for dogs, but, thanks to the diffusion of intelligence, there were some persons in Catalina who knew the importance of preserving such a rarity, and who advised the fishermen to take it to St. John's. After being exhibited there for two days, it was packed in half-a-ton of ice in readiness for transmission to Professor Verrill, in the hope that it would be placed in the Peabody or Smithsonian Museum; but at the last moment its owners violated their agreement, and sold it to a higher bidder. The final purchase was made for the New York Aquarium, where it arrived on the 7th of October, immersed in methylated spirit in a large glass tank. Its measurements were as follows: length of body 10 feet; length of tentacles 30 feet; length of shorter arm 11 feet; circumference of body 7 feet; breadth of caudal fin 2 feet 9 inches; diameter of largest tentacular sucker 1 inch; number of suckers on each of the shorter arms 250.

The November 17, 1877, issue of *The Penny Illustrated Paper and Illustrated Times* featured the Catalina giant squid on its front cover.

Still on the matter of giant squid in Newfoundland, Lee commented as follows:

The appearance of so many of these great squids on the shores of Newfoundland during the term of seven years, and after so long a period of popular uncertainty as to their very existence had previously elapsed, might lead one to suppose that the waters of the North Atlantic Ocean which wash the north-eastern coasts of the American Continent were, at any rate, temporarily, their principal habitat, especially as a smaller member of their family, *Ommastrephes sagittatus*, is there found in such extraordinary numbers that it furnishes the greater part of the bait used in the Newfoundland cod fisheries. But that they are by no means confined to this locality is proved by recent instances, as well as by those already cited.

Stories poured into Lee's mailbox, one of which was based on the words of his source's story:

When the French expedition was sent to the Island of St. Paul, in 1874, for the purpose of observing the transit of Venus, which occurred on the 9th of December in that year, it was fortunately accompanied by an able zoologist, M. Ch. Vélain. He reports that on the 2nd of November a tidal wave cast upon the north shore of the island a great calamari which measured in total length nearly 23 feet, namely: length of body 7 feet; length of tentacles 16 feet. There are several points of interest connected with its generic characters, and M. Vélain's grounds for regarding it as being of a previously unknown species, but they are too technical for discussion here.

A Sergeant Thomas O'Connor, of the Royal Irish Constabulary, contacted the *Zoologist* with a startling account of a giant squid, an encounter that occurred just one year after the one detailed directly above. The story goes as follows:

On the 26th of April, 1875, a very large calamary was met with on the north-west of Boffin Island, Connemara. The crew of a "curragh" (a boat made like the "coracle," with wooden ribs covered with tarred canvas) observed to seaward a large floating mass, surrounded by gulls. They pulled out to it, believing it to be a wreck, but to their astonishment found it was an enormous cuttle-fish [which, like the giant squid, belongs to the class *Cephalopoda*] lying perfectly still, as if basking on the surface of the water. Paddling up with caution, they lopped off one of its arms. The animal immediately set out to sea, rushing through the water at a tremendous pace. The men gave chase, and, after a hard pull in their frail canvas craft, came up with it, five miles out in the open Atlantic, and severed another of its arms and the head. These portions are now in the Dublin Museum. The shorter arms measure, each, eight feet in length, and fifteen inches round the base: the tentacular arms are said to have been thirty feet long. The body sank.

We turn back now to Henry Lee and the highly traumatic encounter of one Captain Jean Magnus Dens, who, Lee stated, was "said to have been a respectable and veracious man, who, after having made several voyages to China as a master trader, retired from a seafaring life and lived at Dunkirk." Lee continued:

A model of a giant squid at the Peabody Museum of Natural History in New Haven, Connecticut, gives you an idea of just how monstrously large these cephalapods are!

Whilst crossing from St. Helena to Cape Negro, he was becalmed, and took advantage of the enforced idleness of the crew to have the vessel scraped and painted. Whilst three of his men were standing on planks slung over the side, an enormous cuttle rose from the water, and threw one of its arms around two of the sailors, whom it tore away, with the scaffolding on which they stood. With another arm it seized the third man, who held on tightly to the rigging, and shouted for help. His shipmates ran to his assistance, and succeeded in rescuing him by cutting away the creature's arm with axes and knives, but he died delirious on the following night. The captain tried to save the other two sailors by killing the animal, and drove several harpoons into it; but they broke away, and the men were carried down by the monster.

The horrific story continued:

The arm cut off was said to have been twenty-five feet long, and as thick as the mizen-yard, and to have had on it suckers as big as saucepan-lids. I believe the old sea-captain's narrative of the incident to be true. The belief in the power of the cuttle to sink a ship and devour her crew is as widely spread over the surface of the globe, as it is ancient in point of time. I have been told by a friend that he saw in a shop in China a picture of a cuttle embracing a junk, apparently of about 300 tons burthen, and helping itself to the sailors, as one picks gooseberries off a bush.

Moving on to places new and varied, Lee said:

Traditions of a monstrous cuttle attacking and destroying ships are current also at the present day in the Polynesian Islands. Mr. Gill, the missionary previously quoted, tells us that the natives of Aitutaki, in the Hervey group, have a legend of a famous explorer, named Rata, who built a double canoe, decked and rigged it, and then started off in quest of adventures. At the prow was stationed the dauntless Nganaoa, armed with a long spear and ready to slay all monsters. One day when speeding pleasantly over the ocean, the voice of the ever vigilant Nganaoa was heard: "O Rata! yonder is a terrible enemy starting up from ocean depths." It proved to be an octopus (query, squid?) of extraordinary dimensions. Its huge tentacles encircled the vessel in their embrace, threatening its instant destruction. At this critical moment Nganaoa seized his spear, and fearlessly drove it through the head of the creature. The tentacles slowly relaxed, and the dead monster floated off on the surface of the ocean.

Lee was far from being done. In his personal papers is this exciting story:

We have also the statement of the officers and crew of the French despatch steamer, *Alecton*, commanded by Lieutenant Bouyer, describing their having met with a great calamary on the 30th of November, 1861, between Madeira and Teneriffe. It was seen about noon on that day floating on the surface of the water, and the vessel was stopped with a view to its capture. Many bullets were aimed at it, but they passed through its soft flesh without doing it much injury, until at length "the waves were observed to be covered with foam and blood." It had probably discharged the contents of its ink-bag; for a strong odor of musk immediately became perceptible—a perfume which I have already mentioned as appertaining to the ink of many of the cephalopoda, and also as being one of the reputed attributes of the Kraken [author's note: the very same legendary, massive beast that we have already addressed].

Harpoons were thrust into it, but would not hold in the yielding flesh; and the animal broke adrift from them, and, diving beneath the vessel, came up on the other side. The crew wished to launch a boat that they might attack it at closer quarters, but the commander forbade this, not feeling justified in risking the lives of his men. A rope with a running knot was, however, slipped over it, and held fast at the junction of the broad caudal fin; but when an attempt was made to hoist it on deck the enormous weight caused the rope to cut through the flesh, and all but the hinder part of the body fell back into the sea and disappeared. M. Berthelot, the French consul at Teneriffe, saw the fin and posterior portion of the animal on board the *Alecton* ten days afterwards, and sent a report of the occurrence to the Paris Academy of Sciences. The body of this great squid, which, like Rang's specimen, was of a deep-red colour, was estimated to have been from 16 feet to 18 feet long, without reckoning the length of its formidable arms.

Lee also had the following to impart:

I have recently had an opportunity of inspecting a most curious Japanese book, in the possession of my friend Mr. W. B. Tegetmeier, which is chiefly

An illustration from Henry Lee's 1883 book, *Sea Monsters Unmasked* depicts the crew of the *Alecton* nabbing a giant squid.

devoted to the representations of the fisheries and fish-curing processes of the country. It is in three volumes, and is entitled, *Land and Sea Products*, by Ki Kone. It is evidently ancient, for it is slightly worm-eaten, but the plates, each 12 inches by 8 inches, are full of vigour. Two of these illustrate in a very interesting manner the subject before us, and by the kindness of Mr. Tegetmeier I am able to give facsimiles of them, which appeared with an article by him on this book, in the *Field* of March 14th, 1874.

It represents a fisherman in a boat out at sea: a gigantic octopus has thrown one of its arms over the side of the boat; the man, who is alone, has started forward from the stern of the boat, and has succeeded, by means of a large knife attached to a long handle, in lopping off the dangerous limb of his enemy. As Mr. Tegetmeier says, "From the extreme matter of fact manner in which all these engravings are made, and the total absence of exaggeration in any other representation, I cannot but regard the relative sizes of the man, the boat, and the octopus, as correctly given, in which case we have evidence of the existence of gigantic cephalopods in Japanese waters."

The only doubt I have is whether the fisherman correctly described his assailant as an octopus, and whether it was not a calamary. [There] is a vivid picture of a fishmonger's shop in a market, under the awning of which may be seen two arms of a gigantic cuttle hung up for sale as food. These are evidently of most unusual size, judging from the action of the lookers on; the one to the left, with a tall stand or case on his back, like a Parisian cocoa-vendor, is holding out his hand in mute astonishment; whilst the attention of the smaller personage in the right-hand corner is directed to the suspended arms of the cuttle by the man nearest to him, who is pointing to them with upraised hand. In another plate in this most interesting work a Japanese mode of fishing for cuttles is delineated. A man in a boat is tossing crabs, one at a time, into the sea, and when a cuttle rises at the bait he spears it with a trident and tosses it into the boat.

> Although such reports were seen as credible, there still remained a "residuum of doubt in the minds of naturalists and the public concerning the existence of gigantic cuttles...."

Although such reports were seen as credible—and provided by trustworthy seafarers, as Lee noted—there still remained a "residuum of doubt in the minds of naturalists and the public concerning the existence of gigantic cuttles until, towards the close of the year 1873, two specimens were encountered on the coast of Newfoundland, and a portion of one and the whole of the other, were brought ashore, and preserved for examination by competent zoologists." Lee tells the story:

The circumstances under which the first was seen, as sensationally described by the Rev. M. Harvey, Presbyterian minister of St. John's, Newfoundland, in a letter to Principal Dawson, of McGill College, were, briefly and soberly, as follows: Two fishermen were out in a small punt on the 26th of October, 1873, near the eastern end of Belle Isle, Conception Bay, about nine miles from St. John's. Observing some object floating on the water at a short distance, they rowed towards it, supposing it to be the *débris* of a wreck. On reaching it one of them struck it with his "gaff," when immediately it showed signs of life, and shot out its two tentacular arms, as if to seize its antagonists. The other man, named Theophilus Picot, though naturally alarmed, severed both arms with an axe as they lay on the gunwale of the boat, whereupon the animal moved off, and ejected a quantity of inky fluid which darkened the surrounding water for a considerable distance. The men went home, and, as fishermen will, magnified their lost "fish." They "estimated" the body to have been 60 feet in length, and 10 feet across the tail fin; and declared that when the "fish" attacked them "it reared a parrot-like beak which was as big as a six-gallon keg."

All this, in the excitement of the moment, Mr. Harvey appears to have been willing to believe, and related without the expression of a doubt. Fortunately, he was able to obtain from the fishermen a portion of one of the tentacular arms which they had chopped off with the axe, and by so doing rendered good service to science. This fragment, as measured by Mr. Alexander Murray, provincial geologist of Newfoundland, and Professor Verrill, of Yale College, Connecticut, is 17 feet long and 3½ feet in circumference. It is now in St. John's Museum. By careful calculation of its girth, the breadth and circumference of the expanded sucker-bearing portion at its extremity, and the diameter of the suckers, Professor Verrill has computed its dimensions to have been as follows: Length of body 10 feet; diameter of body 2 feet 5 inches. Long tentacular arms 32 feet; head 2 feet; total length about 44 feet. The upper mandible of the beak, instead of being "as large as a six-gallon keg" would be about 3 inches long, and the lower mandible 1½ inch long. From the size of the large suckers relatively to those of another specimen to be presently described, he regards it as probable that this individual was a female.

ATTACKED BY MONSTERS OF THE SEA

Henry Lee—without whose diligent research in the nineteenth century we would be sorely lacking in high-caliber reports of lake monsters—spent some of his time addressing one of the most controversial issues of all: namely, the disturbing issue of people being attacked—maybe even killed and eaten—by strange, unknown, and huge creatures of the sea. Of this particular issue, Lee said in his book *Sea Monsters Unmasked*:

I have often been asked whether an octopus of the ordinary size can really be dangerous to bathers. Decidedly, "Yes," in certain situations. The holding power of its numerous suckers is enormous. It is almost impossible forcibly to detach it from its adhesion to a rock or the flat bottom of a tank; and if a large one happened to fix one or more of its strong, tough arms on the leg of a swimmer whilst the others held firmly to a rock, I doubt if the man could disengage himself under water by mere strength, before being exhausted. Fortunately the octopus can be made to relax its hold by grasping it tightly round the "throat" (if I may so call it), and it may be well that this should be known.

Lee continued with his position on all of this: "That men are occasionally drowned by these creatures is, unhappily, a fact too well attested. I have elsewhere related several instances of this having occurred. Omitting those, I will give two or three others which have since come under my notice. Sir Grenville Temple, in his "Excursions in the Mediterranean Sea," tells how a Sardinian captain, whilst bathing at Jerbeh, was seized and drowned by an octopus. When his body was found, his limbs were bound together by the arms of the animal; and this took place in water only four feet deep."

Lee was not done; his files were voluminous on this matter: "Mr. J. K. Lord's account of the formidable strength of these creatures in Oregon is confirmed by an incident recorded in the *Weekly Oregonian* (the principal paper of Oregon) of October 6th, 1877. A few days before that date an Indian woman, whilst bathing, was held beneath the surface by an octopus, and drowned. The body was discovered on the following day in the horrid embrace of the creature. Indians dived down and with their knives severed the arms of the octopus and recovered the corpse."

While they are both cephalopods, an octopus is quite different from a squid. Squid, for one thing, have ten arms versus eight for an octopus. As you can see from this diagram, the body shapes of the two are quite distinctive (octopus on the left, squid on the right).

Lee also cited the work of Clemens Laming, the author of a book titled *The French in Algiers*. In its pages, as Lee learned, was a case that could have resulted in overwhelming tragedy. Thankfully, it didn't quite get to that point: "The soldiers were in the habit of bathing in the sea every evening, and from time to time several of them disappeared no one knew how. Bathing was, in consequence, strictly forbidden; in spite of which several men went into the water one evening. Suddenly one of them screamed for help, and when several others rushed to his assistance they found that an octopus had seized him by the leg by four of its arms whilst it clung to the rock with the rest. The soldiers brought the 'monster' home with them, and out of revenge they boiled it alive and ate it. *This adventure accounted for the disappearance of the other soldiers* [italics mine]."

Lee was hardly done:

The Rev. W. Wyatt Gill, who for more than a quarter of a century has resided as a missionary amongst the inhabitants of the Hervey Islands, and with whom I had the pleasure of conversing on this subject when he was in England in 1875, described in the *Leisure Hour* of April 20th, 1872, another mode of attack by which an octopus might deprive a man of life. A servant of his went diving for "poulpes" (octopods), leaving his son in charge of the canoe. After a short time he rose to the surface, his arms free, but his nostrils and mouth completely covered by a large octopus. If his son had not promptly torn the living plaister from off his face he must have been suffocated—a fate which actually befell some years previously a man who foolishly went diving alone.

Lee recounted the following anecdotes as well:

In Appleton's *American Journal of Science and Art*, January 31st, 1874, a correspondent describes an attack by an octopus on a diver who was at work on the wreck of a sunken steamer off the coast of Florida. The man, a powerful Irishman, was helpless in its grasp, and would have been drowned if he had not been quickly brought to the surface; for when dragged on to the raft from which he had descended, he fainted, and his companions were unable to pull the creature from its hold upon him until they had dealt it a sharp blow across its baggy body. A similar incident occurred to the government diver of the colony of Victoria, Australia. Whilst pursuing his avocation in the estuary of the river Moyne he was seized by an octopus. He killed it by striking it with an iron bar, and brought to shore with him a portion of it with the arms more than three feet long.

There is a lesson to be learned here. Be very careful when you go swimming in oceans and seas. You may not be aware of what lurks below you, ready to strike—perhaps fatally so.

CTHULHU LIVES?

H. P. Lovecraft, who was born in Providence, Rhode Island, in 1890, is one of the most revered of the many and varied horror novelists the world has known. It's a tragedy that he overwhelmingly failed, in the 1920s and 1930s, to see his work achieve the massive levels of popularity that it has today. Lovecraft, who died at the age of forty-six from a combination of cancer and malnutrition, was in many ways the definitive starving artist. He was also a deeply weird, complex, and controversial character: he shunned the opposite sex (but was not gay), had a near-nonexistent sex life, was a racist, and was very much a loner. While Lovecraft's numerous stories never made him famous or wealthy during his brief lifetime, few writers today have achieved such fame—and infamy, in Lovecraft's case. There is also no doubt that Lovecraft's most famous, fictional creation of all was the hideous creature of the oceans called Cthulhu.

> It's a fact that many of Lovecraft's creations ... came to him in a dream state or while in the throes of terrifying nightmares in the dead of night.

The monster first appeared in "The Call of Cthulhu," a story that was published in the pages of *Weird Tales* in 1928. Detailing the appearance of the hellish thing, Lovecraft described it as "a monster of vaguely anthropoid outline, but with an octopus-like head whose face was a mass of feelers, a scaly, rubbery-looking body, prodigious claws on hind and fore feet, and long, narrow wings behind." An entire mythos surrounds Cthulhu and associated monsters and concepts that keep Lovecraft's devotees busy day and night.

Some of those devotees postulate that Lovecraft may not have written his stories himself—at least, not in the way most of us might assume. It's a fact that many of Lovecraft's creations—including the aforementioned Cthulhu and other such fiendish creatures as Nyarlathotep, Shub-Niggurath, and Ithaqua as well as ancient cities and strange landscapes—came to him in a dream state or while in the throes of terrifying nightmares in the dead of night. Maybe, so the theory goes, Lovecraft's ideas were prompted by glimpses—deep in a state of sleep—of all-too-real monsters, creatures, and strange worlds. Perhaps, his dream state was actually a state of astral travel.

The writers at *Gaia* explain astral travel as follows:

Call it what you like—dream body, astral body, energy body, Buddhist light body, Taoist diamond body, Egyptian ka, Tantric subtle body, Hindu body of bliss—and in Christianity, the experience of different "heavens," i.e. "I know a man who was caught up to the third heaven. Whether it was in or out of body, I do not know," from Corinthians 12:1–4. The subtle body is a universal human experience, and apparently part of our standard human design like toenails and kidneys. It is this subtle body that projects astrally and is active during unconscious and lucid dreaming; astral projection and dreaming often go hand-in-hand as "out-of-body" experiences, or OBEs. The subtle body, when cultivated, can survive the physical body as a matrix for consciousness, and astral projection and lucid dreaming are part of spiritual training paths for subtle body cultivation. Neophytes confuse the subtle body with the soul or spirit, two additional aspects of multi-dimensional humans.

This brings us to a fantastic and highly controversial question: Do Cthulhu-like creatures really exist? Were they more than merely the warped dreams of a man who spent far too much time living in a world of fantasy and unearthly monsters? Let us address this weird scenario.

To get to the heart of this issue, we have to focus our attention on one Donald Tyson, an acknowledged expert on the life and writings of Lovecraft. Tyson's books include *The Dream World of H. P. Lovecraft* and *The 13 Gates of the Necronomicon*. Tyson's combined writings make a strong and eerie argument that Lovecraft did

Horror fiction author H. P. Lovecraft wrote of many bizarre and twisted monsters, including the Octopus-headed demon god Cthulhu.

indeed open doors, so to speak, while deep in his nightly slumber. Tyson also demonstrates, by addressing the life of Lovecraft from childhood to death, that this curious situation did not begin during adulthood. No; it went right back to Lovecraft's boyhood, with awful dreams that would continue to plague him until his final moments.

In his childhood, Lovecraft was tormented by what he came to call the "Night Gaunts." They would appear when he had fallen asleep and would manifest as what he described as a dark silhouette, not unlike a self-aware, intelligent shadow. The creatures that Lovecraft dreamed of (or saw in an astral state) sound very much like what today are referred to as the shadow people. The website *Crystal Links* says of these dangerous entities:

> Shadow people (also known as shadow men, shadow folk, or shadow beings) are said to be shadow like creatures of supernatural origin that appear as dark forms in the peripheries of people's vision and disintegrate, or move between walls, when noticed.... Most accounts of shadow people describe them as black humanoid silhouettes with no discernible mouths, noses, eyes, or any expression whatsoever, though purported witnesses have also described child-sized humanoids or shapeless masses. Some

reports also include glowing red eyes. Generally, they are described as lacking mass, though their specific nature varies from a two-dimensional shadow to a vaporous or distorted three-dimensional form. Their movement is often described as being very quick and disjointed; they may first move slowly, as if they were passing through a heavy liquid, and then rapidly "hop" to another part of a witness' surroundings.

Lovecraft shared these experiences, in 1916, with a friend, Rheinhart Kleiner. We're told the following by the H. P. Lovecraft website: "Rheinhart Kleiner (1892–1949) was one of H. P. Lovecraft's earliest correspondents. The recipient of the first issue of Lovecraft's amateur paper, *The Conservative*, in 1915, Kleiner challenged Lovecraft to reconsider his dogmatic views on race, literature, and society. A poet of exquisite skill and sensitivity, Kleiner inspired Lovecraft to write a number of poems directly addressed to him or inspired by his own poems."

It was in one of these letters that Lovecraft referred to the Night Gaunts as "living shadows" and to creatures with faces that lacked eyes, noses, mouths, and ears. They were, then, faceless. The scenario was almost always the same: the Night Gaunts would steal Lovecraft from his bed, haul him into the skies above, and then drop him from a tremendous height. As the ground below came ever closer, Lovecraft would awaken in a cold sweat and in a state of terror.

Donald Tyson's work takes matters far away from the norm, positing the following: "Lovecraft was more than merely a dreamer. Night after night he engaged in intuitive astral projection." And these words from Tyson are highly revealing: "At the start of his career as a writer of cosmic horror tales, Lovecraft did little more than set his dreams and nightmares down on the page, and indeed he sometimes wondered if he could even claim credit as the author of the stories, since he was not so much composing them as narrating what he had seen in sleep."

Notably, in time, Lovecraft's mother, Susie, came to see the Night Gaunts as well, but she did so while wide awake—something that suggests Lovecraft's dreams were far more than they seemed to be. It also suggests that Susie was able to penetrate the same realm of monsters that Lovecraft himself had stumbled upon as a child. Now we get to the heart of the controversy: If the Night Gaunts were real, then maybe Cthulhu was, too. After all, the legendary monster itself was "created" by Lovecraft's tormented dreams as he surfed the astral plane on a nightly basis. If Cthulhu, in some form, does exist, then where is it? One answer to that question is that it might be deep in our waters—and not just in the pages of decades-old stories. Let us now address that theory that Cthulhu, or something significantly like it, may exist. And, furthermore, perhaps there are those in the U.S. government who know the

An artist's rendition of Cthulhu.

truth. It all revolves around a thing (creature, beast—call it what you will) with the decidedly nonhorrific name of Bloop!

It's rare that a story of a monster crosses paths with the world of conspiracy. But that's exactly what happened when it came to the matter of a mysterious creature—or, rather, an alleged mysterious creature—said to have surfaced in the 1990s. It quickly became the subject of U.S. Navy interest. To fully understand the controversy, it's necessary to go back in time to the 1960s, when the Cold War was still in full force. It was in that decade that the Navy established a top-secret program known as SOSUS: the Sound Surveillance System. Essentially, it was a vast network of underwater microphones that spanned much of the planet and that was designed to monitor for Russian submarines, particularly those equipped with atomic weapons. Today, the Cold War is over. The world, however, is still a dangerous place—maybe even more so than back in the old days when the United States had only one enemy, the Soviets, to worry about. At any rate, the SOSUS detectors still exist, picking up on sound waves in what is termed the deep sound channel, a certain ocean layer in which sound can travel especially far.

It's not just Russian (and, today, Chinese) subs that the U.S. military has recorded on its SOSUS equipment. Ships, earth tremors, and whales have been detected by the highly sophisticated technology. The technology has been significantly improved upon since the old days and is now overseen by the National Oceanic and Atmospheric Administration (NOAA), which is a section of the U.S. Department of Commerce. This brings us to a certain, deeply puzzling event that occurred in 1997. That was the year in which NOAA recorded a very weird, and very large, "something" in the waters of the South Pacific Ocean, west of South America's most southern tip.

Before we get to that, let's take a look at the work of NOAA. In the administration's own words:

> NOAA provides timely and reliable information based on sound science to communities and businesses every day. From daily weather forecasts, severe storm warnings, and climate monitoring to fisheries management, coastal restoration and supporting marine commerce, Americans rely on NOAA.... The National Ocean Service [NOS] provides data, tools, and services that support coastal economies and their contribution to the national economy. NOS is dedicated to advancing the following priorities: Ships move $1.5 trillion worth of products in and out of U.S. ports every year. Every ship moving in and out of U.S. ports relies on navigation charts and water level information that NOS alone provides. All mapping, charting, and transportation activities and infrastructure are founded on a reliable, accurate national coordinate system. NOS is solely responsible for maintaining that system, which provides more than $2.4 billion in potential annual benefits to the U.S. economy. Businesses in the maritime community rely on NOS for a range of decisions, from how much cargo to load to choosing the safest and most efficient route between two points. They use NOS data, tools, and services to plan seasonally for ship schedules to service global trade more safely and efficiently as significantly larger vessels transit through U.S. ports as a result of the Panama Canal expansion.

All of which brings us to Bloop.

Whatever "it" was, it caught the attention of NOAA and the military, who nicknamed the anomaly "Bloop." It was of a certain amplitude to be picked up on tracking equipment more than five thousand kilometers from where its movements were recorded. More intriguing, within both NOAA and the Navy, there were those who claimed the signature was suggestive of Bloop being a massive, unknown animal, such as a squid of unparalleled proportions—one might even be justified in saying something akin to H. P. Lovecraft's Cthulhu or the legendary kraken.

Needless to say, the controversy surrounding Bloop attracted a great deal of interest. One of those who took a great deal of interest in the matter was Phil Lobel, a marine biologist based at Boston University. Although Lobel was admittedly doubtful of the hypothesis that Bloop was a huge squid, he did not dismiss the possibility of it being something living. In fact, Lobel suggested it probably was some form of animal.

When the media latched on to the story, NOAA admitted that this was far from being the first occasion upon which such anomalies—which may well have been giant, unknown animals—had been detected in the world's oceans. Every one of them had been given specific names, such as Whistle, Upsweep, Train, and Slowdown. As for NOAA's stance on the matter of Bloop today, the prevailing theory within the agency is that Bloop was nothing weirder than a large iceberg that was beginning to collapse, provoking the sounds that were recorded by the tracking equipment. True or not, the legend of Bloop lives on, giving hope to some that Cthulhu is something more than just fiction.

At its governmental website, NOAA explains the nature of Bloop is as follows:

> In 1997, researchers listening for underwater volcanic activity in the southern Pacific recorded a strange, powerful, and extremely loud sound. Using hydrophones, or underwater microphones, that were placed more than 3,219 kilometers apart across the Pacific, they recorded numerous instances of the noise, which was unlike anything they had heard before. Not only was it loud, the sound had a unique characteristic that came to be known as "the Bloop."
>
> Scientists from NOAA's Pacific Marine Environmental Laboratory (PMEL) were eager to discover the sound's origin, but with about 95 per-

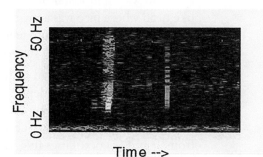

A spectogram of the Bloop that was recorded by the National Oceanic and Atmospheric Administration was, when analyzed in 2012, believed to be a large animal of some unknown sort.

cent of the ocean unexplored, theories abounded. Was the Bloop from secret underwater military exercises, ship engines, fishing boat winches, giant squids, whales, or some sea creature unknown to science?

As the years passed, PMEL researchers continued to deploy hydrophones ever closer to Antarctica in an ongoing effort to study the sounds of sea floor volcanoes and earthquakes. It was there, on Earth's lonely southernmost land mass, that they finally discovered the source of those thunderous rumbles from the deep in 2005. The Bloop was the sound of an icequake—an iceberg cracking and breaking away from an Antarctic glacier! With global warming, more and more icequakes occur annually, breaking off glaciers, cracking and eventually melting into the ocean.

PMEL's Acoustics Program develops unique acoustics tools and technologies to acquire long-term data sets of the global ocean acoustics environment, and to identify and assess acoustic impacts from human activities and natural processes on the marine environment.

Massive, Cthulu-like monster or the cracking of an iceberg? The choice is yours. And, the story is not alone. Let us now take a trip to Oklahoma and a certain lake where monsters dwell.

It's a deeply strange story that is very much dominated by myth, folklore, and urban legend, but it just might have at its heart a genuine mystery of cryptozoological proportions. It goes like this: In the waters of Lake Thunderbird, Oklahoma, something monstrous and weird is said to dwell. It's described as being octopus-like—hence the memorable moniker the creature now has—and is somewhat akin to horror maestro H. P. Lovecraft's most famous creation, Cthulhu, but scaled down. In Lovecraft's own words, you will recall that Cthulhu was "a monster of vaguely anthropoid outline, but with an octopus-like head whose face was a mass of feelers, a scaly, rubbery-looking body, prodigious claws on hind and fore feet, and long, narrow wings behind." The wings aside, that is not a bad description of the Oklahoma Octopus.

Most of the claimed sightings of the Oklahoma Octopus have been reported from within the depths of Lake Thunderbird. This is curious in itself for three reasons: (a) Lake Thunderbird is a freshwater lake; (b) the lake wasn't built until 1962 (which begs the question: where did the beast come from?); and (c) octopuses live in saltwater environments—unless, against all odds, an octopus or several have managed to cope with and adapt to a freshwater world.

There are other notable aspects to the story, too. The lake itself is named after another legendary creature of cryptozoological proportions, the

Thunderbird, a staple part of Native American lore and history. Plus, the Native Americans who called the area their home centuries ago told stories of monstrous, Cthulhu-esque, octopus-like water beasts in the area long before the Oklahoma Octopus was on anyone's radar. The specific locations were the Illinois River (which snakes its way through parts of eastern Oklahoma) and the Verdigris River.

As for the witness reports, they typically revolve around sightings of large tentacles seen breaking the surface of the lake. Seldom is a complete creature encountered, but there are several such cases that, collectively, point to an intriguing situation.

NESSIE AND NESSIE-LIKE MONSTERS

You will note in the sections ahead that a great deal of attention has been given to what is, without a doubt, the most famous of all creatures of the deep: Nessie of Loch Ness, Scotland, or, to put it more correctly, the Nessies, since there clearly cannot be just one of them. The fact that Loch Ness is not in some remote, hard-to-find location means that hundreds of thousands of people can—and do—visit Loch Ness every year, all of them hoping to see a monster or two. Not only can we learn a great deal from the witness testimonies, photos, and film footage concerning the Nessies, but we can also apply the findings to other lakes that are home to monsters but that may be isolated and hard to get to. By spending a great deal of time trying to understand what the Nessies are, we might also come to understand—and classify—similar monsters seen in the lakes of Russia, Scandinavia, and Canada and, possibly, Nessie's very own Scottish cousin, Morag of Loch Morar.

NESSIE OFFICIALLY COMES TO LIFE

There's no doubt that, despite the undeniably large body of lore and legend of strange, supernatural animals—kelpies—living in Loch Ness and dating back centuries, it was not until 1933 that the phenomenon of Nessie caught the attention of the general public and the media. And, it happened not just in Scotland but around the world. Many researchers of the Loch Ness controversy who are doubtful that the stories have merit make much of the fact that, until the 1930s, things were relatively tame on the monster front. They use this as ammunition to suggest that Nessie is a product specifically of the twentieth century, designed to titillate tourists, boost Scotland's revenue, and ensure media attention for the area. This is an outrageous and disingenuous approach to take for two reasons. First, as we have seen, legends of the animals date back more than 1,500 years. Second, there is a very simple reason why the Nessie phenomenon didn't take off—as in stratospherically—until the 1930s, and it has nothing whatsoever to do with tourism, hoaxing, or the press.

Prior to 1933, there was only one road that permitted travel around the loch, despite the gargantuan size of that famous body of water. It was the General Wade's Road that went from Inverness to Fort Augustus and was constructed way back in 1715. That was it. Nothing else. At all. Plus, much of the road ran through the surrounding hills, thus obscuring a good, close view of the loch. In addition, even in those parts of the loch where the road came close to the water, it did so in some heavily forested areas. This meant that a good view of Loch Ness was barely available. For all these reasons, it's no wonder that the Nessies only attracted the attention of the locals. And let's remember that many of those same locals were extremely reluctant to say too much to outsiders about their encounters with the monsters. That all began to change, and massively so, in 1932.

It was in that year that an ambitious project began to construct a brand-new road that would run along the length of the loch's north shore. What

Field Marshal George Wade constructed a number of rather crude military roads in Scotland that were the only means of travel in some parts before the 1930s. Crude stone trails like this one near Melgrave were why not many people ventured to Loch Ness and why, consequently, not many sightings occurred before the 1930s.

made this road so significant in the story of Nessie is that it provided the average car driver, truck driver, or motorcyclist a practically wide-open view of the loch along its entire length *for the very first time ever*. Finally, anyone passing by Loch Ness could see its massive, watery expanse—and, as history has graphically shown, more than a few monsters in it. As all of this demonstrates, there is nothing at all suspicious about the sudden increase in Nessie sightings in 1933, regardless of what the skeptics and the debunkers might wish us to believe.

There is something besides clearer vistas that may have provoked more monster sightings in the early 1930s. While constructing the new road, the workmen involved had to resort to a great deal of blasting to create a route amid the dense, stony environment. That the massive, and very loud, explosions may have disturbed the beasts—and prompted them to surface more often than usual to see what on earth was afoot—is a theory that many Nessie seekers adhere to. It's certainly not out of the question: locals spoke of deafening booms and almighty bangs and of massive chunks of rock hurtling into the air and coming splashing down into the waters of Loch Ness.

Keeping this in mind, it's interesting to note that in February 1932, when the new road was in the early stages of construction, a local mailman saw in the loch something strange that he described as looking like a boat, albeit an upturned one. The man, James Cameron, was sure that whatever he encountered at Shrone Point was a living, unknown animal. Perhaps it was a Nessie, concerned and curious about all the new commotion.

The year 1933 brought the birth of Nessie; of that there is no doubt. One year earlier, however, there was a very strange occurrence at Loch Ness, but it is one that is very often overlooked or ignored. The reason, you will see, is very easy to fathom. It is at extreme odds—in terms of the description of the creature—with other reports. It does not, therefore, sit well with many Nessie investigators. This is too bad. High strangeness is at the very heart of this book, something that ensures the case gets the airing it richly deserves. The witness was a Lieutenant McP Fordyce, and the occurrence happened in April 1932, two months after James Cameron's sighting at Shrone Point.

He added that the beast moved like an elephant but resembled a strange combination of a camel and a horse, to the point of having a camel-like hump on its back and a small head positioned on a long neck.

At the time, Fordyce was living in the English county of Kent, and, with his fiancée, he had traveled by car to Aberdeen, Scotland, to attend a family wedding. Given that the drive was such a long one, instead of simply driving immediately all the way back home, Fordyce decided to show his fiancée a bit of his homeland. The young lovers had a late evening, a romantic dinner, and a stroll through the town, where they encountered a band of men playing bagpipes. It was a perfect slice of ancient Scottish tradition, one that Fordyce's girl would never forget. There was also something else she would never forget, and neither would Fordyce.

The next morning, the pair decided to hit the road running and hopefully make the journey back to Kent in good time. It was a bright and sunny day for the drive, which took them past Loch Ness as far as Foyers, at which point they turned onto the road to Fort William, away from the loch side and into the heart of the wooded areas that dominate certain portions of the loch. According to Fordyce's memory, he was driving about twenty-five miles per hour at the time, when he and his fiancée were shocked and amazed by the sight of a large animal appearing from the dense woods and then making its way across the road at a distance of around 450 feet. He added that the beast moved like an elephant but resembled a strange combination of a camel and a horse, to the point of having a camel-like hump on its back and a small head positioned on a long neck. Displaying welcome gumption, the adventurous Fordyce stopped the car, jumped out, and decided to pursue the monster on foot. As he got closer, while still keeping a respectful distance—just in case the creature turned violent—Fordyce could now see that the rear of the animal was gray in color and had wild and shaggy hair, and its long neck reminded him very much of the trunk of an elephant.

Unfortunately, and surely to the consternation of monster seekers everywhere, Fordyce had left his camera in the car. He then realized the somewhat precarious position he was in, stalking a large and unknown animal in the woods, and decided that pursuing the thing was perhaps not such a good idea after all. A worm-slaying, armored knight of old, Fordyce was most definitely not, by his own admission. He and his fiancée spoke about the amazing event for the entire journey back home. The only theory they could come up with was that the animal had escaped from a zoo. He admitted that he was sure that such a large creature would be easily seen by others and quickly caught. As history has shown, the Nessies remain as elusive today as they were back in 1932, when Fordyce's one-in-a-million, chance encounter occurred.

Aside from confiding in family members, Fordyce stayed silent on his sighting until 1990 when, finally, as an old man, he contacted the media, and his story became public knowledge. The camel-like and hairy descriptions of the beast are, admittedly, at odds with many other reports, but not all. So was Fordyce's observation that it had an elephantine gait. The latter comment suggests that the creature walked on legs, rather than moving around using flipper-like appendages, which are so very often reported in Nessie encounters. Whatever Fordyce encountered, it remains practically unique in terms of its physical appearance. Of course, if the Nessies are shapeshifting kelpies that can take on multiple forms and guises, then the strange appearance of the animal is not quite so strange after all. In fact, it would be exactly what one would expect.

The wave of encounters in 1933 prompted a Miss K. MacDonald to come forward with her account of a strange-looking creature in Loch Ness that looked *nothing* like the classic humped, long-necked monster that was all the rage. It didn't resemble Fordyce's monster, either. According to Miss MacDonald, she saw a six- to eight-foot-long animal swimming the River Ness, approaching the Holm Mills weir. Very bizarrely, she described it as looking somewhat crocodile-like and added that it seemed to have very large teeth or possibly even elephant-like tusks!

The date on which history was *really* made—as the newspapers and the public saw it, anyway—was April 14, 1933. Admittedly, the facts didn't surface until May 2. The latter was the date when a man named Alex Campbell

Mysterious, large waves such as these on Loch Ness make up one kind of sighting that occurs in Nessie sightings. Witnesses saying they have gotten a full view of the creature are rare.

splashed the story across the pages of the *Inverness Courier* newspaper. And what a story it was. Campbell told of the encounter of a then-anonymous, well-known businessman and his wife who lived near Inverness. They had apparently been driving along the north side of the loch when they saw to their amazement a huge splashing in the water. They watched in complete shock as a massive animal, with a body not unlike that of a whale, broke the water. Campbell upped the intrigue and sensational nature of the story when he added that the water churned as the terrible thing surfaced, provoking cold fear in the pair.

There were, inevitably, those who were skeptical of the encounter, particularly when the identities of the mystery man and his wife were revealed. They were John Mackay and his wife, who just happened to be the owners of a hotel at Drumnadrochit. The press, including the *New York Herald Tribune*, were openly suspicious of the story and suggested that the Mackays had concocted the tale to draw tourists to the loch—and to the hotel, of course. The theory was vehemently denied by the Mackays. Had the case been a solitary one, the media might have had a valid point. But the reports flooded in. That denizen of the deep, as Alex Campbell so famously labeled it, was here to stay.

Nine days after the Mackay story was publicized, a beastie was seen again. This time, those lucky enough to see the animal were Alexander Shaw and his son. At Whitefield House, which offers a splendid, panoramic view of the loch from a height in excess of one hundred feet, the pair saw a large wake develop, followed by the sight of an impressively sized back breaking the surface. The MacLennan family, residents of Temple Pier, also encountered strange animals in Loch Ness in 1933 on more than one occasion. They were adamant that the long-necked beast sported flippers and was around thirty feet in length. A pair of large humps was seen in Loch Ness on May 27 by Nora Thompson, who stood, transfixed, watching the animal until it quickly sunk beneath the waves amid an almighty splash.

Maybe the strangest of all the stories was one the media highlighted on June 7. It was a sighting by none other than a pilot who, while flying over the loch near Urquhart Castle, saw below him something distinctly alligator-like in appearance that was around twenty-five feet long and four feet wide. It's interesting that the word "alligator" was used since Miss K. MacDonald, mentioned above, had described seeing a crocodile-like animal in the River Ness, albeit an animal of a much smaller size to that seen by the pilot.

The world was amazed by the events of the early summer of 1933. And the press could not get enough of it. To everyone's delight, the beastly best was yet to come.

There's no doubt that, in terms of Nessie lore, July 22, 1933, was both history-making and groundbreaking. That was the date upon which Mr. and Mrs. George Spicer had an encounter with a large and lumbering beast at Loch Ness that clearly, as Mr. Spicer's words demonstrated, they wished had never occurred. Many people would love to see one of the Nessies. Not the Spicers: it was a traumatic and terrifying event they tried their best, unsuccessfully, to forget. George Spicer was a busy man as the director of a well-respected tailor in London called Messrs. Todhouse, Reynard and Company. When the opportunity came up for a vacation, therefore, he and his wife jumped at the opportunity. They chose to take a trip to Scotland for a bit of tranquility and relaxation. What a mistake that turned out to be.

Toward the end of their holiday, around four o'clock in the afternoon, the Spicers' final day in Scotland turned into a veritable nightmare. As the pair drove south along the road that links Foyers and Dores, Mrs. Spicer suddenly screamed—and with good reason. Somewhere in the region of six hundred feet in front of them, a bizarre-looking animal loomed out of the bushes that dominated the roadside. At first, all that could be seen was what looked like a large trunk. As they got closer, however, the situation quickly changed.

George Spicer described the animal as being hideous, an absolute affront against nature. What particularly struck Spicer was the way the thing moved. It did not do so like any normal animal. Rather, it lumbered across in a series of odd jerks and coils—something that, for Spicer and his wife, was reminiscent of a massive worm. By the time the shocked pair reached the section of the road where the monster had appeared, it was already gone. Nevertheless, evidence of its presence was still there. The surrounding bracken had clearly been flattened by something large and heavy; that much was certain.

Of two other things the Spicers were also certain: the beast was at least five feet in height and could easily have inflicted severe damage on their car. Spicer added that its skin was a gray color, not unlike the dark gray skin of an elephant. Oddly, Spicer also said that the monster seemed to be carrying something on its back. Spicer admitted that both he and his wife remained traumatized by the awful sight for weeks.

While skeptics suggest that the Spicers saw nothing stranger than a line of otters or deer, for the monster-hunting community, the case remains a classic. It must be said that the story has been expanded over the years—although not by the Spicers, it should be stressed. The issue of the beast carrying something on its back has led to controversial assertions that the thing was the body of a lamb. True or not, it's an intriguing thought that the monsters, on rare occasions, may take to the land to secure a tasty meal.

Six months later, a Nessie was once again seen on land. On this occasion, the witness was a man named Arthur Grant, of Glen Urquhart. That Grant was studying to be a veterinarian added to the weight and credibility of his report. A keen motorcyclist, twenty-one-year-old Grant was on the road, heading home at around one o'clock in the morning, when he very nearly became the first person ever to have a head-on collision with a Nessie! Fortunately, however, neither monster nor motorcyclist was injured.

The fact that the night sky was dominated by a powerful, eerie moon meant that Grant had a very good view of the beast as it loomed before him

A number of reports indicate that Nessie is capable of venturing onto land (artist's portrayal).

and then caught the glare of his motorbike's headlight. It was at a distance of around 120 feet that Grant caught sight of something unusual in front of him. Exactly how unusual it was became almost immediately apparent. Grant said he was practically on top of the monster when its tiny head, which sat atop an elongated neck, suddenly turned in his direction. Evidently just as shocked as Grant was, the monster made two bounds across the road, headed down to the loch, and vanished into its depths with an almighty splash. Grant brought his motorbike to what was literally a screeching halt and, demonstrating his spirited character, gave chase. It was quickly clear to Grant, however, that, as a result of the huge splash, the monster had made good its escape. Nevertheless, in the time between when he first saw the thing and when it fled for the dark waters, Grant was able to get an excellent view of his quarry. He described the monster as having a bulky body, flippers rather than legs, and an approximately six-foot-long, thick tail that looked like it could inflict significant damage. As for its overall size, Grant suggested somewhere close to twenty feet.

Skeptics claim that Grant fabricated the story; however, it should be noted that he was insistent that he saw a monster and even made a statement to that effect to the Edinburgh-based Veterinary Society. Given that Grant was a student veterinarian, it seems unlikely that he would have taken the risk of recklessly lying to the Veterinary Society. A prank on the press is one thing. Risking one's future career in front of the society would have been quite another. Grant's statement is an important one, as it adds some additional, intriguing data to his original report.

As he said, given his profession, he knew more than a bit about the world of natural history. As a result, he pondered deeply on the nature of the monster. Interestingly, Grant said that the beast seemed to be a chimera—a combination of several creatures. The head of the monster, explained Grant, was eel-like or snakelike; he wasn't altogether sure. The body resembled that of a plesiosaur. The eyes were large—although, admittedly, Grant only saw one. Logic dictates, however, that both eyes would have been uniform in nature and appearance. The skin of the animal was like that of a whale.

It was reports like those of Arthur Grant and the Spicers that quickly led to the development of the theory that the Loch Ness Monsters represent nothing less than a relic population of plesiosaurs. There's no doubt that this is the most popular and engaging theory for the Nessies, one that the Scottish tourist industry, Hollywood, and the media love to promote. Unfortunately for those willing to put their money on this admittedly likeable theory, the chances of the Nessies being plesiosaurs are slim to none.

First, there is the not insignificant fact that the plesiosaur surfaced around 250 million years ago and died out around sixty-six million years ago. Plesiosaurs, the fossil record has conclusively shown, lived in saltwater environments—our planet's oceans. Loch Ness, however, is a freshwater lake. Yes,

The plesiosaur, which lived during the Mesozoic Era, closely resembles descriptions of modern-day Nessie, giving birth to the theory that the lake monster is somehow a survivor of the last mass extinction event.

there is evidence of the occasional plesiosaur in a freshwater environment, but the bulk of the cases are not suggestive of entire colonies of the beasts inhabiting freshwater bodies. It's far more likely and plausible that they wandered into them and died there. And, yes, there are both a freshwater crocodile and a saltwater crocodile. But the comparison is meaningless without evidence that plesiosaurs were 100 percent comfortable in both fresh water and salt water.

On the matter of extinction vs. nonextinction, let's take note of the fact that, as the fossil record shows, there is not a single bit of evidence to suggest plesiosaurs (anywhere on the planet) survived beyond sixty-plus million years ago. Yes, we have fossilized examples of plesiosaurs. But, no, they don't date from—for example, hypothetically—twenty million years ago, or even five million or one million years ago. They all date from the precise period in which science tells us they came to an end.

And even if plesiosaurs did survive—against just about all the odds conceivable—into the modern era, they could not have made their way into Loch Ness until around the end of the last Ice Age. This is for one simple reason: Loch Ness didn't exist until then. Up until that time, the area (the Great Glen) was, for all intents and purposes, a vast block of ice. So, if they didn't enter the loch until approximately ten thousand years ago, until that point, they must have lived in the ocean waters. But if they did, then there's the problem of why we haven't found any ocean-based remains of plesiosaurs dating back, for example, thirteen thousand or twenty thousand years.

If evidence *had* been found of plesiosaurs off the coast of Scotland just before the end of the last Ice Age, every one of us should have been impressed. But, no, the evidence is always tens of millions of years old. If the plesiosaur survived beyond sixty-five million years ago, why is the evidence to support such a scenario 100 percent absent? Because there is no evidence, that's why.

And now we come to the final observation on this monster matter. Plesiosaurs, despite what some might assume, were not fish. They were reptiles. That means they had to surface to take in oxygen. Crocodiles—which, of course, are also reptiles—can remain underwater for up to two hours or so at a time. So, keeping that in mind, how about a bit of hypothesizing?

If the Nessies are plesiosaurs, then let's say that at any given time, there are around twenty of them in the loch, ranging from young and small to large and old. That would be a reasonable figure to ensure the continuation of a healthy herd. Let's also say that they, like crocodiles, can stay submerged for up to two hours at a time. This means that in any given day, each plesiosaur would have to surface around twelve times. Twenty plesiosaurs, surfacing twelve times a day (at a minimum, I should stress), would equate to 240 surfacing events every single twenty-four-hour-long period. Multiply that by a week, and the figure is elevated to 1,680. Then multiply that by fifty-two weeks in a year, and the figure becomes a massive 87,360 annually.

Even if 90 percent of the surfacing events went unnoticed or unreported (for fear of ridicule, perhaps), that would still mean in excess of *eight thousand reports per year*, every year. But the fact is that the number of sightings reported per annum equates to barely a handful. Or, let's say there are only around ten plesiosaurs at any particular time in the loch, rather than my suggested twenty. That still means a potential 43,680 cases of the animals surfacing across 365 days. Finally, there is the matter of Nessie's famously long neck.

A study of fossilized remains of plesiosaurs has demonstrated that the animals simply were not built to raise their necks high out of the water in the proud and prominent fashion that has been attributed to the Loch Ness Monsters.

Clearly, there is something very wrong here. And what is wrong is the reliance on the plesiosaur theory, which is without doubt woefully inadequate when it comes to trying to explain what lurks deep in Loch Ness. If only this inadequate theory could become as extinct as the plesiosaur itself. Yet, it has endured since the year in which Nessie became world renowned, 1933, without a single shred of evidence to support it. Ironically, a fascinating piece of evidence—a photograph—turned up in 1933 that adds further weight to the argument that the monsters are not plesiosaurs.

Famous Photos and Film

Sunday, November 12, 1933, was the date upon which the most curious and controversial photograph of an alleged Nessie was taken. It remains controversial more than eighty years after it was taken not because it is perhaps too good to be true but because the creature in the photo is so weird looking. Indeed, it is at extreme odds with what so many other eyewitnesses claim to have encountered at the loch. The witness was one Hugh Gray, an employee of the British Aluminum Company. The hot and sunny location of the encounter was near where the mouth of the River Foyers and Loch Ness come together, and the time was around noon. It can be said that Gray was the perfect person to see the creature, as the company he worked for had its premises within walking distance of where the encounter occurred—which was a nearly sheer bluff about fifty feet high. It overlooked the loch and was dominated by dense woods.

According to Gray, after attending a Sunday morning mass, he went for a walk, as he did every Sunday. It was a sunny day, said Gray, and the loch was glistening. Suddenly, something broke the surface of Loch Ness. And it was of large proportions—very large proportions. As luck would have it, Gray had a camera with him and managed to get a shot of the animal as it surfaced and seemed to float almost completely on top of the water. An utterly amazed Gray stood staring at the odd spectacle until the animal submerged, with a thrashing of its tail.

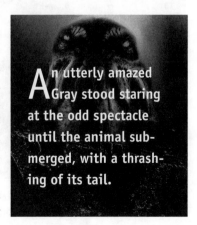

An utterly amazed Gray stood staring at the odd spectacle until the animal submerged, with a thrashing of its tail.

Hugh Gray's picture is, admittedly, an odd one. As a result, it has been interpreted in wildly varying ways. For the skeptics, the most obvious popular answer is that the photo is an innocent, unintended double exposure of a portion of the loch and of a dog swimming toward the camera holding a stick in its mouth, horizontally. It's also a theory that has been endorsed by the mainstream media—unfortunately without any meaningful critical analysis. There are, however, very good reasons why it can be said that the photo clearly is *not* a double exposure and does not show a faithful hound returning a stick to its master.

Yes, one can see what looks like the face of a dog facing the camera, if one chooses to do so. This is, however, undeniably a case of nothing more than pareidolia, the phenomenon that occurs when the brain attempts to interpret random imagery as something familiar and recognizable. Examples might include seeing faces in clouds or the visage of Elvis in a peanut butter and jelly sandwich. The Gray photo does not portray a dog, but it does show a creature that is clearly large, curiously floating atop the water, and lacking the long neck that so many witnesses of Nessie have reported. It is, you may surmise, the

The blurry photo taken by Hugh Gray has been criticized as a fake. With some enhancement, it appears to some to be a dog paddling in the water with a stick in its mouth.

oddly missing extended neck that provokes so much controversy. So, if Hugh Gray's photo doesn't show a dog, then what does it show? Let's take a look.

To the left of the photo is an oddly positioned, thick-looking tail. That there is a degree of haziness present in the photo suggests the tail may have been thrashing violently at the time the picture was taken (which Gray suggested), an act that caused water to spray into the air and make the image appear slightly out of focus and misty. Plus, it is slightly overexposed, which further limits the clarity. Nevertheless, we see a fairly thick body that clearly shows a pair of small appendages on its right side. The obvious and logical presumption is that two identical appendages are on the left side, too, although we admittedly cannot be 100 percent sure of that since the photo only shows one view of the animal.

The most important part of the photo is its extreme right-hand side. There is very little doubt that what is captured on celluloid, for all to see, is the face of a Nessie. It very much resembles the head of a turtle and has a distinct beaklike appearance. One can even make out what looks like a small eye and an open mouth that seems to show evidence of a tongue. Possibly most important of all, the shadow of the head can clearly be seen below it, reflecting off the rippling waters of the loch. Then there is the matter of how high the animal is. It is practically completely *out* of the water.

Loch Ness Monster authority Roland Watson has noticed and commented on this curious aspect of the Gray photo. He has suggested the monsters of Loch Ness may possess a form of internal buoyancy, which would allow the creatures to float on the surface in the very odd fashion as described by Gray.

Ted Holiday was a dedicated seeker of Nessie who started out as a believer that the Nessies are flesh-and-blood animals but, in the early 1970s, radically changed his views—as we shall see later. Before his mind swung over to the supernatural side, Holiday was a champion of the theory that Hugh Gray had filmed a living, breathing creature of unknown origins and identity. He also concluded that the monster captured by Gray was somewhere between twenty and thirty feet in length.

Roy Mackal, also fascinated by the Loch Ness Monster, commented on a theory that has relevance to one specific aspect of Hugh Gray's photo: the turtle-like head. He noted, correctly, that the leatherback turtle can grow to impressive sizes and weights: up to ten feet in length and a ton or more. Problematic, however, is the fact that leatherback turtles do not have long tails. Also, like all turtles, they give birth on land. This latter issue effectively rules out turtles as being the guilty parties since, by now, at least one of the millions of people who have visited Loch Ness would surely have stumbled on at least one sizeable egg of such an immense beast.

A far more thought-provoking theory has been suggested by Steve Plambeck. He suspects the Nessies may be giant salamanders, and he has diligently studied the Gray photo. The salamander theory dates back to the earliest years of Nessie lore, but no one has dug quite so deeply and dedicatedly into it as Plambeck. Salamanders are amphibians that are noted for their long tails, blunt heads, and short limbs. In addition, as in the case of the Chinese giant salamander, they can reach lengths of six feet. But is it possible that some salamanders could grow much larger, even to the extent of fifteen to twenty-five feet? Incredible? Yes. Implausible? Maybe not.

> **O**nly on occasion, Plambeck suggests, do the animals venture to the higher levels, which would account for the occasional sightings and images caught on sonar.

Steve Plambeck says that the Nessies are likely to be creatures that derive their oxygen from the water. Add to that the relatively low number of reports, and what we have, believes Plambeck, is some form of creature that spends the bulk of its time on or near the bed of the loch. Only on occasion, Plambeck suggests, do the animals venture to the higher levels, which would account for the occasional sightings and images caught on sonar. He also suggests that when the monsters do take to the higher levels of Loch Ness, they do so along its sides, the primary location of Loch Ness's fish populations. In other words, the monsters surface chiefly when they are feeding. Plambeck notes: "Such behavior is only consistent with a fish, or aquatic amphibian, which can extract all of its needed oxygen directly from the water."

In that sense, Plambeck makes a persuasive argument when it comes to the matter of the creatures of Loch Ness possibly being huge salamanders or, at the very least, another kind of large, unknown amphibian. It's a theory also noted by researcher "Erika." She says of such a scenario that China's giant salamander is hardly noted for its speed or its time spent out of the water. Indeed, as she correctly states, the creature spends much of its life at the bottom of large bodies of water, where it lies in wait of passing fish that are destined to become tasty meals. She makes the point that taking into consideration the fact that the Chinese giant salamander is a rarely seen bottom-dweller, it's not impossible that a similar creature in Loch Ness could remain largely unnoticed.

Loch Ness Monster authority Roland Watson has also waded into this controversy and admits, "I am a bit partial to a fish-like amphibian or amphibian-like fish theory myself."

There can be absolutely no doubt that of all the many and varied photographs that have been taken that purport to show a mysterious creature in the waters of Loch Ness, the one that provokes controversy on an unparalleled scale is known, somewhat incorrectly, as the "surgeon's photograph." It was taken one year after the Nessie hysteria began. I say "somewhat incorrectly" because the surgeon in question took two photos, and this is just one of the pair that has become famous. The other languishes in relative obscurity, even to this day. For decades the famous photo was championed by Nessie seekers as hard evidence that Loch Ness harbors monsters. Today, however, its reputation is in tatters.

The story dates back to April 19, 1934, when Colonel Robert Kenneth Wilson claimed to have both seen and photographed one of the Nessies. The story seemed solid since Wilson was a respected, London-based gynecologist who was hardly the sort of person to perpetrate a hoax. It was a story that the *Daily Mail* newspaper was more than happy to share with its readers. Although, at the time, Wilson flatly refused to have his name attached to the story, preferring instead to focus on how he came to be in the right place at the right time.

There's no denying the photo was taken at Loch Ness, and there's no doubt that it shows what appears to be a prominent head and neck above the surface of the water. But here's the problem: the famous, arguably iconic photo that was originally presented by the *Daily Mail* is actually a carefully cropped version of the original. It was deliberately cropped in a close-up fashion to make the neck look impressively large. When one looks at the original, panoramic image, however, and when one compares both the head and neck to the size of the surrounding ripples on the loch, it's easy to see that the monster is not only small but ridiculously small.

> When one compares both the head and neck to the size of the surrounding ripples on the loch, it's easy to see that the monster is not only small but ridiculously small.

It was in 1994 that the complicated and convoluted truth was finally made public. The monster was discovered to be a sculptured head, one that was affixed to a toy submarine! It all began with a man named Marmaduke Wetherell. He was a big-game hunter, and in December 1933, the *Daily Mail* pretty much assassinated Wetherell's character after he loudly stated that he had found footprints of a monster at Loch Ness, but it turned out that Wetherell had been the victim of a hoax. The prints were those of a hippopotamus, most likely created by an umbrella stand that had a hippo foot attached to the bottom. Wetherell was both enraged and embarrassed and decided to get his revenge on the *Daily Mail*.

Wetherell's son-in-law was Christian Spurling, who was a sculptor. Using materials purchased by Wetherell's son, Ian, Spurling created a Nessie-like head and neck, which was then carefully attached to a toy submarine. Also in on the act was an insurance agent named Maurice Chambers. The game, as Sherlock Holmes was so fond of saying, was afoot. After a test run conducted in a small pond was successful, it was time for the conspirators to perform the final act. The stretch of water where the famous photos were taken was, by all accounts, somewhere near the Altsaigh Tea House.

With the submarine carefully placed in the water, and with the neck and head standing proud and tall, the photos were quickly taken, after which the monster was scuttled and disappeared beneath the water, never to be seen again. It was then Chambers' role to provide the less-than-priceless pictures to his friend, Colonel Robert Kenneth Wilson, who became the fall guy in the saga and who sold the famous picture to the *Daily Mail*. The photo remained a matter of controversy until 1994, when then-ninety-year-old Christian Spurling finally confessed. Five years later, a book titled *Nessie: The Surgeon's Photo Exposed* by David M. Martin and Alastair Boyd was published, and the entire sordid saga exploded.

It's important to note, however, that this unfortunate state of affairs did not prevent credible sightings from continuing to be reported.

As a new era dawned, Loch Ness's reputation as a place of infinite strangeness and malignancy reached new levels. It was in 1960 that the then-owner of Boleskine House—a retired British army major named Edward Grant—shot himself in the very bedroom in which Aleister Crowley engaged in occult rites, wild orgies, and supernatural summoning. Grant's housekeeper, Anna MacLaren, was the unfortunate soul who, having had a sudden and curious premonition that he was not long for this world, stumbled on the body of the major. When she ran to the room after hearing a single, loud shot while gardening at the back of the house, she was to be confronted by a nightmarish scene.

Upon reaching the house, MacLaren could see standing by the door the major's little dog, Pickiwig. He was playing with a small piece of bone. She asked him where he got it. Pickiwig's only reply was a friendly wag of his tail.

Commonly known among Nessie experts as the "surgeon's photo," this now iconic picture of the Loch Ness creature has been widely debunked by experts.

MacLaren grabbed the bone and then headed to the bedroom. The sight before her was shocking in the extreme. Edward Grant was sitting in front of a large mirror, his head almost completely blown off his shoulders. Blood was splattered everywhere. Although in a state of hysteria, MaLaren had the presence of mind to call the police before fleeing the house. It turned out that Pickiwig's little treat was actually a portion of the major's skull and brain matter. Major Grant's distraught wife, Mary, was left to pick up the pieces, so to speak.

In a curious fashion, this is not the only occasion upon which suicide and Boleskine House have gone together. Only a few years before Grant's suicide, the house was owned by a famous British actor named George Sanders. His attempts to establish a pig farm on the grounds of the house failed miserably, and his partner, a Scottish member of Parliament named Dennis Lorraine, was jailed on fraud charges. Sanders later, in April 1972, died of a self-induced drug overdose just after completing his final movie, a supernatural tale of the dead returning to life called *Psychomania*.

Back to the year 1960: it was also the year in which one of the most famous and controversial pieces of film footage of an alleged Loch Ness Monster was taken. It was the early morning of Saturday, April 23, and acclaimed Nessie seeker Tim Dinsdale was several days into an expedition at the loch when something remarkable and, for Dinsdale, life-changing occurred. It was the final day of Dinsdale's trip, so it was a case of now or never. Very fortuitously, for the man himself, it turned out to be *now*.

As the creature began to suddenly move, Dinsdale could see ripples developing in the water, and, in his own immortal words, "I knew at once I was looking at the extraordinary humped back of some huge living creature."

At roughly 8:30 in the morning, Dinsdale, who had risen early, decided that as nothing unusual or amazing had happened in the previous five days, he might as well cut short his last day. He bid both the loch and the monster farewell and headed off to his hotel. It was while driving through Upper Foyers, however—and still in the direction of his hotel—that Dinsdale saw something amazing. It was something dark, moving across the surface of the loch at a distance of what Dinsdale calculated was around four thousand feet. Given the circumstances, Dinsdale remained surprisingly calm and collected.

Indeed, he did his best not to get overexcited: he brought the car to a halt, turned off the engine, and reached for his binoculars. Whatever the thing was, Dinsdale could see that it was of appreciable size. It was of a mahogany color and somewhat egg shaped. On its left side was a dark patch—of what, Dinsdale had no idea. Interestingly, Dinsdale's instant thought was that the contour and color reminded him of an African buffalo, with plenty of girth, and standing noticeably out of the water. As the creature began to suddenly move, Dinsdale could see ripples developing in the water, and, in his own immortal words, "I knew at once I was looking at the extraordinary humped back of some huge living creature."

Dinsdale's calm was now utterly gone. He raced to grab and turn on his 16mm Bolex cine-camera, which had a 135mm telephoto lens and was already perched on its tripod in the car, right next to him. In seconds, Dinsdale was filming the mysterious blob. He later said that, as he watched, he couldn't fail to notice that the thing left a definite V-shaped wake in the water and appeared to be submerging very, very slowly. That's when things turned from exciting to stressful. Dinsdale was extremely low on film and realized that if he kept filming from his current position, he might use up all the film but without capturing a clearer, close-up shot of the assumed animal. So, he made a sudden decision. Dinsdale stopped filming, jumped into his car, and shot away at high speed, careering along the road to Lower Foyers, across a field, and finally down to the water's edge. Disastrously, the thing was no longer in sight. Mind you, there was still the approximately four minutes of film Dinsdale had taken.

Despite Dinsdale's determination to keep the affair and the footage secret, word soon got out within the monster-hunting community. It wasn't long before the British media was hot on the trail of the monster, of Dinsdale, and of his potentially priceless film. On June 13, 1960, the *Daily Mail* newspaper ran Dinsdale's story, along with four stills from the footage. He also appeared on the BBC's popular current-affairs show *Panorama*. Dinsdale and his monster film were big news. He was deluged with mail, phone calls, and personal visits—not just from the media but from the public, too. It was a wild and crazy time for the monster hunter, which ensured that Dinsdale's pursuit of Nessie was destined to go from strength to strength.

A major development in the story of Tim Dinsdale's forty feet of film occurred in 1965, thanks to a man named David James. As well as being a persistent pursuer of the Nessies, James was also a former member of the British Parliament. As such, he had a lot of contacts and influence in the government, including personnel from what was called JARIC, the Joint Air Reconnaissance Intelligence Center, based at Royal Air Force Brampton in Huntingdon, England. JARIC's five hundred or so staff members were experts at studying film footage, including hazy and hard-to-define footage, which was certainly a good way to describe Dinsdale's film. Plus, studying film of an alleged Loch Ness Monster was a welcome break for the JARIC people, whose work was generally focused on analyzing footage of Russian fighter planes, bombers, and missile bases.

Not only did JARIC carefully scrutinize Dinsdale's footage, they also came to a remarkable conclusion. Noting that the object was likely "not a surface vessel," such as a small boat, the team said, "One can presumably rule out the idea that it is any sort of submarine vessel for various reasons which leaves the conclusion that it is probably an animate object."

Although critics, such as Dr. Maurice Burton, suggested the whole thing was a case of mistaken identity—of nothing more remarkable than a boat—the monster-hunting community was delighted. Roy P. Mackal said: "The JARIC analysis is important as an independent and expert study, free of either pro or con monster bias."

Loch Ness expert Peter Costello noted something important when he said that "the pattern of the wake and wash" were "very different" from those of a boat that was seen and filmed by Dinsdale shortly afterward. And things didn't end there. David James, who both served with the government and was a member of the Loch Ness Investigative Bureau (LNIB), persuaded JARIC to look at additional footage—specifically that was secured by the LNIB.

From around thirty seconds of film taken of something in Loch Ness on October 18, 1962—something that was humped and clearly animate—JARIC concluded it did not show a wave but a solid body that had a glistening appearance. Additional film, also taken in 1962, impressed JARIC, leading to their belief that the object was possibly a living creature. Then, in August 1965, a woman named Elizabeth Hall—also of the LNIB—filmed nine seconds of footage that showed two wakes on the water, moving parallel to each other. JARIC couldn't say what made the wakes, but the staff was pretty certain that the wakes were around nine feet from each other—which effectively rules out small boats due to the danger of collision—and one was around seven and a half to eight feet in front of the other. It all amounted to a significant period in the decades-long search for Nessie.

From around thirty seconds of film taken of something in Loch Ness on October 18, 1962 ... JARIC concluded it did not show a wave but a solid body that had a glistening appearance.

The 1960s were also noted for being the period in which the supernatural aspect of the Loch Ness Monster resurfaced and the old days of the supernatural kelpies returned.

NESSIE INTO THE 1980S, '90S, AND THE NEW CENTURY

Operation Deepscan was a highly ambitious effort in October 1987 to seek out the Nessies with sonar that might have had some degree of success. No fewer than two dozen boats were utilized to scan the depths of Loch Ness with echo-sounding equipment. Some of the presumed anomalies recorded were actually nothing stranger than tree stumps. Others may have been a seal or two that had wandered into the loch. Nevertheless, there was a moment of excitement when something large and unidentified was tracked near Urquhart Bay at roughly six hundred feet below the surface.

It prompted Darrell Lowrance of Lowrance Electronics—whose echo-sounding equipment was used in Operation Deepscan—to say: "There's something here that we don't understand; and there's something here that's larger than a fish, maybe some species that hasn't been detected before. I don't know."

Today, Jonathan Downes is the director of the Centre for Fortean Zoology, one of the few full-time organizations in the world that investigates unknown animals—such as the Loch Ness Monster, the Abominable Snowman, and Mothman—on a full-time basis. Back in 1992, however, Downes was spending his time working as a psychiatric nurse, as a trader of rare vinyl records, and as the publicist for a famous British rocker of the 1970s, Steve Harley, a vocalist with the band Cockney Rebel. It was while Downes was busy selling albums and singles at a record-collecting fair in the English town of Brentwood that he crossed paths with a man named Spike, who told Downes something remarkable.

Spike—clad all in black, elegantly waisted, and pale as a vampire—was what is known as a chaos magician. Magician Andrieh Vitimus describes chaos magic as "an attitude, a philosophy that promotes experimentation, play, and creativity while discarding dogmatic rules."

Downes related what happened when he invited the gothic Spike to take a seat at the record fair: "[Spike] told me how—together with his friends—he had carried out experiments to raise demonic entities. He ... had been involved in a series of rituals designed to invoke the Babylonian snake goddess, Tiamat, on the shores of Loch Ness. He claimed that as a result of his magical incantations, he had seen a head and neck of the Loch Ness Monster looming at him out of the misty lake."

Tiamat, remember, had become part and parcel of the story told by Ted Holiday after studying a certain curious tapestry found near Boleskine House

in 1969. Not long after speaking with Spike, Jon Downes had the opportunity to visit Loch Ness and chose to go where Spike had gone some years earlier: in search of a monster.

Downes continued that as he and his ex-wife, Alison, and two friends—Kim and Paul—drove alongside Boleskine House, he got a distinct chill, realizing that he was deep in the black heart of Aleister Crowley territory. After checking out the exterior of the old house and taking a few photos, the four headed off to find a suitable place to camp for the night, which they did on Loch Ness's north side.

Once home to Aleister Crowley (and, later, Led Zeppelin guitarist Jimmy Page), Boleskine House was severely damaged by two fires in 2015 and 2019, but it is currently undergoing restoration.

After a night out, fine wine and dining, and much talk in a local pub of the Loch Ness Monster variety, Downes decided to take the plunge, as it were. Dawn had barely arrived on the scene when Downes quietly and stealthily crawled out of his sleeping bag, trying not to disturb the others or alert them to what he was about to do. He dug into his rucksack, pulled out a tape recorder, and took it and his briefcase on a brief walk down to the loch's edge. As he crept past the tent in which Kim and Paul were sleeping, Downes could hear the distinct sounds of snoring. That was a very good sign: no one knew what he was up to.

There was an issue involved in using chaos magic to invoke a Nessie that Downes found, admittedly, a little controversial. He explained, "All the celebrants in an invocation to Tiamat had to be naked. Furthermore, an offering of 'the male essence' had to be made in supplication." This was, to say the least, a highly alternative way of catching sight of a Nessie. Cameras and sonar equipment had worked on occasion. Downes, however, was about to enter what was, for him at least, uncharted territory. To say that his nerves were jerky would be an understatement. Indeed, Downes notes, "I had brought a bottle of wine with me to steady my nerves and although it was only just after six in the morning, I took a hearty swig."

Fortunately or otherwise, the sounds of voices from other campers interrupted Downes's plans. The moment—and the task in hand—had come and gone. The invocation that never was may not have reached its—ahem—climax, but the affair is notable for one specific reason: Jon Downes is one of the United Kingdom's leading monster hunters, and even *he* was compelled to go after Nessie according to the teachings of magic—in this case, chaos magic. More and more as time advances, the futile attempts to find and identify Nessie via sonar and photography are giving way to far more esoteric means. And this was not the only occasion in the 1990s when Downes sought to cross paths with supernatural serpents of the deep.

In the summer of 1998, Downes—along with Richard Freeman, the zoological director of the Centre for Fortean Zoology (CFZ), and sundry members of the CFZ—sought to raise from the seas off the coast of Devon, England, the supernatural form of Morgawr. This was the clearly paranormal, long-necked sea serpent that Doc Shiels had pursued back in 1976, one year before he photographed a Nessie. The CFZ had received a request, just a week earlier, from a local television company making a documentary on sea serpents. Downes and his crew were pleased to oblige. On the morning in question, Freeman took to the shore. He stood with his legs spread wide, looking impressive in a long, black robe and brandishing a fierce-looking sword toward the sea. He chanted an ancient invocation in a mixture of Gaelic and old English in an attempt to summon the ancient sea beast from its lair.

This was no casual, last-minute action on the part of Freeman, who as well as being a zoologist is a full-fledged ritual magician. He had prepared well in advance. Four large candles were positioned on the sand—which amazingly stayed alight, despite the rain and a powerful wind. The candles were not merely there for effect. A red-colored candle represented fire. A green one, the earth. The air was portrayed in the form of a yellow candle and the sea by a blue one.

Then, with the time, the setting, and the atmosphere all in alignment, Freeman tossed a bunch of elderberries into the water, essentially as a gift to Morgawr, and screamed at the top of his lungs: "Come ye out Morgawr; come ye out ancient sea dragon; come ye out great old one!"

He chanted an ancient invocation in a mixture of Gaelic and old English in an attempt to summon the ancient sea beast from its lair.

The entire CFZ team, as well as the television crew, turned slowly and apprehensively away from Freeman—whose face briefly became like that of someone deep in the throes of demonic possession—and toward the harsh, pounding waves. Unfortunately, Morgawr failed to put in an appearance that day. Just like Downes's experience at Loch Ness in 1992, however, this particular episode demonstrates that for seekers of monsters of the deep waters, technology is increasingly giving way to the occult traditions of the days of old. Today, it's far less about photographing and recording the Loch Ness Monsters and their ilk and far more about supernaturally invoking them.

Among the significant twenty-first-century developments in relation to the mystery of the Loch Ness Monster was the destruction of a legendary site at Loch Ness—none other than Boleskine House, the abode of the late Aleister Crowley, the "Great Beast" himself. Just before Christmas 2015, the old house was engulfed in fire. It had been spotted on fire in the early afternoon by a motorist on the A82 road running from Inverness to Fort William. Close to three dozen firefighters were quickly on the scene, but to no avail. The owner, Annette MacGillivray, said: "When we bought it, it was a hovel. Just a shell and we paid too much for it. We spent a lot of money, stripping it back to the bare walls and re-roofing it. It had four bedrooms, four bathrooms, a huge drawing room, dining room, library and various smaller rooms. It is unlikely it will ever be rebuilt unless there is someone out there with an interest in the occult wanting to spend a lot of money."

Staff at the *Scotsman*, reporting on the event, shared with their readers some of the weirdness that happened at Boleskine House: "Local legend has it that the house was built on the site of a church which was burned down, killing the entire congregation who were attending mass.... Unexplained and unconfirmed stories of the time include those of a local butcher cutting off his own hand with a cleaver after reading a note from Crowley written on a piece of paper with a spell on the reverse. There are rumors of a tunnel from the cellars of the house to the burial ground which lies below the house by the loch side."

The BBC got in on the controversy of Nessie in late 2017. In an article titled "2017 Has Been a 'Record Year' for Sightings of the Loch Ness Monster," the BBC said:

The Loch Ness monster has had a busy 2017, with more "official" sightings than any other year this century. Admittedly, the number of official sightings logged is eight, but that's a lot for a mythical beast.

The eighth sighting is a photo of a strange "fin" in the water, taken by Dr. Jo Knight from Lancaster University, after a recent visit to the loch. She had taken her nine-year-old son to visit Loch Ness because of his interest in the monster. "My son is interested in all sorts of possible creatures like yetis and Tasmanian tigers," Jo tells *Newsbeat*. "Scotland is slightly easier to get to than the places he wanted to go to look for yetis."

In July 2018, the *Inverness Courier* ran an interesting story about plans to give the matter of Nessie a big boost in local publicity. The article was titled "Businessman Pushes for 'Monster Trail' to Show Nessie at Her Best." It went as follows:

Businesses around Loch Ness are being urged to help create a new monster trail by sponsoring special plaques relating stories and anecdotes about the area's most famous resident.

Despite countless reported sightings of Nessie—as well as several infamous hoaxes—little information is available at locations around the 23-mile long stretch of water. Drumnadrochit company Cobbs has now seized the initiative by installing an engraved plaque at its lochside Clansman Hotel, relating the 1934 sighting by motorcyclist Arthur Grant who reported seeing a long-necked creature in the water on a January night.

Company director Willie Cameron is now urging other businesses and organizations to sponsor plaques relating to more tales of Nessie through the years. 'The majority of people who come to Loch Ness come here for one reason—the Loch Ness Monster,' he said. 'Yet when you go round the loch, there is very little indication relating to the mystery.'

He envisages the installation of plaques at 25 different locations, depending on permission from agen-

The last couple of years have seen a rise in the number of Nessie sightings, according to sources such as the BBC.

cies including Highland Council, Bear Scotland and landowners. The ultimate aim is to develop an app which would contain further details as well as information about any sponsors. 'It is good for business and it is excellent for exceeding customer expectations relative to the sense of place,' he said.

On June 22, 2018, Roland Watson, the author of two books on Nessie, *The Water Horses of Loch Ness* and *When Monsters Come Ashore*, wrote: "It was back in February that I gave a talk on the monster to the SSPR [Scottish Society for Psychical Research], a society founded by Glasgow University's Emeritus Professor of Astronomy, Archie Roy. Coincidentally, he taught me the mathematical delights of Celestial Mechanics many moons ago. After the talk, I made my acquaintance with Sandy, a monster believer for years and one with a story to tell. He recounted his experience to me and was happy to e-mail it to me for general dissemination."

Sandy told Watson that it was in October 2010 that he and his wife had the shock of their lives as they were canoeing on the loch. He stated:

> About half way back I noticed a lighter patch in the water which I took for cloud reflection. My wife had stopped paddling to tell me about a difficult incident she had experienced in the past and was mid-story when I saw the light patch. We were passing close by the light patch soon after I spotted it. When I realized it was a fairly large thing right at the surface I was absolutely petrified; we were half a mile from the shore in the dark, slowly passing a large strange object in Loch Ness. I paddled like mad trying to get past it and away but it was too late to do anything but go right by it with only a couple of meters between it and the canoe.

The mystery remains that: a mystery.

Also in the summer of 2018, Nessie expert Gary Campbell posted the following to his *Loch Ness Monster Sightings* website: "30 April 2018—Eoin

O'Faodhagain said: "I couldn't believe my eyes and started recording it on my phone. It was certainly something big."

O'Faodhagain from Co Donegal took a ten minute video from the Loch Ness webcam at 1207 hours. The creature moves from right to left and there were no boats visible on the water when he first noticed it but as it swam towards Urquhart bay, two cruisers came down the middle of the loch from the north and it sank briefly then came up again, but seemed to be lower in the water than when it first appeared. As the cruisers got closer to the object, it sank completely and never came back up."

The *Daily Record* newspaper was soon on the story: "Eoin O'Faodhagain was given a 'terrific shock' after appearing to capture Nessie diving down before resurfacing. The clip has been accepted by the Official Loch Ness Monster Sightings Register, according to *The Mirror*."

O'Faodhagain said: "I couldn't believe my eyes and started recording it on my phone. It was certainly something big. It dived down and up again and dived and disappeared. It was not a boat. I would say it was Nessie."

Campbell gave his thoughts on the matter: "As far as Nessie footage goes, this is a feature film. Normally you only get videos of one or two seconds. It is remarkable in its length. Clearly it is something that dives in and out of the surface with water splashes and reflections. The object would be no larger than 20 feet."

Then, on July 21, 2018, a long-forgotten newspaper article surfaced; it had largely been lost to the fog of time since the early 1980s. The article appeared in the pages of the U.K.'s *Daily Star* newspaper and read as follows: "Prince Charles has joined the great Scottish monster hunt. He has asked to see a film made last year that is said

Prince Charles of Wales has been said to have an interest in Nessie research.

to 'prove conclusively' that there are monsters in some Scottish lochs. And monster hunter Sidney Wignall said last night: 'By the time he's finished watching it, the Prince will no longer be in any doubt that these creatures are real and not just a figment of people's imagination.'"

It's intriguing to note that the footage was not taken at Loch Ness but at Loch Morar, which, as you will recall, is the home of the mysterious monster known as Morag, which features prominently in the pages of this book. The article continues:

> Sidney, 59, shot the seven-minute cine film from a powered hang glider last September at Loch Morar in the Western Highlands. He claims it shows Morag, a relative of the Loch Ness Monster. "Part of the film shows two creatures leaving wakes behind them in the otherwise still water." he said. "Another part shows a 1,000 yard wake similar to a torpedo's. But the most frightening bit shows a creature—or something—lying perfectly still at the side or the loch. Whenever I get to that bit, my hair stands on end—and I'm sure it will do the same to the Prince."

Sidney, of Old Colwyn, North Wales, has spent £4,000 on his hunt for the monsters, and he has sent several reports on his activities to Prince Charles. The film, which was shot over a period of five weeks, will be rushed to the prince as soon as it is returned from Japan, where it is being studied at the moment. A Buckingham Palace spokesman said last night: "The Prince has said he is interested in seeing the film. But no date has been fixed yet. I don't want to say too much—or we'll be deluged with Loch Ness monster things from now on."

By 2020 the film appeared to have vanished, which is unfortunate. But we do have the words of one man who saw it, Nessie expert Rip Hepple. He said: "The piece of film was shown, and while it was very short it was most impressive. It was not stated which stretch of water it was, but from the glimpse of shoreline we had it did not seem to be Loch Ness. I thought it may have been one of the tree covered islands at Loch Morar; the very clear water seemed to support this. But what was on the film? It was as close as anyone could wish, to being a silhouette of a plesiosaur."

They mystery of Nessie and its cousins elsewhere in Scotland is surely destined to continue.

AN ALEISTER CROWLEY CONNECTION

Much has been written over the years regarding the monsters of Loch Ness and the notorious Aleister Crowley, who was known as the "Great Beast." Crowley, who lived at the loch for a while, has been accused of manifesting the monsters, of having secret knowledge of their supernatural nature, and of much more. The most accurate aspect of the Crowley–Nessie connection came from none other than Crowley himself. In late 1933, Crowley was invited to write an article on the Loch Ness Monster controversy for the English newspaper *Empire News*, which was founded in 1884 and is no more. Crowley took up the challenge, and his article was published on November 12, 1933. Under the heading "The Magician of Loch Ness: Uncanny Happenings at Manor of Boleskine—Evil Influence," Crowley began:

> I have been very intrigued by the recent stories concerning the appearance of some fearsome monster, about 30 feet long, with eyes reported to be "like the headlights of a motor-car," which is alleged to lurk in the depths of Loch Ness. Interested because at one time during the pursuit of my investigations into magic I owned the notorious manor of Boleskine and Abertarff, situated on the south-east side of Loch Ness half-way between Inverfari-

gaig and Foyers. I say notorious because long before I purchased the Manor it was already the place around which a score of legends had been woven. All of them of a mysterious nature. Thus the head of old Lord Lovat, who was beheaded after the '45, was believed to roll up and down the corridors of the rambling old place. There was another legend that a lunatic had murdered his mother by smashing her brains out against the wall, and that she returned at times to pick them up again. These alone had sufficed to give Boleskine an evil reputation, and my own experiences there by no means diminished that evil reputation.

So you will appreciate my interest in the latest story of Loch Ness, about which there have been so many speculations. I notice that the monster has been seen by a number of reputable people, who speak in awed tones, some suggesting that it may be a survival of some prehistoric creature released from some fastness in the earth by recent blasting operations in the district. Others that it is some mysterious monster from the deep which has made its way to the loch from which it cannot now escape. I know not. I only know that all the time I have known Loch Ness it has always been regarded by those living in the vicinity as "the loch which never gives up its dead." Divers who have gone down as far as 200 feet have told of huge fissures and holes in the bottom of the lake, whilst the deepest soundings have yielded over 700 feet as its depth in places. I have no knowledge of this monster, but I have knowledge of the Manor of Boleskine, where many uncanny events happened during the time I lived there.

Crowley then addressed the controversial matter of Boleskine House itself:

It was in the early days of my magical studies that I decided to look around for a suitable place where I could prepare myself for the great "Operation of Sacred Magic." It had to be a house in a secluded situation, with a door opening to the north from the room in which I was to make my ora-

Occultist and founder of the Thelema religion, Aleister Crowley (1875–1947) once lived near Loch Ness and was accused of giving rise to the monster within its depths.

tory. Outside the door I had to construct a terrace covered with fine river sand, and at the end of the terrace I was to construct a lodge where the spirits might congregate. All these instructions I had gleaned from my secret Master of the Lodge of which I was an initiate. At the time I was a young man with a fortune of 40,000 prepared to spend every penny of it on the achievement of my purpose, but I had scoured the country for a suitable residence in vain before I lighted upon Boleskine, which fulfilled all my requirements. The great "Operation" was to be commenced at Easter. I set aside the south-western part of the long, low building for my work, constructing my terrace and lodge outside the largest room there, in which I set my "Oratory" proper. This was a large wooden structure, lined with mirrors, which I had brought with me from my temple in London.

There was much more to come, as Crowley made abundantly clear:

The work would take me at least six months, and in view of certain dangers and interferences which I had already experienced from a rival magician, I invited another initiate to stay with me by way of company. He had not been there a month before he felt the strain unendurable. One morning I came down to breakfast to find him gone. The butler was surprised that I did not know that he was going away by early boat that morning. He had come down in a rush and simply vanished, and it was years before I saw him again. One day I returned from a wander over the hills to find a priest in my study. He had come to tell me that my lodge-keeper, a life abstainer from any form of alcoholic liquor, had been raving drunk for three days, and had tried to kill his wife and children. I got an old Cambridge friend to come down and stay with me, but within a few weeks he began to display symptoms of panic and strange fears, stating that there were "presences" in the place of an evil nature. At length he left me, and I carried on alone.

I devoted myself to the task of preparing certain talismans, squares of vellum inscribed in Indian ink, and in order to make my task easier I did this work in the sunniest room of the house. Yet even on the brightest days I had to use artificial light on account of the eerie darkness which could be felt. It was as if the faculty of vision suffered from some interference. But I completed my talismans and then sent to the Chiefs of the Second Order in London for certain documents to which an initiation in Paris entitled me. These were refused and I made a special journey over to Paris. It was at this time that there occurred a revolt among certain members of the Order, and as a result my "Operation" was delayed, as it meant waiting for the following Easter before I could continue with it.

Moving on (quite literally), Crowley wrote in his article for the *Empire News*:

> I traveled for a time, climbing mountains in Mexico with that great climber Eckenstein. At length I returned to Boleskine, to find it a place with a greater reputation for evil than ever. The natives would not pass the house after dark. Yet for myself I shall always feel a little grateful to Boleskine for giving me my wife, although in later years this union which held so much for both of us whilst it lasted became a domestic tragedy. I was invited to go over from Boleskine to stay with a friend, and it was then that I met Rose. She was engaged to marry a wealthy American whom she did not love, at that time being enamored of a flabby sort of individual over here. The American was coming over in a few weeks and she confided to me that she hated the thought of marrying him whilst in love with the other man. "We can soon remedy that," I said: "Marry me—that will put an end to the American romance—and you can settle down with your lover."

> A crazy suggestion, but Rose jumped at the idea. We were married at a lawyer's in Dingwall by that simple process of declaring that we regarded ourselves as man and wife. To add a touch of romance to the commonplace, I took out my dirk and kissed it as a pledge. I did not kiss Rose. It was at this moment that my bride's brother burst in upon us to stop the folly, but suddenly Rose took command of affairs, and she told him to go to the devil, as she was going off with me. I don't know whether it was my indifference to her and a sort of gratitude for getting her out of a hole which purged her heart of any infatuation for her lover, but the fact is that Rose fell in love with me. What is more, the fine flight of her rapture evoked my love in return. She was a beautiful and fascinating woman of high intelligence, and the honeymoon which followed was an uninterrupted beatitude. We traveled. From Cairo we went out and spent a night sleeping in the King's Chamber of the Great Pyramid, and thence up country for some big game shooting.

"One of the workmen had become suddenly maniacal and attacked my wife, who was making her usual morning inspection. We overpowered him and shut him in the coal-cellar until the police arrived."

Crowley, coming close to the end of his article, wrote:

> Rose was deeply interested in my magical work, and on my return to Boleskine I started to prepare once more for the great

"Operation." Suddenly I knew that the rival magician to whom I have referred was attacking me. At this time I kept a pack of blood-hounds, and he succeeded in killing them off one after another. There was absolutely no sign of any sort of disease. They simply died. The servants, too, were continually becoming ill one with this complaint, one with the other. Action was necessary. One morning we heard screams and oaths from the direction of the kitchen. One of the workmen had become suddenly maniacal and attacked my wife, who was making her usual morning inspection. We overpowered him and shut him in the coal-cellar until the police arrived.

He wrapped up: "Maybe the lake of Loch Ness is suffering from the same phenomena as the Manor of Boleskine. I do not know. But I am extremely interested in the ultimate end of the investigation into the existence of the monster which has created such excitement." So there you have it: Crowley and his very own words concerning Loch Ness, Boleskine House, and those mysterious monsters.

BANISHING A MONSTER

On the night of June 2, 1973, Loch Ness played host to something truly extraordinary. It was nothing less than a full-blown exorcism that was designed to forever banish the malignant monsters from the deep and dark waters. It was all the work of Donald Omand, both a doctor and a reverend, who had substantial knowledge and experience in the domain of all things supernatural. Of his thoughts on the Nessie phenomenon, Reverend Omand said: "Each year I drive along most of the long, somewhat tedious, shore of Loch Ness in traveling from the Kyle of Lochalsh to Inverness, and never yet have I observed the monster."

We should not interpret this to mean that Omand was a skeptic when it came to the Loch Ness creatures. In fact, quite the opposite is the case. He believed that one had to be at the loch at the right time to encounter one of the monsters. His reasoning was simple: the Nessies are supernatural entities that can only be encountered when the circumstances are conducive to an encounter. For Omand, the monsters were projections of something large and terrifying from a bygone era—monsters that may have existed millions of years ago but that continue to manifest, albeit in paranormal form.

For the God-fearing reverend, the supernatural beasts had to be cast out, and the sooner the better. He was helped in his venture by none other than Nessie seeker Ted Holiday. Holiday's interests in Omand's opinions on the monsters of Loch Ness were prompted by the latter's book *Experiences of a Present-Day Priest*. It's a book that details the reverend's nagging and worrying suspicions that lake monsters have supernatural, rather than physical, origins. Omand had also focused his attentions on combating black magic and witch-craft, and he had even exorcised bears, lions, and tigers believed to have been in the throes of dark, demonic possession. He was, then, hardly your average priest. But, he was exactly the kind of priest needed to rid Loch Ness of its strange inhabitants.

It's worth noting how and why Reverend Donald Omand became so deeply immersed in the Loch Ness Monster controversy. In 1967, he had his own sighting of a black-humped beast in Loch Long, which is located in Argyll & Bute, Scotland. It was only in view for moments, but even so, it was long enough for Omand to have gotten a clear look at it and to realize it wasn't anything as simple as a wave or a rotting tree trunk. It was a monster—and one that seemingly had the ability to boil and bubble the water.

Omand was further exposed to the mysteries of water monsters in the following year, 1968—the same year in which Ted Holiday was coming around to the idea that the Nessies had supernatural origins. Omand had confided in a friend what he had seen at Loch Long in 1967. That friend was a Norwegian sailor named Jan Andersen. The upshot of this revelation was that Captain

Loch Long in western Scotland is another lake that might host a Nessie-type monster, according to Reverend Donald Omand, who reported seeing a black-humped beast there.

Andersen invited Omand to accompany him, in June 1968, on a trip through the Fjord of the Trolls, otherwise known as the "eeriest waterway in Norway." Omand jumped at the opportunity. Had he known what was going to happen, Omand might have declined the invitation.

As the pair negotiated the mysterious waters, the water began to boil and bubble, as it had at Loch Long one year earlier. As if right on cue, a pair of large, dark-colored humps rose from the depths and headed directly for Andersen's boat. The humps were so large that Omand was deeply afraid that the leviathan might actually capsize the vessel and send the pair to Davy Jones's locker.

Captain Andersen reassured Omand that the animal would bring no harm to them. Sure enough, at the last moment, the creature abruptly changed course and sank beneath the surface. Andersen stressed to Omand the importance of recognizing that although the monster did no physical harm, it was definitely malevolent. Puzzled as to how the monster could be considered evil when it hadn't hurt them, Omand was told by Andersen that such creatures did not bring physical harm to anyone, as they wished to be perceived as nonmalevolent. This, however, was nothing more than a cunning and callous ruse. Omand asked Andersen what he meant by that, and the seafarer replied that it was not the bodies of the witnesses that the creatures were set on disrupting but their minds and characters—to the point of provoking anxiety, paranoia, and, finally, mental collapse.

> Puzzled as to how the monster could be considered evil when it hadn't hurt them, Omand was told by Andersen that such creatures did not bring physical harm to anyone, as they wished to be perceived as nonmalevolent.

Ted Holiday could personally relate to Andersen's words and how his personal mindset had been radically altered and manipulated by exposure to the Nessies. Holiday wasted no time in sending Omand a letter, applauding him on his train of thought. It was the letter and the praise that led Omand to invite Holiday to spend a weekend with him at his home in Devon, England. Holiday didn't need to be asked twice: he jumped at the opportunity. During the course of their monster-themed meeting, Holiday learned that Omand had already spoken with the Bishop of Crediton about performing an exorcism at Loch Ness, which the bishop thought was an excellent idea. Given his dramatic change of opinion on the nature of the lake monsters of Loch Ness, Holiday, too, thought it would be a very wise move.

Holiday had another reason for contacting Omand: 1973 marked the publication of Holiday's second book on lake monsters, *The Dragon and the Disc*. Holiday gave his book just about the most relevant and applicable subtitle as possible: "An Investigation into the Totally Fantastic." It was in the pages of *The Dragon and the Disc* that Holiday finally bid farewell to his earlier, and far more down-to-earth, theories for the things of Loch Ness. His new book encompassed not just the paranormal side of lake monsters in general, and the Nessies in particular, but UFOs in both ancient and modern times. So, keeping all this in mind, Holiday set a date to meet with Reverend Omand—the one man who, more than any other, shared Holiday's deep conviction that the Loch Ness Monsters were not what they seemed to be. They were worse. Much, much worse. And now it was time to confront them—maybe even head-on.

A decision was reached to undertake a number of exorcisms: several on the shore at various points along the loch and one in the dead center, on the water itself. A small boat was generously provided by Wing Commander Basil Cary, who lived with his wife near the shore of the loch and who was particularly intrigued by the monster legend. The BBC was intrigued, too, and was determined to be on the scene to capture the exorcism on camera—or, as it transpired, a recreation of it since the camera crew turned up late.

As the ritual began, the seriousness of the affair quickly became apparent. When Omand and Holiday—along with Tony Artus, a captain in the British Army with an interest in the controversy of Nessie, and a photographer friend of Omand—arrived at Lochend, Omand asked Holiday and Artus to kneel, which they did, and holy water was sprinkled on their foreheads in the shape of a cross. As if right on cue, a chilled wind suddenly enveloped the area. That was not necessarily a good sign—at all. With that act performed, Omand approached the mysterious waters, lowered his head, and said in quiet and deliberate tones:

> I exorcise thee, O Creature of Salt, by the living God, by the true God, by the Holy God, by that God who by the prophet Eliseus commanded thee to be cast into the water to cure its barrenness: that thou mayest by this exorcism be made beneficial to the faithful, and become to all those who make use of thee healthful both to soul and body: and that in whatsoever place thou shalt be sprinkled, all illusions and wickedness and crafty wiles of Satan may be chased away and depart from that place; and every unclean spirit commanded in His name, who is to come to judge the living and the dead and the world by fire.

It was quite a statement, to be sure! Omand continued, asking for Loch Ness and its surroundings to be free of malevolent, supernatural spirits and that the monsters be forever dispatched to a paranormal realm far away from the loch. Just for good measure, Omand sprinkled a liberal amount of holy water into the loch. The same ritual was undertaken, and the same words were spoken, at a pebbled stretch of beach, at Borlum Bay, and at Fort Augustus. These particular exorcisms had a profound effect on Ted Holiday. Looking back on that night a few years later, he said that while he held no particular, firm beliefs when it came to the matter of religion, "I felt a distinct tension

Reverend Omand attempted an exorcism of the Loch Ness monster but apparently to no avail.

creep into the atmosphere at this point. It was as if we had shifted some invisible levers and were awaiting the result."

In addition, Holiday recalled that the photographer looked very worried. Tony Artus had plunged into a state of complete silence. Only the reverend seemed unaffected by the unusual situation all four found themselves in. By the time the final land-based exorcism was over, evening was nearing its end, and the all-enveloping darkness of night was beginning to blanket the area. There was no time to waste; the intrepid mariners headed for the waters of Fort Augustus, intent on bringing the matter of Nessie's presence to a hopeful closure. Whitecaps and a howling wind appeared, seemingly out of nowhere. Yet again, it appeared, a bad sign was the order of the day—or, rather, of the night. Holiday felt a distinct air of menace envelope him, and he took a deep breath. If there be monsters, now was possibly the time for them to make their presence known and engage the reverend in a battle of good versus evil. Once again, the reverend had words to intone as he called for the reign of the monsters to end and for their banishment from Loch Ness.

The last of the holy water was then poured into the loch amid hopes that it would help to drive the paranormal presence away for good. Instead, something else happened: Reverend Omand visibly, and suddenly, paled, shivered, and appeared close to passing out. The group raced to get the boat to the shore, and there then followed a torturously slow walk across the surrounding hills, now grown dark. It was a walk that saw Holiday and Tony Artus constantly supporting Omand to prevent him from keeling over into the grass. Despite the seemingly serious nature of the situation, Omand later explained that feeling drained and light-headed were two of the classic after-effects of performing an exorcism and nothing to overly worry about. After a while, Omand was fully recovered, and the group retired to their beds, earnestly hoping and praying that the Nessies would never again darken Loch Ness. As history has shown, however, they did—time and time again.

Perhaps as some form of malignant backlash against the valiant attempts to banish the monsters, dark forces seemed to hover ominously around the area for almost a week afterward. Several days after the exorcism, Holiday took a nighttime drive to the home of Basil and Winifred Cary to solicit their views on the Sundberg UFO encounter at Loch Ness in August

1971. A psychic with notable powers of precognition and someone who had spent time in India and had worked for the Special Operations Executive during World War II, Mrs. Cary did not encourage delving into the domain of the unknown. In fact, she did her utmost to discourage it.

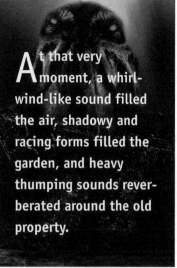

As Holiday brought up the matter of the UFO encounter, Mrs. Cary's face took on a deeply furrowed frown, then a look of concern, and finally one of downright fear. In no uncertain terms, she quietly cautioned Holiday to keep away from the reported landing site of the allegedly alien craft, warning him that the only outcome of such an action would be disaster—or worse. An evil presence was apparently hovering around and listening intently to her words.

At that very moment, a whirlwind-like sound filled the air, shadowy and racing forms filled the garden, and heavy thumping sounds reverberated around the old property. The plume of a black, smokelike substance appeared amid the garden's flowers and plants. An ear-splitting scream from Mrs. Cary filled the living room. The entire household was briefly enveloped by a cloak of terror and mayhem. After twenty seconds or so, however, normality was returned, and the brief atmosphere of paranormal terror was gone.

A Cousin of Nessie

Make mention of Scottish lake monsters to most people, and they will inevitably conjure up imagery of the world's most famous unknown water beast, the Loch Ness Monster. What they probably don't know is that there are more than a few Scottish lakes with legends of diabolical creatures attached to them. While many of the stories are decidedly fragmentary in nature, one of them is not. Welcome to the world of Morag, the resident beastie of Loch Morar.

At just over eleven and a half miles in length and just over one thousand feet deep, it has the distinction of being the deepest body of fresh water in the British Isles. Unlike Loch Ness, the water of which is almost black, Loch Morar can boast of having practically clear water. It takes its name from the village of Morar, situated close by and at the western side of the loch, where the Battle of Morar took place in 1602—a violent, death-filled confrontation between the Mackenzie and MacDonell clans.

As for the monster, Morag, the tales are many. What makes them so different from the ones coming out of Loch Ness is not the descriptions of the creatures but that such reports are often hard to uncover. Unlike Loch Ness, Loch Morar is an isolated, seldom-visited loch. It is bereft of a large population and not particularly easy to access. The result is that tourists to Scotland—or even native Scots—rarely visit it. For that reason, as is said of Las Vegas, what happens at Loch Morar is usually destined to stay there. Nevertheless, there are enough classic cases on record to strongly suggest strange things lurk in Loch Morar.

One of the earliest reports came from a man named James McDonald, who claimed a sighting of a three-humped creature snaking through the waters late one cold, dark night in January 1887. Rather ominously, superstitious locals perceived this as a distinctly ill omen: the three humps or sections were said to represent death, a coffin, and a grave—such was the fear that the villagers had of the monster in their midst. Eight years later, Sir Theodore Brinckman and his wife were fishing at the loch when a long thing, shaped like an upturned boat, surfaced from the depths. "It'll just be the monster," said one of the locals, a man named MacLaren.

An astonishing sighting occurred in 1948, when a man named Alexander MacDonnell sighted one of the Morags actually on the bank of the shore at Bracorina Point. In a few moments, it practically belly-flopped back into the water and vanished. It was a beast described as the size of an elephant. Needless to say, there is no known, indigenous creature in the British Isles that rivals an elephant in size. In the same year, a number of people, led by a Mr. John Gillies, caught sight of an approximately thirty-foot-long animal, displaying no fewer than four humps. Then, in August 1968, John MacVarish had

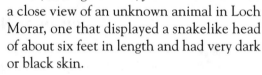

a close view of an unknown animal in Loch Morar, one that displayed a snakelike head of about six feet in length and had very dark or black skin.

Without doubt, the most amazing—and, for the witnesses, nerve-racking—encounters occurred on the night of August 16, 1969. That was when William Simpson and Duncan McDonnell were traveling on the waters near the west end of the loch. Suddenly, as if out of nowhere, a large animal—possibly thirty feet in length—loomed into view and actually collided with their motorboat. Perhaps *rammed* would be a better term to use. When Simpson tried to blast the creature with his shotgun, it sank

Loch Morar in Lochabar, Highland, Scotland, is home of Morag, a less-well-known cousin of Nessie.

beneath the waves—a result of the ear-splitting sound of the gun, both men concluded, rather than as a result of Simpson having actually shot the monster.

As for what the Morags might really be, monster hunter Richard Freeman says: "As with the Nessie, I think the best bet are giant sterile eels. The common eels swim out to the Sargasso Sea to breed and then die. The baby eels follow scent trails back to their ancestral freshwater homes, and the cycle begins again. Sometimes, however, a mutation occurs, and the eel is sterile. These stay in fresh water and keep on growing. They are known as eunuch eels, and no one knows how old they get or how big. One theory suggests that these rare, naturally occurring mutations may be on the increase due to pollution. PCBs and beta-blocker chemicals have long been implicated in causing sterility in fish. Could they be causing more eunuch eels in the deep lakes of Scotland? For now, we just don't know."

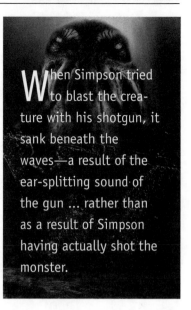

When Simpson tried to blast the creature with his shotgun, it sank beneath the waves—a result of the ear-splitting sound of the gun ... rather than as a result of Simpson having actually shot the monster.

THE RIVER NESS MONSTER AND EARLY YEARS

Yes, that's right: before the Loch Ness Monster, there was the River Ness Monster, inhabiting the waterway leads into the famous loch. Considering the many attempts that have been made by monster hunters to suggest the Nessies are plesiosaurs, salamanders, or giant eels, it seems interesting that even the very first reported encounter with one of the creatures of Loch Ness was steeped in occult mystery. It's a certain Saint Adomnán, whom we have to thank for bringing this intriguing case to our attention. The story can be found in book 2, chapter 27 of Saint Adomnán's *Vita Columbae*. To say that it's quite a tale is an understatement. Born in the town of Raphoe, Ireland, in 624 C.E., Saint Adomnán spent much of his life on the Scottish island of Iona where he served as an abbot, spreading the word of the Christian god and moving in highly influential circles. He could count among his friends King Aldfrith of Northumbria and Fínsnechta Fledach mac Dúnchada, the High King of Ireland. And he, Saint Adomnán, made a notable contribution to the world in his tale of a certain famous lake monster.

Saint Adomnán's *Vita Columbae* (*Life of Columba*) is a fascinating Gaelic chronicle of the life of Saint Columba. He was a sixth-century abbot, also of Ireland and then Iona, who spent much of his life trying to convert the Iron Age Picts to Christianity. In 563, Columba sailed to Scotland and two years later happened to visit Loch Ness while traveling with some comrades to meet with King Brude of the Picts. It turned out to be an amazing and notable experience, as *Vita Columbae* most assuredly demonstrates. Adomnán began his story thus:

> When the blessed man was staying for some days in the province of the Picts, he found it necessary to cross the river Ness; and, when he came to the bank thereof, he sees some of the inhabitants burying a poor unfortunate little fellow, whom, as those who were burying him themselves reported, some water monster had a little before snatched at as he was swimming, and bitten with a most savage bite, and whose hapless corpse some men who came in a boat to give assistance, though too late, caught hold of by putting out hooks.

If the words of Adomnán are not exaggeration or distortion, then not only was this case the earliest on record, it's also one of the very few reports we have in which one of the creatures violently attacked and killed a human being. Adomnán continued that Saint Columba ordered one of his colleagues—a man named Lugne Mocumin—to take to the River Ness, swim across it, pick up a boat attached to a cable on the opposite bank, and bring it back. Mocumin did as Saint Columba requested: he took to the cold waters. Or, more correctly, to the lair of the deadly beast.

Saint Columba was an Irish abbot who spread Christianity to the Picts in Scotland during the sixth century C.E. The saint supposedly confronted Nessie after a man was found dead by the lake with an enormous bite wound.

Evidently, the monster was not satisfied with taking the life of just one poor soul. As Mocumin swam the river, a terrible thing ominously rose to the surface and, with its huge mouth open wide, gave an ear-splitting roar. Saint Columba's party was thrown into a state of collective panic as the monster quickly headed in the direction of Mocumin, who suddenly found himself swimming for his life. Fortunately, the legendary saint was able to save Mocumin. He quickly raised his arms into the air, made a cross out of them, called on the power of God to help, and thundered at the monster to leave Mocumin alone and be gone. Amazingly, the monster did so.

Invoking God apparently had quite an adverse effect upon the Nessie, something which the pages of *Vita Columbae* makes very clear. Saint Adomnán wrote that immediately after Saint Columba made the sign of the cross and called on the supernatural power of God to save Mocumin, the creature fled for safety and vanished below the surface. This was very good news for Mocumin, who was barely ten feet away from the monster when it decided to cease its attack. The amazed group fell to their knees, praising God for having saved their friend. Even what Saint Adomnán referred to as the local "barbarous heathens" were impressed by the astonishing spectacle of the monster being denied a second victim.

One could make a rational case that the story was simply a parable, a fable—perhaps one designed to demonstrate the power of the word of God over the domain of evil. After all, Saint Columba, as noted above, spent years trying to convert the Picts to Christianity, and what better way to persuade people than to suggest that God had the power to repel deadly Scottish lake monsters? On the other hand, it's decidedly curious that of all the large bodies of water in Scotland where the story could have been set, it turned out to be none other than Loch Ness or, at any rate, the River Ness, an approximately twelve-mile-long waterway that flows out of the loch's northern end.

A little-known fact in this story is that this was not the only close encounter Saint Columba had with a Nessie: Saint Adomnán told of how one

Urquhart Castle on the banks of Loch Ness is a popular tourist traction as well as a lookout point for a number of Nessie sightings.

of the animals allegedly towed the saint's boat—a currach, a wooden vessel coated in animal skins and used frequently by the Celts of that era—across the loch, which led Columba to give the monster its freedom in the loch. A variant on this story suggests that Columba confronted the beast in the waters near Urquhart Castle, which is a hotspot for Nessie sightings today and has been for many decades.

The paranormal mystique surrounding the Loch Ness Monsters and Saint Columba and his boat do not end there. None other than the ghostly form of Saint Columba's ancient currach has been seen traveling on the expansive waters on more than a few occasions. Just two years into the twentieth century, the supernatural currach was seen by one Finlay Frazer, a resident of Strathenick. Colin Campbell, the brother of Alex Campbell—a man who played a major role in the development of the Loch Ness Monster controversy, as we shall later see—had a close encounter with the spectral craft during the Second World War. And a man named Thomas O'Connell saw its spectral shape in 1962, near Invermoriston.

Colin Campbell said of his extraordinary and eerie sighting that it was a dark night when, quite out of the blue, he saw at a distance of around ninety feet a stationary boat on Loch Ness. It was, however, no ordinary boat. It lacked any illumination itself but was bathed in an eerie, mysterious, white-blue glow. Campbell was sure that what he saw was the spectral form of an ancient, primitive craft constructed millennia earlier. From the very outset, then, the saga of Nessie—and those that were exposed to it almost one and a half thousand years ago—was absolutely steeped in matters of a paranormal nature. And it still is.

The next report of a Nessie dates from around nine hundred years later, in 1520. It should be stressed this does not mean there was a complete absence of encounters in the intervening years. It suggests that, possibly, no one chose to speak about what they may have seen. More likely, if the details of sightings were passed down orally and among close-knit communities close to the loch, they may have become forgotten and lost to the fog of time.

The details of the 1520 case come from a man named David Murray Rose, a respected antiquarian who was particularly active from the late 1800s to the 1930s. It was in 1933, when Nessie mania was in full swing, that Rose contacted the *Scotsman* newspaper about his knowledge of an early episode of the Nessie variety. In a letter dated October 20, 1933, Rose stated that post-Saint Columba, the next reference to the presence of strange creatures in Loch Ness harked back to 1520. He cited as his source an old manuscript that was filled with tales of all manner of strange and legendary creatures, such as fire-breathing dragons and ghostly hellhounds. According to Rose's research, the book in question described how one Fraser of Glenvackie slaughtered such a dragon—in fact, what was said to be the very last Scottish dragon—but not before the beast managed to scorch much of the landscape. Interestingly, Rose said that the author of the book made a comment to the effect that although the dragon was slain, the creature of Loch Ness lived on.

While Rose's account is unfortunately brief, it does demonstrate that more than five hundred years ago, there existed a tradition of monstrous animals in Loch Ness, long before the term "Nessie" was coined.

CHAMP, BIG WALLY, PEPIE, OGOPOGO, AND PADDLER

Located on the U.S.–Canada border covering parts of Vermont, Quebec, and New York State, Lake Champlain has long been the reputed domain of a huge serpent known as Champ. Indeed, reports extend back more than 150 years. One of the most fascinating developments in the story of Champ occurred in 1881. That was the year in which a huge skeleton was unearthed by one H. H. Burge. Of this sensational discovery, a reporter recounted in the May 27, 1881, issue of the *Middlebury Register*:

> The proprietors of the Champlain Granite Works, located near Barn Rock on Lake Champlain claim to have uncovered a petrified sea serpent of mammoth proportions, being about 8 inches in diameter and nearly fifty feet long. The surface of the stone bears evidence of the outer skin of a large serpent while the inner surface shows the entrails. The proprietors are intending soon to begin excavations along the place where it lies embedded in the dirt and granite, to ascertain its size.

Additional data surfaced on June 8 of the following year, 1882, in the *Elizabeth Town Post & Gazette* with this first-person account:

> The report of finding a monster in the limestone deposit of the "North Shore" I heard many times and considered it a story originating with someone anxious to be the author of a sensation.

> Last summer, a party, part of whom were scientific gentlemen by education and profession, called at the cottage and almost demanded admission to the apartments of the monster. The Superintendent was busy at the time superintending his many laborers engaged in the quarry, and told the gentlemen he could not leave his business and go down to the house, and furthermore, he was not prepared to exhibit what he had found, as there was so little of it, but at some time in the future he would be glad to show to all his serpent. I had heard the above from one of the party, and

Beautiful Lake Champlain spans the border between New York and New Hampshire, but the northern edge also reaches into Quebec, Canada.

made my mind up to say nothing of the serpent when I went there. Just about to bid the good folks good-day, the Superintendent said: "I am not in show business, as many have thought, neither am I showing snakes, but I have something to show you."

On the carpet in an upper room lay six or seven feet in length, pieces of an enormous petrified snake. Some portions were six inches long and some fifteen or more. The pieces were placed together and fitted so nicely that was no room for doubt of their having been broken apart. The largest end was eight or nine inches in diameter, and only three or four feet from the terminal of the entrails, and two or three feet beyond. The entrails were petrified, but much darker and quite open or porous and containing many bright and glistening crystals. The vertebra was visible at each broken end, and the flesh part showed traces of what had at one time been veins.

The skin was readily distinguished from the flesh as would have been had the monster been cut in two whilst living. After an examination of each piece, and comparing the gradual enlargement of the cavity, thickness of flesh and skin on the belly, and the gradual thickening towards the back, left no room in my mind to entertain the thought that it was an accident or freak of nature with molten rock. During this hour of examination at the south side of the window with bright sunlight, the Superintendent had sat quietly and had said nothing but answer a very few questions. I said I did not want to be inquisitive, but would like to know in what kind of rock he was found and his general position. He said he was not in the rock but was merely attached to the limestone, and his position was as if he had placed himself for rest or sleep, and he had traced his body by actual measurement over sixty feet, and his weight to several tons when all removed. The portions the Superintendent has removed he has secured alone, but will be obliged to have help in getting the remainder or leave the monster to rest in his slumber of death. When the proper time comes the scientific men of different localities will be called upon to make an examination and publish to the world their verdict.

Cryptozoologist Richard Freeman, who has taken a deep, personal interest in this particularly intriguing saga, says: "The remains are next mentioned in the *Burlington Free Press* of November 4th, 1886, and apparently were on show at a bank-sponsored exhibition held in Vergennes, Vermont. They were subsequently purchased by the famous showman P. T. Barnum (1810–1891) for his museum. From then on the specimen seems to have vanished. Searches of Barnum's records have so far been fruitless. Barnum's collections were twice ravaged by fire, but both of those incidents were before he bought the remains."

Freeman speculates: "What was the skeleton? Some kind of fossil? The strata around Lake Champlain is too young for dinosaurs or their contemporary marine reptiles. Archaeocetes are also much too old for the strata. The only fossil whales that have been uncovered in the area are modern species such as the beluga (*Delphinapterus leucas*). The presence of skin and soft organs is unusual. These are only preserved under exceptional circumstances. This raises the possibility that it was a sub-fossil or, in other words, fairly recent in origin."

A Champ made out of stone that someone assembled along the shore of Lake Champlain.

It's not often that one sees a story of a giant monster splashed across the front page of the *New York Times*. Nonetheless, that is exactly what happened on July 1, 1908. The article was headlined: "200-FOOT SEA SERPENT. Seen at 3 Bells in Gulf of Mexico—Enormous Rattles on Its Tail." *Times* staff wrote:

> What is confidently believed to be a sea serpent has been sighted and narrowly inspected by the officer's crew and fifteen passengers of the steamship *Livingstone* of the Texas-Mexican Line. All of the witnesses made a sworn affidavit to this effect before United States Consular Agent Charles W. Rickland at Frontera, Mexico.

> The statement is signed by Capt. G. A. Olsen and the other officers, George Thomas of Denver, Albert Dean of Memphis, H. B. Stoddard of Bryan, Texas, Mrs. Jessie Thornton of Chicago, and eleven other passengers. In substance it declares that at three bells on the evening of June 24, the *Livingstone*, bound from Galveston to Frontera, Mexico, making good weather, and about fifty miles north of Frontera, in the Gulf of Mexico, the serpent was sighted off the port bow.

> The ship got within sixty feet of the creature, and for fifteen minutes stood while all on board viewed the serpent through the glasses. It was apparently sleeping, and not less than 200 feet long, of about the diameter of a flour barrel in the centre of the body, but was not as round. The head was about six feet long by three feet at the widest part.

> The color was dark brown, and near its tail were rings or circles that appeared larger in circumference than the body at that point. As it swam away the tail was erected, and a rattling noise as loud as that made by a gatling gun in action startled the watchers on the *Livingstone*.

On November 5, 1885, the *Wallowa Chieftain* newspaper ran an article on its resident monster, which has been given the distinctly nonmonstrous name "Big Wally." It is said to dwell in Wallowa Lake, Oregon, an approximately fifty-one-square-mile body of water with a depth of around three hundred feet. The article states:

> A prospector, who refuses to give his name to the public, was coming down from the south end of the lake on last Friday evening in a skiff shortly after dusk, when about midway of the lake he saw an animal about fifty yards to the right of the boat, rear its head and neck up out of the water ten or twelve feet, but on setting him it immediately dived. He ceased rowing and gazed around in astonishment, for the strange apparition which he had just seen, when it raised about the same distance to the left, this

time giving a low bellow something like that of a cow. It also brought its body to the surface, which the prospector avers was one hundred feet in length. The monster glided along in sight for several hundred yards. It was too dark to see the animal distinctly, but it seemed to have a large, flat head, something like that of a hippopotamus, and its neck, which was about ten feet in length, was as large around as a man's body.

Farther north, a Nessie-like creature, Caddy—an abbreviation of *Cadborosaurus willi*—has struck a deep chord with the people of Cadboro Bay, British Columbia, Canada. It's a chord with a long history. For the skeptics, sightings of the Caddies can be explained away as whales, sharks, sea lions, and serpent-like oarfish. Not everyone, however, believes the monsters of Cadboro Bay can be dismissed quite so easily. Take, for example, the 1933 encounter of two duck hunters, Cyril Andrews and Norman Georgeson. They were in the bay's Gowlland Head. What began as a duck hunt rapidly changed into something very different, as Andrews noted shortly afterward, when he went public with the story. He stated:

> I succeeded in shooting a golden-eye duck, but as I had only broken its wing, it began swimming to a kelp bed about fifty yards from shore. Seeing I could not get the wounded bird I sent Norman home for a small punt, five feet long. Returning, he was paddling across the bay towards me as I walked over a little rise to see if he was coming. As I looked across the water I heard a disturbance some distance out. From where I was standing I could plainly see the whole body of a sea monster just moving a foot underneath the surface.

The giant oarfish *Regalecus glesne* is a type of lampriform fish (such as the ribbonfish) that could understandably be mistaken for a sea serpent. The one in this 1996 San Diego photo is 23 feet (7 meters) long.

Thinking I might alarm Norman I did not draw his attention to what I saw, so he came along and picked me up at the point from which we had shot the bird. From there we paddled to the wounded bird in the kelp bed. I was sitting in front of the punt ready to pick the bird up, when about ten feet away from it, out of the sea rose two coils. They reached a height of at least six feet above me, gradually sinking under the water again, when a head appeared. The head was that of a horse, without ears or nostrils, but its eyes were in front of its head, which was flat just like a horse.

While Nessie in Loch Ness, Scotland, is certainly the world's most famous lake monster, it most assuredly does not stand—or swim—alone. Numerous lakes around the world are said to be the lairs of monstrous serpents of the deep. In all likelihood, some sightings of such alleged creatures are due to mistaken identity—perhaps of catfish and sturgeon, both of which can grow to impressive sizes. But other reports simply cannot be dismissed with such down-to-earth explanations. Take, for example, Ogopogo of Okanagan Lake in British Columbia, Canada.

It's interesting to note that Okanagan Lake is, like Loch Ness, a place of considerable size, one in which a colony of predominantly underwater creatures could survive and thrive. It is more than eighty miles long, three miles wide, and just short of 250 feet deep.

Like its Scottish cousin, Nessie, Ogopogo has a long and rich history of sightings. We may never know for sure how far back into history the creatures of Okanagan Lake extend, but we can say for sure that the Native Americans who lived in the area as early as the 1700s knew that the waters of the lake were home to something monstrous and terrifying. That much is evident by the name they gave to the beast—or, far more likely, beasts. They called it the *n'ha-a-itk*. Appropriately, it translates into English as "Lake Demon."

Perhaps "Lake Demon" was too horrific for the locals, and they settled upon "Ogopogo." The story of the name is an intriguing and winding one, as the late cryptozoologist Mark Chorvinsky noted: "The name Ogopogo might suggest to some that it is an Indian word, but all evidence points to a modern origin. According to Mary Moon, author of *Ogopogo: The Okanagan Mystery* (1977), in 1924 a local named Bill Brimblecomb sang a song parodying a popular British music-hall tune at a Rotary Club luncheon in Vernon, a city in the northern Okanagan Valley. H. F. Beattie adapted the lyrics."

Among the lyrics are the following: "I'm looking for the Ogopogo. His mother was a mutton, his father was a whale. I'm going to put a little bit of salt on his tail."

When it comes to the eyewitness accounts of Ogopogo, the list is impressive. Most witnesses describe a large creature—anywhere from fifteen to

A statue of the famous Ogopogo lake monster greets visitors at City Park in Kelowna, British Columbia, Canada.

twenty-five feet and, on occasion, even as long as fifty feet—serpentine in appearance, and sometimes displaying undulating "humps" and a neck that occasionally rises out of the water to a height of six to seven feet. If true, then this effectively rules out sturgeon or catfish as being the guilty parties. With that said, let's now take a look at the evidence in support of the theory that Okanagan Lake is a domain of monsters.

It was on September 16, 1926, that Ogopogo was thrown into the limelight. Literally dozens of people—in no fewer than thirty vehicles—saw a mysterious creature in the vicinity of Okanagan Mission Beach. They were unanimous in their belief that the beast was an immense serpent-like animal.

On July 2, 1947, a Mr. Kray got a good look at an Ogopogo and said the creature had "a long sinuous body, 30 feet in length, consisting of about five undulations, apparently separated from each other by about a two-foot space, in which that part of the undulations would have been underwater. There appeared to be a forked tail, of which only one-half came above the water. From time to time the whole thing submerged and came up again."

Jumping forward more than forty years, there is the case of Ernie Giroux, a hunting guide, who spotted a fifteen-foot-long creature in the waters of the lake in the summer of 1989. Whatever the beast was, it was like nothing Giroux had ever seen before: it "swam real gracefully" and had a head shaped like a football and a long neck. To date, the number of reports of Ogopgo are in the hundreds. As to what the monsters may be—surviving creatures from the Jurassic Era, giant eels, or something entirely unknown to science—the answers continue to elude both monster hunters and those that have been fortunate enough to encounter the famous monster.

In 2015, Chad Lewis and Noah Voss wrote a book titled *Pepie: The Lake Monster of the Mississippi River*. It is an excellent study of the little-known beast (or beasts) of Lake Pepin, which borders Wisconsin and Minnesota. As the authors demonstrated, it's a story that dates back not just decades but centuries. And how did Lewis and Voss demonstrate this? By getting into the heart of the action and launching full-blown investigations, that's how. This meant road trips to the lake itself, archival research, and securing witness testimony. As the authors noted, it's not just the monster itself that is weird; so is the lake: "As a lake on a river, Lake Pepin is somewhat of a geological oddity." They add: "Sediment buildup from the mouth of the Chippewa River forms a delta that obtrudes into the Mississippi River causing a backup of water, which is Lake Pepin." It's a large lake, too, running at approximately twenty-two miles.

Pepie the monster gets its name from Lake Pepin, a bucolic vacation spot near the Mississippi River between Minnesota and Wisconsin.

As for Pepie the monster, like so many other lake monsters, this one is large, serpentine, and mysterious. Sightings of the beast, it's revealed to us, date back to the earliest years of Native American times, and a chapter titled "Pioneer Sightings" details a number of fascinating cases from the nineteenth century. One such case concerns a beast described by the local media of the day as a "living curiosity" and "the size of an elephant and rhinoceros."

A wave of encounters with Pepie occurred in the 1960s, and a variety of reports later surfaced in the 1980s. It's important to note, however, that the story of Pepie is not purely historical; sightings have been made throughout the 2000s and right up until at least 2010. We're also given the strange and controversial story of an alleged photo of Pepie, and Lewis and Voss describe their 2011 and 2013 expeditions to the lake. Particularly intriguing is the chapter in *Pepie* on various additional unknown animals seen in the Mississippi River. The reports are chiefly from old newspapers, which chronicle encounters with a "mysterious reptile," a huge beast with a head like "a dog or wolf," an animal described as "half horse, half alligator," and much more.

One of the most important sections of the book presents the theories for what the Pepies might really be. Misidentification is suggested in some cases—possibly of otters, swimming deer, and snakes. The authors demonstrate, however, that such examples do not explain the bulk of the genuinely weird cases. The matter of witness suggestibility—based on the expectation of seeing Pepie when visiting the lake—is also discussed, as is the angle of hoaxing.

When those down-to-earth issues are dealt with, Lewis and Voss offer up candidates for what the animals might be. Plesiosaurs, whales, and long-necked seals all come to the surface (so to speak) in this particular chapter.

Things then go down a more mysterious path into the realm of significant UFO activity alleged in the area. If, like me, you're a fan of the work of John Keel—who concluded that many of the weird and mysterious things of our world are somehow all interconnected—you'll particularly enjoy this chapter.

For those monster hunters who might want to seek out Pepie for themselves, it's worth noting there's a $50,000 reward on offer for those who can provide conclusive proof of the existence of the beast. Our authors then provide us with a "Final Thoughts" section, in which they look back on their investigations and share some welcome thoughts and observations.

Zoologist and monster hunter Richard Freeman shared with me his research into sightings of lake monsters that are especially appropriate to mention here. He said:

> In one of my earliest blogs I wrote about cryptid material turning up in museums and the possibility of unlabeled or "lost" material in collections around the world. In the state of Wisconsin some strange material, possibly related to a lake monster, was uncov-

Lake Mendota, one home of the water spirits called the Wak Tcexi, is right in the heart of human civilization. This photo shows the University of Wisconsin and downtown Madison right on the lakeshore.

ered not once but twice. The Winnebago Indians believed in two distinct types of dragon-like monster inhabiting lakes. The Wak Tcexi was a paranormal entity and was evil. The Winnebozho was flesh and blood, and benign. There are a number of "monster lakes" in the state but this story is linked to two in particular. Lake Mendota is close to Wisconsin's capital, Madison. Sightings of the creatures date back to the 1860s. W. J. Park and his wife were boating on the lake when they came across what looked like a large log. Mr. Park poked the "log," which dived, churning up the water.

Lake Mendota is linked to Lake Monona via the Yahara River. Monsters are seen here too. In July 1892 Darwin Boehmer and a friend were boating on the lake when they saw the monster swimming off towards Ott's Spring with an undulating motion. It showed 14 feet of its back above the surface.

On October 7th of the same year an anonymous man claimed that a 20-foot monster had tried to tip up a boat he had hired from John Scott's boat livery. He said he would never venture onto the lake again for all the money in the capital. Nor would he return to Madison without a Winchester rifle and two revolvers. Mr. Scott saw the beast for himself. He and his two sons described a hump twice the length of the boats they hired out, and he refused to row two ladies across the lake having seen the beast. He was convinced it was dangerous.

Ten days later, back at Lake Mendota, twelve men spotted a 35-foot serpent whilst in the connecting river. A man claimed that a creature shaped like a "living log" had attempted to overturn his boat. The anonymous man may have used his Winchester rifle and two revolvers on the monster with no effect, because that is what occurred in Lake Monona on June 11th, 1897. Eugene Heath said the beast he saw looked like an upturned boat and his bullets had no effect whatsoever on it. He hastily retreated from the lake as the thing came for him. A few days earlier he claimed to have seen it eating a swimming dog.

Back in Lake Mendota in 1899, a tourist from Illinois was anchored in the lake when he saw the water swell about 100 feet from his boat. A beast 60 to 70 feet long, with a snake-like head, rose up. It seemed to be sunning itself. In the summer of 1917 a monster with blazing eyes and a snake-like head was seen off Picnic Point, Lake Mendota, by a fisherman who ran away leaving his rod and basket behind him.

The same year a young couple were sunning themselves by the pier at Lake Mendota. As they lay on their backs and hung their feet over the edge, the girl felt something tickle the sole of her bare foot and thought it was her boyfriend. However, on turning over she saw what she called "a huge snake or dragon" in the water. The couple fled to a nearby fraternity house. That year piers were damaged and boats overturned—the monster was blamed.

Shortly before that wave of sightings a large, thick scale was washed up on the shore near Picnic Point. It was sent to the University of Wisconsin, where it baffled experts. The State Historical Society records that one anonymous professor believed it was from a sea serpent. Part of the lake was dredged back in 1890, near Olbrich Park, and some massive vertebrae were uncovered.

The scale might have come from a sturgeon, and the bones may well have been fossils, but one would have thought that a university professor would have recognized these. It might be interesting to enquire if the scale is still in the possession of the

University of Wisconsin, and whether the State Historical Society recorded what became of the bones as well as if they were ever examined properly. If there are any readers in Wisconsin that fancy pursuing this, it may be a worthwhile endeavor.

Situated in Idaho, Lake Pend Oreille is a huge expanse of water that extends in excess of forty miles in length and one thousand feet in depth. The lake also might be home to a creature not unlike Nessie, the famed monster of Loch Ness, Scotland. Then again, Lake Pend Oreille's lake monster, known locally as Paddler, might be something even stranger.

Sightings of the prehistoric-looking thing date back to the 1940s and continue to the present day. A particularly spectacular encounter with Paddler occurred on Memorial Day in 1985.

Sightings of the prehistoric-looking thing date back to the 1940s and continue to the present day. A particularly spectacular encounter with Paddler occurred on Memorial Day in 1985. On that day, a woman named Julie Green was on the lake with several friends when they all caught sight of something huge and fantastic: a large, gray-colored thing racing across the lake, seemingly partially above and below the surface of the water. That the thing was only around six hundred feet away meant Green and her friends were able to determine that whatever it was, it wasn't a wave.

Then, in 1996, the Groves family of Pasadena, California, while vacationing with family who lived in the lake area, reported seeing early on a Sunday morning a large, gray-colored object break the waters. It was described as resembling the back of an elephant in both color and size. Needless to say, Lake Pend Oreille isn't home to a herd of elephants that enjoy taking morning swims.

While monster hunters are content to suggest that Paddler (or the Paddlers) is either an unknown animal or one from the Jurassic Era that survived extinction, there is another explanation for the presence of the monster. It's a very alternative explanation, too. Patrick Huyghe has undertaken extensive research into the saga of Paddler, and he has noted something that might be significant: "The very first mention of Paddler came straight from the Navy's own Farragut Naval Training Station, established on the southwestern end of Lake Pend Oreille in 1942."

Built in response to the terrible and tragic events at Pearl Harbor in December 1941, the FNTS was created at Lake Pend Oreille as the hostilities with the Axis powers grew, and about 290,000 servicemen and women have passed through it. What is particularly interesting, however, is that in the postwar era—that is to say, after 1945—the U.S. Navy's presence on the lake began to change. The one arm that began to play a more substantial role was the Navy's Acoustic Research Department. The ARD says of its work:

"Unique experimental hardware and floating platforms have been developed" at the naval facilities on Lake Pend Oreille, and "future plans include continuation of sonar dome development and submarine silencing and target strength reduction experiments using large-scale models."

One has to wonder if some of these "unique experimental hardware," "floating platforms," and "large-scale models" have been responsible for at least some sightings of what the witnesses believed was Paddler.

Huyghe notes something that is supportive of this particular theory: "In 1949 and 1950, a few years after this secret Navy test site opened, the next two accounts of the lake monster appeared in local newspapers."

It's not at all unlikely that the U.S. Navy might secretly spread tales of lake monsters, such as Paddler, to divert people from learning the truth of what was afoot deep in Lake Pend Oreille, such as the covert testing of new subsurface military vehicles of a highly classified, experimental nature.

OTHER INLAND WATER MONSTERS

We know from an abundance of witness testimonies that our oceans are teeming with amazing and unknown animals. Some of them, as we've seen, are deadly, marauding predators. We can find evidence of similar creatures living within multiple inland environments, too. It's vital that we come to appreciate the nature of these largely land-locked leviathans. They include aquatic insects that have grown to incredible sizes, huge turtles, massive frogs, violent pike that reach the size of an average person, unidentified animals that dwell in the lakes and lagoons of Africa, and huge lizards hiding in the dense realms of Australia. They may never be able to leave their land-based environments, but they will always be monsters of the waters.

AFRICAN LAKE MONSTERS

For more than one hundred years, tales have circulated concerning a dangerous and potentially deadly beast that has made its water-based home in the heart of the Congo Basin in Central Africa. Its name: Mokele-Mbembe. It bears a superficial resemblance to a *Brontosaurus* a herbivore that existed in the Jurassic period, weighed up to sixteen tons, and could grow to approximately seventy-two feet in length. Like the rest of the dinosaurs, the brontosaurus was violently taken out of circulation around sixty-five million years ago, possibly by a collision between Earth and a massive comet, the result of which was worldwide chaos, massive flooding, the plummeting of the hot

A sketch of a Mokele-Mbembe based on descriptions. The animal has never been photographed to date but is said to look rather like a brontosaurus.

temperatures that existed during that era, and the inevitable extinction of the dinosaurs. But did they really die out? Is it possible that at least some of the massive monsters from the distant past managed to survive? If so, could they be with us to this very day? Could the Mokele-Mbembe be one of those survivors? Such a scenario sounds incredible and unlikely. That doesn't make it impossible, however. What do we know about this mysterious, huge creature that is said to live both on land and in the water?

The name Mokele-Mbembe translates into English as "the one who stops the flow of rivers," which is a highly apt moniker for a creature of highly impressive proportions. Although it is said to be large, the Mokele-Mbembe is nowhere near the size that the brontosaurus was millions of years ago; most witnesses describe it as being the size of an African elephant, at most. It's not at all impossible that over millions of years, nature has led the Mokele-Mbembe to scale down—something that might explain why we don't see too many reports of the monster. Something the size of an elephant, which spends a lot of time in the water, could, in theory, hide from us to a highly successful degree—even if there is a colony of, let us suggest, twenty animals at any given time. It's highly unlikely, however—indeed, nearly impossible—that herds of animals around seventy feet long could feed and live in the Congo and not have been found and identified by now.

Now let us take a look at the available evidence that exists in relation to this particularly intriguing creature and the incredible lore and legend that surrounds it. Our story begins with a man named Carl Hagenbeck. The *Circuses and Sideshows* website states:

> Carl Hagenbeck was a German merchant of wild animals who supplied many European zoos, as well as P. T. Barnum. He created the modern zoo with animal enclosures without bars that were closer to their natural habitat. The transformation of the zoo architecture initiated by him is known as the Hagenbeck revolution. Hagenbeck founded Germany's most successful privately owned zoo, the Tierpark Hagenbeck, which moved to its present

location in Hamburg's Stellingen quarter in 1907. He was a pioneer in displaying humans next to animals in as human zoos.

He was born on June 10, 1844, to Claus Gottfried Carl Hagenbeck (1810–1887), a fishmonger who ran a side business buying and selling exotic animals. When Hagenbeck was 14, his father gave him some seals and a polar bear. His collection of animals grew until he needed large buildings to keep them in. Hagenbeck left his home in Hamburg to go with hunters and explorers to jungles and snow-clad mountains. He captured animals in nearly every land in the world.

In 1909, Hagenbeck's autobiography was published. Its title: *Beasts and Men*. It's in the pages of Hagenbeck's book that he describes encounters with a large, unknown animal that was reputed to live in Rhodesia and that was "half elephant" and "half dragon." A formidable monster, no doubt! Hagenbeck said: "It can only be some kind of dinosaur, seemingly akin to the brontosaurus." The legend had well and truly begun.

It's interesting to note that this was not the only mysterious water animal that was being discussed in this same time frame—and in Africa. For example, there are the intriguing words of Paul Gratz, a German explorer who said in 1911: "The crocodile is found only in very isolated specimens in Lake Bangweulu, except in the mouths of the large rivers at the north. In the swamp lives the *nsanga*, much feared by the natives, a degenerate saurian which one might well confuse with the crocodile were it not that its skin has no scales and its toes are armed with claws. I did not succeed in shooting a *nsanga*, but on the island of Mbawala I came by some strips of its skin."

Next we come to the matter of Captain Ludwig Freiherr von Stein zu Lausnitz, a German who had a passion for exploring and exotic animals. In 1913, in what is now the Republic of Cameroon, Captain von Stein learned the following. In his very own words:

> The animal is said to be of a brownish-gray color with a smooth skin, its size is approximately that of an elephant; at least that of a hippopotamus. It is said to have a long and very flexible neck and only one tooth but a very long one; *some say it is a horn*. A few spoke about a long, muscular tail like

Carl Hagenbeck was a dealer in wild animals who was a supplier for the circus owner P. T. Barnum. He was also instrumental in developing the modern, cageless zoo.

that of an alligator. Canoes coming near it are said to be doomed; the animal is said to attack the vessels at once and to kill the crews but without eating the bodies. The creature is said to live in the caves that have been washed out by the river in the clay of its shores at sharp bends. It is said to climb the shores even at daytime in search of food; its diet is said to be entirely vegetable. This feature disagrees with a possible explanation as a myth. The preferred plant was shown to me, it is a kind of liana with large white blossoms, with a milky sap and apple-like fruits. At the Ssombo River I was shown a path said to have been made by this animal in order to get at its food. The path was fresh and there were plants of the described type nearby. But since there were too many tracks of elephants, hippos, and other large mammals it was impossible to make out a particular spoor with any amount of certainty.

Moving into more modern times, there is the work of adventurer and explorer Dr. Roy P. Mackal, which began in 1980 and succeeded in bringing an awareness of the Mokele-Mbembe into the rest of the world. Mackal, who died in 2013, was no fool. Indeed, he was a biologist and biochemist who spent much of his life working at the University of Chicago.

Mackal was lucky to speak with numerous natives who had encountered a Mokele-Mbembe or who knew of its reputation as a dangerous, bad-tempered, large beast to be avoided at all cost. To his amazement, Mackal quickly realized that what the local people were describing was nothing less than a sauropod—a herbivorous dinosaur with four legs, a long tail, and a huge body. Mackal's quest led him to write a book on the subject and on his search for evidence that such animals really did exist. Its title: the highly apt *A Living Dinosaur? In Search of Mokele-Mbembe*.

Mackal was not alone. J. Richard Greenwell, who had a similar fascination for the monsters of the Congo, discovered a number of giant tracks at the Likouala River. Greenwell, utterly amazed, was sure that the Congo harbored giant-sized animals of an unknown kind. In 1986, a man named Rory Nugent was lucky enough to see one of the animals, its prominent, long neck protruding out of the Likouala Swamp. Nugent even managed to photograph the creature, but the locals insisted that he destroy the pictures. They said that if the photos were not destroyed, the monster would come for all of them. Nugent felt it was wise to do as he was told, and the priceless pictures were lost to history. The story of the Mokele-Mbembe was far from being over, though. Bill Gibbons uncovered a notable incident that occurred in the 1960s and said about the occurrence:

> Around 1960, the forest dwelling pygmies of the Lake Tele region (the Bangombe tribe), fished daily in the lake near the molibos, or water channels situated at the north end of the lake. These channels merge with the swamps, and were used by

Mokele-mbembes to enter the lake where they would browse on the vegetation. This daily excursion into the lake by the animals disrupted the pygmies' fishing activities. Eventually, the pygmies decided to erect a stake barrier across the molibo in order to prevent the animals from entering the lake.

When two of the animals were observed attempting to break through the barrier, the pygmies speared one of the animals to death and later cut it into pieces. This task apparently took several days due to the size of the animal, which was described as being bigger than a forest elephant with a long neck, a small snake-like or lizard-like head, which was decorated with a comb-like frill.

Are dinosaurs really living deep in the Congo? While the theory is a credible one, it's also one that is controversial in the extreme. With that said, is there another potential explanation? Yes, there is. It comes from a man who has traveled much of the world in search of monsters: Richard Freeman, a former keeper at Twycross Zoo in England, mentioned in earlier chapters. I had the good fortune to interview Freeman about his views on the Mokele-Mbembe and what they might be. Freeman told me:

An English ex-pat that gathered information on a supposed horned giant animal said to lurk in Lake Bangweulu [situated in

Could the deep jungles of the Congo, with its warm climate, have served as a refuge for brontosaurus? Or descendants of those dinosaurs?

the upper Congo River basin in Zambia], J. E. Hughes was born in Derbyshire in 1876 and attended Cambridge [University, England]. The British South Africa Company offered him a job as assistant native commissioner in the newly formed civil service of north-east Rhodesia. After seven years of service Hughes resigned and became a hunter/trader. He lived for the next eighteen years on the Mbawala islands on Lake Bangweulu. He recorded his life in a book, *Eighteen Years on Lake Bangweulu*, in which he writes of the monster.

Let's now see what Hughes had to say himself about the matter of monsters in Africa from his 1933 book:

For many years there has been a persistent rumour that a huge prehistoric animal was to be found in the waters of our Lake Bangweulu. Certainly the natives talk about such a beast, and "Chipekwe," or "Chimpekwe," is the name by which they call it. I find it is a fact that Herr Hagenbeck sent up an expedition in search of this animal, but none of them ever reached the Luapula or the Lake, owing to fever, etc.; they had come at the wrong time of the year for newcomers.

Mr. H. Croad, the retired magistrate, is inclined to think there is something in the legend. He told me one night, camped by the edge of a very deep small lake, he heard a tremendous splashing during the night, and in the morning found a spoor on the bank—not that of any animal he knew, and he knows them all.

Another bit of evidence about it is the story Kanyeshia, son of Mieri-Mieri, the Waushi Paramount Chief, told me. His grandfather had said that he could remember one of these animals being killed in the Luapula in deep water below the Lubwe.

A good description of the hunt has been handed down by tradition. It took many of their best hunters the whole day spearing it with their "Viwingo" harpoons—the same as they use today for the hippo. It is described as having a smooth dark body, without bristles, and armed with a single smooth white horn fixed like the horn of a rhinoceros, but composed of smooth white ivory, very highly polished. It is a pity they did not keep it, as I would have given them anything they liked for it.

I noticed in Carl Hagenbeck's book *Beasts and Men*, abridged edition, 1909, p. 96, that the Chipekwe has been illustrated in bushman paintings. This is a very interesting point, which seems to confirm the native legend of the existence of such a beast.

Lake Young is named on the map after its discoverer, Mr. Robert Young, formerly N.C in charge of Chinsali. The native name of the lake is "Shiwangandu." When exploring this part in the earliest days of the Administration, he took a shot at an object in some floating sudd that looked like a duck; it dived and went away, leaving a wake like a screw steamer. This lake is drained by the Manshya River, which runs into the Chambezi. The lake itself is just half-way between Mipka and Chinsale Station.

Mr. Young told me that the natives once pulled their canoes up the Manshya into this lake. There were a party of men, women, and children out on a hippo-harpooning expedition. The natives claimed that the Guardian Spirit of the lake objected to this and showed his anger by upsetting and destroying all the men and canoes. The women and children who had remained on the shore all saw this take place. Not a single man returned and the women and children returned alone to the Chambezi. He further said that never since has a canoe been seen on Lake Young. It is true I never saw one there myself. Young thinks the Chipekwe is still surviving there.

Hughes concluded: "My own theory is that such an animal did really exist but is now extinct."

Another bit of hearsay evidence was given me by Mr. Croad. This was told to him by Mr. R. M. Green, who many years ago built his lonely hermitage on our Lulimala in the Ilala country about 1906. Green said that the natives reported a hippo killed by a Chipekwe in the Lukula—the next river. The throat was torn out.

I have been to the Lukulu many times and explored it from its source via the Lavusi Mountain to where it loses itself in the reeds of the big swamp, without finding the slightest sign of any such survival of prehistoric ages.

When I first heard about this animal, I circulated the news that I would give a reward of either £5 or a bale of cloth in return for any evidence, such as a bone, a horn, a scrap of hide, or a spoor, that such an animal might possibly exist. For about fifteen years I had native buyers traversing every waterway and picking up other skins for me. No trace of the Chipekwe was ever produced; the reward is still unclaimed.

Hughes concluded: "My own theory is that such an animal did really exist but is now extinct. Probably disappearing when the Luapula cut its way to a lower level—thus reducing the level of the previously existing big lake, which is shown by the pebbled foothills of the far distant mountains."

Now let's return to the words of Freeman:

Perhaps, if we are to believe Mr. Young's tale, the creature's ferocity kept it from being hunted very often. A picture is emerging of a huge, dangerous, semi-aquatic animal with a single horn and an antipathy towards hippos. Many have come to the conclusion that these are Ceratopsian dinosaurs. These were a suborder of Ornithischia—bird-hipped dinosaurs—and contained such well-known horned dinosaurs as *Triceratops* and *Styracosaurus*. They were all herbivores and were typified by bearing horns and a bony frill like an Elizabethan ruff that grew from the rear of the skull to protect the animal's neck. The number of horns varied between the species; some such as *Monoclonius* bore only one horn on the snout.

There are two main stumbling blocks with the dinosaur theory. First and foremost there is no fossil evidence for any species of non-avian dinosaur surviving beyond the Cretaceous period (which ended 65 million years ago). Secondly there is no indication of any species of being aquatic, let alone Ceratopsians. So we need to look elsewhere for this beast's identity.

On the matter of that identity, Freeman shares with us his views: "The idea of a water-dwelling rhino may seem strange but the great Indian rhino (*Rhinoceros unicornis*) spends almost as much time in water as a hippopotamus. It feeds mainly on lush water plants such as reeds and water lilies. The Indian rhino also bears only one horn, much like the *Emela-ntouka* and unlike the two savannah-dwelling African species, who both bear two horns."

Freeman winds matters up as follows: "One group of rhinos the *Amynodontids* specialized in an aquatic lifestyle. These flourished in the Oligocene epoch 38 to 25 million years ago finally dying out around 10 million years ago. Could one species have survived into the present? This is by no means impossible, but it is perhaps more likely that our unknown giant is a modern species that has avoided detection, rather than a prehistoric survivor."

THE DEADLIEST LAKE MONSTERS OF ALL

The most important aspect of the sixth-century saga of Saint Columba is that which suggests an unfortunate soul was violently slaughtered by a monster in Loch Ness. The reason the incident is so important is as intriguing as it is disturbing. Within the folklore of Loch Ness and much of Scotland, there are centuries-old legends and myths concerning supernatural, violent, shapeshifting creatures known as kelpies. In English they are called water horses. In most respects, they are the same creature, but there is one noticeable difference between the tales that specifically refer to kelpies and those that talk about water horses. Typically, water horses are far more at home in deep, sprawling lakes, while kelpies prefer pools, rivers, marshes, and small, compact lakes. There is also a variant of the kelpie known as the *each-uisge*, which is a far more murderous monster than the kelpie but is clearly of the same supernatural stock.

The term "kelpie" has unclear origins, but it is probably a distortion of the Gaelic *calpa*, which translates as heifer. Kelpies are terrifying, murderous creatures that lurk in the depths of Scottish lochs, canals, and rivers—more than a few in Loch Ness. Not only that, like werewolves, kelpies are definitive shapeshifters: creatures that can take on multiple guises, including hideous serpentine monsters, horses, hair-covered humanoids, beautiful maidens of the mermaid variety, and horselike creatures. The kelpie is driven by a crazed goal to drown the unwary by enticing and dragging them into the depths, killing them in the process.

While numerous old bodies of water in Scotland have kelpie legends attached to them, it's surely no coincidence that the bulk of the legends are focused upon Loch Ness. And, as we'll see later, there is good evidence to suggest that the creatures of the loch do indeed have the ability to change their form and morph and mutate into numerous states. It's also notable that many reports of Loch Ness Monsters suggest they have manelike hair flowing down the back of their head and neck—not unlike the mane of a horse, which may have prompted both the name and imagery of the water horse. Before we get to the matter of Loch Ness, let's take a deeper look at this malevolent, demonic entity of darkest Scotland: the kelpie.

Reports of, and legends pertaining to, strange creatures in the large lochs of Scotland date back centuries—specifically to the sixth century, as we have seen with the Saint Columba affair of 563 C.E. With hindsight, they sound very much like kelpies, even though they had quite different names

Kelpies can take on different forms, being shapeshifters, including everything from a horselike creature to human, as in this 1895 painting by Thomas Millie Dow. Whatever the guise, they are water creatures who favor drowning human victims.

and titles. In 1900, Alexander Carmichael, for example, told of a beast known as the glaistic. It was a hideous monstrosity. Half-human and half-goat, it dwelled in isolated bodies of water, always ready to pounce on and slaughter the unwary and unfortunate.

Moving on, we have the lavellan, described by some as a shrewlike animal and by others as a lizard-style beast. Both its saliva and breath were said to be deadly to both man and beast. Note that the reference to the lavellan having deadly breath echoes the old story of the wyvern of Wales' Llyn Cynwch Lake. Loch Tummel, in Perthshire, Scotland, has its own kelpie, although it goes by another name, the buarach-bhaoi. Highland Perthshire Tourism says of this fearsome thing that it resembled nothing less than a gigantic leech, which typically wrapped itself around horses and then dragged them into the depths of its underwater abode to drain the unfortunate animals of blood in definitive vampire style.

Loch Lindie was the deadly domain of Madge, a violent, murderous monster that, said Edward Nicholson in 1897, had the power to morph into numerous forms, including those of a raven, a cow, a horse, and a hare. Similarly, Loch Leathan was the lair of the deadly boobrie, yet another body-altering thing with nothing but coldhearted killing on its crazed mind.

So far as can be determined, it was in the late 1700s that the words "kelpies" and "water horses" first appeared in print. The story is a bit older, however, dating to the 1740s. That was when a renowned poet, William Collins, who died while still in his thirties, made mention of the kelpie in one of his many odes. It was not until 1788, however, that Collins's poem was published in the pages of Alexander Carlyle's *An Ode to the Popular Superstitions of the Highlands. Written by the Late William Collins.*

Eighteenth-century records demonstrate there was some degree of disagreement regarding whether kelpies lived within the deep waters of lakes like Loch Ness or lurked at their very edges in shallow, marshy waters and possibly even on the land. This is worth noting since there have been more than a few sightings of the Nessies being seen near the shore, basking, lying on the shore itself, and even lurking in the surrounding woods, as strange as such a thing might sound. This suggests a collective body of data, and an enduring and attendant tradition, of the kelpies being creatures that chiefly lurked in the water but on occasion moved about the landscape, which is exactly what we have been told about the Nessies since the early 1930s.

While, as I mentioned earlier, the kelpie can take on the guise of numerous animals, there is no doubt that the horselike kelpie is the one most often reported. And generally, it is a black horse. The downfall of the unwary traveler occurs when he or she, generally late at night, is walking past some large expanse of water. Suddenly, just such a horse appears out of the darkness and beckons the victim, in an inviting fashion, to climb onto its back. That so many ill-fated people did exactly that suggests they were under some form of supernatural spell. This echoes the medieval tales of shapeshifting fairies that could place people into a state of being "pisky-led" or "pixie-led," meaning that their minds were enslaved and their actions controlled by the magic of the wee folk. Perhaps, and in view of the shapeshifting abilities of both, the fairies and the kelpies of old were actually one and the same.

When the entranced person mounts the horse, the tranquil atmosphere changes immediately and terrifyingly. The infernal beast charges into the water, plunging into its depths and dragging its victim to his or her violent death. On other occasions, the kelpie will take on the form of a beautiful woman who invites people to walk to the water with her, much like the centuries-old stories of men becoming hypnotized by the visions of voluptuous fairy queens in the ancient English woods. Similarly, the kelpie will appear as a dashing young man to capture and drown young women.

In 1807 a poet named James Hogg, who studied in depth the folklore and legend of Scotland, said that a creature similar to the kelpie was the water cow. It dwelled in the allegedly bottomless Saint Mary's Loch, a three-mile-long body of water located in what are termed the Scottish Borders. Although nowhere near as dangerous as the kelpie, the water cow could also transform itself into multiple forms and was best avoided at all costs, largely as a result of its penchant for enticing people to walk to the shore and then violently dragging them into the water, where they would drown.

In Falkirk, Scotland, is this 100-foot (30-meter) statue of two kelpies by artist Andy Scott.

A perfect example of this enticing aspect of the kelpie's manipulative character and powers comes from Christian Isobel Johnstone (1781–1857) of Edinburgh, Scotland. With her husband, a printer named John Johnstone, she ran the *Edinburgh Weekly Magazine*. In 1815 she told a chilling story of how, one day some years earlier, a group of young boys decided to go swimming in a particularly wild and dark loch on a mountain in the vicinity of Glen Ogle. In no time at all, a powerful-looking, white horse rose from the depths and swam to shore. Upon reaching land, the horse stretched itself out, as if beckoning the boys to climb on its back. Feeling adventurous, as young boys do, they did exactly that. It was not just a big mistake; it was also the last mistake any of them would ever make. When the young friends were atop the horse, it suddenly reared up and shot into the lake, drowning them as it speedily propelled itself below the surface and into the inky depths.

When the young friends were atop the horse, it suddenly reared up and shot into the lake, drowning them as it speedily propelled itself below the surface and into the inky depths.

On other occasions, the kelpie will manifest not as a horse but as something akin to a hair-covered wildman—or, one might be justified in saying, a Bigfoot. This latter description is absolutely personified by an 1879 encounter at Bridge 39 on England's old Shropshire Union Canal. Here, late one January night, a man and his horse were attacked by a crazed, half-human, half-apelike animal that leapt out of the shadowy surrounding woods. Shaggy and covered in hair, it became known as the Man-Monkey. Local police associated the presence of the creature with the recent death of a local man who had drowned in the canal under mysterious circumstances. It is clear from a study of the affair that the locals and even the police believed the man in question was dragged to his death into the waters of the canal by the English equivalent of a Scottish kelpie.

As the kelpies became both more prevalent and reported, so did their presence in popular culture. Renowned poet Robert Burns said in "Address to the Devil" in 1876:

When thowes dissolve the snawy hoord
An' float the jinglin icy boord
Then, water-kelpies haunt the foord
By your direction
An' nighted trav'llers are allur'd
To their destruction.

Despite its supernatural, malignant powers, the kelpie was not a creature of indestructible proportions. If one knew its weaknesses, one could defeat it. It's fascinating to note that one of the primary ways that a kelpie could be killed was with silver, particularly with a silver bullet. Most people will, of course, be familiar with the legends that a silver bullet is the one thing guaranteed to put down the world's most famous shapeshifting monster of all time, the werewolf. There is a vampire parallel, too: kelpies had deep aversions to Celtic crosses.

Deadly lake monsters have appeared outside the British Isles as well. Cryptozoologist Richard Freeman, in a personal interview, shared with me his lake monster-based research in Russia, saying:

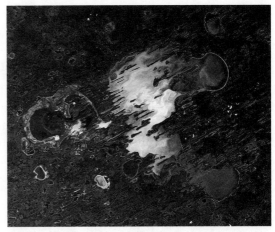

Remote Lake Chany, just north of Russia's border with Kazakhstan, covers a remarkable 770 square miles but is relatively shallow, making it a nice environment for wildlife, including a large snake that evidently consumes unwary fishermen.

> One of Russia's largest lakes seems to be the home of a large, powerful, and dangerous creature that locals say has killed nineteen fishermen. Lake Chany is virtually unknown in the West but it is a vast expanse of water covering 770 square miles. Its is fifty-seven miles long by fifty-five miles wide but is fairly shallow, at only twenty-three feet deep, with an average depth of only six feet. Lake Chany is in the southern part of the province of Novosibirsk Oblast close to the borders of Kazakhstan. The creature involved in the attacks is described as serpentine and huge. The beast claimed its latest victim, a fifty-nine-year-old fisherman, last week [in July 2010]. Sixty-year-old Vladimir Golishev was in the boat, then the creature overturned it and dragged his friend away.

Freeman secured the words of the witness: "I was with my friend some 300 yards from the shore. He hooked something huge on his bait and stood up to reel it in. But it pulled with such force it overturned the boat. I was in shock—I had never seen anything like it in my life. I pulled off my clothes and swam for the shore, not daring hope I would make it. He didn't make it, and they have found no remains. It's time to find out the truth."

Freeman continued to me: "In 2007 a twenty-three-year-old special services soldier, Mikhail Doronin, was lost when something capsized his boat. His eighty-year-old grandmother Nina was watching from the shore and said that the lake was calm. Her eighty-one-year-old husband, Vladimir, said, 'Something on an awesome scale lives in the lake, but I have never seen it.' Official figures say that nineteen people have vanished in the lake in the past three years. Locals say the figure is actually much higher and that remains have washed ashore with bite marks showing large teeth."

Undeniably, deadly lake monsters are a global phenomenon.

GIANT INSECTS

Most aquatic insects, including dragonflies, diving beetles and caddisflies, live in fresh water. In this environment, their number and diversity are 12 times greater than other animals that share the same habitat, including fish, amphibians and crustaceans. Very few insects live in saltwater. The most common saltwater dwellers are insects that look like water striders, called halobates or sea skaters, which "surf" the waves of the ocean!

Most aquatic insects live in shallow water near shorelines, where light is still visible from the bottom. They live in all kinds of places, from mountain streams and rivers to lakes and tranquil ponds. The more rich in nutrients the habitat is, the greater the diversity of insects that live there.

Those are the words of the ecological website *Espace pour la vie Montréal.* These facts provide significant food for thought for what you will read in this chapter.

Is it possible that the southwest region of the United States is home to giant-sized insects—living deep underground—that feed upon us, the human race? Such a thing sounds unlikely and incredible, similar to the scenario presented in the classic 1954 sci-fi move *Them!* In the movie, massive, radioactive ants terrorize and slaughter the people of a small New Mexico town, and they threaten to do likewise not just to the rest of the country but to the entire planet. This brings us to an important question: might truth be stranger than fiction? Yes, just possibly.

Danielle B. is a woman who, for a number of years, lived in the New Mexican town of Aztec. Like the far more famous New Mexican town of Roswell, Aztec has a crashed-UFO legend attached to it. It's a legend that dates back to March 1948, when, reportedly, a near-intact flying saucer and its crew of diminutive dead pilots were found. Danielle, however, says she encountered something far stranger at Aztec than deceased extraterrestrial dwarfs and a wrecked flying saucer.

It was on one particular day in May 2004 that Danielle decided to spend a few hours hanging out in Aztec's Hart Canyon—which, curiously enough, is exactly where the alleged UFO is said to have fallen to Earth back in the 1940s. It was also where Danielle had an encounter with something far worse than aliens. On a warm and sunny day, Danielle found a place to sit and read a book, with her snacks and drinks at hand. It was a perfect way to spend a day off work, at least for a while.

All was normal for a couple of hours until Danielle noticed a small, black helicopter approaching her in the distance. More correctly, she assumed that it was a helicopter, since at a distance that's what it appeared to be. As it approached, it became clear that it was no normal helicopter: there was no "thud-thud" sound that one associates with the fast-moving blades of a helicopter. On top of that, it appeared to be carrying below it a small calf, held tightly in place by thick ropes! It was most definitely not the kind of thing you see every day. When the helicopter got close to Hart Canyon, Danielle could see that the helicopter was actually nothing of the sort. It was a large, obscene-looking insect about four meters in length. The presumed rotor blades of the helicopter were actually the fast-beating wings of the creature. As for the ropes, they were nothing less than powerful-looking, black limbs.

Danielle could only stare—in a mixture of awe, fascination, fear, and horror—as the huge creature flew overhead, dropped the poor calf on a nearby peak, and then swooped to the ground with frightening speed, pounced on the animal, and viciously tore into it. In less than half an hour, the giant insect was done feasting and took to the skies. Danielle had been too shocked to flee the area, and as a result, the terrible event was forever embedded in her memory. Suspecting, probably correctly, that if she told local law enforcement offi-

The *Meganeura monyi* was a real dragonfly that lived about three hundred million years ago and had a wingspan of over two feet. Such large flying insects were possible back then because there was much more oxygen in the atmosphere than there is now.

cials of what she saw, she would likely be booked for wasting police time, Danielle finally made her shaky way home. She stayed silent on the matter until she confided in me roughly three years later.

Even I have to admit that Danielle's story stretches credibility to the max, despite the fact that she came across as nothing less than absolutely credible, down-to-earth, and normal. And while many might be inclined to dismiss such a bizarre account, I don't. Not because, in *X-Files* style, "I want to believe," but because of something very different. It may come as a surprise to a lot of people to learn that, in the distant past, huge insects—not unlike the one described by Danielle—really did exist.

For example, in the Jurassic Era, there existed in what today is the United States a dragonfly called *Meganeura monyi*. This was no regular dragonfly, however, for it had a wingspan in excess of three feet. As another example, in 2001, Ohio State University geologists discovered the fossilized remains of a five-foot-long centipede in an old mine. Then there were the ancient remains of a sea scorpion unearthed from a German quarry in 2007; an arthropod, the sea scorpion is of the same group as insects and spiders. There was something notable about this particular sea scorpion, however: it was slightly more than eight feet in length.

Of course, none of these oversized things were alive at the time of their discovery. Indeed, they lived, walked, and flew millions of years ago. Nonetheless, is it feasible that in certain parts of the United States—perhaps in underground caves and caverns—certain similar things exist today? Most people would probably say no. But try asking Danielle, and you will get a very different response. To this day, she has no doubt that these things are real. At the time of this writing, she is working on her own book, which ties in the predations of these hideous things with the so-called "cattle mutilation" phenomenon, which has plagued and puzzled ranchers, police officers, and even the FBI for decades, particularly in the Southwest. In Danielle's scenario, the cattle mutilators are not satanic cults, aliens, or covert military units conducting biological warfare operations. No: the mutilators are giant creatures from eras long gone that are feeding on the nation's cattle herds late at night.

Perhaps one day, Danielle's story will finally be vindicated. If such a thing does happen, let's hope it's not because the huge insects have decided to turn their predatory attentions toward us, the human race. The possibility that *Them!* may one day become reality, rather than the stuff of science fiction, is as chilling as it is disturbing.

It's important to note that cattle and other animal mutilation is quite real, even if you don't buy into accounts of giant insects living underground. Since at least 1967, reports have surfaced throughout the United States of animals—chiefly cattle—slaughtered in bizarre fashion. Organs are taken, and significant amounts of blood is found to be missing. In some cases, the limbs of the cattle are broken, suggesting they have been dropped to the ground from a significant height. Evidence of extreme heat, to slice into the skin of the animals, has been found at mutilation sites. Eyes are removed, tongues are sliced off, and, typically, the sexual organs are gone.

While the answers to the puzzle remain frustratingly outside of the public arena, theories abound. Potential culprits include extraterrestrials, engaged in nightmarish experimentation of the genetic kind; military programs involving the testing of new biowarfare weapons; occult groups that sacrifice the cattle in ritualistic fashion; and government agencies secretly monitoring the food chain, fearful that something worse than "mad cow disease" may have infected the U.S. cattle herd and, as a result, the human population.

Extraordinary Beavers and Bears

John Warms, who has extensively studied reports of monstrous beasts in Manitoba, Canada, has uncovered tales of giant, marauding beavers in not just Manitoba but also in areas stretching from Alaska to Florida. The term "giant" is not an exaggeration, as we're talking about beavers the size of people and even larger. As incredible as it may sound, such beasts really did once exist. Warms says: "Today we know from recovered bones that the giant beaver is in a separate classification from the one we know so well as *Castor canadensis*. It has been named *Castoroides ohioensis* after the state where its remains were first documented."

Warms also notes that he has a number of reports on file of "bear-sized beavers" as well as sightings of huge beaver lodges that come close to the size of an average house. It's hardly surprising that their lodges would be so huge. After all, not much else would be suitable for creatures that reached heights of seven feet and weights in excess of 250 pounds. Although the giant beaver is believed to have become extinct around ten thousand years ago—along with the mammoth and the mastodon—modern sightings suggest that remnants of the population have survived.

It's important to note that reports like those obtained by Warms are nothing new. One can find reports of huge, violent beavers that cover both the United States and Canada and date back centuries. As a perfect example, in 1808, Alexander Henry the Younger was exploring the Red River in Manitoba when he encountered a Native man near the forks of the Red and Assiniboine Rivers—today, the site of the city of Winnipeg. Henry's journal for that time contains a notable entry that confirms a giant beaver story having been told to him by his Native friend, a member of the Salteaux Nation:

> A Salteaux, who I found here tented with the Courtes Oreilles, came to me this evening in a very ceremonious manner, and after having lighted and smoked his pipe informed me of his having been up a small river, a few days ago, upon a hunting excursion, when one evening while upon the water in his Canoe, watching the Beaver to shoot them, he was suddenly surprised by the appearance of a very large animal in the water. At first he took it for a Moose Deer, and was preparing to fire at it accordingly. But on its approach towards him he perceived it to be one of the Kitche Amicks or Large Beavers. He dare not fire but allowed it to pass on quite near his canoe without molesting it. I head already heard many stories concerning this large Beaver among the Saulteaux, but I cannot put any faith in them. Fear, I presume, magnifies an ordinary size Beaver into one of those monsters, or probably a Moose Deer or a Bear in the dark may be taken for one of them as they are seen only at night, and I am told they are very scarce.

One can find reports of huge, violent beavers that cover both the United States and Canada and date back centuries.

While Henry's words clearly demonstrate his skepticism, they are important in the sense that they confirm that accounts of giant beavers existed centuries ago. As for John Warms's extensive research, it suggests that the giant beaver is still with us, albeit in deep stealth.

In 1903, a man named Oscar Frederickson of Winnipegosis, Manitoba, Canada, wrote a fascinating and extensive report on his knowledge of huge lake monsters in the early decades of the twentieth century. His information came from witnesses, both first- and secondhand. He began his account like this:

> In 1903, I lived with my parents on Red Deer Point, Lake Winnipegosis. Our house was situated about two hundred yards from the shore. About a mile south of our place lived a man by the name of Ferdinand Stark. One day Stark was down by the lake shore when he saw what he thought was a huge creature in the lake. It was moving northward along the shore, a short distance out.

> Stark wanted someone else to see the strange animal, and as we were his nearest neighbors, he came running along the lake to our place. All the while, he could see the creature moving in the same direction as he was, only going a little slower than he was running.

> Stark arrived at our home very much excited and breathing heavily, and asked my dad and mother to hurry down to the lake to see

Castoroides ohioensis was a large beaver that lived during the Pleistocene Era (mounted skeleton of a specimen at the Minnesota Science Museum is shown here), grew to be six to seven feet long and could weigh over two hundred pounds. Might stories of the Kitche Amicks be survivors of that species?

a strange animal in the water. By the time my parents got down to the lake shore, there was nothing to be seen. Whatever Stark had seen had disappeared. Looking somewhat bewildered, but still visibly excited, Stark began to describe what he had seen.

All he could see of the creature was its big back sticking out of the water, and it was very dark or black in color. A number of gulls followed it and kept flying down to it as if they were picking at it. My parents did see quite a number of gulls still flying around.

In 1935, Mr. Cecil Rogers of Mafeking and I made a trip to Grand Rapids on Lake Winnipeg. While there, I called on Mr. Valentine McKay, a resident of Grand Rapids for many years. As we were talking, the conversation drifted to strange animals that had existed at one time. To my surprise, McKay said he had seen some such animal in Lake Winnipegosis.

McKay, very pleased by the fact that Frederickson took his story seriously and did not poke fun at him, prepared a carefully written statement for the monster hunter, which read as follows:

In September 1909, I was traveling alone in a canoe from Shoal River on Lake Winnipegosis to Grand Rapids on Lake Winnipeg. At the time I saw this animal I was standing on the lake shore. I had stopped at Graves' Point to make tea. I was at the edge of the bush getting willows for a campfire, when I heard a rumbling sound like distant thunder. As I looked out on the glassy surface of the calm water, I saw a huge creature propelling itself on the surface of the water about four hundred yards out from shore. A large part must have been submerged, judging by the great disturbance of the water around it.

The creature's dark skin glistened in the autumn sun, and I estimated it was moving at the rate of two to three miles an hour. As I watched it, a member of the body shot up about four feet, vertically, out of the water. This portion seemed to have something to do with the creature's method of locomotion. The course it was taking was toward Sugar Island or Sleep Rock. I watched it till it went out of sight. The number of gulls, hovering around this creature, followed it as far as I could see.

Frederickson had something notable to say on this particular story: "Mr. McKay said he had described this creature to a geologist by the name of Craig who said it was quite possible that it was a remaining specimen of a prehistoric animal that was once plentiful."

On the matter of the two men in question—Ferdinand Stark and Valentine McKay—Frederickson made a number of observations and comments: "A great many people will think these two men just made up a story about seeing some strange animal or creature in Lake Winnipegosis, but it is hardly probable that both men would think up a yarn about the gulls. Stark and McKay never met, as far as I could find out. Stark moved from Winnipegosis about 1904 or 1905, and where he is now, if still living, I have not been able to find out."

Frederickson had yet another account to relate on this particular matter of unidentified, large beasts on the loose in the early part of the twentieth century:

In 1934, Captain Sandy Vance lived on Graves' Point. One day he was over at Sitting Island, which is on the northeast side of the point. He saw what he thought was a huge animal a short distance off shore. Vance said it was the biggest living creature he had ever seen in water. Mr. Vance had been captain on freight tugs for many years on Lake Winnipeg and Lake Winnipegosis. He said he had often seen moose and deer in water, so there is no reason not to believe that he saw some strange living creature. Captain Vance died some years ago. He was well known here.

Finally, there is the following short but intriguing account from Frederickson: "There are quite a few Natives who have seen some strange thing. They call it 'the big snake.' Those of Shoal River claim that a monstrous animal was seen often off Sugar Island and Steep Rock in Dawson Bay during the latter part of the 19th century."

Tales of giant, water-dwelling bears, like the thirty-foot Kinik and the ten-legged Kokogiak, are told in the frozen North as well. "Nathaniel Neakok, the mighty hunter of polar bears, has quit scoffing at reports about the great Kinik being seen in this northernmost region of North America," reported the Idaho Falls, Idaho, *Post-Register* on May 15, 1958. The story continued:

A Kinik is a polar bear that has grown to such immense proportions that it is too difficult for it to live out of the water, so it adopts a purely aquatic lifestyle.

A Kinik is the name Eskimos give to a bear they say is too big to come out of the water. Its size varies with the individual story. But all agree he is a monster of great size and strength and appetite. Several weeks ago, Neakok laughed so loudly when told Raymond Lalayauk had reported seeing a 30-foot bear that his hearty guffaws echoed and re-echoed across the great, frozen polar wastes. But Neakok isn't laughing anymore. He has seen a Kinik with his very own eyes.

This Kinik, Neakok says, was grayish white and only its head was visible as it swam through the water. It was so large he did not attempt to shoot it. Neakok said its head alone must have been five or more feet long—and almost as wide. This was not the first time a monster was reported by respected men of the village. Floyd Ahvakana and Roxy Ekownna, elders in the Presbyterian Church and men of undoubted veracity, tell of seeing a tremendous sea monster in 1932 while hunting with a third Eskimo, now deceased. All three thought it was a Kokogiak or 10-legged bear which occupies a prominent role in Eskimo legend.

Until now there have been many scoffers in the village, especially about Kokogiak. And … white men have been known to make reference to the "coming tourist season" or "another abominable snowman." But since the respected Neakok added his testimony, the scoffers are strangely quiet. Even fearful. You don't even hear much about how the Arctic's strange mists distort distances or size, creating weird optical illusions. But you do hear told and retold stories about Kokogiak, the 10-legged bear of Eskimo legend.

The stories could go something like this:

"Once upon a time there was a lazy Eskimo. He was the laziest man in the village. One evening after he had heard the village hunters tell of their experiences, the lazy one went out on the ice. He came to a large hole where some seal lungs were floating, showing that a large bear had eaten seal, leaving only the lungs. The man watched and waited by this hole and, sure enough, a monstrous bear came up. As he started out onto the ice, the man rammed his spear in first one eye and then the other, blinding the bear.

"However, the bear came right on out of the water and following his scent gave chase after the fleeing hunter. The man ran and ran, dodging among the humps of ice but he could not shake his pursuer. Finally, he saw ahead two towering walls of ice, with only a narrow corridor between.

"Through this pass he ran but the bear, following close upon his heels, was too big and he stuck fast, unable to back out. The hunter ran around and succeeded in killing the giant, 10-legged bear."

Many Eskimos—possibly even some white men—still believe there are Kokogiak out there somewhere in the Arctic vastness. And, says wide-eyed Nathaniel Neakok, a 30-foot polar bear too big to shoot.

Beginning in the Cascades of southern Oregon and extending down to Copco Lake, south of the California–Oregon border, the river is some 250 miles in length and takes its name from the Native American term for "swiftness." However, the creature that Jeffrey Shaw and his wife claim to have seen on a summer's day more than forty years ago can hardly be described as "swift."

According to Shaw, he and his wife had rented a pleasant, wooden cabin on a stretch of the river and would most days sit near the water's edge with a couple of bottles of white wine and a well-stocked picnic basket. As someone whose schedule with the military was incredibly hectic, said Shaw, the pair relished some much-welcome peace and quiet while communing with nature.

The Shaws had taken a ten-day vacation, and all was normal for the first half of the week; however, six or seven days into their break from the rigid confines of the Air Force, matters took a very weird and dramatic turn. On the day in question, the Shaws had driven fifteen or twenty miles in search of a particular sandbank they had been told was the perfect area for a private waterside feast. Unfortunately, they failed to locate the place in question, and so, as fate would have it, they stopped at a shady, grassy area some two to three hundred yards from the edge of the water. And with blankets, wine, and a plentiful supply of food laid out, they enjoyed a romantic lunch under a warm and sunny sky.

It was perhaps a little more than two hours into their day of fun when Jeffrey Shaw's wife saw out of the corner of her eye what she first thought was a large black bear ambling along at the edge of the woods and heading in the direction of the water. Concerned, she whispered to her husband and pointed toward the creature maneuvering among the trees and the bushes. But a closer look revealed that it was no black bear.

Jeffrey Shaw explained to me that as the trees and bushes became less dense, he and his wife were able to get a much clearer view of the animal that was "shuffling" toward the lake. At first glance, he said, the creature was continually obscured by the woods and therefore initially appeared to be only about six or seven feet in length—which is what had led his wife to assume it had been a black bear on all fours. Now, however, they could see that it was closer to thirty feet long and appeared to resemble either a giant snake or a monstrous eel.

> The Shaws stated that they did not feel frightened in the presence of the unknown creature, only awestruck.

Both of the Shaws confirmed to me that the creature seemed to have great trouble moving on land, hence their "shuffling" description, and they added that it seemed to "wriggle from side to side" as it moved, while its body appeared to be "continually vibrating" as it did so. They were unable to discern the nature of the beast's head, said Jeffrey Shaw, adding that "the whole thing reminded us of a big black pipe."

The Shaws stated that they did not feel frightened in the presence of the unknown creature, only awestruck. And while they did not actually see it enter the water, they were sure that this was its ultimate destination. At no time did it make any noise as it passed by, said the couple, and it appeared not to notice them in the slightest. On the following two days, they returned to the same spot, hoping to see the remarkable animal once again, and Jeffrey Shaw even camped out one night near the water's edge, hoping for a truly close encounter.

It was unfortunately (or fortunately, depending on your perspective) not to be, however. Whatever the true nature of the beast, it summarily failed to appear again for Jeffrey Shaw and his wife. The Klamath waters continued—and continue to this day—to keep a tight grip on their dark secrets, it would appear.

MONSTER MADNESS AND MEDIA MAYHEM

It is important to note that not all monster investigations result in the finding of an actual monster. On occasion, such accounts and the resulting inquiries are whipped up by the local media, eager for sensational tales of mysterious things in their midst. That does not remove the possibility that something may have happened or that a strange creature might really have put in an appearance, but it can complicate the matter. The story I will now share amounts to a perfect example of all the above.

On April 3, 2003, something very strange happened in a body of water in central England near the bustling town of Cannock, Staffordshire. Known locally and unofficially as Roman View Pond, it was very soon to become famous—or perhaps infamous. In no time at all, not only were the local media on the scene of the reportedly crazy antics but most of the national media, too. I should stress that I know the area well, having grown up only about fifteen minutes' drive from the pond, which is actually much bigger than its name suggests. By the time the saga took off, however, I was already living in the United States, having moved from the United Kingdom in early 2001.

With that all said, I will now share with you the fantastic story, as told by the Centre for Fortean Zoology's (CFZ) director, and my good friend, Jonathan Downes, who operates out of Devon, England, and who very generously shared the following with me for inclusion in the pages of this book:

The affair started with an e-mail message from Nick Redfern. He is living in Texas now—living proof that one can take the boy out of the West Midlands, but the fact that he still keeps a finger on the pulse of the events of his hometown proves that one cannot take the West Midlands out of the boy! The story comes from the Wolverhampton *Express and Star* dated June 16, 2003, written by Faye Casey, and titled "Mystery as 'Croc' Spotted at Pool."

The article reads as follows:

A Staffordshire community was today trying to unravel a pool monster

Author, naturalist, and cryptozoologist Jonathan Downes is director of the Centre for Fortean Zoology in Devon, England.

mystery after reported sightings of a 7ft "crocodile" type creature rising from the deep. Police officers, RSPCA inspectors and an alligator expert from Walsall were called to the pool in Roman View, Churchbridge, Cannock, on Saturday afternoon when reports of the sighting were first made.

They searched the area and found nothing, coming to the conclusion that the creature must have been a fish or possibly a snapper turtle. But locals are not convinced and youngsters have designed their own "croc on the loose" posters to stick on lampposts. One man, who did not wish to named, said he called the emergency services because what he saw in the pool was not a large fish. He and members of his family had been feeding the swans when the creature emerged.

"We were there looking at the two swans and their baby cygnets," said the man. "And there was a commotion in the water and lots of turbulence. It was far too big to be caused by a fish. As the creature went past I saw it had a flat head, a 5ft long body, and 2ft tail. It was not smooth and was moving in a snaking action—my initial reaction was it was a crocodile or alligator and so I called the police." Linda Charteras, from nearby Cheslyn Hay, was also feeding the swans on Saturday afternoon. "I saw the creature first—a large pool of dirt came up. It looked as though it was after one of the cygnets. I saw its head and long nose and thought there was no way it was a fish," she said. Natalie Baker, who lives on nearby Nuthurst Drive, said her children and their friends had been designing the posters. "There has got to be something in it for the police and RSPCA to come out."

But despite growing local interest in the creature—a group were out with their binoculars scanning the water last night—the RSPCA say it is highly unlikely the beast was an alligator or croc. Nick Brundrit, field chief inspector for the RSPCA, said the team kept up observations at the pool for around an hour and a half on Saturday, but there were no obvious signs of an alligator-type creature. He said the sighting was more likely to be a group of basking carp swimming together, or possibly a snapper turtle.

After quoting the *Express & Star* article, Jon Downes resumes the tale:

Following on from the excellent preliminary fieldwork carried out by Mark Martin, the main CFZ expedition finally reached Cannock in the early afternoon of 21st July. After a rendezvous at our digs, the Exeter contingent and Mark Martin drove in convoy to the pond at the end of Roman View.... The pond where the crocodile had been reported was surprisingly wild looking. It seemed an oasis of sanity in an increasingly desolate and unattractive West Midlands environment—especially considering that on the far side of the pond from where we set up our temporary base camp, a new section of the M6 was under construction. What looked as if it had once been virgin woodland on the hillside opposite had been flattened in order to build a featureless and rather nasty out-of-town shopping centre, so the ground immediately surrounding the pond looked even more inviting.

A wide range of butterflies and other flying insects fluttered, hovered, and buzzed their way around the thick vegetation, which was about 800 yards long and 300 yards across and was fringed by reeds and bull-rushes. A contemplative-looking heron sneered down at us from a large bush at one end of the pond, and, indeed, spent most of the weekend there gazing down at us with a particularly supercilious manner. The pond was also home to a pair of swans and their three cygnets who cruised up and down the water like majestic galleons and totally ignored us for the duration of our stay.

From CFZ headquarters in Exeter came me, Richard Freeman (who had been back in the country for only four days after his first expedition to Sumatra), Graham Inglis, John Fuller, and Nigel Wright (on his first CFZ expedition for some years). We were joined by the aforementioned Mark Martin, Peter Channon (from the Exeter Strange Phenomena group), Chris Mullins (from Beastwatch UK), Neil Goodwin (from Mercury Newspapers), and Wilf Wharton (the CFZ Wiltshire representative who was soon to be immigrating to the Antipodes).

Much to my amazement, everybody turned up roughly on time, and we gave three short briefings: one from me, giving a general overview of the events; one from Mark, who provided additional background data; and the third from Richard, who cautioned on the do's and don'ts of handling crocodiles.

I split the available personnel into three field groups. There was the boat team (Mark and Graham); the away team (Richard, Wilf, Chris, Neil and Peter); and the shore team (me, John and Nigel). The initial idea was that the boat team would spend Monday and Tuesday carrying out intensive sonar sweeps of the lake, with the intention of determining the depth of any large fish or errant crocodilians. In the meantime, the shore team would scour the shoreline in search of signs of a large beast and to determine the entry and exit points of the pond.

Even as John, Graham, and Mark struggled to get our trusty dinghy, the *Waterhorse* (named after Loch Ness Monster hunter Tim Dinsdale's boat), inflated and onto the water, the first set of eyewitnesses arrived. They were a motley gaggle of teenage boys who came up to us and in thick Brummie accents asked "whether you're here for the crocodoile, loike?" We replied in the affirmative, and they told us that they had also had an encounter with a scaly creature in Roman View Pond. Richard quickly interviewed them.

This interview proceeded as follows:

Richard Freeman and several other friends from the Centre for Fortean Zoology were passing by Roman View Pond when they saw an enormous splash that could only have been made by a very large aquatic animal.

RICHARD FREEMAN: "I gather that you've actually seen this animal and fed it? Could you please tell us exactly what happened?"

BOYS: "We came down at just after the RSPCA had been here. We saw what looked like the animal in the water; and so Elliot went and got some chicken and we lobbed it into the water to feed it. Some of it went too far away. But then we threw one piece and it landed just next to it, and there was a massive splash, and we could see both the head and the tail. We actually thought that we had seen two of the animals in the water but then remembered there is at least one massive pike in here and that the other animal was a fish."

FREEMAN: "And what did this animal look like?"

BOYS: "It was dark and about five feet long, including the tail."

FREEMAN: "Did you see scales or ridges on the tail, or anything like that?"

BOYS: "We didn't see its tail properly but there did seem to be a few spikes."

FREEMAN: "And have you seen the animal since?"

BOYS: "No. We stopped coming down here after the TV people had been. We have been told to keep away from the pond by some of the local residents." [Note from Jon Downes: "There then followed an amusing teenage rant about one of the women whose house overlooks the pond and whom the gang of lads seem to cordially dislike, before Richard managed to bring the conversation back on course."]

FREEMAN: "Do you know anybody else who has claimed to have seen it?"

BOYS: "Yeah, a couple of our friends. One of our friends had been out walking her dog and spotted it. This was the first time that it was seen. Also, a lot of kids from our school have been bunking off at lunchtimes it and coming down here. Some of them say that they have seen it. One day, we came down and there were about fifty kids sitting on the bank."

FREEMAN: "Do you know whether it has ever been seen on land?"

BOYS: "Not to our knowledge. No."

FREEMAN: "Does anybody—not necessarily you—have any ideas about where it might have come from?"

BOYS: "We were told that it might have been a pet that got too big and was thrown out."

FREEMAN: "There seem to be a lot of little streams and pipes which come in and out of the pond. Do you have any idea where they go to?"

BOYS: "Not really."

FREEMAN: "Prior to this there has not been anything odd reported in this lake before?"

BOYS: "I don't think so. I seem to remember that there was some speculation about something in this pond a few years ago but can't remember the details."

Here, Downes continues his story:

The group of teenagers went about their business, and we went about ours. However, at least at first some of the other local residents were not as friendly. From the moment we arrived the net curtains began to twitch, and soon a procession of residents walked past us, nonchalantly, to find out what we were doing. Nigel spent much of his time in conversation with these people, explaining the details of our mission and reassuring them that we were perfectly harmless.

There was one slight problem, however. Despite having made every effort to contact the owners of the pond (we had even instituted a search with Her Majesty's Land Registry), we had been unable to find them. After we had been at the pond for less than an hour, one irate local who claimed to be a friend of the owner approached us in a combative and pugnacious manner. For a brief few moments if looked at us if we were going to be embroiled in an unpleasant scene. However, John Fuller and I managed to calm the situation down, and the man disappeared, reasonably mollified.

Finally, we managed to get the boat onto the water, and the away team was dispatched to the far side of the pond. Then pay dirt! Nigel, by luck more than by judgment, ran into the lady whose family had been renting the property for thirty-eight years. She could not have been more helpful; and despite the fact that we were trespassing on her property, she granted us permission in writing to carry out whatever investigations we felt were necessary.

At about 6:15, after a series of false alarms, Mark Martin—in the boat—had a sighting of what appeared to be the eighteen-inch-long, dark blackish-green head of a large animal. It was not a positive sighting of a crocodile, but it was the best that we had managed to achieve. At the same time, the away team found an area of flattened reeds, which looked like a place where a large animal had made itself comfortable after emerging from the waters of the pond. Unlike other such areas around the shores of the pond, there were no downy feathers from one of the swans; and as the area of flattened vegetation was too big for any known mammal species from the area, it seemed quite possible that this had been the resting place of our mystery crocodilian.

As soon as we had permission to survey the pond and its surroundings and were no longer conducting a covert operation, we laid a series of navigation lines across two sections of the lake. We took a series of sonar readings to determine the depth of the lake along the lines and found, to our surprise, that the depth of the lake seemed to change by the minute. The next day we found that the lake was fed by a series of sluice-gates from connective channels that crisscross the entire area. We discovered that the bottom of the lake was mostly fairly thick silt, and found that the influx of water from the north end was causing waves in the silt itself, which meant that the depth of the lake fluctuated in some places from between 2.5 and 4.5 feet. Then in the early evening, John Mizzen, one of the original witnesses who had been interviewed by Mark Martin, turned up.

Again, we turn the reins over to Freeman:

FREEMAN: "Basically, can you recount the story from scratch?"

JOHN MIZZEN: "We were over on the other side of the pond feeding swans, when about five feet from the water's edge my daughter-in-law was looking down this way while I was looking at the lake. She saw the—whatever it was—and said: 'That's never a fish.' It then swam along the water's edge, where I reckon that the water is no more than two feet deep, and it was about five feet long and that's including the tail. When it got five or ten feet away from us, it came up and broke the surface. Its head was flat, as was its jaw and its nose, and it was dark greenish black in colour and about eighteen inches wide. The tail had a scaly appearance, and then it went underneath the water and we just lost contact with it. It had been on the surface for about three or four seconds, and in that time it covered about fifteen to twenty feet."

This muskie fish is a somewhat rare fish from North America that can reach a length of up to four feet long and looks somewhat like what Freeman described at Roman View. The only problem is that they were in England at the time.

FREEMAN: "On its head did you notice anything about the eyes?"

MIZZEN: "I didn't see anything of that; not the eyes sticking out of their head or the water or anything. I only saw it from behind, and the surrounding parts to its eyes were not visible as far as I could tell."

Downes once more picks up the story:

Later that afternoon at Richard spoke to a number of other elderly gentlemen who requested anonymity. One of them told us that there had been a series of incidents at a slaughterhouse that was on the shores of one of the other ponds connected to Roman View Pond by a watercourse. Apparently, this establishment, which dealt predominantly with the dispatching of elderly and ill horses, supplied meat to local zoos. Some of the meat was hung in a concrete pit to prepare it for consumption by zoo animals. Whilst it was hanging, something had taken enormous bites out of the carcasses.

On another occasion, a horse was attacked. Apparently, in the vicinity there is a training stable at which horses learn to draw old-fashioned hearses. One of the ways that they trained these animals to walk slowly is to swim them in another of the local ponds, which is connected by a watercourse to Roman View Pond itself. On one occasion, whilst one of these horses was swimming, it was attacked by something. When they got it out onto the bank it had a massive bite on one of the back legs. It was eight to ten inches deep and went right down to the bone. The horse was immediately taken to the knackers yard and shot.

By this time it was beginning to get quite late in the evening, so the team decamped to the local pub to partake of one of the most unpleasant-tasting fish suppers that it has been my misfortune to eat. Later in the evening, as it was approaching dusk, we returned to the pond and spent three hours searching the surface of the pond with three 1.5-million candlepower spotlights. The away team, with head torches strapped on, scoured the bank, and out in the middle of the lake Mark and Graham sat patiently in the boat waiting for a scaly monster to surface. Needless to say, all these searches were fruitless, and at about one in the morning we packed up for the night.

The next day the CFZ posse was up and about relatively early. After an excellent breakfast we arrived at the lake soon after ten o'clock in the morning. Within twenty minutes everybody else had joined us (except for Wilf, who had been forced by the pressure of work to drive down to the south at the end of the previous night's escapades). In many ways the second day seemed, at first, to be a slight disappointment after the adventures of the first. When you look back, it's easy to see that we achieved even more, but at the time it didn't feel like it. Whereas on the first day we had been rushing about and had even logged a sighting, much of the second day was spent hanging about, waiting for something to happen.

The boat party continued their sonar sweeps of the lake, while the shore party continued their explorations of the bank in search of footprints and signs of crocodilians. Sadly, no such signs were found. Indeed, although on the previous day we had managed to log one pretty good sighting by Mark Martin, today we had none at all. However, this did not mean that the day was a complete waste of time. In the original newspaper report, a local lady called Natalie Baker was quoted as saying that her children and their friends had been so excited by the media activity following the initial crocodile sightings that they had spent some time making colored posters of the animal as part of a school project.

Now, Nigel has been working with me for nearly seven years now, and over the years I have asked him to do some extraordinary things for me. I had never before said to him: "Dude, I want you to find me a little girl who draws pictures of crocodiles." But I did, and—not at all to my surprise; because over the years I have known him I have come to rely on his powers of deduction a great deal—he not only found me the little girl, but managed to persuade her to give me one of the aforesaid posters. Flushed with success after that particular triumph, Nigel and I went off to try to solve another mystery, which we felt was likely to have a pivotal importance in solving the case of the Cannock crocodile once and for all.

Richard and I have been members of what I like to call the "UK Animal Mafia" or the "Zoo Mafia" for some years. This is a weird sort of freemasonry that consists of people on the fringes of the pet trade, the zoo trade, and the professional zoology trade. These people—even when it would seem that they should have completely opposing agendas—often co-operate to a surprising extent. One of the foremost members of the Zoo Mafia in the Midlands had warned us about the activities of a particularly unscrupulous reptile dealer who was allegedly operating in the

Cannock area. Nigel and I left the shore party and the boat party doing their own respective things and went undercover.

It was surprisingly easy to track this fellow down. He had left a trail of debts a mile long, and whenever we went, we couldn't find anybody who would say a good word about him. We found the shop where he had once operated a business, which, according to one of our informants, had been closed down on animal welfare grounds.

We spoke to his erstwhile landlord and found that when he closed shop, he had left large sums of money owing. We found that he had then set up business under another name in another part of town, but this too had gone the way of all flesh. After two failed businesses, we discovered that the person question had most recently been sighted working part-time for a pizza delivery company and selling the remnants of his stock through small ads in the local paper. Although we cannot prove it, we were convinced that this discovery had essentially solved the provenance of the Cannock crocodile. It was obvious that somebody had

One theory about crocodilians in the Cannock area is that they were escapees from illegal trade in animals.

been dumping exotic reptiles in the district. Only a couple of days before we arrived, the Wolverhampton *Express and Star* had carried a story about a large common snapping-turtle which had been captured in a local brook.

The newspaper report claimed that the turtle, named "Lucky" by the RSPCA inspector who captured him, could have been over twenty years old and had "probably lived most of his life in the wild," having inspected the brook in question, and furthermore knowing that when snapping turtles achieve the size of the specimen fished out of this tiny brook in Staffordshire they are very sedentary creatures who on the whole sit on the bottom of a stream waiting for something to swim into their open mouths. I feel it is far more likely that "Lucky" was dumped into the stream in question within the last few weeks.

Feeling rather pleased with ourselves for having completed what we regarded as a rather tidy piece of detective work, we returned to the lake. We discovered that in our absence the CFZ operatives there had discovered some useful data about the age of the lake. Apparently, it had begun life as a pit from which locals dug coal. When the coal petered out in the mid-1930s, it had begun to fill with water. However, it was a long and slow process, and it wasn't until after the war that the water was deep enough to swim in.

We also spoke to one of the head honchos of the local angling society, and we discovered that although there were some very big carp in the pond, the largest pike that anyone had managed to catch was only about nine pounds in weight. However, according to the local water bailiff, there was at least one massive pike weighing in excess of twenty-three pounds and probably more than three and a half or four feet in length. The shore team had managed to identify a number of other small ponds in the area and found of that most of these were interconnected, either by culverts or by open-water courses. One of the strangest things we discovered was that somebody had been dumping koi carp into several of these ponds.

As some of you may know, I used to write a column for *Koi Carp* magazine, and so with these very limited credentials Nigel, Richard, John, and I paid a visit to a small koi farm about half a mile away. They too had heard the stories about koi carp—some of them quite sizeable and worth a lot of money—being dumped into these local ponds. But they were completely unable to let us know who had been dumping them and why. The next day, we found ourselves in the middle of Cannock Chase and deep in conversation with local wildlife officers who told us that koi had been turning up in isolated ponds across Cannock Chase as well. It seems as if there is some kind of strange, piscine Johnny Appleseed at work, doing his best to stock the waterways of the West Midlands with these large ornamental fish.

Back at the pond, we were ready to do a reconstruction of the original sighting by John Mizzen, Linda Charteris, and her children. Sometime before, we had instituted the practice of performing reconstructions of sightings filmed from two or three different angles, much in the manner of the BBC television program *Crimewatch*. We have found that using these methods is an invaluable tool in field investigations, and although we had already interviewed both John and Linda in some depth—as had Mark right at the beginning of the investigation—we decided to carry out one of these reconstructions are at the pond. We filmed it from three angles: Neil on one side, Mark on the other, and Graham filming from the boat. It is always interesting carrying out one of our *Crimewatch* reconstructions, and we have never yet done one where we didn't learn something new.

John Mizzen is probably one of the most professional and accurate eyewitnesses that it has ever been my pleasure and privilege to work with. During our *Crimewatch* reconstruction, we discovered that his estimates of the distance that the crocodile had been from the shore and our measured distance differed by only a few inches.

After the *Crimewatch* reconstructions, we slowly began to break camp. John and Neil lit a barbecue, which had been donated to us by Chris Mullins, and soon the fragrant smell of slowly charring burgers drifted over the evening wind. Someone produced the remains of a bottle of Scotch, and Nigel appeared from Sainsbury's with two dozen bottles of beer. The CFZ drank, ate, and watched the sun go down. Neil disappeared back to Liverpool, and the rest of us went down the pub. Tomorrow was another day; but, unfortunately, we had not caught a crocodile. From the eyewitness descriptions, Richard and I were fairly convinced that the elusive creature was a spectacled caiman of between three and five feet in length. Sadly—unless it was very lucky, and somebody managed to fish it out of one of the connecting streams—it was doomed to a slow and ignominious death as soon the first chills heralded the advent of the season of mists and mellow fruitfulness. And all because of some stupid, selfish person who wanted an exotic pet! C'est la vie; unfortunately.

GIANT TURTLES AND OTHER GOLIATHS

If you think about Japanese monster movies, the chances are good that you'll think almost immediately of Godzilla. The monster first appeared in the 1954 movie titled—what else?—*Godzilla*. The four-hundred-foot-tall creature has an "atomic heat beam" that allows it to raze to the ground city upon city—something it has done on numerous occasions, particularly throughout Japan's landscape. It has a very bad temper and a huge tail that can flatten skyscrapers—in fiction, of course. Another huge monster, too, has become famous in the world of Japanese monster movies. His name is Gamera, and he is a gigantic turtle. A contributor to the website *Fandom* says of Gamera:

> Unlike any other species of turtles, Gamera has the habit of walking bipedally rather than on all fours, though he occasionally walks quadrupedally in his first three films. Gamera is capable of using his upper limbs in the same manner as Godzilla, as his forelegs have appendages much closer in construction to hands than feet, and is capable of grappling with opponents and manipulating objects. His mouth is filled with teeth, unlike any living modern turtle (several types of extinct prehistoric turtles were toothed, however), with a pair of large tusks protruding upward from his lower jaw. Gamera is also usually seen with very large human-like eyes, adding intelligence to his overall appearance. In the Heisei trilogy, Gamera has retractable bone spikes in each of his elbows.

It barely needs saying that Gamera, like Godzilla, is just a cinematic creation. It should be noted, though, that there are real-life equivalents of the mighty turtle. Writing at the website of the Pine Barrens Institute of Wisconsin, Adam Benedict says:

> First reported in 1494 by explorer Christopher Columbus near the Dominican Republic, the Father of All Turtles was described as being the size of a whale, while also possessing a long tail with a fin on each side to help with movement through the water. The giant turtle was said to have kept its head out of the water the entire time it swam within close proximity of Columbus's ship, the *Santa Maria*. Eventually, the Turtle felt it had spent enough time on the surface and dove back below the surface of the Atlantic where it was seen no more by the explorer and his men.

Scientific American has also addressed the possibility that our oceans may be home to turtles of gigantic proportions—maybe not the size of Gamera but still highly impressive in scale. A writer for *Scientific American*, back in 1883, wrote:

> Captain Augustus G. Hall and the crew of the schooner *Annie L. Hall* vouch for the following: On March 30, while on the Grand Bank, in latitude 40° 10', longitude 33°, they discovered an immense live trunk turtle, which was at first thought to be a vessel bottom up. The schooner passed within twenty-five feet of the monster, and those on board had ample opportunity to estimate its dimensions by a comparison with the length of the schooner. The turtle was at least 40 feet long, 30 feet wide, and 30 feet from the apex of the back to the bottom of the under shell. The flippers were 20 feet long. It was not deemed advisable to attempt its capture.

Darren Naish, a cryptozoologist and the author of a number of books, including *Hunting Monsters* and *Dinosaurs: How They Lived and Evolved*, tells of a fascinating case from September 1959. He states:

> The case occurred off the coast of Soay, an island—famous for sheep!—just south of Skye off the west coast of Scotland, and concerns basking shark fisherman Tex Geddes and engineer James Gavin. On seeing a large, dark, approaching object from their boat, Geddes and Gavin first heard it breathing and then had a reasonably close-up view of a large, hump-backed, scaly creature with a rounded, tortoise-like head, a "large red gash of a mouth," and a prominently serrated back. It was likened at one point to a "hellish monster of prehistoric times," was described as opening and closing its large mouth, of breathing through said mouth, and of having hanging structures of some sort within the mouth. They described the exposed part of the body as between 6 to 8 feet (Gavin) or 8 to 10 feet (Geddes) long and likened the head to that of a donkey in size, so this was a sizeable creature.

Contributors to *Astonishing Legends* have looked into this matter of oversized turtles and cite Naish's work:

> The sighting and accompanied story soon gained traction, and was fea-

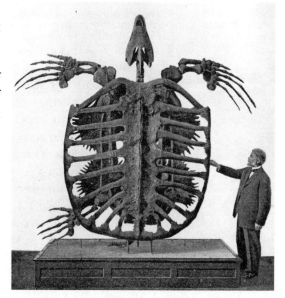

During the Cretaceous Period, a huge sea turtle called the *Archelon* swam the warm oceans of Earth.

tured in national news media in outlets such as the *Illustrated London News*. Tex was the main catalyst for this, and wrote about the encounter to prominent zoologist and writer Maurice Burton. But did they truly seem some kind of primitive sea-dragon, a curiously deformed large animal … or just a sea turtle? Well, writer Darren Naish, who looked into the case, believed it to be the Occam's Razor of answers: a sea turtle. According to Naish, some sea turtles are known for having tall(ish) triangular dorsal structures, beak-like mouths, and long necks. However, he does concede that no sea turtles of the sizes the two men reported have ever been found. So, he admits, there is a chance that it is an unknown species of large marine reptile. The proposed existence of a giant sea-turtle is not impossible.

Now we'll turn our attentions to the matter of the huge alligator gar, a creature most often seen in the rivers of the Lone Star State. The Texas Parks and Wildlife staff are well acquainted with these creatures. The TP&W website provides a concise background on these massive fish: "Alligator gar get big—really big—and they look like something that should be swimming around with dinosaurs, not bass and crappie. But it is not just their looks that are unique. Alligator gar are like few other fishes that swim in our rivers, reservoirs and estuaries. Even among the four species of gar that occur in Texas—longnose, spotted, shortnose and alligator gar—this species is unique." The description continues:

> Gars are easily distinguished from other freshwater species by their long, slender, cylindrical bodies, long snouts, and diamond-shaped interlocking (ganoid) scales. The tail fin is rounded. Dorsal and anal fins are placed well back on the body and nearly opposite each other. Alligator gar is the largest of the gar species. It can grow up to 8 feet long and weigh more than 300 pounds. Adults have two rows of large teeth on either side of the upper jaw. Coloration is generally brown or olive above and lighter underneath. The species name *spatula* is Latin for "spoon," referring to the creature's broad snout. Alligator gar can live for many decades. They grow very fast when young, but growth slows with age. In general, for every additional foot the fish grows, its age doubles. A 3-foot gar is typically about 2.5 years old; a 4-foot gar about 5, and a 7-foot trophy catch might be 40 years old. The world record, caught in Mississippi in 2011, weighed 327 pounds and was probably at least 95.

On the matter of that ancient, 327-pound creature that the TP&W referenced, blogger J. R. Absher at *Outdoor Life* was highly enthused by the story, writing:

The alligator gar, which can be found in Texas, can survive out of water for up to two hours. They are known to grow to six feet in length and weigh about one hundred pounds.

A 327-pound alligator gar caught by rod-and-reel angler Kenny Williams from Chotard Lake in Issaquena County, MS [in February 2011] may surpass the standing IGFA record for the species— by nearly 50 pounds! Williams' fish measured 8-feet, 5.25 inches, with a 47.95-inch girth. According to the International Game Fish Association web site, the current all-tackle world record alligator gar weighed 279 pounds and was caught from the Rio Grande River in Texas in 1951. "At first I didn't think he was that big. But as I was getting him into the boat, it was like, 'How big is this thing?' It was a lot of effort just to get him into the boat," Williams told WAPT-TV in Jackson, Miss. "I don't even know how to describe it. It was just huge and hard to get into the boat."

What about crocodiles and alligators? They can grow to absolutely fearsome sizes. Jeanna Bryner at *Live Science* provides important information about the differences between crocodiles and alligators:

Alligators have wider, U-shaped snouts, while crocodile front ends are more pointed and V-shaped.... When their snouts are shut, crocodiles look like they're flashing a toothy grin, as the fourth tooth on each side of the lower jaw sticks up over the upper lip. For alligators, the upper jaw is wider than the lower one, so when they close their mouths, all their teeth are hidden.... Crocodiles tend to live in saltwater habitats, while alligators hang out in freshwater marshes and lakes. They belong to the subgroup *Eusuchia*, which includes about 22 species divided into three families: the fish-eating gavials or gharials, which belong to the *Gavialidae*; today's crocodiles or the *Crocodylidae*; and the *Alligatoridae*, or alligators. Eusuchians appeared on the scene during the late Cretaceous some 100 million or so years ago.

At the website *Our Planet*, a writer reveals: "Five members of the Stokes family captured and killed a giant alligator at the Alabama River on August 16, 2014, which measured 15 feet and 9 inches long and weighed 1,011.5 pounds (~458.8 kg). Most sources pick this one as the largest alligator ever recorded."

A contributor to the website *Jurassic Dreams* unleashes even bigger monsters upon us, writing:

Depending on who you ask, the answer is different. Unfortunately, giant prehistoric crocodiles' fossils aren't found complete, and only isolated parts of the skeleton and fragments form this puzzle. For the time being, we are sure about three species competing for the top on this peculiar ranking. Deinosuchus ... lived 75 millions of years ago, at the end of the Cretaceous. It's important to note that actually it's not a crocodile, as it's kin to the American alligators. It has a broad, robust mouth, which allowed this species turn on itself to dismember the meat of its preys, as today's crocodiles do. Based on its features, paleontologists assume it fed on land animals, dinosaurs. It stalked them from the water. The fossils of some herbivorous dinosaurs show teeth marks by the Deinosuchus, which is a definitive proof about its diet. Regarding its size, it went from 10 to 12 meters.

Ten to twelve meters? That's formidable in the extreme.

A DEADLY FISH IN THE WATERS OF WALES

Deep in the heart of North Wales exists a large expanse of water called Lake Bala. You may say, well, there's nothing particularly strange about that. You would be correct. Lake Bala is not out of the ordinary—not in the slightest. But what is rumored to dwell in its dark depths is, most assuredly, out of the ordinary. Bala is the domain of a violent lake monster called Teggie. Or, perhaps, it is the domain of secret military experiments. It all very much depends on whom you ask and whom you believe.

Before we get to the matter of Teggie, it's worth noting that within Lake Bala, there lurks another creature called the gwyniad. This one can hardly be termed a monster, as it's just a small fish. Nonetheless, it does have a bearing upon the matter of Teggie. The gwyniad dates back to the prehistoric era and is found in Lake Bala and nowhere else—at all. This has, quite naturally, given rise to a thought-provoking question: What else of a prehistoric nature might be in Lake Bala? And how big might it grow? The questions are intriguing. The answers are even more so.

Whereas sightings of the Loch Ness Monster date back more than 1,500 years, Lake Bala's resident unknown beast has only been reported for just over a century. Some locals, who claim to have seen not just one but several Teggies at close quarters, say the creatures resemble huge, violent northern pike. Pike are ferocious fish that can easily grow to four feet in length, occasionally five, and, rumor has it, even six. If, however, the Teggies are indeed northern pike, then they would have to be true giants, since witnesses claim that the creatures they encountered were on the order of ten to fifteen feet. No one, surely, needs telling that a too-close encounter with such a creature could result in a swift and bloody death.

There are equally baffling reports of a reptilian monster that vaguely resembles a crocodile. Such a scenario is unlikely, as a colony of crocodiles would stand little chance of adapting to and surviving a harsh North Wales winter—never mind centuries of such winters. There is, however, a third theory for what the Teggies might be. It's just as strange and controversial as the crocodile and northern pike scenarios but in a very different fashion.

There are long-standing rumors in and around the Bala area that in the build-up to the First World War, the British Royal Navy clandestinely let loose a group of seals into the lake. Their intention was reportedly to strap them with dynamite and train them to attack specific targets, namely warships. It should be noted that the dynamite was not real, and the "warships" were just

Bala Lake in Wales is the home of Teggie, another cousin to Nessie, say some, but just a large northern pike, according to others.

small rowing boats. In other words, the project was a test run in the event that the Royal Navy might find itself at war with Germany (which it did in 1914, when the First World War broke out), and suicidal seals, strapped with explosives, might be required to fight for their country.

As the story goes, the seals proved impossible to train, and the project was abandoned. And so today, what people are seeing are brief glimpses of descendants of the original seals. Of course, it's very possible this is nothing more than a tall tale, passed on through the generations and without any actual facts to support it. And, it must be said, it would be very difficult to mistake a seal for a crocodile or a huge, violent pike. Thus, the legend of Teggie continues to thrive.

After the publication of an article I wrote on Teggie in 2017, Roland Watson—the author of an excellent book, *The Water Horses of Loch Ness*—wrote his own article on the Bala Lake affair. Roland stated: "Having seen Nick Redfern's recent interesting article on the Lake Bala Monster, it brought to my mind an article I had on the creature from years back plus some recent thoughts I had on the phenomenon. The article is from issue 82 of the *Fortean Times* dated August 1995."

The *Fortean Times* article that Roland referred to is titled "Teggie & Other Beasts of Bala." It states, in part: "Early last March [1995], brothers Andrew and Paul Delaney from London were fishing on Lake Bala in Gwynedd, North Wales. 'It was very calm and we were about to finish when we noticed something coming up to the surface about 80 yards from the boat. At first we thought it was a tree trunk. Then it straightened up and towered 10 feet in the air. It had a small head and a long neck, like pictures of the Loch Ness Monster.'"

The large northern pike, a fish that makes its home in the British Isles and North America, can weigh up to forty-five pounds.

Interestingly, at the time, the article prompted feedback from one of the readers of *Fortean Times*. It was feedback concerning a sighting of a large, unidentified animal in Bala Lake "about 12 years ago," which would have been around 1983. The letter writer told *Fortean Times*: "The car park attendant at the lake side told me he'd once witnessed an animal swim from one side of the lake to the other. 'It was as long as three dogs swimming together,' he told me, and resembled a hump protruding from the water." Interestingly, the same *FT* source added that around 1990, he or she was back at Bala Lake and discussed the matter with staff at the local tourist center. One of them said that she suspected what people were seeing was a large pike.

A drawing of the monster was done by Craig Boscombe of the *Liverpool Echo* newspaper, about which Roland Watson says: "Nick's article about a possible 10 foot pike does in fact make some sense looking at the sketch … done by Craig Boscombe. After all, a crocodile head is not too dissimilar to that of a pike. Having said that, the Delaney brothers' account is distinctly more in line with the traditional long neck ascribed to lake cryptids."

None of this definitively proves that the Bala Lake monster is a pike—and, admittedly, there is the issue of the long neck to which two witnesses referred. But, that single case aside, the chances are looking more and more likely that the creatures are indeed pike. I say "creatures" rather than "creature" because most pike have a maximum life span of around five to ten years at most, but the reports of monstrous fish in the lake date back decades. Therefore, either we are dealing with one extraordinarily large and incredibly long-lived pike, or there must be more than a few of them. That still doesn't explain how or why the pike of Bala Lake might be reaching such incredible lengths of around ten feet or, as some have suggested, even longer. I'm as certain as I can be that we are not dealing with unknown animals, but there is definitely a mystery to be solved.

> I'm as certain as I can be that we are not dealing with unknown animals, but there is definitely a mystery to be solved.

One such mysterious incident, which I'd noted in my earlier article on Teggie, involved "a story which dates back to 1973, and that is related in issue 22 of the Centre for Fortean Zoology's magazine, *Animals & Men*. That was the year in which a team of divers surveyed Norton Mere, a body of water located in Shropshire, England. While checking out the mere, the group was shocked by a brief, shadowy encounter with an enormous beast, one which churned the waters and created a huge wake. It was the conclusion of the group that what they had encountered was a northern pike of very large proportions."

This brings me to the latest development in the saga of Bala Lake and Teggie. In 2017, I received a communication from a resident of Dublin, Ireland. In 2015, "Colin M." traveled to North Wales with his wife and children. They spent a week checking out the landscape and seeing all the sights. That included Bala Lake, which is less than four miles in length, barely half a mile wide, and slightly less than 140 feet deep.

There was a good reason why the family was there: Colin is a keen fisherman who has a love of the water. While his wife and kids went to grab lunch,

Colin hired a kayak from a local firm and took a trip around the lake. He reasoned that its small size ensured that a trip around the lake would be brief and uneventful. He was wrong. According to Colin, in one shallow part of the water, as he was returning to shore, he saw what he is absolutely sure was a pike. It was, however, a pike like most have never seen. The largest pike ever officially caught in the United Kingdom was one hooked by a fisherman named Roy Lewis back in 1992. It weighed forty-six pounds. Pike are vicious things and not to be messed with.

Colin, however, estimated that the pike he saw in the shallows of Bala Lake was around nine to ten feet in length. If true, then Bala Lake really does have a monster in its depths. Of course, skeptics will likely refer to "a fisherman's tale" and the legend of "the one that got away" and assume that Colin was mistaken about the length of the monster. I have to say, though, that it's hard to mistake something three to four feet in length with something one and a half times longer than the average adult man. Plus, Colin didn't weave a sensational tale of having to fight the beast off, nor did he claim it tipped him out of his kayak, and so on. Rather, said Colin, the whole thing was somewhat surreal: he saw the creature close by and barely below the surface of the shallows and "didn't know what to do so I just sailed past." And that was it: a very brief encounter with something truly monstrous.

Could giant, highly dangerous pike be the cause of the old legends of monsters in Lake Bala? Why not?

CREEPY CREATURES

A new mystery began on Valentine's Day 2002 when a Lancashire, England, newspaper announced that "something" had been attacking swans at a picturesque, otherwise tranquil nature reserve in the north of England. Eyewitnesses reported that a giant, unknown creature had been seen dragging fully grown swans beneath the water, never to be seen again. The location was the Wildfowl and Wetlands Trust Reserve at Martin Mere, Ormskirtk, Lancashire. Once the media started reporting that the beast was "the size of a small car," things really took off in the publicity stakes.

Pat Wisniewski, the reserve's manager, said: "Whatever it was out there must have been pretty big to pull a swan back into the water. Swans weigh up to thirteen kilos. This could be an extremely large pike or a Wels catfish." Wisniewski had good reason to take the matter seriously, as four years previously, in 1998, he had spotted something large and dark circling in the mere, or lake, much to his consternation and concern. It didn't take long for a team of intrepid investigators from Britain's pre-mier monster-hunting group, the Centre for Fortean Zoology, to head from their home base in the south of England to Martin Mere. It was an ambitious project, led by CFZ director Jon Downes, with backup pro-vided by Richard Freeman, a former head keeper at England's Twycross Zoo.

In no time at all, the story went from one of a mystery fish to a tale involving "dragons," "unexplained ancient human mutilation," and even "a resident mermaid." Of course, much of this was due to media hype and sensationalism, but people were clearly seeing something out of the ordinary. The CFZ was determined to know exactly

Flamingoes roam the grounds of the Wildfowl and Wetlands Trust Reserve at Martin Mere, where a number of swans were mysteriously killed.

what it was. Freeman and Downes undertook numerous interviews with local folk who had seen the beast. They were pretty much unanimous that it was a powerful, fast-swimming creature with a slick, shiny, muscular back that moved with astonishing speed.

It was thanks to Freeman's dedication that, in July 2002, he finally caught sight of the monster fish. Although it was only in view for moments, Freeman was pretty sure that what he encountered in the dark waters was a Wels catfish. This was no ordinary Wels, however. It was huge. In all likeli-hood, said Freeman, it was very old, probably no less than a century in age. The older the Wels, the bigger its size. Freeman opined that it had probably managed to successfully avoid one and all for decades, happily living on the local fish and bird population. And, of course, if someone occasionally report-ed seeing a monster fish in Martin Mere, who would believe it? Probably no one until, for reasons unknown, the great beast began to make its presence known more in the summer of 2002.

Sightings have subsided in recent years, leading to the possibility that the immense, car-sized creature has died or, perhaps more likely, retreated to the lower, muddy depths of the mere to avoid detection and media attention. Keep that latter possibility in mind should you ever visit Martin Mere and decide to go for a paddle. You may do so at your cost—possibly at the expense of a few toes or even your very life.

In August 2010, English author, good friend, and seeker of all things weird Elizabeth Randall reported that, according to a sensational article that appeared in the British *Daily Mail* newspaper that month, "a picture has been circulating on the Internet purporting to show a sea monster that so far seems to have eluded identification. It was seen off Saltern Cove, Devon, U.K., and has been dubbed by many as a 'new Nessie.' The image appears to show a greenish-brown, long-necked 'something,' with a reptilian-like head, that was trailing a shoal of fish just 30 yards offshore. According to reports the fish beached themselves just a few seconds later."

Elizabeth continued: "The photo was sent to the Marine Conservation Society, who have still to decide exactly what it is. Theories range from a sea serpent to a saltwater crocodile. The lady who took the photograph at first thought that it might be a turtle but the Marine Conservation Society (MCS) says that not only do turtles not chase fish, but the description doesn't fit."

Others maintained, despite the skepticism of the MCS, that a turtle was the culprit. Photographs that were taken by one of the witnesses, Gill Pearce, however, clearly demonstrated that the neck of the creature was much too long for it to be that of a regular turtle. Pearce took the photos on July 27 and subsequently reported the details of the encounter to the Marine Conservation Society; a spokesperson for whom, Claire Fischer, told the press:

> Gill Pearce spotted the creature about 20 meters from the bay at Saltern Cove, near Goodrington. It was observed at about 15.30 on 27 July but by the time she had got her camera it had moved further out. She spotted it following a shoal of fish which

Saltern Cove in Devon, England, appears to be too peaceful to be the home of a sea monster, but some kind of long-necked, Nessie-like creature is said to lurk there.

beached themselves in Saltern Cove. The creature remained in the sea, then went out again and followed the shoal—this indicates it's not a turtle as they only eat jellyfish. We would love to know if other people have seen anything like this in the same area and can help clear up the mystery.

Of the affair, Jonathan Downes of the Centre for Fortean Zoology, who is an expert on reports of strange and unknown animals, said: "Me? I think it is a basking shark; I think that what appears to be its back is its tail, and the 'head' is the tip of its nose, but golly, wouldn't I love to be proved wrong!"

It's possible that what was seen was Morgawr, a sea serpent-style beast that has been reportedly seen for decades in and around Falmouth Bay, Cornwall, England—which, notably, is situated only one county away from where this latest incident occurred. Variously described as looking like a giant serpent, a monstrous eel, or even a supposedly extinct plesiosaur, Morgawr was first viewed in September 1975 by two witnesses who claimed to have seen a humped animal with "stumpy horns" and bristles that ran along the length of its long neck, which apparently had a conger eel in its huge mouth.

A whole wave of startling encounters with the creature allegedly occurred during the period of 1975–1976, and such reports continue to surface sporadically from time to time from this location. Did Morgawr possibly decide to take a trip along the coast for a brief vacation and to entertain the nation's media? Maybe so!

An approximately mile-long body of water in Clwyd, North Wales, Cynwch Lake is renowned for the story of its resident monster, a wyvern—a story that dates back centuries. According to ancient legend, the wyvern was a dragon-like animal to be avoided at all costs. Reptilian, and sporting large and membranous wings of a batlike appearance, it stands on two powerful legs and has a strong tail that it uses to sting and kill its prey, not unlike a scorpion. In some cases, and just like the dragon of old, the wyvern was said to occasionally breathe fire. This brings us to the monster of Cynwch Lake.

For as long as anyone could remember, the lake and its surrounding landscape made for a peaceful and relaxing environment. That all changed when the deadly wyvern decided to swoop down on the lake and make it its home. Tranquility was no more. The creature was undeniably monstrous. It was described by fearful locals as looking like a huge, coiling, and writhing monster with a humped back and an undulating neck. On its back were two wings, and its feet displayed razor-sharp claws that could tear a person to pieces. Its breath was reportedly poisonous and green. In no time, the Welsh wyvern began to eat its way through the local populations of sheep, cattle, and pigs. Terrified village folk stayed behind locked doors after the sun set, which was when the beast surfaced from the waters of the lake. The time came, however, when enough was enough.

A local warlock, known as the Wizard of Ganllwid, believed he stood a good chance of slaying the deadly beast. As he knew, all previous attempts to kill the animal had failed, for its noxious breath caused instant death to anyone and everyone exposed to it. But the wizard had a brainwave: he decided to round up a team of archers who could shoot the wyvern from a distance. It was to no avail, however. It was as if the beast had a sixth sense about it, and whenever the bowmen were around, the wyvern would stay steadfastly below the waters.

At last there was a breakthrough, which proved to be the turning point in the tumultuous affair. On one particular morning, a bright and sunny one, the wyvern left the waters of the lake and slithered its way onto the shore, where it proceeded to bask under a hot sun. As luck would have it, a young shepherd boy, named Meredydd, happened to be in the area and saw the beast, asleep, as he was directing his sheep to his father's farm.

Fortunately, the monster was deep in its slumber, as was evidenced by its hideous, skin-crawling snoring, which was more like the hiss of a gigantic snake. Its body moved rhythmically, its strange form glistening like wet leather. Realizing that this was quite possibly the only time the wyvern could be killed, Meredydd raced to nearby Cymmer Abbey and breathlessly told the monks what he had just seen. He asked for a much-revered axe that hung in the abbey, suggesting that if anything could kill the wyvern, it was surely the axe, which allegedly possessed magical powers. The monks agreed, and in mere minutes, Meredydd was heading back to Cynwch Lake for a battle to the death. Of whose death, exactly, Meredydd was not so sure. Nevertheless, he was determined to do his very best to rid the area of the loathsome beast.

A wyvern is a dragon-like creature that has wings but, apparently, can also lurk about lakes and slither out to menace people.

Fortunately, when Meredydd returned to the spot where the monster slept, he could see that it had not moved. There was no time to lose. The young shepherd used all his might to raise the axe over his head and then brought it down hard and fast on the neck of the sleeping monster. In a spilt second, its head and neck were severed. The jaws of the severed head snapped wildly and widely, in the fashion of a headless chicken, while the neck thrashed around for a few moments before falling limp on the grass. The nightmare was over, no thanks to a powerful warlock, but all thanks to a young shepherd.

The idea that there could be monstrous, man-eating beasts of an unknown nature lurking in the wilder parts of our planet is not at all implausible. But what about man-eating plants and trees? As incredible as it may sound, there is no shortage of reports of flesh-eating flora. They thrive in lush, wet, watery environments, like so many of the world's monsters.

In 1878 a German explorer named Carl Liche traveled to the island of Madagascar, where he witnessed nothing less than a human sacrifice to a tree. The horrific details were laid out in a letter penned by Liche and sent to the *South Australian Register* in 1881. According to Liche, the unfortunate victim was a woman of the Mkodo tribe who was tied to the terrible tree, seemingly as a gift to it. Liche said:

> The slender delicate palpi, with the fury of starved serpents, quivered a moment over her head, then as if instinct with demoniac intelligence fastened upon her in sudden coils round and round her neck and arms; then while her awful screams and yet more awful laughter rose wildly to be instantly strangled down again into a gurgling moan, the tendrils one after another, like great green serpents, with brutal energy and infernal rapidity, rose, retracted themselves, and wrapped her about in fold after fold, ever tightening with cruel swiftness and savage tenacity of anacondas fastening upon their prey.

"The tree possessed white, transparent leaves that reminded Liche of the quivering mouthparts of an insect."

Researcher Brent Swancer says that the flesh-devouring tree "was described as being around 8 feet in height, and having an appearance reminiscent of a pineapple, with eight long, pointed leaves that hung down from its top to the ground. The trunk of the tree was topped with a sort of receptacle that contained a thick liquid said to have soporific qualities that drugged potential prey and was believed to be highly addictive. Surrounding this receptacle were long, hairy tendrils with six white palpi resembling tentacles. The tree possessed white, transparent leaves that reminded Liche of the quivering mouthparts of an insect."

Moving on, the *American Weekly* on January 4, 1925, included in its pages an article titled "Escaped from the Embrace of the Man-Eating Tree." It described an encounter in the Philippines in which a man—referred to only as Bryant from Mississippi—and his native guide came across a truly unusual tree, around thirty-five feet in height and roughly ninety feet in diameter. Rather ominously, the tree stunk of rotting flesh, and a human skull could be seen at its base. It was the curious dimensions—which gave it something of a bulbous shape—that first caught the attention of the man; it wasn't long before something else grabbed his attention, literally. As the man stood and stared at the tree, he realized to his horror that it was reaching out to him. The *American Weekly* writer said of what happened next:

The whole thing had changed shape and was horribly alive and alert. The dull, heavy leaves had sprung from their compact formation and were coming at him from all directions, advancing on the ends of long vine-like stems which stretched across like the necks of innumerable geese, and, now that the old man had stopped his screaming, the air was full of hissing sounds. The leaves did not move straight at their target, but with a graceful, side-to-side sway, like a cobra about to strike. From the far side, the distant leaves were peeping and swaying on their journey around the trunk and even the tree top was bending down to join in the attack. The bending of the trunk was spasmodic and accompanied by sharp cracks.

The effect of this advancing and swaying mass of green objects was hypnotic, like the charm movements of a snake. Bryant could not move, though the nearest leaf was within an inch of his face. He could see that it was armed with sharp spines on which a liquid was forming. He saw the heavy leaf curve like a green-mittened hand, and as it brushed his eyebrows in passing he got the smell of it—the same animal smell that hung in the surrounding air. Another instant and the thing would have had his eyes in its sticky, prickly grasp, but either his weakness or the brown man's strength threw them both on their backs. The charm was broken. They crawled out of the circle of death and lay panting in the grass while the malignant plant, cracking and hissing, yearned and stretched and thrashed to get at them.

Carnivorous plants such as the famous Venus flytrap do, of course, exist, but could there be plants so large and voracious that they eat human beings?

Despite the incredible nature of the story, it's important to note that it was written for the *American Weekly* by a very credible source: a botanist and naturalist named Willard Nelson Clute, who was the author of numerous books, including *The Useful Plants of the World* and *A Dictionary of American Plant Names*. Who knows? Perhaps the deadly, people-eating plant of the Philippines still exists, still luring the unwary into its deadly embrace.

Finally, there is the 1881 account of Philip Robinson, who, in *Under the Punkah*, wrote of his uncle's near-death experience with a plant hungry for human flesh somewhere along the Nile River:

> This awful plant, that rears its splendid death-shade in the central solitude of a Nubian fern forest, sickens by its unwholesome humors all vegetation from its immediate vicinity, and feeds upon the wild beasts that, in the terror of the chase, or the heat of noon, seek the thick shelter of its upon the birds that, flitting across the open space, come within the charmed circle of its power, or innocently refresh themselves from the cups of its great waxen flowers; upon even man himself when, an infrequent prey, the savage seeks its asylum in the storm, or turns from the harsh foot-wounding sword-grass of the glade, to pluck the wondrous fruit that hang plumb down among the wondrous foliage. And such fruit!

> Glorious golden ovals, great honey drops, swelling by their own weight into pear-shaped translucencies. The foliage glistens with a strange dew, that all day long drips on to the ground below, nurturing a rank growth of grasses, which shoot up in places so high that their spikes of fierce blood-fed green show far up among the deep-tinted foliage of the terrible tree, and, like a jealous body-guard, keep concealed the fearful secret of the charnel-house within, and draw round the black roots of the murderous plant a decent screen of living green.

IN SEARCH OF A MIGHTY FISH

It was in late July 2002 that the U.K.-based Centre for Fortean Zoology (CFZ) carried out an investigation into the strangest story to filter out of Lancashire, England, in years. In February many reliable witnesses, all seasoned bird watchers, saw overwintering swans being attacked and dragged underwater by some powerful, unseen predator at Martin Mere bird reserve. Luckily, all the birds managed to fight off the aquatic assailant and make it to shore. One, however, had its wing feathers so badly bitten that it could not migrate to Iceland in the summer and remained on the mere, or lake. The fifty thousand or so swans and geese were so spooked that they left the mere on several occasions.

I'll now hand you over to Jonathan Downes, who tells the story of the investigation:

Fearing a hoax, we rang the Mere [the Martin Mere nature reserve] and spoke to the chief warden Pat Wisniewski, who confirmed the odd yarn and had even seen some immense animal swimming in the mere. Pat welcomed the idea of a CFZ investigation. Hence Jon Downes, Graham Inglis, Richard Freeman, and new addition John Fuller took the 300-mile-plus trip to track this titan from the abyss in its inky watered lair. We intended to sweep the lake with an electronic fish finder and attempt to bait the animal to the surface and hopefully photograph and identify it. We agreed that a giant wels catfish was the most likely candidate. A pike would need to be exceptionally large to attack a swan and would have probably left lacerations with its teeth, unlike the sucking bite of the catfish.

Pat turned out to be one of the very nicest blokes we have met. Anyone who includes Doctor Who, H.P. Lovecraft, and Hawkwind amongst his likes must be a good egg. He had arranged for us to sleep in the Rains hide overlooking the deepest part of the mere. Though the mere was very beautiful, our hearts fell as we walked around it on the evening of our arrival. The mere was shallow, muddy, and only a few hundred feet across. Richard especially doubted that it could support a large predator. By 9:30 that night, he was eating his words.

Whilst walking around the mere's edge, Richard came upon a massive fish basking in the shallows. Its black, oily, scale-less back bore a small dorsal fin. Disturbed, the massive animal made off and dove in a tremendous swirl, to reappear briefly further out close to a small island. It dove again in amidst a huge disturbance. Its length was hard to estimate as only the back broke the surface, but if it was attacking swans the team agreed it would have to be around eight feet long.

Next day the dinghy, *Waterhorse* (named after Nessie seeker Tim Dinsdale's boat), was inflated and the fish finder deployed to gauge the depth of the mere. In summer the depth is far less than winter. Many areas of the mere were only eighteen inches or so deep and badly silted up. A couple of areas, including where the sighting had occurred, were deeper.

Graham set out to map the lake and its islands as this had not been done in detail before. We intended to make a 3-D map of the mere's depth as well. This was swiftly abandoned after the second sighting that took place in the same place as the first. At eleven A.M. Richard saw the fish again. This time it was just beneath the surface. It threw its elongate body into a violent S-shaped curve and thrashed the water as it disappeared. The description fitted none of the fish known to be resident in the mere but recalled a wels.

The wels, sheetfish, or European catfish (*Silurus glanis*) is indigenous to continental Europe east of the river Rhine; it appears to be particularly common in eastern Europe, especially in the basin of the river Danube. It has a slimy, scale-less, elongated body and a broad, flat head with a wide mouth. Writing in *Naturalized Animals of the British Isles*, Sir Christopher Lever notes that it has a "distinctly sinister appearance." He goes on to describe the creature in some depth:

The wels catfish (*Silurus glanis*) is a large European fish that can reach a length of 16 feet (5 meters) and weigh 660 pounds (300 kilograms).

"The head, back and sides are usually some shade of greenish-black spotted with olive-green, and the underside is yellowy-white, with an indistinct blackish marbling; the head and back may sometimes be a deep velvety black and the sides occasionally take on a bronzy sheen. Two long barbels depending from the upper jaw, and four short ones from the lower jaw, help to give the catfish its name. There is no adipose fin, but an enormously elongated anal fin: a tiny dorsal fin is situated half-way between the bases of the pectoral and pelvic fins. The largest authenticated wels, taken from the river Dnieper in the Ukraine in the southern U.S.S.R., measured over 16 ft. (5 m) in length and weighed 675 lb (306 kg); elsewhere in Europe and in England, however, the wels seldom exceeds 5 ft (152 cm) in length and 25 lb (11 kg) in weight."

The wels is a solitary fish. It lives mostly in the still, deoxygenated waters of lakes, marshes, and lagoons, but can also be found in the lower reaches and backwaters of slow-flowing rivers. Unusually for a catfish, it is tolerant of both heavy industrial pollution and saltwater and is found naturaly in the brackish water of certain parts of the Black and Baltic Seas. Wels are nocturnal, choosing to feed after dark. They are voracious predators, especially when adults. Lever lists prey species as including "turbot, bream, crayfish, eels, frogs, roach, tench, ducklings, goslings and occasionally water-voles."

They have even been reported as maneaters. Lever cites an authority called Valenciennes (presumably the eminent nineteenth-century ichthyologist) as saying: "In the year 1700, on the 3rd of July, a countryman took one near Thorn for Torun, Poland, which had the entire body of an infant in its stomach." Lever also quotes someone called Grossinger (whom I have been unable to identify further) as saying that a Hungarian fisherman discovered the corpse of a woman in another "having a marriage ring on her finger and a purse full of money at her girdle."

The evidence available to us leads us to conclude that the giant fish may have been introduced to Lancashire by Frank Buckland of the Acclimatization Society after his visit to Southport in the 1870s.... After this the mapping of the Mere's depth was abandoned to concentrate on the area we believed to be the monster's lair. We set up a rope between the shore and a small island. From this we dangled the fish finder's transducer into the water and set up the display screen on land. John Fuller kept watch with a camera, and we baited the area heavily.

Firstly we used duck pellets, which were roundly ignored. Later we tried bait balls made from corn beef and sardines (our staple diet for the mission). Still the monster did not rise. Finally the cadaver of a dead lapwing was employed, but even this mouthwatering morsel could not tempt the beast. However, four large soma contacts were recorded by John Fuller over the next few days.

During the course of the next few days Graham completed a map of the lakeshore and islands, and we carried out over sixty interviews with media from around both the country and the world, including Radio Free Iran! The media circus reached its zenith with several live broadcasts on Sky News.

Though we did not photograph the monster, we confirmed its existence and are confident that it is in fact a wels catfish. We also filmed they eyewitness testimonies of many of the birdwatchers who saw the attacks including Pat himself. On return to Exeter we called on by GMTV within twenty-four hours. They paid for us to return to the mere for a live broadcast. They set up underwater cameras (next to useless in the pitch waters of the mere) and interviewed us throughout the morning. At one point something large broke the surface of the water behind the presenter, but this may have been a large carp. Nothing further was gleaned on this extra day at the mere.

If the monster causes as much disruption this winter as it did over the last, Pat is considering calling us in again to net the beast and move it to a smaller pool not used by overwintering waterfowl. The beast has become quite a tourist attraction, upping the numbers of visitors to the mere. In the tradition of giving lake and sea monsters awful names, the CFZ have christened Martin Mere's monster "Marty."

MONSTERS FROM A LAND DOWN UNDER

A creature believed by many to have supernatural or even hellish origins, the bunyip is a monster that lurks within the creeks and swamps of Australia. It has been known to the Aboriginal people for centuries or even longer. As for its appearance, in 1845 the *Geelong Advertiser* told its readers:

> The Bunyip, then, is represented as uniting the characteristics of a bird and of an alligator. It has a head resembling an emu, with a long bill, at the extremity of which is a transverse projection on each side, with serrated edges like the bone of the stingray. Its body and legs partake of the nature of the alligator. The hind legs are remarkably thick and strong, and the fore legs are much longer, but still of great strength. The extremities are furnished with long claws, but the blacks say its usual method of killing its prey is by hugging it to death. When in the water it swims like a frog, and when on shore it walks on its hind legs with its head erect, in which position it measures twelve or thirteen feet in height.

One of the most fascinating reports of an encounter with a bunyip came from a man who has taken on near-legendary status in Australia. His name was William Buckley. Born in Cheshire, England, in 1780, Buckley was an unforgettable and imposing figure, standing around six feet, eight inches tall with a head of wild, long, black hair. He enlisted in the King's Foot Regiment and fought against the army of none other than French emperor Napoleon Bonaparte. In what was certainly a miscarriage of justice, Buckley was found guilty of theft and given a sentence of fourteen years. Buckley was shipped off to Australia to serve his time in jail. He did not remain in jail for long. In December 1803, Buckley managed to escape and, as a result, spent an incredible thirty years living with the Wathaurung Aborig-

> One of the most fascinating reports of an encounter with a bunyip came from a man who has taken on near-legendary status in Australia. His name was William Buckley.

ines, taking two wives. In July 1835, Buckley finally came out of hiding and was soon thereafter pardoned for the crime that never was.

In 1852, a man named John Morgan wrote a celebrated and highly entertaining book on Buckley, appropriately titled *Life and Adventures of William Buckley*. One of the highlights of the book was Buckley's claim to Morgan that while living in the wilds of Australia, he encountered a bunyip. Buckley told his chronicler:

> We next went about forty miles, I should think, to a place they call Kironamaat; there is near to it a lake about ten miles in circumference. It took us several days to accomplish this march, as we hunted all the way; we halted near a well of fresh water, the lake being brackish, and there was a great plain near us. We here made nets with strips of bark, and caught with them great quantities of shrimps. We lived very sumptuously and in peace for many months at this place, and then went to the borders of another lake, called Moodewarri: the water of which was perfectly fresh, abounding in large eels, which we caught in great abundance.

> In this lake, as well as in most of the others inland, and in the deep water rivers, is a very extraordinary amphibious animal, which the natives call Bunyip, of which I could never see any part, except the back, which appeared to be covered with feathers of a dusky grey color. It seemed to be about the size of a full grown calf, and sometimes larger; the creatures only appear when the weather is very calm, and the water smooth. I could never learn from any of the natives that they had seen either the head or tail, so that I could not form a correct idea of their size; or what they were like.

Buckley later stated, of an adventure at a lake named Jerringot:

> Here, the Bunyip—the extraordinary animal I have already mentioned—were often seen by the natives, who had a great dread of them, believing them to have some supernatural power over human beings, so as to occasion death, sickness, disease, and such like misfortunes. They have also a superstitious notion that the great abundance of eels in some of the lagoons where animals resort, are ordered for the Bunyip's provision; and they therefore seldom remain long in such neighborhoods after having seen the creature....

> When alone, I several times attempted to spear a Bunyip; but, had the natives seen me do so, it would have caused great displeasure. And again, if I had succeeded in killing or even wounding one, my own life would probably have paid forfeit—they

considering the animal, as I have already said, something supernatural.

The Australian office of the Centre for Fortean Zoology (CFZ) notes the following on this very unusual animal:

> Naturalist George French Angas collected a description of a bunyip as a "water spirit" from the Moorundi people of the Murray River before 1847, stating it was "much dreaded by them.... It inhabits the Murray; but ... they have some difficulty describing it. Its most usual form ... is said to be that of an enormous starfish." Robert Brough Smyth's *Aborigines of Victoria* of 1878 devoted ten pages to the bunyip, but concluded "in truth little is known among the blacks respecting its form, covering or habits; they appear to have been in such dread of it as to have been unable to take note of its characteristics."

The bunyip is an Australian water spirit that has been described as appearing in a variety of forms, ranging from starfish-like to more seal-like in nature, as in the illustration above.

The CFZ notes that although the Australian Aborigines believed the bunyip was a monster of supernatural proportions (and still believe that to be the case), there may be a more down-to-earth explanation: "In many 19th-century newspaper accounts the bunyip was variously attributed a dog-like face, dark fur, a horse-like tail, flippers, and walrus-like tusks or horns or a duck-like bill. Many modern-day researchers now believe the descriptions may have referred to seals or walruses, or even a cultural memory of megafauna such as the diprotodon."

Whatever the truth of the bunyip, the legend and lore that surrounds it is, today, as robust as it always has been.

Is it feasible that the subtropical rain forests of Australia (for, contrary to popular belief, the continent is not merely desert) are home to gigantic, man-eating lizards of twenty to thirty feet in length? Do such monsters lurk in the swamps, lagoons, and inland waters of Australia? Could such *Jurassic Park*-like beasts really remain hidden, undetected, and free to rampage in unstoppable fashion? The Australian government's wildlife department scoffs at such scenarios. Witnesses, however, strongly suggest otherwise. As for the creature itself, it's not something created out of the minds of the fantasy-driven and the deluded. Thousands of years ago, Australia really was home to such immense beasts. The big question is: Do they still live, despite the fact that they have been declared completely and utterly extinct in the long-gone past? Maybe they are still with us.

The creature in question, *Megalania prisca*, was a huge, vicious monitor lizard that roamed Australia at least as late as forty thousand years ago. It was named by one Richard Owen, a paleontologist of the 1800s—a man who has gone down in history as coining the term *Dinosauria*, or "terrible reptile." Generally referred to as just *Megalania*, its title very appropriately translates to "ancient, giant butcher."

The Australian government's wildlife department scoffs at such scenarios. Witnesses, however, strongly suggest otherwise.

Many might consider it utterly absurd to believe that packs of thirty-foot monster-lizards could still exist in stealth in the wilds of modern-day Australia and not be found. Nonetheless, let's take a look at what we know of this undeniably controversial saga. For decades, reports have surfaced out of Australia of such creatures—to the extent that Australian monster hunter Rex Gilroy has been able to put together an extensive dossier of such accounts. One in particular is well worth noting.

Gilroy, during the course of his investigations into claims that *Megalania* still lives, had the good fortune to meet with a solider named Steve, who told Gilroy a fascinating and terrifying story. It was in October 1968 that Steve, serving in the Australian military at the time, was taking part in an exercise in Queensland on what was termed the Normandy Range. One part of the exercise required Steve's unit to negotiate a particularly treacherous and dense, swampy area.

As the team did so, they came upon something highly disturbing: the viciously ripped-to-pieces body of a cow. Not only that, but from the surrounding ground, Steve and his comrades could see that something had dragged the cow for a considerable time before savagely eating huge chunks out of the poor animal. More significant, lizard-like prints were found in the muddy ground— all of which were close to two feet in length—as was an area of flattened ground, which suggested to the group that the unknown beast had a long, heavy tail that dragged behind it. No one needed to be told twice: the soldiers got the hell out of the swamp as quickly as possible.

As amazing as Steve's story was, and still is, it may well have been nothing less than a close and highly hazardous encounter with a marauding monster that science and zoology assure us became extinct tens of thousands of years ago—but which, against all the odds, might still be with us. Remember that if you ever choose to take a trek through the subtropical terrain of Australia.

The Australian Museum website says of this immense monster, which moved as easily and effortlessly in swamps and lagoons as it did on land:

"*Megalania prisca*, the largest terrestrial lizard known, was a giant goanna (monitor lizard). First described from the Darling Downs in Queensland by Sir Richard Owen in 1859, *Megalania* lived in a variety of eastern Australian Pleistocene habitats—open forests, woodlands and perhaps grasslands. *Megalania* would have been a formidable reptilian predator like its relative the Komodo Dragon of Indonesia, and may have eaten large mammals, snakes, other reptiles and birds."

The people at *Mythology.net* provide us these insightful words on *Megalania*:

In many Aboriginal stories that have been handed down through oral record and cave paintings that have been discovered, it is suggested that some of these reptiles were capable of bringing fire and other destruction along with them. Additionally, the fossils of these creatures suggest they were not purely terrestrial creatures, but may also have aquatic abilities. This thought is supported by an Aboriginal tale that speaks of a *Megalania prisca* who wandered into the ocean. The story claims that the *Megalania prisca* happened to wander into the ocean and began to swim. While in the ocean, it was attacked by a Great White Shark and the two creatures began to fight each other. The *Megalania* was able to overcome the shark and dragged the carcass of the Great White back to shore. The story ends with the depiction of the *Megalania* feasting on the carcass of the shark.

As amazing as Steve's story was, and still is, it may well have been nothing less than a close and highly hazardous encounter with a marauding monster....

Moving on, Owen Quinn reports at the website *Following the Nerd*:

In 1890 in the village of Euroa, Victoria, a thirty foot lizard terrorised the villagers, resulting in a squad of forty men armed to the teeth going out to hunt it down only to find it had disappeared. They called it a monstrous goanna, something that the Aborigines recorded in their history as the horny-skinned bunyip goanna and it goes right back to the Dreamtime. Now a goanna is a name for a monitor lizard, but nothing the size of these things. Settlers to Australia were warned by the native people to beware of this variety of goanna. These could grow to thirty feet in length and had powerful jaws. To the people these really were dragons come to life and a threat like nothing they had ever faced.

In May 1899, the *Sydney Evening News* waded into the controversial matter of huge lizards with an article titled "A Tale of Central Australia." It was written by a man named Ernest Favenc, who, as well as being a journalist, was a historian and explorer. Favenc detailed in his feature a frightening confrontation between Aborigines and a massive monster-lizard known to the locals as the Gonderanup:

> It was a brilliant moonlight night and the party were smoking after their meal, when they were startled by an agonised cry from one of the horses. There is no sound more startling and painful to hear than the semi-human cry of a horse in mortal pain and terror, and the men, starting to their feet, picked up their firearms, and hastened in the direction of the sound. One horse, a grey, was plunging frantically in its hobbles, rearing and uttering the terrified scream of pain that had startled them. As they approached they saw, clinging to the horse's throat, with claws buried in the shoulders, and its jaws having a firm grip on the poor creature's throat, what appeared to be a monstrous lizard. The horse, as they approached, stood still, trembling all over, but the horrible thing fastened on it never moved.
>
> Putting his carbine close to its head at an angle that would not hurt the horse, Murray fired. The claws of the thing relaxed, but the jaws never opened, and the frightened horse began turning round and round with the dead creature hanging on to its throat. Then it staggered, fell, and, with a shuddering gasp, died. The creature that had attacked it was, in fact, an enormous sort of lizard, with a huge disproportionate head. The iron jaws, armed with cruel teeth, still retained their death grip on the dead horse's throat from which the blood was now pouring.
>
> While engaged in looking at it Dandy was seized in the side by another of the horrible creatures. Rafter, the other man, killed it, but not before it inflicted a terrible wound. Murray called to them to catch the horses and get away as soon as they could, for others of the brutes were coming. Dandy could do nothing but stagger to camp; while Murray and Rafter ran after the horses to drive them up. Dandy heard shouting and shots, but the others did not come back. He heard another of the creatures crawling towards him, and, overcome with blind terror, he fled.
>
> Dandy and Rafter would soon die out there in the hot desert from the wounds inflicted by the Gonderanup. And of the

A 1935 illustration of the bunyip portrays a truly alien, bizarre water monster.

horses that had been attacked, only their skeletons remained, the ferocious reptiles having picked the flesh clean.

> When they approached the camp all was silent. Martin shouted for Dandy, but got no answer. Poor Dandy was dead. The bite of the *Gonderanup* seemed to be fatal. Murray never would tell the whole details of his fight with the lizards on the bank of the salt lake…. The subject seemed repulsive to him, and he swore that you could hack the bodies off the creatures, and their jaws would still remain fixed. They were not natural, he said, and old black fellows of that part who remember them say so too.

That was far from being the end of the story, as further accounts of these dangerous giants continued to surface. In January 1940, the *Northern Standard* newspaper (which covered the Australian city of Darwin) made significant page space for its readers to tell their tales of monsters under the headline "Seeking an 18ft Lizard." It told of the ambitious and dangerous plan of one Fred Blakeley to capture one of the giant creatures, which he called a prenty. The journalist who wrote the article said:

> He hopes to bring back one alive. He claims to be one of the few white men who have seen a giant Prenty. He describes it as a mammoth lizard about 18 feet from snout to tail-tip. Its claw tracks are about 6 feet apart. The claws are sharp and poisonous and inflict a wound which festers quickly and rarely heals. The giant Prenty, he says, attacks chiefly with its tail. It can fell an ox with a sweeping blow. It is faster than a crocodile and its gait resembles a gallop. The Aborigines call the Prenty a *debil debil*, Blakeley told the *Northern Standard*.

Writing for *Weird Australia*, Andrew Nicholson stated:

> In the Cessnock district of the Hunter Valley in NSW [New South Wales], a local farmer reported seeing a giant reptile in a paddock on his property in 1978. The monster reptile was apparently ripping into the flesh of a cow with its massive jaws and teeth. Using the spacing of fence posts just beyond the carnivorous lizard, the farmer estimated its length at an astounding 35 feet, and around 9 feet tall on all fours. After arranging a search party of local farmers, the incredible beast could not be found. The bloody remains of the poor cow and some large indistinct tracks in the grass were all that remained.

The appropriately named *Weird Australia* people also noted that on August 14, 1931, the *Cairns Post* newspaper reported: "There is no room for doubt about the existence of the prenty, a gigantic lizard of Central Australia." The story continued:

An early caller at *The Telegraph* office was Mr. B. W. G. Phillips, a great friend of the late T. C. Wollaston, who discusses the Prenty in his book, *Opal—We of the Never Never.* The Prenty, according to Wollaston, "has leisure and space to grow properly. It is powerful in limbs, beautiful in skin, its reach exceptional, eight feet in length when its tongue is fully extended." Its color is gamboge yellow, with blackish-grey markings; and perfectly round spots—as large as a shilling—adorn the sides and neck like a pedigree Ayrshire. The prenty has a long head and brilliant eye, and when it stands up with stiffened legs and arched body, its head bent forward, it looks a formidable beast.

Walsh was shocked to fleetingly see the approximately four-foot-tall animal emerge from the watery depths and shuffle into the heart of nearby scrubland.

Without a doubt, Sydney, Australia, can lay claim to having played host to one of the most mystifying and bizarre of all creatures ever encountered, and I do not use those two words—mystifying and bizarre—lightly. How else would one describe a diminutive beast that looks like an elephant, walks on its hind legs, and surfaces from the depths of nothing less than a dark lagoon? That was exactly what a woman named Mabel Walsh encountered in Narrabeen—a beachside suburb of Sydney—back in the late 1960s.

While driving home late one April 1968 evening with her nephew John, Walsh was shocked to fleetingly see the approximately four-foot-tall animal emerge from the watery depths and shuffle into the heart of nearby scrubland. It was a creature that Walsh would never forget, even though it was in view for mere seconds. Gray in color with what looked like a tough, leathery skin, it had a snout resembling that of an anteater, a slim trunk, long back legs, and a pair of short forelimbs that dangled as it waddled along—sideways, no less—by the edge of the road before vanishing into the scrub.

The local newspaper, the *Daily Telegraph*, recognizing the publicity the story would surely create, splashed the details across its pages. In an article titled "And now it's the Monster of Narrabeen!"—and with the subtitle of "Loch Ness was never like this"—the details of Mabel Walsh's story tumbled out, which provoked yet more reports of the fantastic creature.

Some of them sounded decidedly sensationalized, since they suggested the monster of the deep had taken to dragging sheep, cows, and even horses to their horrific deaths in the heart of the lagoon—a most unlikely action for a creature barely four feet in height. Others spoke in near-hysterical tones of seeing a bright red, clawed hand come out of a hole in the ground at the lake and try to grab a terrified youngster.

The final word on the matter went to Mabel Walsh, who started the controversy, and who told newspaper staff that people might call her crazy, but she was absolutely sure there was a bizarre creature in Narrabeen Lake.

SOLIMÕES RIVER SNAKE

In October 1907, a frightening face-to-face encounter with an unknown animal of the deep took place on the Solimões River, Colombia. The source of the story was Franz Herrmann Schmidt, a German explorer. Along with a friend, Captain Rudolph Pfleng, Schmidt spent more than a month trekking around wild areas of Colombia. It was while doing so that Schmidt and Pfleng crossed paths with a monster. Almost two weeks into their trip along the Solimões River, Schmidt, Pfleng, and their Colombian guides came across an isolated valley surrounded by lush vegetation fed by a small body of water nearby. The two were amazed and concerned when, out of the blue, they came across gigantic prints in the mud and wet grass. Not only that, there was clear and undeniable evidence that something had been feeding on the surrounding trees—something that had the ability to reach heights of approximately thirteen to fifteen feet. Clearly, this was a formidable beast and, possibly, a highly dangerous one.

Less than twenty-four hours later, there was a major, hair-raising development: As the group took to the waters of the Solimões River in their trusty canoes, the sounds of apparently huge animals could be heard in the trees near the bank; crashing noises and the sounds of trees uprooted in violent fashion were only the start. Notably, the locals who had been hired to take Schmidt and Pfleng on their adventure made it clear that they knew of the animal and headed away from the bank and into the middle of the river in the hope that the lumbering animal would not follow.

As for how the story went from there, let's take a look at it in Schmidt's own words:

> There was a sudden outcry among them, a large dark something half hidden among the branches shot up among them and there was a great commotion. One of the excited Indians began to paddle the boat away from the shore, and before we could stop him we were one hundred feet from the waterline. Now we could see nothing and the Indians absolutely refused to put in again, while neither Pfleng nor myself cared to lay down our rifles to paddle. There was a great waving of plants and a sound like heavy slaps of a great paddle, mingled with the cries of some of

While navigating Brazil's Solimões River, German explorer Franz Herrmann Schmidt and his party encountered an enormous, snakelike river creature.

the monkeys moving rapidly away from the lake. One or two that were hurt or held fast wore shrieking close at hand, then their cries ceased. For a full ten minutes there was silence, then the green growth began to stir again, and coming back to the lake we beheld the frightful monster that I shall now describe.

Schmidt could not forget the appearance of the terrible leviathan:

The head appeared over bushes ten feet tall. It was about the size of a beer keg and was shaped like that of a tapir, as if the snout was used for pulling things or taking hold of them. The eyes were small and dull and set in like those of an alligator. Despite the half dried mud we could see that the neck, which was very snakelike, only thicker in proportion, as rough knotted like an alligator's sides rather than his back.

Evidently the animal saw nothing odd in us, if he noticed us, and advanced till he was not more than one hundred and fifty feet away. We could see part of the body, which I should judge to have been eight or nine feet thick at the shoulders, if that word may be used, since there were no fore legs, only some great, heavy clawed flippers. The surface was like that of the neck. For a wonder the Indians did not bolt, but they seemed fascinated.

As far as I was concerned, I would have waited a little longer, but Pfleng threw up his rifle and let drive at the head. I am sure that he struck between the eyes and that the bullet must have struck something bony, horny or very tough, for it cut twigs from a tree higher up and further on after it glanced. I shot as Pfleng shot again and aimed for the base of the neck.

The animal had remained perfectly still till now. It dropped its nose to the spot at which I had aimed and seemed to bite at it, but there was no blood or any sign of real hurt. As quickly as we could fire we pumped seven shots into it, and I believe all struck. They seemed to annoy the creature but not to work any injury. Suddenly it plunged forward in a silly, clumsy fashion. The Indians nearly upset the dugout getting away, and both Pfleng and I missed the sight as it entered the water. I was very anxious to see its hind legs, if it had any. I looked again only in time to see the last of it leave the land—a heavy blunt tail with rough horny lumps. The head was visible still, though the body was hidden by the splash. From this instant's opportunity I should say that the creature was thirty-five feet long, with at least twelve of this devoted to head and neck.

In three seconds there was nothing to be seen except the waves of the muddy water, the movements of the waterside growth and a monkey with its hind parts useless hauling himself up a tree top. As the Indians paddled frantically away I put a bullet through the poor thing to let it out of its misery. We had not gone a hundred yards before Pfleng called to me and pointed to the right.

Above the water an eighth of a mile away appeared the head and neck of the monster. It must have dived and gone right under us. After a few seconds' gaze it began to swim toward us, and as our bullets seemed to have no effect we took to flight in earnest. Losing sight of it behind an island, we did not pick it up again and were just as well pleased.

Answers for what the beast might have been never surfaced. Could its descendants still be there, skulking in those dense trees and lurking in the nearby waters? Maybe they are. Perhaps it's time for someone else to pick up where Schmidt and Pfleng left off.

DRAGONS AND WURMS

Wurms: There are some creatures that, due to the passage of time, have become true enigmas. They were dangerous and huge in size and roamed the woods and lakes of what is now the United Kingdom. The spelling of their names varied: wurms, wyrms, and worms. We know they existed, but as to what they were, well, that is quite another issue. It's my view that we should address the matter to try to get a full understanding of their identities. During the Middle Ages, reports spread of large, wormlike animals that slithered their way across the landscape, killing and even eating people, and, when they needed to, hiding in deep rivers and lakes. That the Nessies of Scotland have been seen briefly on land suggests that Scotland's most famous monsters and those ancient worms were and still are the very same things. So, to develop a solid understanding of at least some lake monsters, we must go back in time to the old world of the wurms—and, after that, to see how—in relatively modern times—these coiling, crawling monsters play a role in conspiracy theories.

SEA BEASTS IN THE TWENTIETH CENTURY

A terrifying confrontation with a huge, unknown animal took place on May 30, 1903. The witnesses were Captain W. H. Bartlett, Second Officer Joseph Ostens Grey, and the rest of the crew of the cargo steamer *Tresco*. Bartlett and his men had left Philadelphia two days previously. The journey was a normal one; that is, until an enormous animal appeared on the scene. When they reached a point around ninety miles off of Cape Hatteras, North Carolina, those aboard could not fail to see something very strange: more than thirty sharks were being furiously pursued by a gigantic creature, as evidenced by a large hump that broke the waves. It must be stressed that only a monster of immense power, enormous size, and ruthless killing techniques would even consider taking on not just one shark but dozens of them! When a head and neck of a massive scale quickly appeared, one and all knew there was a monster in their midst.

At this point, the captain and the crew got a good look at the astounding thing of the deep. It was easily in excess of one hundred feet in length. Its body was "as thick as a cathedral pillar" and looked very much like a classic dragon of Chinese mythology. Second Officer Grey prepared a report for the November 1903 issue of the *Wide World Magazine* that reads like fantasy but was only too real:

> There was something unspeakably loathsome about the head, which was five feet long from nose to upper extremity. Such a head I never saw on any denizen of the sea. Underneath the jaw seemed to be a sort of pouch, or drooping skin. The nose, like a snout upturned, was somewhat recurved. I can remember seeing no nostrils or blow-holes. The lower jaw was prognathous, and the lower lip was half projecting, half pendulous. Presently I noticed something dripping from the ugly lower jaw. Watching I saw it was saliva, of a dirty drab color. While it displayed no teeth, it did possess very long and formidable molars, like a walrus's tusks. Its eyes were of a reddish color. They were elongated vertically. They carried in their dull depths a somber baleful glow, as if within them was concentrated all the fierce menacing spirit that raged in the huge bulk behind.

> Luckily for all of those on the ship, the monster soon decided to exit the area—but not before creating a huge wave that shook the ship in chaotic fashion, almost as if it was warning the crew to come no closer. They understood the message and hastily left the area. And who can blame them for that?

The traditional Chinese dragon is very serpent-like in form and is traditionally described as being intelligent.

In 1916, one Irwin J. O'Malley revealed his discovery of a huge, fossilized creature of unknown origins and huge proportions. In the April 15 issue of *Scientific American* that year, he recorded:

> During the latter part of a holiday trip to the Yangtze Gorges undertaken by my wife and self in November, 1915, we met Mr. M. Hewlett, British Consul at Ichang, and his wife, and in their company spent a day in the Ichang Gorge, landing at various points to climb the cliffs and explore some of the numerous caves. While exploring a large cave on the right of the bank of the river, and about one mile above the Customs Station at Ping Shon Pa, we discovered the fossils about to be described. The cave is reputed by the Chinese to extend some twenty miles to a point near Ichang.
>
> It is reported that a party from H.M.S. *Snipe* spent three days in the cave some years ago and that they failed to reach the end. Evidence that the party penetrated beyond the point where the discovery was made exists in the name of their ship painted on the cave walls at a point considerably further in.
>
> The Chinese name of the cave is Shen K'an Tzu, which means "The Holy Shrine," and one of the characters forming the word K'an is the Chinese character for "dragon." A large rock is seen at the entrance, and some eight to ten yards behind this there is a peculiar piece of curved rock bearing some slight resemblance to a portion of a dragon's body; the resemblance is possibly suggestive enough to impress the Chinese mind, but altogether fails to impress the foreigner.
>
> After proceeding some hundreds of yards inside the cave we found ourselves walking on a peculiar ridge in order to avoid the surrounding pool of water. The ridge curved backward and forward across the width of the cave like the curves of a large serpent, the suggestion being so strong we lowered our lamps in order to examine the ridge more closely. To our astonishment and delight, we found that we were in very truth walking along a perfect fossil of some huge reptile. Further inspection revealed the presence of six or eight of these enormous monsters. Having taken a few small specimens of loose portions of scale for examination in a better light, we left, to return the following morning for the purpose of measurement.
>
> On our return the following morning we selected one of the largest fossils lying for a great part of its length isolated from the others, the coils of the remainder being rather entangled. The

isolated portion measured seventy feet, so that is absolutely certain that the length is at least seventy feet, and as far as we could ascertain, this same specimen extended for another sixty or seventy feet. However, I admit that error is possible here, owing to the interlacing coils of the reptiles. The depth of the body seen in the foreground is two feet. The head is partially buried in the cave wall and appears to be a large, flat head similar to that of Morosaurus comperi.

About twelve or fourteen feet from the head two legs are seen partially uncovered, and again to more about fifty feet from the head. The fact that several persons have penetrated this cave in former years beyond the point where the discovery was made seems to indicate the fossils have been but recently uncovered, probably by a heavy discharge of water through the cave. It seems probable that these reptiles were trapped by some volcanic disturbance and starved to death; the size of the bodies compared to their length would indicate this.

A point of peculiar interest is the resemblance to the Chinese dragon of these fossils. I believe that it has therefore been supposed that the Chinese borrowed their idea of the dragons from Western mythology. The discovery has created a great stir among the local Chinese and foreigners, who are daily flocking to view the fossils. I am attempting to interest the Chinese authorities in Pekin and also the Chinese Monuments Society in order that the specimens may be preserved from damage.

Cryptozoologist Richard Freeman is director of the Centre for Fortean Zoology in Woolfardisworthy, Devon, England. He has investigated the dragon-like fossils discovered in China.

Cryptozoologist Richard Freeman suspects that what O'Malley came across were the remnants of a China-based dinosaur named Mamenchisaurus. That O'Malley said the creature's remains resembled a "Chinese dragon" has led Freeman to ponder on the incredible notion that dragons were not just creatures of legend and folklore but real monsters, which brings us to Freeman's personal views on dragons that were said to spend significant amounts of time on the ocean waters. He says, from his home in Exeter, England:

I started my career as a zoologist—so I had a grounded training. But cryptozoology was my passion. Now, I have had a particular passion—an obsession, I suppose—for years with dragons. But there was something that always puzzled me: no one had ever thought, for more than a hundred years, to publish a definitive, nonfiction book on the subject. And as I am a qualified zoologist, I thought: why not me? It's important to note that I've traveled the world pursuing these creatures—the Gambia, Mongolia, Thailand, and right here in England with some of the old legends from past centuries. And of one thing I can be certain: there isn't just one answer to the question of what dragons are or what they may be.

There are many creatures that have become linked to the lore and legend of what today we perceive and view as dragons, and some of these creatures are distinctly different to each other. But that should not take away from the fact that dragons are a real phenomenon. I am absolutely certain, having reviewed many ancient reports of dragon activity, that many sightings—perhaps two or three hundred years ago and probably further back—were genuine encounters, but where the witnesses were seeing what I believe to have been huge snakes, giant crocodiles, and the Australian "monster lizard" *Megalania*.

Any mention of dragons always conjures up images of fire-breathing monsters, and there are definitely reports that fall into that group. *But, when you look into many of the earliest, ancient legends, you find that the dragon is more often associated with water. So, I have a theory that some of the better lake monster accounts from centuries ago may well have influenced dragon tales* [italics mine]. Personally, I also believe that some classic tales of dragons in England in medieval times, and tales of beasts such as the Lambton Worm, probably have their origins in lake monster accounts, giant eels, etc., that have then mutated into tales of dragons on the loose. But the important point is that this shouldn't detract from the fact that people did see something.

I would pretty much stake my life on the fact that *Megalania* still exists—or did until very recently—in the large forests and lagoons of Australia, and that it also roamed New Guinea. This was a huge, killer-beast; a massive monitor lizard that exceeded thirty feet in length. In literal terms, this was a classic dragon-type animal.

There is no excuse for not getting out into the field and doing firsthand investigations; none at all. In fact, it's vital. I have no time for the armchair theorist. And one of the experiences that I will remember for the rest of my life was traveling to Thailand with the Discovery Channel in 2000, where we chased giant snakes—the Naga—in the caves and tunnels that exist deep below Thailand. It's very easy to see why the inhabitants in times past considered them to be dragons. The Naga is apparently a large snake, a very large one—maybe on the order of literally tens of feet in length, oil-drum-sized bodies, and definitely big enough to take a whole man.

There have come reports from the Congo of an animal known as Mokele-mbembe. Again, it has crossover qualities with dragon legends, but I'm sure that it will be shown in time to be some sort of giant monitor lizard, too.

> "Dickinson suggested that these animals developed large, expanded stomachs that would fill with hydrogen gas...."

Back in 1979 Peter Dickinson wrote a book that was titled *The Flight of Dragons*. Dickinson had come up with this idea—an excellent theory, in fact—that real-life dragons did exist and that they were the descendants of dinosaurs such as the *Tyrannosaurus rex*. Dickinson suggested that these animals developed large, expanded stomachs that would fill with hydrogen gas, which would come from a combination of hydrochloric acid found in the juices of the digestive system that would then mix with calcium found in the bones of their prey.

Then, from there, the hydrogen—a lighter-than-air gas—allowed these creatures to take to the skies and then control their flight by burning off the excess gas in the form of flame. Anyone seeing this would be seeing the closest thing to the image of the dragon that we all know and love. Dickinson's theory is an excellent one, and may well be a perfect explanation for sightings of real dragons—in times past, and perhaps today, I believe.

The dragon has its teeth and claws deep into the collective psyche of mankind, and it's not about to let go. Our most ancient fear still stalks the earth today. Beware: this is no fairytale. When your parents told you that there were no such things as dragons, they lied.

A Canadian military officer in British Columbia, F. W. Kemp, had an extraordinary encounter of the beastly variety with his wife in 1932. In the wake of their sighting of something terrifying, Kemp wrote down the whole story, which ensured it would be preserved for posterity—and it certainly was. It reads as follows:

On August 10, 1932, I was with my wife and son on Chatham Island in the Strait of Juan de Fuca. My wife called my attention to a mysterious something coming through the channel between Strong Tide Island and Chatham Island. Imagine my astonishment on observing a huge creature with head out of the water traveling about four miles per hour against the tide. Even at that speed a considerable wash was thrown on the rocks, which gave me the impression that it was more reptile than serpent to make so much displacement.

The channel at this point is about 500 yards wide. Swimming to the steep rocks of the Island opposite, the creature shot its head out of water on the rock, and moving its head from side to side, appeared to taking its bearings. Then fold after fold its body came to surface. Towards the tail it appeared serrated with something moving flail-like at the extreme end. The movements were like those of a crocodile. Around the head appeared a sort of mane, which drifted round the body like kelp.

The Thing's presence seemed to change the whole landscape, which make it difficult to describe my experiences. It did not seem to belong to the present scheme of things, but rather to the Long Ago when the world was young. The position it held on the rock was momentary. My wife and sixteen-year-old son ran to a point of land to get a clearer view. I think the sounds they made disturbed the animal. The sea being very calm, it seemed to slip back into deep water; there was a great commotion under the surface and it disappeared like a flash.

In my opinion, its speed must be terrific and its senses of smell, sight and hearing developed to a very high degree. It would be terribly hard to photograph, as its movements are different from anything I have ever seen or heard of. I should say its length to be not less than eighty feet. There were some logs on Strong Tide Island which gave me a good idea as to the size of monster as it passed them. I took a measurement of one the next day which was over sixty feet in length, and the creature overlapped it to a large extent at each end. I put a newspaper on the spot where it rested its head and took an observation from our previous point of vantage. The animal's was very much larger than the double sheet of newspaper. The body must have been at least five feet thick, and was of a bluish-green color which shone in the sun like aluminum. I could not determine the shape of the head, but it was much thicker than the body.

LINDORMS AND OTHER SCANDINAVIAN BEASTS

Scandinavian history and folklore is filled with tales of all manner of monsters, rampaging beasts, and deadly creatures of a fantastic nature. Very few, however, were as feared as the lethal lindorm. It was a huge, wriggling, snakelike animal that, like today's lake monsters such as Nessie, Champ, and Ogopogo, chose to live in deep, massive lakes. There was one big difference between the lindorms and similar monsters, however. The lindorm never stopped growing. This, rather ironically, was its very own downfall: as it grew bigger and bigger, it got heavier and heavier, which eventually ensured it could no longer support its own weight and would sink to the lake bed, unable to move its massive bulk, where it would eventually die.

There are stories in Scandinavian legend of lindorms having a particular hatred of Christian churches and chapels, which they would reportedly coil around and crush into rubble with their powerful, flexible bodies. Perhaps this was a result of the fact that the dragon was a beast revered in pagan times, but this was far less so when Christianity was brought to Europe. There are also tales of huge bulls reared to fight lindorms, even to death. Fortunately for the bulls, they were well trained and very often killed the snakelike monstrosities with their powerful horns.

While the lindorm is today a creature relegated to the world of myth, Scandinavia can boast of being home to a multitude of lake monsters and sea serpents. With that in mind, perhaps the lindorm is still with us but just under another name.

Reverend Sabine Baring-Gould (1834–1924) had a deep fascination for stories of strange creatures, including werewolves, ghouls, and a menacing phenomenon known as *eigi einhamir*. In Baring-Gould's own words in his *Book of Were-Wolves*:

In Norway and Iceland certain men were said to be *eigi einhamir*, not of one skin, an idea which had its roots

Of Scandinavian origin, linworms were snakelike monsters typically having two front legs and no hind legs. They were either described as land creatures or, sometimes, as inhabiting the ocean. This ninth-century Swedish runestone depicts the lindorm.

in paganism. The full form of this strange superstition was, that men could take upon them other bodies, and the natures of those beings whose bodies they assumed. The second adopted shape was called by the same name as the original shape, *hamr*, and the expression made use of to designate the transition from one body to another, was at *skipta hömum*, or *at hamaz*; whilst the expedition made in the second form, was the *hamför*. By this transfiguration extraordinary powers were acquired; the natural strength of the individual was doubled, or quadrupled; he acquired the strength of the beast in whose body he travelled, in addition to his own, and a man thus invigorated was called *hamrammr*.

But how, exactly, was transformation achieved? Baring-Gould researched this matter extensively and offered the following:

> The manner in which the change was effected, varied. At times, a dress of skin was cast over the body, and at once the transformation was complete; at others, the human body was deserted, and the soul entered the second form, leaving the first body in a cataleptic state, to all appearance dead. The second hamr was either borrowed or created for the purpose. There was yet a third manner of producing this effect—it was by incantation; but then the form of the individual remained unaltered, though the eyes of all beholders were charmed so that they could only perceive him under the selected form.

> Having assumed some bestial shape, the man who is *eigi einhammr* is only to be recognized by his eyes, which by no power can be changed. He then pursues his course, follows the instincts of the beast whose body he has taken, yet without quenching his own intelligence. He is able to do what the body of the animal can do, and do what he, as man, can do as well. He may fly *or swim, if he is in the shape of bird or fish* [italics mine]; if he has taken the form of a wolf, or if he

Sabine Baring-Gould, an Anglican priest, was a novelist, hagiographer, and collector of folk songs. An antiquarian, he also had a fascination with stories of werewolves, sea monsters, and other cryptid beasts.

goes on a *gandreið* or wolf's-ride, he is fall of the rage and malignity of the creatures whose powers and passions he has assumed.

While many of the sightings are somewhat vague and open to interpretation, one which occurred in 1878 is not. It came from a man named Martin Olsson, a mechanic at a sawmill in Ostersund, Sweden, who lived in a cabin at the edge of the lake. He described his dramatic encounter with the monster:

> I was fishing near Forson Island when I got a strange feeling someone was watching me. I looked behind me and the lake creature was not more than forty meters behind my boat. I dropped my pole and line in the lake when I saw it. The weather was bright and sunny and I got a good view of the animal. The neck was long, about as round as a man's body at the base where it came up out of the water. It tapered up about six feet to a snake-like head that was larger than what I figured the neck could support. There was a hairy fringe just back of the neck. Hanging down the back. This "ribbon" was stuck close to the neck, possibly because of the wetness. The color was greyish brown. The thing had two distinct eyes that were reddish in appearance. There were a couple of dark humps visible beyond the neck. Both of these humps, and the part that was out of the water, glistened in the sunlight. I did not see scales. There was a skin on the animal that resembled the skin of a fish.

> I didn't want to alarm the animal, but I did want to get away as quickly as possible. Moving very cautiously, I took my oars and pulled slowly away from the spot. I became even more frightened when I had rowed about ten meters' distance and the animal began to swim towards me. I stopped rowing, and the thing just lay there in the water staring at me. This must have gone on for about five minutes. I'm uncertain because my mind was on anything but the passage of time. There was no doubt in my mind that this thing could have overturned my little boat. I thanked god when he dropped beneath the water and I saw a blackish hump move out in the opposite direction.

Although far less well known than its counterpart in Loch Ness, Scotland, the mysterious beast of Lake Storjson, Sweden, has been seen on far more than a few occasions. The late cryptozoologist Mark Chorvinsky said to me in an e-mail:

> Fisheries officer Ragnar Björks, 73, was out checking fishing permits on Sweden's Lake Storsjön when he had the fright of his life. From the placid waters a huge tail suddenly broke the surface near Björk's 12-foot rowboat. The colossal creature attached

to the tail appeared to be 18 feet long, grey-brown on top with a yellow underbelly. When Björks was alongside the monster, he struck at it with his oar, hitting it on the back. Angered, the creature slapped the water with its tail and the rowboat was thrown nine to twelve feet into the air. "At first I didn't believe that there was any monster in the Storsjön … but now I am convinced." Does Nessie have a relative in Lake Storsjön in the mountains of Northern Sweden? A large unknown creature has been seen in the lake for over 350 years. Since 1987 the Society for Investigating the Great Lake has collected some 400 reports of "Storsjöodjuret," as the Swedes call the monster. There is no clear picture of the beastie. Some witnesses describe a large neck undulating back and forth that looks like a horse's mane; others observed a large wormlike creature with recognizable ears. Reports of the creature's size range from 10 to 42 feet in length. Like the Loch Ness Monster, one of the numerous theories is that during the Ice Age 15,000 years ago, the monster may have become trapped in the Swedish lake.

Located in the middle of Sweden, Lake Storsjön has been the source of lake monster tales since the seventeenth century.

It's intriguing to note that the story of the monster of Lake Storsjön dates back to the seventeenth century, demonstrating that this is no recent hoax. Indeed, the first reference to the huge beast dates from 1635. A priest, Andreas Plantin, said:

> A long, long time ago two trolls, Jata and Kata, stood on the shores of the Great-Lake brewing a concoction in their cauldrons. They brewed and mixed and added to the liquid for days and weeks and years. They knew not what would result from their brew but they wondered about it a great deal. One evening there was heard a strange sound from one of their cauldrons. There was a wailing, a groaning and a crying, then suddenly came a loud bang. A strange animal with a black serpentine body and a cat-like head jumped out of the cauldron and disappeared into the lake. The monster enjoyed living in the lake, grew unbelievably larger and awakened terror among the people whenever it appeared. Finally, it extended all the way round the island of Frösön, and could even bite its own tail. Ketil Runske bound the mighty monster with a strong spell which was carved on a stone and raised on the island of Frösön. The serpent was pictured on the stone. Thus was the spell to be tied till the day someone came who could read and understand the inscription on the stone.

Later on in the seventeenth century—specifically 1685—there was this: "It is said that beneath this [rune]stone lies a dreadfully large head of a serpent and that the body stretches over Storsjön to Knytta by and Hille Sand where the tail is buried. The serpent was called a rå and therefore shall this stone be risen. Since no one peacefully could cross [Storsjön], the ferryman and his wife states, along with many others, that in the last turbulent time this stone was tore down and broken in two. As long as this stone laid on the ground many strange things occurred in the water, until the stone was risen and assembled anew."

Furthermore, Anne Adsen notes on the website *Adventure Sweden* that for anyone who wants to find vital information on the mysterious creature, there is no shortage of material:

> By the southernmost tip of Lake Storsjön there is a small community called Svenstavik. By the community grocery store and next to the liquor store there is an interactive research and visitor's center for all curious to know more about the monster. The center is always [ready] in case there is a monster sighting via the monitors on the bottom of Lake Storsjön. Young and old researchers are welcome to sit down by the large tablelike touch screens to find out all the known facts of the monster. In one corner you can watch films of true witnesses telling their stories and

you can draw your own monster, process it through the "Monster Making Machine" and see your own monster swim off on the wall of the center.

A writer at the *Columbia* travel blog, writing about the Lake Storsjon Monster, shares further data and leaves us with a pair of intriguing questions: "There are numerous designated monster-spotting points where you can sit with your binoculars and scan across the lake in hopes of a glimpse of the beast. In winter, as the ice ebbs and flows with a gentle groan, you can surely envision the large serpent like creature slowly moving about beneath the surface. Will he break through the ice beneath you and say hello? Do you want him to?"

Fully aware of the legends surrounding the kraken of Scandinavia, Henry Lee neither ignored nor dismissed tales of sea serpents coming out of Norway, Denmark, Finland, and Sweden. He stated: "We will now consider the accounts given by Scandinavian historians, of the sea-serpent having been seen in northern waters. Here, I suppose, I ought to indulge in the usual flippant sneer at Bishop Pontoppidan. I know that in abstaining from doing so I am sadly out of the fashion; but I venture to think that the dead lion has been kicked at too often already, and undeservedly."

Lee continued: "Whether there be, or be not, a huge marine animal, not necessarily an ophidian, answering to some of the descriptions of the sea-serpent—so called—Pontoppidan did not invent the stories told of its appearance. Long before he was born the monster had been described and figured; and for centuries previously the Norwegians, Swedes, Danes, and Fins had believed in its existence as implicitly as in the tenets of their religious creed."

A 1555 illustration of Olaus Magnus's sea worm.

Moving away from Lee, Olaus Magnus, the archbishop of Uppsala, Sweden, penned the following words in 1555:

They who in works of navigation on the coasts of Norway employ themselves in fishing or merchandize do all agree in this strange story, that there is a serpent there which is of a vast magnitude, namely 200 foot long, and moreover, 20 foot thick; and is wont to live in rocks and caves toward the sea-coast about Berge: which will go alone from his holes on a clear night in summer, and devour calves, lambs, and hogs, or else he goes into the sea to feed on polypus (octopus), locusts (lobsters), and all sorts of sea-crabs. He hath commonly hair hanging from his neck a cubit long, and sharp scales, and is black, and he hath flaming, shining eyes. This snake disquiets the shippers; and he puts up his head on high like a pillar, and catcheth away men, and he devours them; and this happeneth not but it signifies some wonderful change of the kingdom near at hand; namely, that the princes shall die, or be banished; or some tumultuous wars shall presently follow. There is also another serpent of an incredible magnitude in an island called Moos in the diocess of Hammer; which, as a comet portends a change in all the world, so that portends a change in the kingdom of Norway, as it was seen anno 1522; that lifts himself high above the waters, and rolls himself round like a sphere. This serpent was thought to be fifty cubits long by conjecture, by sight afar off: there followed this the banishment of King Christiernus, and a great persecution of the Bishops; and it shewed also the destruction of the country.

Back to Henry Lee:

The Gothic Archbishop, amongst other signs and omens, also attributes this power of divination to the small red ants which are sometimes so troublesome in houses, and declares that they also portended the downfall, A.D. 1523, of the abominably cruel Danish king, Christian II.... His curious work is full of wild improbabilities and odd superstitions, most of which he states with a calm air of unquestioning assent; but as he wrote in the time of our Henry VIII., long before the belief in witches and warlocks, fairies and banshees, had died out in our own country, we can hardly throw stones at him on that score. It is a most amusing and interesting history, and gives a wonderful insight of the habits and customs of the northern nations in his day.

Amongst his illustrations of the sea monsters ... a sea-serpent is seen writhing in many coils upon the surface of the water, and having in its mouth a sailor, whom it has seized from the deck of a ship. The poor fellow is trying to grasp the ratlins of the shrouds, but is being dragged from his hold and lifted over the bulwarks by the monster. His companions, in terror, are endeavoring to escape in various directions. One is climbing aloft by the stay, in the hope of getting out of reach in that way, whilst two others are hurrying aft to obtain the shelter of a little castle or cabin projecting over the stern. I am strongly of the opinion that this is but the fallacious representation of an actual occurrence.

Read by the light of recent knowledge, these old pictures convey to a practiced eye a meaning as clear as that of hieroglyphics to an Egyptologist, and my translation of this is the following: The crew of a ship have witnessed the dreadful sight of a serpent-like form issuing from the sea, rising over the bulwarks of their vessel, seizing one of their messmates from amongst them, and dragging him overboard and under water. Awe-stricken by the mysterious disappearance of their comrade, and too frightened and anxious for their own safety to be able, during the short space of time occupied by an affair, which all happened in a few seconds, to observe accurately their terrible assailant, they naturally conjecture that it must have been a snake.

It was probably a gigantic calamari, such as we now know exist, and the dead carcasses of which have been found in the locality where the event depicted is supposed to have taken place. The presumed body of the serpent was one of the arms of the squid, and the two rows of suckers thereto belonging are indicated in the illustration by the medial line traversing its whole length (intended to represent a dorsal fin) and the double row of transverse septa, one on each side of it.

One Captain Lawrence de Ferry wrote, back in August 1746, to a John Reutz:

The latter end of August, in the year 1746, as I was on a voyage, on my return from Trundhiem, on a very calm and hot day, having a mind to put in at Molde, it happened that when we were arrived with my vessel within six English miles of the aforesaid Molde, being at a place called Jule-Naess, as I was reading in a book, I heard a kind of a murmuring voice

The beak of a giant squid, *Mesonychoteuthis hamiltoni*, gives one an idea of how immense this animal is and how it could have been seen as a sea monster by mariners of old.

from amongst the men at the oars, who were eight in number, and observed that the man at the helm kept off from the land. Upon this I inquired what was the matter, and was informed that there was a sea-snake before us. I then ordered the man at the helm to keep to the land again, and to come up with this creature of which I had heard so many stories.

Though the fellows were under some apprehension, they were obliged to obey my orders. In the meantime the sea-snake passed by us, and we were obliged to tack the vessel about in order to get nearer to it. As the snake swam faster than we could row, I took my gun, that was ready charged, and fired at it; on this he immediately plunged under the water. We rowed to the place where it sunk down (which in the calm might be easily observed) and lay upon our oars, thinking it would come up again to the surface; however it did not. Where the snake plunged down, the water appeared thick and red; perhaps some of the shot might wound it, the distance being very little.

The head of this snake, which it held more than two feet above the surface of the water, resembled that of a horse. It was of a greyish colour, and the mouth was quite black, and very large. It had black eyes, and a long white mane, that hung down from the neck to the surface of the water. Besides the head and neck, we saw seven or eight folds, or coils, of this snake, which were very thick, and as far as we could guess there was about a fathom distance between each fold.

I related this affair in a certain company, where there was a person of distinction present who desired that I would communicate to him an authentic detail of all that happened; and for this reason two of my sailors, who were present at the same time and place where I saw this monster, namely, Nicholas Pedersen Kopper, and Nicholas Nicholsen Anglewigen, shall appear in court, to declare on oath the truth of every particular herein set forth; and I desire the favour of an attested copy of the said descriptions. I remain, Sir, your obliged servant, L. de Ferry.

MONSTROUS, MASSIVE WORMS

Malcolm Lees enlisted in the British Royal Air Force in the early 1950s and retired in the late 1960s. In 1962 he received a posting to an RAF station in the county of Wiltshire, England, which he declined to name, and worked in the prestigious and secretive world of intelligence gathering. Most of the work, Lees explained, was routine and even mundane, and he laughed heartily at the idea, spouted by many, that intelligence work was a glamorous one full of James Bond-style escapades. Nevertheless, Lees said, there was one aspect of his career that really was stranger than fiction. Early one September morning in 1962, a call came to the base from someone who had seen a UFO hovering in the vicinity of the ancient standing stones in the historic Wiltshire village of Avebury.

UFO reports reached the base from time to time, said Lees. They were always handled by the RAF's Provost and Security Services. For the most part, they were mind-numbingly mundane and related to little more than sightings of unidentified lights in the sky that could have been anything or nothing. Invariably, he said, the reports were a week old, or even more, by the time they were received. As a result, they were simply filed and passed up the chain of command, which was then at Government Buildings, Acton, and was relocated to Rudloe Manor in 1977. But this particular case was a little different, said Lees.

As she slowly rose to her feet, the creature's head turned suddenly in her direction, and two bulging eyes opened.

The witness was a middle-aged lady who had lived in Avebury all of her adult life and was fascinated by archaeological history. A "spinster" (as the files describe her), she would often stroll among the Stonehenge-like formations at night, marveling at their creation and musing upon their history. On the night in question, she had been out walking at around 10:30 P.M. when she was both startled and amazed to see a small ball of light, perhaps two feet in diameter, gliding slowly through the stones. Transfixed and rooted to the spot, she watched as it closed in on her at a height of about twelve feet. The ball stopped fifteen feet or so from her, and small amounts of what looked like liquid metal slowly and silently dripped from it to the ground. Then, in an instant, the ball exploded in a bright, white flash.

For a moment, she was blinded by its intensity and instinctively fell to her knees. When her eyes cleared, however, she was faced with a horrific sight. The ball of light had gone, but on the ground in front of her was what she could only describe as a monstrous, writhing worm.

The creature, she said, was about five feet long, perhaps eight or nine inches thick, and its skin was milk-white. As she slowly rose to her feet, the creature's head turned suddenly in her direction, and two bulging eyes opened. When it began to move unsteadily toward her in a caterpillar-like fashion, she emitted a hysterical scream and fled the scene. Rushing back home, she slammed the door shut and frantically called the air base, having been directed to them by the less than impressed local police.

The Provost and Security Services department was used to dealing with UFO reports, said Lees, and a friend of his in that department was dispatched early the next day to interview the woman—amid much hilarity on the part of his colleagues, all of whom thought that the story was someone's idea of a joke. On returning, however, Lees's friend and colleague had a grim look on his face and informed him guardedly that whatever had taken place, it was definitely no hoax.

The woman, he said, had practically barricaded herself in her home, was almost incoherent with fear, and only agreed to return to the scene after lengthy coaxing. Lees's colleague said that he found no evidence of the UFO. The worm, or whatever it was, was clearly long gone. On the ground near the standing stone, however, was a three-foot-long trail of a slimelike substance, not unlike that left by a snail. Lees's colleague quickly improvised and, after racing back to the woman's house, scooped some of the material onto a spoon and into a drinking glass.

> On the ground near the standing stone, however, was a three-foot-long trail of a slimelike substance, not unlike that left by a snail.

After assuring the woman that her case would be taken very seriously and requesting that she discuss the events with no one, he headed back to the base, the slimy substance in hand. A report was duly prepared and dispatched, along with the unidentified slime, up the chain of command. For more than a week, said Lees, plainclothes military personnel wandered casually among the stones, seeking out evidence of anything unusual. Nothing else was ever found, however.

Lees said that he was fascinated by this incident because it was one of the few UFO-related cases he heard about that was taken very seriously at an official level and that had some form of material evidence in support of it. He did not know the outcome of the investigation, but he never forgot about it.

The River Wear is a sixty-mile-long body of water that dominates much of northern England. In medieval times, it is said to have been the lair of a marauding, giant, wormlike monster that provoked unrelenting terror across the land, devouring animals and people and causing mayhem wherever it crawled until, at last, its reign of fear was brought to a fatal halt when a brave hero decided the creature had to die. One person who dug deeply into the strange but engaging saga of the Lambton Worm was Joseph Jacobs, a noted Australian folklorist who, in the 1800s, focused much of his research and writings on the matter of strange creatures, fabulous beasts, and marauding monsters reported throughout the British Isles. We turn now to Jacobs and his personal, nineteenth-century account of this legendary monster of the deep:

> A wild young fellow was the heir of Lambton, the fine estate and hall by the side of the swift-flowing Wear. Not a Mass would he hear in Brugeford Chapel of a Sunday, but a-fishing he would go.

And if he did not haul in anything, his curses could be heard by the folk as they went by to Brugeford.

Well, one Sunday morning he was fishing as usual, and not a salmon had risen to him, his basket was bare of roach or dace. And the worse his luck, the worse grew his language, till the passers-by were horrified at his words as they went to listen to the Mass-priest.

At last young Lambton felt a mighty tug at his line. "At last," quoth he, "a bite worth having!" and he pulled and he pulled, till what should appear above the water but a head like an elf's, with nine holes on each side of its mouth. But still he pulled till he had got the thing to land, when it turned out to be a Worm of hideous shape. If he had cursed before, his curses were enough to raise the hair on your head.

"What ails thee, my son?" said a voice by his side, "and what hast thou caught, that thou shouldst stain the Lord's Day with such foul language?"

Looking round, young Lambton saw a strange old man standing by him.

"Why, truly," he said, "I think I have caught the devil himself. Look you and see if you know him."

But the stranger shook his head, and said, "It bodes no good to thee or thine to bring such a monster to shore. Yet cast him not back into the Wear; thou has caught him, and thou must keep him," and with that away he turned, and was seen no more.

The young heir of Lambton took up the gruesome thing, and taking it off his hook, cast it into a well close by, and ever since that day that well has gone by the name of the Worm Well.

For some time nothing more was seen or heard of the Worm, till one day it had outgrown the size of the well, and came forth full-grown. So it came forth from the well and betook itself to the Wear. And all day long it would lie coiled round a rock in the

An illustration from the 1890 book *English Fairy and Other Folk Tales* by C. E. Brock depicts the Lambton Worm.

middle of the stream, while at night it came forth from the river and harried the countryside. It sucked the cows' milk, devoured the lambs, worried the cattle, and frightened all the women and girls in the district, and then it would retire for the rest of the night to the hill, still called the Worm Hill, on the north side of the Wear, about a mile and a half from Lambton Hall.

This terrible visitation brought young Lambton, of Lambton Hall, to his senses. He took upon himself the vows of the Cross, and departed for the Holy Land, in the hope that the scourge he had brought upon his district would disappear. But the grisly Worm took no heed, except that it crossed the river and came right up to Lambton Hall itself where the old lord lived on all alone, his only son having gone to the Holy Land. What to do? The Worm was coming closer and closer to the Hall; women were shrieking, men were gathering weapons, dogs were barking and horses neighing with terror. At last the steward called out to the dairymaids, "Bring all your milk hither," and when they did so, and had brought all the milk that the nine kye of the byre had yielded, he poured it all into the long stone trough in front of the Hall.

The Worm drew nearer and nearer, till at last it came up to the trough. But when it sniffed the milk, it turned aside to the trough and swallowed all the milk up, and then slowly turned round and crossed the River Wear, and coiled its bulk three times round the Worm Hill for the night.

Henceforth the Worm would cross the river every day, and woe betide the Hall if the trough contained the milk of less than nine kye. The Worm would hiss, and would rave, and lash its tail round the trees of the park, and in its fury it would uproot the stoutest oaks and the loftiest firs. So it went on for seven years. Many tried to destroy the Worm, but all had failed, and many a knight had lost his life in fighting with the monster, which slowly crushed the life out of all that came near it.

At last the Childe of Lambton came home to his father's Hall, after seven long years spent in meditation and repentance on holy soil. Sad and desolate he found his folk: the lands untilled, the farms deserted, half the trees of the park uprooted, for none would stay to tend the nine kye that the monster needed for his food each day.

The Childe sought his father, and begged his forgiveness for the curse he had brought on the Hall.

"Thy sin is pardoned," said his father; "but go thou to the Wise Woman of Brugeford, and find if aught can free us from this monster."

To the Wise Woman went the Childe, and asked her advice.

"'Tis thy fault, O Childe, for which we suffer," she said; "be it thine to release us."

"I would give my life," said the Childe.

"Mayhap thou wilt do so," said she. "But hear me, and mark me well. Thou, and thou alone, canst kill the Worm. But, to this end, go thou to the smithy and have thy armour studded with spear-heads. Then go to the Worm's Rock in the Wear, and station thyself there. Then, when the Worm comes to the Rock at dawn of day, try thy prowess on him, and God gi'e thee a good deliverance."

"This I will do," said Childe Lambton.

"But one thing more," said the Wise Woman, going back to her cell. "If thou slay the Worm, swear that thou wilt put to death the first thing that meets thee as thou crossest again the threshold of Lambton Hall. Do this, and all will be well with thee and thine. Fulfil not thy vow, and none of the Lambtons, for generations three times three, shall die in his bed. Swear, and fail not."

The Childe swore as the Wise Woman bid, and went his way to the smithy. There he had his armour studded with spear-heads all over. Then he passed his vigils in Brugeford Chapel, and at dawn of day took his post on the Worm's Rock in the River Wear.

As dawn broke, the Worm uncoiled its snaky twine from around the hill, and came to its rock in the river. When it perceived the Childe waiting for it, it lashed the waters in its fury and wound its coils round the Childe, and then attempted to crush him to death. But the more it pressed, the deeper dug the spear-heads into its sides. Still it pressed and pressed, till all the water around was crimsoned with its blood. Then the Worm unwound itself, and left the Childe free to use his sword. He raised it, brought it down, and cut the Worm in two. One half fell into the river, and was carried swiftly away. Once more the head and the remainder of the body encircled the Childe, but with less force, and the spear-heads did their work. At last the Worm uncoiled itself, snorted its last foam of blood and fire, and rolled dying into the river, and was never seen more.

Our world has no shortage of modern-day monsters, as we have seen time and again in the pages of this book. The world of the past had no shortage, either, as the strange saga of what became known as the Linton Worm makes very clear. A tale that dates back to the 1100s, it tells of a horrific, man-eating, giant, wormlike beast that terrified the good folk of Linton, Roxburghshire, which is located on the Southern Uplands of Scotland. As will soon become apparent, the monster has parallels with a number of Scottish lake monsters, particularly Nessie of Loch Ness and Morag of Loch Morar.

According to the old tales, the Linton Worm was somewhere between ten and twelve feet in length, which, if true, effectively rules out any known British animal, wild or domestic, as being the culprit. Rather oddly, so the old legend went, the huge worm had two homes. In part, it lived in the heart of Linton Loch—a small, boggy area and the ideal place for a monster to hide. Its other dark abode was Linton Hill, which even today is referred to as Worm's Den, such is the enduring nature of the legend. That the beast apparently had the ability to leave the water and slither across the landscape of Scotland brings to mind the small number of reports of both the aforementioned Morag and Nessie being seen on land.

By all accounts, the worm was a creature to be avoided at all costs: cows, sheep, pigs, vegetables, and even people could be food for the monster. Quite naturally, the people of Linton were thrown into a collective state of fear when the slithering thing decided to target their little village. Residents became petrified to leave their homes lest they become the victims of the marauding beast. Doors and windows remained locked. Farmers stayed home; that is, until a man named John de Somerville came upon the scene.

When told of the nature of the monster that had brought terror to Linton, de Somerville—known as the "Laird of Lariston"—had a local blacksmith create for him a razor-sharp spear, which de Somerville intended using to slay the mighty beast. Fortunately, he did exactly that, by setting the spear aflame and plunging it into the throat of the monster, after seeking it out at Worm's Den. The beast fought back, its

A scene from the story "Worme of Linton" from the 1901 collection *Scottish Fairy and Folk Tales*.

wormy form writhing and turning and twisting violently atop the hill, to no avail. Exhausted and on the verge of death, the beast retreated to its labyrinthine lair within Linton Hill. It was neither seen nor heard of again.

The Linton folk never forgot the valiant act of John de Somerville, and a sculpture commemorating de Somerville's brave act was created in Linton Church, as William Henderson noted in his 1879 book *Notes on the Folk-lore of the Northern Counties of England and the Borders*. He said:

> The sculptured effigy of the monster, which may still be seen with the champion who slew it, at the south-western extremity of Linton church, differs from both accounts. A stone, evidently of great antiquity, is there built into the wall. It is covered with sculpture in low relief, and bears figures which, though defaced by time, can yet be made out pretty clearly. A knight on horseback, clad in a tunic or hauberk, with a round helmet, urges his horse against two large animals, the foreparts of which only are visible, and plunges his lance into the throat of one. Behind him is the outline of another creature, apparently of a lamb. The heads of the monsters are strong and powerful, but more like those of quadrupeds than of serpents. It is perplexing also to see two of them, but not the less does popular tradition connect the representation with the Linton Worm.

It tells the strange, seventeenth-century story of a terrible monster that instilled fear in the people of the English town of Horsham....

Today, both church and effigy remain intact, still provoking wonder and perhaps even a little fear in those who visit the little village of Linton.

And then there's this tale. Printed in 1614 by John Trundle of London is a pamphlet with the extraordinarily long title of *True and Wonderful, A DIS-COURSE Relating A STRANGE AND MONSTROUS SERPENT OR DRAG-ON Lately Discovered and yet living to the great Annoyance and divers Slaughters both Men and Cattell, by his strong and violent Poyson. In Sussex, two Miles from Horsam, in a Woode called St. Leonards Forrest, and thirtie Miles from London, this present Month of August, 1614.*

It tells the strange, seventeenth-century story of a terrible monster that instilled fear in the people of the English town of Horsham and reads as follows in quaint, old-English style:

> In Sussex, there is a pretty market-town called Horsham, near unto it a forest, called St. Leonards forest, and there, in a vast and unfrequented place, heathy, vaulty, full of unwholesome shades, and overgrown hollows, where this serpent is thought to be bred; but, wheresoever bred, certain and too true it is that there it yet lives.

Within three or four miles compass are its usual haunts, oftentimes at a place called Faygate, and it hath been seen within half a mile of Horsham, a wonder, no doubt, most terrible and noisome to the inhabitants thereabouts. There is always in his track or path left a glutinous and slimy matter (as by a small similitude we may perceive in a snail's) which is very corrupt and offensive to the scent, insomuch that they perceive the air to be putrified withal, which must needs be very dangerous.

For though the corruption of it cannot strike the outward part of a man, unless heated into his blood, yet by receiving it in at any of our breathing organs (the mouth or nose) it is by authority of all authors, writing in that kind, mortal and deadly, as one thus saith: Noxia serpentum est admixto sanguine pestis.

The serpent, or dragon, as some call it, is reputed to be nine feet, or rather more, in length, and shaped almost in the form of an axletree of a cart, a quantity of thickness in the midst, and somewhat smaller at both ends. The former part, which he shoots forth as a neck, is supposed to be an ell long, with a white ring, as it were, of scales about it.

The scales along his back seem to be blackish, and so much as is discovered under his belly appeareth to be red; for I speak of no nearer description than of a reasonable occular distance.

For coming too near it hath already been too dearly paid for, as you shall hear hereafter. It is likewise discovered to have large feet, but the eye may be there deceived; for some suppose that serpents have no feet, but glide upon certain ribs and scales, which both defend them from the upper part of their throat unto the lower part of their belly, and also cause them to move much the faster.

For so this doth, and rids way, as we call it as fast as a man can run. He is of countenance very proud, and, at the sight or hearing of men or cattle, will raise his neck upright, and seem to listen and look about, with arrogancy. There are likewise on either side of him discovered two great bunches so big as a large football, and, as some think, will in time grow to wings; but God, I hope, will defend the poor people in the neighbourhood, that he shall be destroyed before he grow so fledged.

He will cast his venom about four rod from him, as by woeful experience it was proved on the bodies of a man and woman coming that way, who afterwards were found dead, being poisoned and very much swelled, but not preyed upon.

Likewise a man going to chase it and, as he imagined, to destroy it, with two mastiff dogs, as yet not knowing the great danger of it, his dogs were both killed, and he himself glad to return with haste to preserve his own life. Yet this is to be noted, that the dogs were not preyed upon, but slain and left whole; for his food is thought to be, for the most part, in a cony-warren [rabbit warren], which he much frequents, and it is found much scanted and impaired in the increase it had wont to afford.

These persons, whose names are hereunder printed, have seen this serpent, beside divers others, as the carrier of Horsham, who lieth at the White Horse, in South wark, and who can certify the truth of all that has been here related.

JOHN STEELE.
CHRISTOPHER HOLDER.
And a Widow Woman dwelling near Faygate.

Possibly connected to the matter of mysterious worms seen centuries ago in Great Britain, there is this fascinating story of a real-life dragon found in the pages of Charles Igglesden's 1906 book, *A Saunter through Kent with Pen & Pencil.* Of a dragon reportedly seen centuries earlier in Cranbrook, Kent, in southern England, Igglesden wrote: "The magnificently wooded park of a hundred and fifty acres is richly watered by a huge lake made in 1812 and a smaller one within the grounds, while further west is an old mill pond that rejoices in a curious legend. It is an old one and the subject of it is very ancient indeed and as rare as it is horrible."

He continued that nothing less than a flying dragon was said to haunt the pond but that "on certain—or uncertain—nights of the year it wings its flight over the park and pays a visit to the big lake yonder. But he always returns to the Mill Pond and it is said to pay special attention of a vicious kind to young men and women who have jilted their lovers. A legend with a moral is this. But a winged dragon! A dragon of the ordinary kind is bad enough. But a flying dragon! Augh!"

Igglesden had more to add to the story: "It is a Mr. Tomlin's opinion that there is stronger evidence of the existence of this dragon than of most of his kind and of his fires gone out in the closing years of the last century. Nothing short of this monster's malign influence could account for the curious fact that, till the coming of Mr. Tomlin's eldest daughter, no child had been born at Angley Park for upwards of a hundred years."

> He continued that nothing less than a flying dragon was said to haunt the pond but that "on certain—or uncertain—nights of the year it wings its flight over the park and pays a visit to the big lake yonder."

Over the years, numerous monster seekers have flocked to the area in question in hopes of encountering the dragon. Its presence is far less today, however, than it was in centuries past. Nevertheless, it's worth noting that in December 1997, a local policeman, on duty during the early hours of a chilly, windy Saturday morning, caught a brief sight of a "bloody great bird, about twenty feet across" in the skies of Cranbrook. Was it the ancient dragon crossing the night sky?

Reports of lake monsters abound across the planet. Among the most famous ones are Scotland's Loch Ness Monster, Ogopogo of Lake Okanagan, and Champ of Lake Champlain. The big question is: If the creatures are real, then what, exactly, are they? Monster hunters suggest they may be relic populations of plesiosaurs, marine reptiles that are believed to have become extinct tens of millions of years ago. Other theorists suggest the creatures might be immense eels. Then there is the giant salamander scenario, which might be a viable candidate for those mysterious, giant "worms" reported in those ancient English texts above.

Salamanders are amphibians noted for their long tails, blunt heads, and short limbs, and they can reach lengths of six feet, as in the case of the Chinese giant salamander. Could they grow larger still? Steve Plambeck thinks it is possible. Plambeck, a noted authority on the giant salamander theory as it relates to the Loch Ness Monster, explains:

Salamanders are a type of amphibian; there are 655 species of salamander currently, the largest of which is the Chinese giant salamander (pictured), which can weigh over sixty pounds and reach nearly four feet in length.

Nessie is a bottom dwelling, water breathing animal that spends very little time on the surface or in mid-water, although just enough to be spotted visually or by sonar on very rare occasions. Its forays up from the depths are most likely made along the sides of the Loch, to feed on the fish which are predominantly found along the sides, in shallower water above the underwater cliffs that precipitously drop off into the 750 foot abyss. Such behavior is only consistent with a fish, or aquatic amphibian, which can extract all of its needed oxygen directly from the water.

Yet as seldom as it happens, and for reasons known only to the animal itself, Nessie also *leaves the water* for apparently brief stretches, as observed most famously in the Spicer and Grant sightings of 1933 and 1934 respectively. It may be said that this is nothing new: it's a centuries old tradition among the Highlanders that the *kelpie* or water horse of Loch Ness comes ashore. That's a key behavioral trait to take into account if we are distinguishing fish from amphibians.

In that sense, Plambeck makes a persuasive argument when it comes to the matter of the creatures of Loch Ness possibly being huge salamanders or, at the very least, another kind of large, unknown amphibian. It's a theory also noted by a researcher identified as "Erika." She says of such a scenario:

> This might seem ridiculous at first, but in China there is a species of giant salamander that can grow up to six feet long. Certainly this is an animal which is long enough, and odd enough, that if it surfaced in a lake, onlookers could be forgiven for mistaking it for a monster.

> There are other similarities which make this a plausible theory. The Chinese giant salamander lives in very cold fresh water, which describes Loch Ness handily. They are found in the rocky streams and mountain lakes of remote northern China, where they are as elusive as they are endangered.

> Best of all (for this purpose), the Chinese giant salamander is a very sluggish animal. It rarely surfaces, and spends most of its time lying at the bottom, waiting for prey to swim past. It strikes quickly and then retreats. This is not an active animal, and it's entirely possible they could live in a lake as big as Loch Ness without ever being seen at the surface.

Loch Ness Monster authority Roland Watson has also waded into this controversy, saying: "Before long neck stories began to dominate peoples' thinking, some held to the view that Nessie was some form of outsized amphibian and in particular the salamander. I am a bit partial to a fish-like

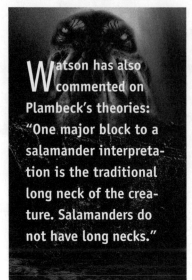

Watson has also commented on Plambeck's theories: "One major block to a salamander interpretation is the traditional long neck of the creature. Salamanders do not have long necks."

amphibian or amphibian-like fish theory myself, so we are in agreement to some degree there. An amphibian has its issues just like any other Nessie theory but I am sure it can hold its own in the Nessie pantheon."

Watson has also commented on Plambeck's theories: "One major block to a salamander interpretation is the traditional long neck of the creature. Salamanders do not have long necks. Steve however suggests that the long tail of the salamander can account for this apparent problem. I can see merit in that idea and have no problem believing that a long tail can be mistaken for a long neck by eyewitnesses."

Seekers of unknown animals might be disappointed by the possibility that some of our most famous lake monsters are merely salamanders and nothing else. But, when actually confronted, at close quarters, by such a creature—one of twenty to twenty-five feet in length—few would probably quibble with the notion that such a thing should be classed as a monster.

SNAKES AND EELS

Snakes and eels are not what one might call literal monsters, but they play an integral part of this overall story, particularly when they grow to incredible sizes and decide to go on rampages. Although eels spend all their lives in the water, when necessary, they can and will briefly move onto land in a fashion not unlike the movements of a snake. Also, on the matter of snakes, it should be noted that they are extremely skillful swimmers. Imagine coming face-to-face with a fifty-foot-long snake or a thirty-foot-long eel in deep and dark waters. Such encounters have been reported for centuries. They have even caught the attention of the CIA, as you will now see!

GIANT SNAKES

It's a fact that all snakes can swim, which has almost certainly led to some lake monsters being mistaken for huge snakes and vice versa. Nonetheless, on many occasions, the witnesses were absolutely sure about what they had encountered: gigantic snakes. Let's take a look at some of the most astonishing cases on record.

In 1868, a Frenchman named Raud made a truly extraordinary statement regarding a monstrous, near-dragon-like snake seen in the California countryside earlier in the year, which he estimated to have a length of around forty feet. Despite the dubious nature of the story, it was supported by his friend and colleague F. C. Buylick, who had been cutting wood and burning charcoal with Raud when the immense creature loomed into view. Raud, who had broken off from the woodcutting to pursue nothing more threatening than a hare, said the following of the beast, which appeared to dwell deep in the woods, swamps, and fields of the area:

I had proceeded twenty-five yards, perhaps, when I emerged into an open space not to exceed thirty feet in diameter. As I entered it the hare dragged itself into the brush on the opposite side, and I quickened my steps in pursuit. Almost at the same instant I was startled by a loud, shrill, prolonged hiss, a sound that closely resembled the escape of steam from the cylinder of a locomotive when starting a heavy train. I stopped as suddenly as if my progress had been arrested by a rifle bullet, and looking toward the upper end of the plat my eyes encountered an object the recollection of which even now makes me shiver with horror.

Coiled up not more than twenty feet from where I stood was an immense serpent—the most hideously frightful monster that ever confronted mortal man. It was a moment before my dazed senses could comprehend the dreadful peril that threatened me. As the truth of my terrible situation dawned upon me, my first impulse was to fly; but not a limb or muscle moved in obedience to the effort of my will. I was as incapable of motion as if I had been hewn in marble: I essayed to cry for help but the effort at articulation died away in a gurgling sound upon my lips.

The serpent lay in three great coils, its head, and some ten feet of its body projecting above, swaying to and fro in undulatory [sic] sinuous, wavy convulsions, like the tentacles of an octopus in the swift current of an ebbing tide. The monster stared at me with its great, hateful, lidless eyes, ever and anon darting its head menacingly in my direction, thrusting out its forked tongue, and emitting hisses so vehemently that I felt its baleful breath upon my cheek. Arching its neck the serpent would dilate its immense jaws until its head would measure at least eighteen inches across, then dart toward me, distending its mouth and exhibiting its great hooked fangs that looked like the talons of a vulture.

Not many people realize that snakes like this Burmese python are not just terrestrial; they are also accomplished swimmers.

As I stood in momentary expectation of feeling the tusks and being crushed in the constricting fold of the scaly monster, my situation was appalling beyond description—beyond the conception of the most vivid imagination. The blood ran down my back cold as Greenland ice and congealed in my veins. Every pulse in my body seemed to stand still and my heart ceased to beat. Even respiration was slow and painful. There was a choking, suffocating sensation in my throat, and my lips became dry and parched. There was a ringing in my ears, dark spots floated before my eyes, and I should have fainted but for the horrifying reflection that if I gave way to such weakness my doom was inevitable. A cold clammy perspiration oozed from every pore, and so intense was my agony of fear that I suffered the tortures of the damned augmented a thousandfold. While all my physical capacities were prostrated and paralyzed, every mental faculty seemed preternaturally sharpened. It appeared as if the terrible tension of my nerve and bodily incapacity immeasurably increased my range of vision, and rendered my perceptive faculties critically acute.

Not the slightest movement of the serpent escaped me, and every detail of its appearance—size, color, shape and position—is, alas! only too strongly photographed upon my recollection. As I stated before, the serpent lay in three immense coils, the triple thicknesses of its body standing as high as my shoulders. The monster was fully twenty inches in diameter in the largest place. Its head was comparatively large. Its tremendous jaws that at times dilated to twice their natural size, having enormous hooked fangs that fitted in between each other when the mouth was shut. The neck was slender and tapering. The belly of the serpent was a dirty whitish color, deeply furrowed with transverse corrugations. With the exception of about ten feet of the neck and contiguous parts which were nearly black, the body of the snake was brown, beautifully mottled with orange-colored spots on the back. How long I confronted this terrible shape I do not know. Probably only a few moments; but to me it seemed ages.

At length the serpent began slowly to uncoil, but whether for the purpose of attacking me or retreating I could not fathom. You can have but a faint conception of my relief and joy when I discovered that it was the latter. Lowering its crest and giving vent to a venomous hiss, the monster went slowly crashing through the chaparral, its head being plainly visible above the jungle. For a moment I could scarcely realize that I was no longer threatened by a death too horrible to contemplate.

There was a tingling sensation through my body from the top of my head to the soles of my feet as the blood again commenced circulating in my veins. I attempted to step forward, but so benumbed were my limbs that I fell heavily to the earth. Recovering, I staggered through the chaparral into the open country. As I emerged from the thicket I saw my partner a short distance up the ridge and motioned him to approach. When he did so he was greatly alarmed at my haggard appearance, and excitedly inquired the cause. In reply I pointed to the serpent, then some 100 yards distant—a sight that threw him into the utmost consternation. We watched the monster until it disappeared from view in the rocky recesses of a cliff that overhangs the river. We were enabled to measure the length of the serpent very exactly by its passing parallel with two trees, its head being even with one while its tail reached the other. Mr. Buylick has since ascertained that the trees are forty feet apart.

The Hagenbecks were a family of collectors of all manner of animals that supplied the world's zoos with a wide variety of exotic animals for more than a century. It's hardly surprising, therefore, that they came across a number of extraordinary tales—and extraordinary animals. Indeed, one of the Hagenbecks' explorers was the very first person to encounter a pigmy hippopotamus, which occurred on February 28, 1913. Another explorer, Lorenz Hagenbeck, had a particular interest in snakes. He was especially fascinated by supersized snakes, to the point where he made it his business to collect as many credible reports as possible. A fascinating story came to Hagenbeck from a pair of Roman Catholic priests, Father Victor Heinz and Father Protesius Frickel. Father Heinz's story was particularly notable, since it revolved around the sighting of a truly colossal monster. Heinz prepared the following statement telling the entire shocking story:

During the great floods of 1922 on May 22—at about three o'clock to be exact—I was being taken home by canoe on the Amazon from Obidos; suddenly I noticed something surprising in midstream. I distinctly recognized a giant water snake at a distance of some thirty yards. To distinguish it from the *sucurijiu*, the natives who accompanied me named the reptile, because of its enormous size, *sucurijiu gigante* (giant boa).

Coiled up in two rings the monster drifted quietly and gently downstream. My quaking crew had stopped paddling. Thunderstruck, we all stared at the frightful beast. I reckoned that its body was as thick as an oil drum and that its visible length was some eighty feet. When we were far enough away and my boatmen dared to speak again they said the monster would have

Hagenbeck Zoo in Hamburg, Germany, was founded by Carl Hagenbeck in 1907 and was the first zoo to create cage-free enclosures to allow wildlife to live in simulated natural settings that were more humane.

crushed us like a box of matches if it had not previously consumed several large capybaras.

Such was the extraordinary nature of the encounter that Father Heinz determined to find all he could on the immense beast and its ilk. He learned that yet another huge boa had been shot and killed, one day previously, as it tried to devour a capybara—the world's largest rodent, which can reach the size of a dog. It wasn't long before Father Heinz had a second sighting of a massive snake:

> My second encounter with a giant water snake took place on 29 October 1929. To escape the great heat I had decided to go down river at about 7:00 P.M. in the direction of Alemquer. At about midnight, we found ourselves above the mouth of the Piaba when my crew, seized with a sudden fear, began to row hard towards the shore. "What is it?" I cried, sitting up. "There is a big animal," they muttered very excited. At the same moment I

heard the water move, as if a steamboat had passed. I immediately noticed several meters above the surface of the water two bluish-green lights like the navigation lights on the bridge of a riverboat, and shouted: "No, look, it's the steamer! Row to the side so that it doesn't upset us."

It was no steamer:

Petrified, we all watched the monster approach; it avoided us and re-crossed the river in less than a minute—a crossing that would have taken us ten to fifteen minutes as long. On the safety of dry land we took courage and shouted to attract the attention of the snake. At this very moment a human figure began to wave an oil-lamp on the other shore, thinking, no doubt, that someone was in danger. Almost at once the snake rose on the surface and we were able to appreciate clearly the difference between the light of the lamp and the phosphorescent light of the monster's eyes. Later, in my return, the inhabitants of this place assured me that above the mouth of the Piaba there dwelt a *sucuriju gigante*.

We also have the following account of Reymondo Zima, a Portuguese merchant, whom Father Heinz had the good fortune to interview. Zima told the priest:

On 6th July 1930 I was going up the Jamunda in company with my wife and the boy who looks after my motor-boat. Night was falling when we saw a light on the riverbank. In the belief it was the house I was looking for I steered towards the light and switched on my searchlight. But then we noticed that the light was charging towards us at an incredible speed. A huge wave lifted the bow of the boat and almost made it capsize. My wife screamed in terror. At the same moment we made out the shape of a giant snake rising out of the water and performing a St. Vitus's dance around the boat, after which the monster crossed this tributary of the Amazon about half a kilometer wide at fabulous speed, leaving a huge wake, larger than any of the steamboats make at full speed. The waves hit our 13-meter boat with such force that at every moment we were in danger of capsizing. I opened my motor flat out and made for dry land. Owing to the understandable excitement at the time it was not possible for me to reckon the monster's length. I presume that as a result of a wound the animal lost one eye, since I saw only one light. I think the giant snake must have mistaken our searchlight for the eye of one of his fellow snakes.

In the summer of 1868, a story came out of Spring Valley, California, of a sixty-foot-long, deadly snake roaming the area. The story was told in the pages of the *Calaveras Chronicle* newspaper, where a writer said:

> On the 12th of August, 1868, the serpent was first seen in the vicinity of Zane's ranch, near Spring valley. Several persons—reputable people—saw the monster on two or three occasions, but always at a considerable distance—never nearer than a quarter of a mile. The reptile created the most intense excitement in the neighborhood, and at one time the getting up of a party to hunt it down was strongly agitated.
>
> What were then thought to be the most extravagant stories regarding the size of the serpent were told, but recent events prove that the truth was not exaggerated. The snake was seen in an open field in broad daylight, and described as "being from forty to sixty feet long, and as large around as a barrel." The mark of the monster in the dust where it crossed the road bore witness to its immense proportions. There was a difference of opinion regarding its method of locomotion, some maintaining that it progressed by drawing itself into immense folds, after the manner of a caterpillar, while others were equally certain that its motion was similar to others of the ophidian family.
>
> The serpent disappeared for several months, and was seen by Mr. W. P. Peek, of this place, while coming up the hill from the Gwin mine. Mr. Peek was driving a two horse team and had got about half way up the steep hill that has to be ascended in leaving the mine, when he heard what he supposed to be the loud "screeching" noise sometimes made by a wagon brake. Certain that a team was coming down the grade, and being in a favorable place for passing, he turned out of the road.
>
> After waiting until out of patience, and no team appearing, he drove on. He had gone but a short distance when a movement in the dense chaparral that lined the road attracted his attention, and, advancing in the direction, he was horrified by the sight of a portion of the body of an immense serpent. At the same time his horse became unmanageable, and while Mr. Peek's utmost endeavors were put forth to prevent the escape of the frightened team, the monarch moved slowly off into the brush, making the hissing sound he had mistaken for the brake of an approaching wagon.
>
> About a year subsequently the serpent was seen by a couple of boys in the vicinity of Mosquito, the youths being so badly frightened that they could scarcely reach home and tell the story.

Giant snakes have been reported all over the world; the reports reached their height in the nineteenth century.

Such is briefly the story of the Calaveras serpent up to Saturday of last week, when the experiences had with it at once settled all doubts as to its reality, and fix the fact beyond question that one of the largest boas of which we have knowledge has its residence in this county.

Since 2017 I have been working on a project that, in part, is focused on worldwide reports of giant snakes. There is very little doubt that the nineteenth century was the period in which sightings of these massive beasts in the United States were at their height in terms of media interest. In fact, a similar situation existed in that same time frame as close encounters with so-called "wild men" abounded. Of course, today those "wild men" are perceived by cryptozoologists and monster hunters as having been Bigfoot creatures by another name. Maybe they were. It should be stressed that some of the reports of giant snakes in the United States were exaggerated. Others proved to be nothing but outright hoaxes, created to entertain readers and boost sales of the relevant newspapers. Trying to determine the category into which the following case should be placed is no easy task. In my view, it falls into that hazy and controversial realm where fact, fiction, gonzo journalism, and exaggeration combine into one amazing tale.

"King of Reptiles: Julius Hamer Meets a Mad Snake of Gigantic Proportions" is the title of the admittedly eye-catching story that appeared in the pages of the *Evening Times* of Monroe, Wisconsin, on August 11, 1894. The story began:

> Julius Hamer is a young man of Plymouth, Ill., who despises rats and mice and especially minks, as the latter have been killing his young chickens very rapidly. Accordingly Julius secured a trap and set it in his barn. He thought to catch the mink or other animal that had been robbing his coops, so baited the trap with a small mouse. Last night Julius was awakened by the snorts and stamping of his horse in the barn, where he had set a trap. He rushed out to be met by the horse, who had broken from his stall halter. The animal was whinnying and quaking with fear and he was made aware of a sickening odor rising from the atmosphere.

That's where things got controversial—*extremely* controversial. The unknown journalist with a flair for all things atmospheric and exciting continued on in fine fashion, complete with the requisite eerie moon: "Rising into the barn his eyes met a sight, by moonlight, which he hopes he will never see again. A monster snake, fifty feet in length, he declares, had been caught in the trap through the neck and the horrid reptile was thrashing around in the barn in a frightful manner."

We can state with a fair degree of certainty that Julius—caught in the heart of the action—exaggerated matters to a significant degree.

Well, that's quite a story. However, the idea that a fifty-foot-long snake was roaming around the United States a little more than 120 years ago stretches credibility to the absolute limit. Not even the mighty Titanoboa reached such a monstrous length! We can state with a fair degree of certainty that Julius—caught in the heart of the action—exaggerated matters to a significant degree. One is reminded of fishermen who talk of failing to catch "the one that got away"—the "one" being a fish of unlikely and gigantic proportions.

Back to the story: "The air was filled with hisses, while the peculiar fetid odor arising from a huge boa when angered permeated the air. The snake became so desperate that it lashed the stalls into kindling wood and broke out several boards in the side of the barn. Julius gave a terrible yell, which aroused some of the neighbors, but the snake had torn the trap loose from its moorings by this time and started for the creek, which is several miles distant. The men were too frightened to follow the animal far, but they saw the huge reptile cutting a wide swath through the corn as it hurried away." Interestingly, there was talk of the giant snake also being the "Thompson's Lake sea serpent" that had then recently been seen near Lewistown, Illinois.

I share this story with you to demonstrate that, by all means, we must dig into the world of the past when it comes to tales of strange and huge beasts, including giant snakes. But we must also be very careful when it comes to the matter of credibility. In the same way that much of today's right-wing media promote what are clearly "untruths" (as lies are called today), so did certain factions of the press back in the 1800s.

GIANT EELS ON THE RAMPAGE

One of the most interesting theories for sightings of lake monsters is that some of them might actually be giant-sized eels. On a September day in 2009, England-based monster seeker Jonathan Downes, his wife, Corinna, and their colleague at the Centre for Fortean Zoology, Max Blake, headed out to Ireland's Lough Leane, a small but engaging body of water. It was late afternoon on September 17, 2009, and Tony "Doc" Shiels, both a creature hunter and an Irish wizard, had invited the trio to spend some time with him. It was fortuitous, indeed, that Downes accepted the invitation. Notably, Shiels said that the trio should keep their eyes focused on one particular stretch of water. As Corinna Downes notes, something very strange appeared before them: "I saw a trail left by something as it made its way from the island to the shore to the east of it.... If I was to be pressed for an answer I would probably suggest a large eel."

Max Blake recorded his thoughts on the encounter, too: "If I had to make a guess, I would say that it was most likely to have been a giant eel."

The experience was not a solitary one.

Taking into account the location of the affair, it may well be the case that the following story, which also originates in Ireland, can be explained by the presence of a massive eel. In 2015, I was fortunate to acquire a wealth of original notes and files belonging to the late monster hunter F. W. "Ted" Holiday, who spent a great deal of time in the 1960s and 1970s investigating the Loch Ness Monster. Among those notes was a summary report of an interview that Holiday had conducted with one Stephen Coyne in July 1968. This one was not at Loch Ness, Scotland, however; it was at Lough Nahooin, Ireland. Holiday's notes report the following:

> At about seven on the evening of 22 February 1968, Stephen Coyne went down to the bog by the lough to bring up some dry peat. With him he took his eldest son, a boy of eight, and the family dog. Although the sun had set it was still quite light. On reaching the peat-bed beside Nahooin he suddenly noticed a black object in the water. Thinking it was the dog he whistled to

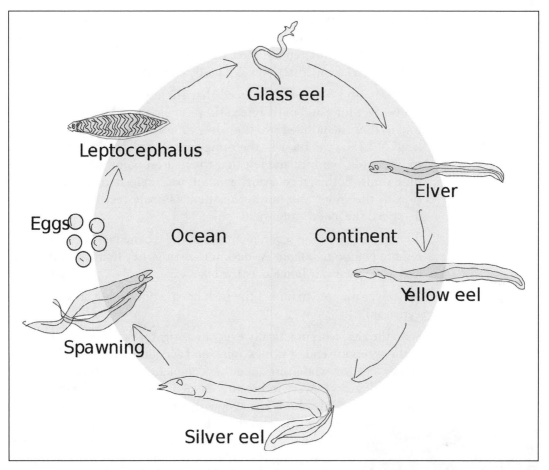

There are about eight hundred species of fresh- and saltwater eels on Earth. A fascinating order of animal, their life cycle is complex, too, as illustrated above. They start as a larval leptocephalus, then become transparent glass eels, elvers, juveniles, and finally adults.

it; however, the dog came bounding along the shore from behind. On seeing the object it stopped and started barking.

He then saw that the object was an animal with a pole-like head and neck about nine inches to a foot in diameter. It was swimming around in various directions. From time to time it put its head underwater; two humps then came into view. Occasionally, a flat tail appeared. Once this came out near the head, which argued length and a high degree of flexibility. The thing was black, slick, and hairless with a texture resembling an eel.

The dog's barking seemed to irritate the monster and it began to move in-shore, its mouth open. However, when Coyne strode over to support his dog, it turned away and resumed swimming around this little lough. At about this point the little boy ran home to bring his mother to see the strange beast. When Mrs. Coyne and the children returned, the Peiste [which is Irish terminology for a lake monster] was still busily patrolling the tiny lake.

Both Mr. and Mrs. Coyne agreed that the creature was about twelve feet long and both agreed they saw no eyes. Mrs. Coyne told us that she noticed two horn-like projections on top of the head. Whereas she thought the thing approached as near as four to five yards, her husband felt that the nearest point was about nine yards. Both agreed that the mouth was underslung in relation to the snout and neither of them saw any teeth. Coyne described the mouth-interior as "pale."

To and fro before the seven members of the Coyne family strutted the Nahooin dragon. As dusk was setting they finally left it and made their way home over the bog.

Whatever the true nature of the Irish beastie of Lough Nahooin, it was never seen again.

As is the case with practically every investigator of the unknown, I am often on the receiving end of stories, tales, and accounts that sound great but are related by a person who insists on either complete or partial anonymity. Of course, such tales can be very interesting indeed, but they can be extremely frustrating, too. Primarily, this is because, without hard evidence that the person really is who they claim to be, very little can be done with the story in terms of investigating or validating it aside from keeping it on file and hoping that by making it public—as I'm doing now—it may encourage others to come forward. The strange story that follows is a classic example.

Needless to say, if the physical details described in the first encounter were not exaggerations on the part of the witness, then it was without a shadow of a doubt a definitive monster.

It comes from a man who claims to be a retired British police constable with personal knowledge of a story of truly monstrous proportions. It focuses on dark goings-on after sunset in the British city of Birmingham in the late 1970s and early 1980s. For what it's worth, here is the tale.

According to the man, who identified himself only by the surname of Sykes, while serving in the British Police Force (service that, he said, began in 1977 and ended in 1988), he heard two tales from colleagues of giant eels seen in the winding canals that run through Birmingham—both of which occurred, he thought, around 1979 or 1980. In both cases, the witnesses had reported seeing very large creatures—the first, amazingly, around twenty feet in length, and both were "very dark" in color. Needless to say, if the physical details described in the first encounter were not exaggerations on the part of the witness, then it was without a shadow of a doubt a definitive monster.

Notably, Sykes said that although he was not the investigating officer in either case, he recalled that around the same time the eels were seen, there had been a spate of mysterious disappearances of pet rabbits in the area. And while some of Sykes's colleagues had attributed this to the work of sadists and nutcases, there had been brief talk at the station that "it was the eels' doing."

There was one other, and very ominous, story that Sykes recalled and related to me as I listened intently. At the height of the rabbit disappearances and the two eel encounters, someone had contacted the police station where Sykes was working to relate a remarkable tale. "It was a local lad, in his twenties; I remember that much," said Sykes. "He hadn't been long married and had just bought a house around here." The storyteller claimed to have heard a huge commotion in his small backyard in the early hours of one particular morning and then quickly phoned the police about it.

The wooden fence at the foot of the yard had been partially smashed down; a large area of grass had been flattened; and something had broken into his rabbit hutch, utterly destroying it in the process. Needless to say, by the time the man got downstairs and into the yard, there was no sign of the unknown intruder. Unfortunately, there was no sign of the rabbits, either.

Continuing his tale, Sykes wondered out loud if the eels, hungry for food, had elected to stealthily leave the confines of the canal and had, under the protective cover of overwhelming darkness, slithered around the yards of the nearby homes in search of a tasty rabbit or several. Well, it was as good a theory as any, I thought. And it was pretty disturbing, too, to think that such beasts might secretly be on the loose in a sprawling, industrialized city like Birmingham, mercilessly prowling the area by night.

As far as Sykes knew, this particularly weird and unsettling incident was never resolved. No more sightings surfaced, and a rigorous search of the canal failed to find anything conclusive at all. And that, in essence, was the tale. Without doubt, it's one that is fascinating, outrageous, and bizarre in equal measures. Taking into consideration the amount of time that has gone by since the events allegedly occurred, it is unfortunately difficult to prove anything with any high degree of certainty; that is, unless anyone reading this knows more.

Lake Granbury, southwest of Fort Worth, Texas, was created in 1969 with the

Some types of eel, such as this European eel, can crawl on land and survive there for short periods. It would be possible, then for them to feed on terrestrial animals.

Texas' Brazos River is 1,280 miles (2,060 kilometers) long, making it the eleventh longest river in the United States. It is home to a diverse population of fish and other wildlife.

construction of the De Cordova Bend Dam on the Brazos River, which is the lake's primary inflow. At more than 1,200 miles long, the Brazos River is the eleventh-longest river in the United States. And Lake Granbury is hardly small, either: it has a surface area of 8,310 acres. The approximately seventy-five-foot-deep lake is home to many and varied kinds of fish, including catfish, bass, gar, and sunfish. It's a popular spot for a bit of fun, too: water-skiing, boating, and fishing are all popular on weekends and holidays. And then, there is the matter of its hideous, terrifying inhabitant. The resident monster goes by the name of One Eye and is described as a classic lake monster: dark gray in color, with a long neck and a humplike back. Irish creature seeker Ronan Coghlan says: "Whether it has attained a one-eyed state by accident or whether it is naturally one-eyed, I cannot say."

Although the lake is less than half a century old, the Brazos River has a long history of sightings of huge fish and mysterious creatures. Native Americans and early Spaniards talked of something terrible and savage lurking in the river. In 2010, a huge gar was hauled out of its waters.

Accounts such as these have given rise to the theory that the association between lake, dam, and river has somehow allowed monsters to find their way into Lake Granbury. Maybe there is some truth to this theory—maybe even a lot of truth. Let us look at a close encounter of the beastly variety that happened on a Saturday afternoon in August 1999. According to the witness, Becky, she was standing on a stretch of shoreline—which, I was later able to determine, was not far from a row of houses—hanging out with her then-boyfriend, now her husband.

Suddenly, out of nowhere and at a distance of about forty feet, a large animal lurched out of the water and, for about ten or fifteen seconds, partially beached itself on the land. It thrashed around violently, finally managing to return to the waters and vanishing into the depths. The utterly shocked couple estimated the animal was around seventeen to twenty feet in length, with a body thickness of close to two feet.

Interestingly, the woman did not describe the creature as resembling a long-extinct plesiosaur, as so many other witnesses have in times past and present. Rather, she had no doubt whatsoever that it was a gigantic eel. As both she and her boyfriend fished regularly, they knew an eel when they saw it. But they had never seen one of this size!

Certainly, the world of conventional zoology will assure you that eels simply do not—and cannot—reach such immense sizes. But that doesn't mean they don't exist. Are the legends of One Eye based on sightings of giant eels? If so, how could the creatures get so monstrously huge? The theories are intriguing, and the sightings are multiple.

One of the most interesting accounts came from one John Weatherley. On April 5, 2007, he contacted me after hearing me interviewed on the popular *Coast to Coast* AM radio show. Weatherley said:

> Greetings. I enjoyed your interview on Coast to Coast AM this morning. I was particularly interest in your theory regarding giant eels in northern lakes, e.g., Loch Ness. Perhaps you could help me identify the creatures that I and many hundreds saw a few years ago?
>
> I am British and live in Florida. My family and I came to Florida by sea from Australia in 1969. [After reaching South America] our ship left Acuapulco and sailed along the west coast towards the Panama Canal. It was the first week of July 1969. The sea was calm, and we were cruising quite slowly because of congestion in the canal.
>
> As we cruised along the west coast of Costa Rica and Panama, we were about seven or eight miles from shore and just a few yards from the flotsam line. It was a clearly defined line of seaweed about 30 feet wide with odd bits of wood and the occasional small tree limb. We cruised along this path for several hours in bright sunshine between about 10 A.M. and 2 P.M. There were many fish visible and some very large turtles, but the significant sighting were huge eels. These creatures were always in pairs, and we saw a pair perhaps every 20 minutes or so.
>
> They averaged about 15 feet long and had a diameter of about 1.5 feet. They were khaki or olive in color and were identical to the eels for which I used to fish as a boy in my hometown of Canterbury, Kent, except they were so large. They were lazily swimming very slowly along through the flotsam or just wallowing at the very surface. The ship was carrying about 1,200 passengers, and most were on deck on this idyllic day, so the eels were seen by many people. Most were engaged in counting the enormous numbers of sharks which were clearly visible around the ship. I wonder if you have any idea what species of eel these were? They could easily have swallowed a child or a small adult.
>
> Regards, John Weatherley

While I was unable to identify the specific eels that Weatherley saw, there is no doubt in my mind that Weatherley saw a unique group of very large eels.

BOLIVIAN SNAKE AND THE CIA

While there are numerous reports of people encountering massive snakes in the jungles, seas, and rivers of the world, one of the strangest cases on record involves none other than the Central Intelligence Agency. The story is an intrigue-filled one, part James Bond and part Indiana Jones. It all began—and violently ended—in 1956.

CIA personnel based at the American Embassy in Bolivia were used to dealing with unpredictable and strange events. But even by their standards, the events that went down in August 1956 were off the scale. In the early days of the month, CIA staff received reports of a gigantic snake on the loose in a nearby, rarely explored cave that was buried deep within the mountainous jungle environment. And when I say gigantic, I mean somewhere between thirty and fifty feet long.

Worse still, a spate of mysterious disappearances of people from a nearby tribe had just about everyone on edge. The tribespeople were sure that the culprit was the deadly beast, and there were even rumors that the monster possessed supernatural powers. Something had to be done, and a call was put into the CIA by local Bolivian authorities, asking for help. While hunting for a giant snake was hardly the kind of thing that CIA agents typically got involved in, they agreed to give it a go.

A six-person team was put together by a man we know only as Lee, who led the group deep into the jungle. They were prepared to take on the man-eater; but, as circumstances would demonstrate, it turned out to be a very close call. The supersized snake was not about to go down without a fight. As Lee's team climbed the heavily

Reports of a gigantic snake were received by the U.S. embassy in La Paz, Bolivia, in 1956.

wooded hill and arrived at the small entrance to the cave where the snake made its lair, one and all stayed as silent as possible and began to prepare for a potentially deadly confrontation with the massive beast.

Every man had several tear gas canisters, and they were all equipped with handguns. They had something else with them, too: a large, canvas sack with zippers at both ends that had been created by CIA employees and that, it was hoped, the snake could be enticed into and then shot and killed before it could do any harm. It sounded frankly like a most implausible situation and something guaranteed to fail.

Nevertheless, the men strategically positioned themselves at various points around twenty feet from the cave entrance. It was then up to Lee to creep up to the shadowy opening. His first action was to encase the entrance with that large sack and, through a small space, hurl one of the canisters into the heart of the cave. He did so and then quickly retreated. It was a very wise move.

Within less than a minute, as the tear gas did its thing, the huge snake came charging out of the cave. The rumors of such a monster living in the cave were suddenly, and chaotically, rumors no more. Even the agents waiting for the beast were shocked by the sight of the coiling thing before them: it was around forty feet in length and had a body thicker than an oil drum. As for its fang-filled head, it was around the size of a horse's head. To their utter consternation, in seconds it tore its way out of the sack, ripping it to shreds in the process. And then it began to move slowly forward. One and all backed away another thirty or forty feet as the huge creature stared malevolently at them—no doubt trying to decide which one to attack and devour first. Lee quickly realized it was a case of now or never, and he fired a salvo of bullets into the snake's head. By all accounts, it took more than several bullets to bring the violent beast down.

One and all backed away another thirty or forty feet as the huge creature stared malevolently at them—no doubt trying to decide which one to attack and devour first.

Of course, it must be said that this entire story has a somewhat unlikely feeling to it—a sense of urban myth or friend-of-a-friend tale. There is, however, good evidence to suggest that the event occurred exactly as described above. This brings us to a man named David Atlee Phillips. A significant figure in the CIA in the 1950s, he spent a great deal of time in Mexico, Cuba, and Chile. Phillips crossed paths with Lee at a cocktail party in La Paz, Bolivia, in 1958. As the pair swapped espionage stories, the matter of the giant snake surfaced. Phillips admitted to Lee that he was dubious of the whole story. Nonplussed, Lee agreed to show him the snake's skin, which Lee had preserved in the embassy's basement! Even when he was finally able to see the evidence, however, Phillips still doubted the story behind how the huge skin was obtained. He suspected Lee had gotten it from a collector and had created the story of a violent confrontation with the monster to impress a girlfriend or two. It turns out that was not the case.

Phillips apparently developed quite an obsession with the snake saga and brought it up, some months later, with one Darwin Mervill Bell, a man who had ties to both the CIA and the Agency for International Aid in Bolivia. Over drinks, Phillips tackled Bell on the matter of the snake legend, since Lee was a friend to both Phillips and Bell. Phillips said, as he discussed the story of how the snake was killed: "To this day, Lee claims they made a canvas sack with zippers at both ends. Now, did you ever hear anything about that?"

For a few moments, Bell was silent, seemingly musing on Phillips's question. Then he answered: "Mr. Phillips, I certainly have heard about that. I was the tail zipper man."

Finally, Phillips was convinced.

As for what the snake actually was, there's a distinct possibility it may have been a surviving relic of a massive snake that lived tens of millions of years ago in what is now Colombia. Its name was *Titanoboa*, and it has a lineage that connects it to both the boa constrictor and the anaconda of today. It could grow to massive lengths. Indeed, William DeLong, writing on the website *All That's Interesting*, says: "Titanoboa, the enormous serpent of legend, thrived in the tropical jungles of South America some five million years after the extinction of the dinosaurs. The death of the giant reptiles left a vacuum at the top of the food chain, and Titanoboa gladly stepped up. This prehistoric species grew up to 50 feet in length and weighed as much as 2,500 pounds. That's as long as a semitrailer you see on highways and about twice as heavy as a polar bear. At its thickest point, Titanoboa was three feet wide, which is longer than a human arm."

It was certainly not a monster one would want to cross paths with. Did secret agents of the CIA, back in the 1950s, take out of circulation the very last of the *Titanoboas*? Possibly, yes.

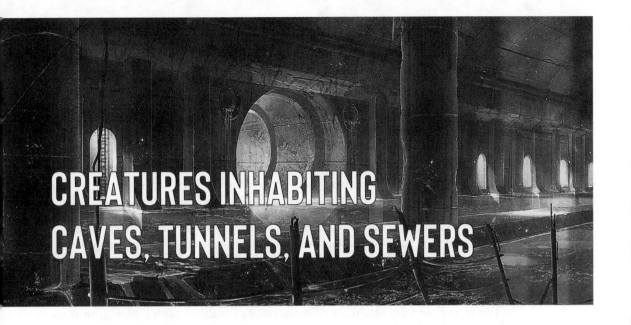

CREATURES INHABITING CAVES, TUNNELS, AND SEWERS

The majority of monsters that appear in the pages of this book spend all of their time deep in the oceans and lakes of Earth. There are, however, other animals that lurk and live far below the surface of the planet in caves, tunnels, and even sewers. In that sense, they are creatures of realms far below us but of a slightly alternative fashion. They include alligators under the sewers and a wealth of strange creatures that roam the London Underground rail system.

ALLIGATORS IN THE SEWERS

Perhaps the most terrifying of all monsters are those that we know exist. And when they are right under our feet—literally—they become even more fear-inducing. Take, for example, the alligators of New York. We're talking about those immense, bone-crunching beasts that lurk deep within the myriad, winding sewers and subways beneath the Big Apple. Most people assume that the stories of New York's people-eating alligators are nothing more than the stuff of myth and urban legend. This could not be further from the truth.

Proof that alligators have been on the loose in the city for decades was provided way back in February 1935 by none other than the *New York Times*. The story was spelled out in an article titled "Alligator Found in Uptown Sewer: Youths Shoveling Snow See the Animal Churning in Icy Water." As the newspaper noted, the gang of boys, led by Salvatore Condoluci, actually managed to capture the approximately seven-foot-long animal after it was seen lurking in the sewers on 123rd Street close to the Harlem River, and they beat and stabbed it to death.

For more than three decades, Teddy May was the commissioner of sewers in New York. He has gone on record stating that he'd heard tales of alligators roaming the sewers of the city as far back as the 1930s—the same time frame in which the *New York Times* reported on the violent encounter at 123rd Street. May conceded that he took little interest in the reports since he felt they were all a matter of folklore and legend and certainly not reality.

As the reports grew in number, however, May decided that enough was enough, and it was time for him to take a look for himself at what might have been going on below New York. To May's amazement and terror, after descending into the darkened, mysterious, subterranean realm, he stumbled upon a number of significantly sized alligators swimming in the sewer waters. The stories, he instantly realized, were not just stories after all. Not surprisingly, May beat a hasty retreat.

Then there is the story of Mark Cherry, a man who maintains that one night in 1966, he was the solitary passenger standing on the platform at the 149th Street–Grand Concourse station when he was forcefully grabbed by a pair of police officers, who told him there had been a flooding in one of the tunnels and he had to leave immediately. The somewhat heavy-handed approach of the officers puzzled Cherry—that is, until he caught sight of something as he was being practically frog-marched away from the platform.

According to Cherry, what he saw was a group of subway employees hauling the body of a large albino alligator out of one of the tunnels, along with a body bag of the type in which a human body would be placed. Significantly, said Cherry, the body bag was clearly not empty. The implication was that the unfortunate soul inside had been attacked and killed by the alligator—which, in turn, had been killed by the police. Realizing that Cherry now knew what had really happened, the officers sternly warned him not to speak of what he had seen—which Cherry did not until 2004. It is a good indication of the fear that was drilled into Cherry back in 1966 that he was still concerned, nearly forty years later, that someone in authority might pay him a visit and silence him again, this time permanently. Fortunately, nothing so conspiratorial ever occurred. Indeed, taking any kind of retaliatory action against Cherry would only have vindicated his story.

While sightings and claims of alligators in the sewers of New York are nowhere near as prevalent today as they were decades ago, the controversy still provokes intrigue and fascination. And maybe, if we are to believe Mark Cherry, more than a few New Yorkers may have become the victims—and the dinners—of huge, vicious alligators.

Across the ocean, the idea that crocodiles might be living in Ireland stretches credulity not just to its limit but far beyond it! Nevertheless, creatures that at least superficially resemble crocodiles have been seen and reported across the land and for centuries, particularly in Ireland's lakes and loughs. A particularly fascinating account of such a monster was chronicled by Roderic O'Flaherty in his 1684 book *A Chronographical Description of West or H-Iar Connaught*. The location was the waters of Lough Mask. O'Flaherty said:

> There is one rarity more, which we may term the Irish crocodile, whereof one, as yet living, about ten years ago [1674], had said experience. The man was passing the shore just by the waterside, and spyed far off the head of a beast swimming, which he took to be an otter, and took no more notice of it; but the beast it seems lifted up its head; to discern whereabouts the man was; then diving swam under the water till he struck ground; whereupon he run out of the water suddenly and took the man by the elbow whereby the man stooped down, and the beast fastened his teeth in its pate, and dragged him into the water.

What had begun for the man as a sighting of an unusual animal was now nothing less than a fight for life and limb. O'Flaherty continued with his

One idea about enormous alligators prowling New York City's sewer system is that they were once young pets that escaped or were abandoned by their owners.

extraordinary account: "Where the man took hold of a stone by chance in his way, and calling to mind he had a knife in his jacket, took it out and gave a thrust of it to the beast, which thereupon got away from him into the lake. The water about him was all bloody, whether from the beast's blood, or his own, or from both he knows not. It was the pitch of an ordinary greyhound, of a black slimey [sic] skin, without hair as he imagines."

O'Flaherty then made an intriguing statement on the nature of the beast and its history to the extent that it was known: "Old men acquainted with the lake do tell there is such a beast in it, and that a stout fellow with a wolf dog along with him met the like there once; which after a long struggling went away in spite of the man and his dog, and was a long time after found rotten in a rocky cave of the lake when the waters decreased. The like they say is seen in other lakes in Ireland, they call it *Dovarchu*, i.e. a water dog, or *Anchu*, which is the same."

Peter Costello, a noted authority on Irish lake monsters, has studied this case carefully and makes a number of thought-provoking comments. Just before we get to Costello, it's important that we first have an awareness of a footnote that appears in an 1866 edition of O'Flaherty's book, which was published by the Archaeological Society based in Dublin, Ireland. The editor of this particular edition said in the footnote: "In these western parts, this animal is generally called *each-uisge*, which means a water horse, and he is described as having 'a black shining skin' and switch tail 'without hair.' The story related by our author is yet told in the neighbourhood of Lough Mask."

On this issue, Peter Costello says:

There seems to be some confusion here. The word "Dovarchu" does sometimes mean an otter in Irish. But [James] Hardiman seems to be mixing up two creatures which are carefully distinguished in the folk tradition. In 1843 the author of *Wild Sports of the West* observed that in Connaught "animals of extra-ordinary [sic] formation, and strange virtues, are supposed to inhabit lakes and rivers. Among these the sea-horse and the master-otter are pre-eminent. By a singular anomaly, the first is said to be found in certain island lochs, and his appearance is imagined to be fatal to the unfortunate person who encounters it."

Costello adds to this: "O'Flaherty's Irish crocodile is presumably the master-otter, while the sea-horse is the *uisge* of Gaelic stories.... It has often been suggested that some reports of lake monsters could be sightings of large otters," and suggestions have been made to the effect that "the Loch Ness animal might be a long-necked otter-like animal."

One of the most fascinating of the monster-themed stories comes from the renowned explorer Marco Polo (1254–1324), who told of animals that dwelt underground and that some likened to dragons in the province of Carajan in the region of Yunnan, in southern China. Polo's description of the beasts is as intriguing as it is bizarre and puzzling. In his own legendary words:

> In this province are found snakes and great serpents of such vast size as to strike fear into those who see them, and so hideous that the very account of them must excite the wonder of those to hear it. I will tell you how long and big they are.
>
> You may be assured that some of them are ten paces in length; some are more and some less. And in bulk they are equal to a great cask, for the bigger ones are about ten palms in girth. They have two forelegs near the head, but for foot nothing but a claw like the claw of a hawk or that of a lion. The head is very big, and the eyes are bigger than a great loaf of bread. The mouth is large enough to swallow a man whole, and is garnished with great [pointed] teeth. And in short they are so fierce-looking and so hideously ugly, that every man and beast must stand in fear and trembling of them. There are also smaller ones, such as of eight paces long, and of five, and of one pace only.
>
> The way in which they are caught is this. You must know that by day they live underground because of the great heat, and in the night they go out to feed, and devour every animal they can catch. They go also to drink at the rivers and lakes and springs. And their weight is so great that when they travel in search of food or drink, as they do by night, the tail makes a great furrow in the soil as if a full ton of liquor had been dragged along.
>
> Now the huntsmen who go after them take them by certain gyn which they set in the track over which the serpent has past, knowing that the beast will come back the same way. They plant a stake deep in the ground and fix on the head of this a sharp blade of steel made like a razor or a lance-point, and then they cover the whole with sand so that the serpent cannot see it.

Famous medieval Italian merchant and explorer Marco Polo told of animals he saw in China that appeared to be just like the dragons in Chinese mythology.

Indeed the huntsman plants several such stakes and blades on the track. On coming to the spot the beast strikes against the iron blade with such force that it enters his breast and rives him up to the navel, so that he dies on the spot and the crows on seeing the brute dead begin to caw, and then the huntsmen know that the serpent is dead and come in search of him.

This then is the way these beasts are taken. Those who take them proceed to extract the gall from the inside, and this sells at a great price; for you must know it furnishes the material for a most precious medicine. Thus if a person is bitten by a mad dog, and they give him but a small pennyweight of this medicine to drink, he is cured in a moment. Again if a woman is hard in labor they give her just such another dose and she is delivered at once. Yet again if one has any disease like the itch, or it may be worse, and applies a small quantity of this gall he shall speedily be cured. So you see why it sells at such a high price.

They also sell the flesh of this serpent, for it is excellent eating, and the people are very fond of it. And when these serpents are very hungry, sometimes they will seek out the lairs of lions or bears or other large wild beasts, and devour their cubs, without the sire and dam being able to prevent it. Indeed if they catch the big ones themselves they devour them too; they can make no resistance.

Even though these creatures that so tantalized Marco Polo seem to be definitive "unknowns," it should be noted that cryptozoologist Richard Freeman feels strongly that they are nothing stranger than crocodiles.

London Underground Horrors

Britain's famous London Underground serves commuters traveling throughout Greater London and select parts of Buckinghamshire, Hertfordshire, and Essex. It claims the title of the world's oldest underground system of its type, given that it opened for business on January 10, 1863. Today, nearly 250 years after its initial construction, the London Underground has no fewer than 268 stations and approximately 250 miles of track, thus making it the longest subsurface railway system on the planet. Moreover, in 2007, a whopping one billion passengers were recorded as having used the Underground since 1863.

According to numerous witnesses, the London Underground has played host to far more than mere tracks, trains, and human travelers. Deep within the winding tunnels of this subsurface labyrinth, bizarre and terrible things—many of a "wild man" variety—are rumored to seethe, fester, and feed. And British authorities are doing all they can to keep the lid on the chaos and carnage that threatens to spread deep below the streets of the nation's historic capital city.

Stories of strange creatures—many of a definitively cryptozoological nature—lurking in the London Underground have circulated for years, chiefly in a fictional, on-screen format. Such examples include:

1. The 1967 production of *Quatermass and the Pit*, in which bizarre, mutated, and diminutive ape-men—who were the subject of advanced genetic experiments undertaken millions of years earlier by visiting Martians—appear in the London Underground of the 1960s in the form of spectral, manifested, inherited memories;

2. *The Web of Fear*—a *Dr. Who* adventure from 1968 that sees the doctor and his comrades doing battle with robotic yetis on the Underground;

Other than trains and passengers, the London Underground is host to residents of the most eldritch kind, including wild men and hungry beasts.

3. *An American Werewolf in London*, a 1981 film in which the beast of the title feasts on a doomed, late-night rail traveler; and

4. *Reign of Fire*, a 2002 production starring Christian Bale and Matthew McConaughey that revolves around literal fire-breathing dragons bursting forth from the old tunnels of the Underground to decimate Britain and, eventually, the rest of the planet.

Some of the older tales of creature-like entities prowling the tunnels under London were incorporated into another film, perhaps less well known than those listed above. Made in 1972, *Death Line* starred horror film stalwarts Christopher Lee and Donald Pleasence and related the fictional saga of a collapse, in the latter part of the nineteenth century, at a station being built at Russell Square, which happens to be a real station on the Underground. Unfortunately, when the disaster occurs, a significant number of workers—both men and women—are presumed killed. And when the company funding the project goes bankrupt, all efforts to dig out the bodies to give them a decent burial are quickly, quietly, and conveniently forgotten.

Had the plans gone ahead, the company would have learned to its horror that the workers did not die. Instead, they found themselves trapped underground and were forced to make new lives for themselves in their permanent, subsurface home, which they do by dining on just about anything and anyone that dares to cross their path or stumble upon their darkened abode.

As *Death Line* tells it, some eight decades on, the final few offspring of the original workers are still valiantly clinging to life. Their existence, however, is a distinctly poor one: afflicted by a host of genetic abnormalities caused by inbreeding and a lack of regular nourishment, their minds are reduced to truly primitive levels, and their bodies are overwhelmingly diseased and corrupted. Their only source of food comes in the form of the occasional, unfortunate user of the Underground who, if the circumstances are in their favor, they can secretly grab, kill, and devour.

Death Line is an entertaining and odd little film that seldom gets the airing it deserves, and it's one that leaves the viewer with much to think about and muse upon when it comes to the matter of wild people living among us. Notably, there are those who believe the film is more than mere fiction. Some are firmly of the opinion that the story it relates is 100 percent fact—albeit, admittedly, a difficult-to-confirm fact—and that far below the capital city, primitive beastmen roam, forage, slaughter, and feed.

Before his passing in 2007, Frank Wiley, who spent his entire working life in the British police forces, told a bizarre and unsettling tale of his personal memories and investigations of a number of very weird killings on the London Underground, always late at night, from 1967 to 1969. The killings, Wiley said, occurred on at least three stations and were hushed up by the police as the unfortunate results of particularly vicious, late-night muggings.

In reality, Wiley explained, the muggings were nothing of the sort and were far more horrific in nature. There were, he recalled, seven such deaths during the time he was assigned to the investigations. As for the cases of which Wiley had personal awareness, he said the modus operandi was always the same: the bodies of the people—a couple of whom were commuters and the rest hobos simply looking for shelter on cold, windswept nights—were found, always after at least ten o'clock P.M., a significant distance into the tunnels, with arms or legs viciously amputated—possibly even gnawed off. Stomachs were ripped open, innards were torn out, and throats were violently slashed. A definitive man-eater—or, worse still, a whole group of man-eaters—was seemingly prowling around the most shadowy corners of London's dark underworld after sunset. And it, or they, had only one cold and lethal goal: to seek out fresh flesh with which to nourish their hungry bellies.

A definitive man-eater—or, worse still, a whole group of man-eaters—was seemingly prowling around the most shadowy corners of London's dark underworld after sunset.

Could the killings have been the work of a rampaging animal, possibly one that had escaped from a London-based zoo or private menagerie, and was now on the loose below the capital city? Or might the deaths have been simply due to desperate, suicidal people who threw themselves under the speeding trains and whose remains were violently dragged into the tunnels under the steel wheels of the racing carriages? Wiley strongly believed that neither of these scenarios provided adequate explanations.

There was a further, very good reason why the deaths were not ascribed to the work of wild beasts or suicides: namely, the presence of a terrifying-looking character seen at some point in 1968 by two workmen who were repairing a particular stretch of track on the Bakerloo Line (a fourteen-mile-long section of the London Underground that was constructed in 1906). The savage character, stated Wiley, was a bearded, wild-haired man, dressed in tattered, filthy clothing.

When one of the workers challenged the mysterious figure with a large ratchet, the man came closer, moving in a weird, faltering, stumbling style. To the horror of the pair, he held his arms out in front of him, bared a mouth of decayed teeth in their direction, and uttered a low and threatening growl. The strange figure then slowly backed away, eventually turning and then suddenly running deeper into the tunnel, until he was finally lost from view. Unsurprisingly, and rather sensibly, the fraught workmen elected not to give chase but instead raced to the nearest police station and summoned the authorities, who, said Wiley, questioned the petrified men vigorously.

Wiley added that secret orders quickly came down to the police investigators on the case—from the British Government's Home Office, the work of which focuses on a host of issues relative to national security—to wrap everything up very quickly. Intriguingly, Wiley maintained that secret liaisons with Home Office personnel revealed that there were unverified rumors of deeper, very ancient, crudely built tunnels far below the Underground that reportedly dated back centuries, long before the advent of trains, railways, and suchlike. There was even some speculation they may have been constructed as far back as the Roman invasion of Britain that began in 43 C.E. Precisely who had constructed the older tunnels, and who might have emerged from them to wreak deadly havoc on the Underground in the 1960s, was never revealed to Wiley's small team of personnel.

> "And when the last killing I was involved in [occurred], in 1969, I didn't hear much after that; just rumours there might have been more deaths in the '70's upward."

He said: "Probably no-one really knew, anyway. Only that someone, like the character seen by the workmen, was coming up from somewhere, killing, taking parts of the bodies, and then they were always gone again. It all got pushed under the rug when the Home Office said so. And when the last killing I was involved in [occurred], in 1969, I didn't hear much after that; just rumours there might have been more deaths in the '70s upward. I don't know."

Wiley's last comments on his controversial claims, in 2004, went as follows: "There's more to the [*Death Line*] film than people know. My thought then, and which it still is today, is someone making the film heard the stories, the deaths we investigated. They had to have; the film was too close to what happened. And I think we didn't have control of the tunnels, and someone up in the government knew. Perhaps it's still going on. That would be a thought."

With Wiley's final sentence, I have absolutely no argument!

The London Underground's British Museum station closed its doors on September 25, 1933. For many years prior to its closure, a local myth circulated to the effect that the ghost of an ancient Egyptian haunted the station. Dressed in a loincloth and headdress, the figure would emerge late at night into the labyrinth of old tunnels. In fact, the story gained such a hold that a London newspaper offered a significant monetary reward to anyone who was willing to spend the night there. Somewhat surprisingly, not a single soul took the newspaper up on its generous offer.

The story took an even stranger turn after the station was shut down. The comedy-thriller movie *Bulldog Jack*, which was released in 1935, included in its story a secret tunnel that ran from the station to the Egyptian Room at the British Museum. The station in the film is a wholly fictional one dubbed

Bloomsbury; however, the scenario presented in the film was based on the enduring legend of the ghost of the British Museum station.

Oddly enough, on the exact same night that the movie was released in British cinemas, two women disappeared from the platform at Holborn—which just happened to be the next station along from the British Museum. Strange marks were later found on the walls of the closed station, and more sightings of the ghost were reported, along with reports of weird moaning noises coming from behind the walls of the tunnels. Not surprisingly, tales began to circulate to the effect that the police had uncovered some dark and terrible secret—maybe about a paranormal killer on the tracks—that had to be kept hidden from the populace at all costs. In other words, there was a strange, yet eerily similar, precursor to the 1960s recollections of Frank Wiley, one that predated his own experiences by more than three decades.

London Underground officials were, for a significant period of time, forced to dismiss the story, and there has always been an outright denial about the existence of a secret tunnel extending from the station to the museum's Egyptian Room. Nevertheless, the story was resurrected in Keith Lowe's novel of 2001, *Tunnel Vision*, in which the lead character states, while trying to impress and scare his girlfriend at the same time: "If you listen carefully when you're standing at the platform at Holborn, sometimes—just sometimes—you can hear the wailing of Egyptian voices floating down the tunnel towards you."

London Underground officials were, for a significant period of time, forced to dismiss the story, and there has always been an outright denial about the existence of a secret tunnel....

Might the loincloth-wearing "Egyptian" actually have been one of Frank Wiley's savage underground cannibals? If so, were the tales of a police cover-up an indication that officialdom may have secretly known about the capital city's wild men for far longer than even Wiley could have guessed?

In some respects, Wiley's story eerily parallels that of a man named Colin Campbell, who maintains that while traveling home on the London Underground in the mid-1960s, he had a nightmarish encounter with a very similar beast. According to Campbell, it was late at night, and, rather surprisingly, he was the only person to get off the train at its scheduled stop on the Northern Line. As the train pulled away from the unusually deserted and silent platform and Campbell made his way toward the exit, he claims to have heard a strange growl coming from behind him. He quickly spun around and was shocked to see a large, hairy, apelike animal lumbering across the platform toward the track, seemingly mumbling to itself as it did so.

Most bizarre of all, the beast was definitively spectral, rather than flesh and blood. Around three-quarters of its body was above the platform, while its legs were curiously near-transparent and, incredibly, passed right *through* the platform. Campbell further asserts that as he stood in awe, too shocked to even try to move, the beast continued to walk through the concrete, right onto the tracks, and then straight through the wall directly behind the tunnel—all the time paying absolutely no attention to Campbell in the slightest.

Are savage, devolved humans *really* living—in literal cannibalistic style—deep under London? And are the old tunnels *really* home to ghostly apemen of the type encountered by Colin Campbell back in the 1960s? Or are such tales simply born out of legends provoked by the likes of *Dr. Who* and *Quatermass and the Pit*? If not the latter, then some might say that such accounts have a significant bearing upon the reports of the British wild man— particularly if the creatures have found ways to exit the tunnels from time to time to make their way around select portions of the city and the surrounding countryside by the camouflage of a dark and disturbing night.

WATER GODS, SPIRITS, AND MYTHOLOGICALS

There is little doubt that most of the creatures described in Monsters of the Deep *are real, living animals—even if they still baffle us as to what they are. There are, however, some monsters that straddle the realms of reality and those of folklore and mythology. Even though we don't know their real identities—and may never will—it's important that we take a look at them, which is what we are about to do in this chapter. They include the multiheaded, snakelike Hydra of Greek mythology; Jonah's whale, which is described in amazing fashion in the pages of the Old Testament; and the huge sea serpent known as the leviathan. Beliefs in similar creatures still exist to this day. For example, in 1968 evidence found at Loch Ness revealed that a secret society was worshipping a mythological Babylonian sea goddess called Tiamat.*

JONAH'S WHALE, THE LEVIATHAN, AND THE HYDRA

Beyond any shadow of a doubt, it is one of the strangest of all the stories in the pages of the Bible. It is the controversial saga of a man named Jonah, who allegedly spent no fewer than three days immersed in the water-filled belly of a large fish or whale. Many biblical scholars and believers are content to accept the bizarre story in wholly literal terms: as an encounter with a massive sea creature. Others adhere to the theory that the tales in the Old Testament are born of distorted accounts of alien visitation and have suggested "that Jonah was not swallowed by a whale but abducted by the extraterrestrial crew of a UFO." Before we get to the alien angle, however, let us first address the matter of what, exactly, the Bible says about Jonah's underwater exploits.

Jonah, the son of Amittai, was a prophet from Gath Hepher, Israel, who, according to the biblical book of Jonah, was instructed by God: "Go to the great city of Nineveh and preach against it, because its wickedness has come up before me"—Nineveh being a Mesopotamian city on the east side of the Tigris River, which flows through the areas that are now Turkey and Iraq.

By all accounts, Jonah was not one to take orders from anyone, not even an all-powerful deity. As a result, he outright ignored God's command and elected to head for Joppa, a seaport, and make his way by ship to Tarshish. As the Bible words it, Jonah "ran away from the Lord."

Given that this is a story from the Old Testament, we can hardly be surprised by God's response: it was one filled with wrath and dire punishment for Jonah. God conjured up an appropriately almighty storm, the huge waves of which, when coupled with violent thunder and lightning, almost battered the ship to the point of complete destruction. The crew, it becomes clear, was a

Jonah and the Whale (1621) by artist Pieter Lastman depicts Jonah being released from a fishy fate.

suspicious bunch and drew lots to determine whose wrongdoing had incurred the fury of God. Jonah came up short and was quickly tossed overboard by the frightened crew. At once, something remarkable happened.

The pounding waves became calm, the skies cleared, and the storm was gone in pretty much an instant. Then something even more astounding occurred: a mighty fish or whale surfaced from the depths and swallowed Jonah, who, up until that point, had been doing his best to stay afloat in the churning waters. As he sat in the fishy, watery belly for a full three days, Jonah came to realize his error and eventually repented for not following God's orders to preach to the people of Nineveh. A satisfied God arranged for Jonah to be deposited back on dry land in a most curious fashion: the whale, rather unceremoniously, vomited him up.

There was, however, something very strange about the newly returned Jonah: the three days in the belly of the whale had bleached his skin and clothes white, giving him a decidedly unsettling, eerie appearance. This may well have had some bearing on why, exactly, the people of Nineveh listened to Jonah when he ordered them to give up their evil, wanton ways, lest God destroy the city. They not only listened, they also did as Jonah had insisted: they changed their behavior, fasted, and repented. God, seeing that the people of Nineveh had indeed changed, forgave them, and the city was spared destruction.

That is the Old Testament version of the story of Jonah and the mysterious whale in which he was inexplicably able to live for three full days. The idea that a person could survive, for around seventy-two hours, in the belly of a whale, deep within the waters of a churning ocean, is, of course, ridiculous. We are therefore required to look in other directions for potential answers to what really lay at the heart of the story.

Michel M. Deschamps, of the organization Northern Ontario UFO Research & Study (NOUFORS), says:

> I did some research and found that it was impossible for a man to be inside of a whale for three days because there is no species of whale that can actually swallow a man whole and then spit him out. The largest whales only eat plankton, which is microscopic in size compared to that of a man.
>
> I kept thinking that maybe Jonah had been taken aboard a vessel of some type … which then brought him to shore, a few days later.
>
> I had read many reports of these black silhouettes that were seen floating on the surface of the ocean during the 1950s and 1960s. Some thought that maybe they were dealing with Soviet submarines. But whatever they were, they always managed to disappear without a trace, leaving the authorities dumbfounded.

At some point in the exercise, Navy personnel tracked the movements of a very curious object deep in the ocean waters. They continued to do so for no fewer than four days....

It is a known fact amongst UFOlogists that USOs (Unidentified Submerged Objects) do exist, and they are of a non-terrestrial origin. They're actually UFOs that have the ability to submerge themselves in our world's oceans and lakes.

So it would not be too surprising for me to find out that this is what lies behind the story of "Jonah and the whale."

That the field of ufology is rife with sightings of so-called USOs is not in doubt. The late author and anomalies researcher Ivan T. Sanderson wrote an entire book on the subject of unidentified craft seen in the world's oceans: *Invisible Residents*. While it would be impossible to summarize all of Sanderson's bulging case files, one will suffice on this topic.

From military sources, Sanderson learned of a fascinating case that occurred off the coast of Puerto Rico in 1963. U.S. Navy personnel were taking part in a military exercise; aircraft, ships, and submarines played significant roles in the operation.

At some point in the exercise, Navy personnel tracked the movements of a very curious object deep in the ocean waters. They continued to do so for no fewer than four days as the object—which was clearly under intelligent control—traveled to the astonishing depth of twenty-seven thousand feet. Whatever the nature of the USO, it remained unidentified.

Researcher John Black, in his 2013 paper "The Story of Jonah," makes good observations on the story of Jonah:

Let us travel back thousands of years to a time when there was no technology and ask ourselves how an advanced, modern vehicle would have been perceived and described using the limited terms and references the civilization had. Is it not obvious that an airplane would have been perceived as a shiny, metallic bird, or a perhaps a chariot of fire?

Similarly, isn't it possible that a submarine would have been perceived as a whale, since whales, even then, were the largest mammals in the sea? A prime example of such a limitation is how we still use the term "flying disc" for unknown vehicles simply because they remain, to us, unknown disc-like shaped objects that fly. If we had this kind of technology then the term we use would be completely different.

Black concludes: "This story makes you wonder whether this 'God' could have just been a supreme being with knowledge and power beyond the author's comprehension, along with a fleet of vehicles at his disposal to force the faith and obedience of his subjects."

It's interesting to note that within alien-abduction lore, there are many accounts of people reportedly taken onboard UFOs and submerged into liquids or gels. They sound eerily like the accounts of Jonah while he was caught in the water-filled belly of a whale. An extract from one such report, taken from an online article called "A True Account of Alien Abduction—1988," reads thus:

> I woke up again, this time naked in a funnel shaped pool filled with a greenish black gel type liquid. The pool had to be 20 yards wide all around. And pretty deep. The pool was made of some kind of shiny metal. With the gel it made the surface very slippery and you would slip under the gel if you tried to get out. I then realized something very odd at that time. I wasn't alone.
>
> There were at least 15 other humans with me. All of them screaming and panicking. This is what scared me. I didn't know what they were screaming about. I thought they knew something I didn't, so I got scared. Some were under the gel moving around I could see. Most were trying to escape.

A second account, related at the *Alien Hub* website, reads:

> I found myself inside a clear glass cylinder, totally submerged in some kind of warm fluid, thicker than water, thinner than oil. To my surprise, I was able to breathe this warm fluid without discomfort. I could also open my eyes without a problem. The solution was clear, of a greenish color and the container was softly lit. I remember, still fully submerged in this solution that I slowly began to recall the abduction that had taken me away from my bedroom, minutes, maybe hours before (impossible to tell). Then I made the connection with the place I was now in and real fear took hold of me. I remember desperately trying to get out of the container, but I could not move a muscle except for my eyelids.
>
> Finally, and all at once by sheer force of will, I was able to regain move-

There are many personal accounts about people being abducted by aliens and submerged in gels or other liquids.

ment of my limbs. I jumped out of the glass container faster than a spring. Apparently, what I had been breathing while submerged was very different than air because I felt the urgent need to take a big breath of air as soon as I came out.

I was naked and dripping this fluid/solution that was sort of a slimy gel. The place was dark, very steamy with a strange, unpleasant smell.

Researcher Helmut Lammer, in "New Evidence of Military Involvement in Abductions," tells the story of an abductee he calls "Lisa." In Lammer's words:

Lisa ... was kidnapped and brought to a military underground facility, where she saw naked humans floating in tubes. Lisa claims that she was forced by humans into some type of pool filled with a golden yellow bubbly fluid, while other humans looked at her. Lisa has traumatic recollections that her kidnappers tried to make her and other victims able to breath in the liquid. In two of the before mentioned cases the abductee was forced to breath the liquid like Lisa. The hypnosis transcripts reveal that the liquid breathing experiences were traumatic for the abductees. Both abductees where totally immersed in the liquid and both reported that they could breath the fluid.

UFO authority Stanton Friedman made a notable observation in "UFO Propulsion Systems":

The amount of acceleration a person can stand depends on many factors; the three most important depend on the duration of acceleration (the greater the force, the shorter the time it can be tolerated), the direction of the force in relation to the body (back to front acceleration is much easier to handle than head to foot acceleration, and for this reason Apollo astronauts have their backs perpendicular to the direction of the thrust, rather then along it as in an elevator), and body environment ... (*a person immersed in fluid can withstand greater acceleration than one not so immersed*).

In light of Friedman's words, we might wish to consider the possibility that Jonah's time spent within the belly was actually time spent immersed in fluids that allowed for his body to cope with the rigors of travel in a craft not normally designed to transport humans. It may well have been a liquid that had an unfortunate side effect: it bleached Jonah's skin as white as a ghost. Perhaps the story of Jonah is, in reality, one of the earliest accounts on record of an alien abduction.

It's intriguing to note that nineteenth-century sea serpent expert Henry Lee addressed the matter of Jonah and the whale. In an 1883 book called *Sea Monsters Unmasked*, he said:

> Leaving these water-snakes of the tropics, we come, next in order of date, upon some very remarkable evidence that there was current amongst a community where we should little expect to find it, the idea of a marine monster corresponding in many respects with some of the descriptions given several centuries later of the sea-serpent.

In an interesting article on the Catacombs of Rome in the *Illustrated London News* of February 3rd, 1872, allusion is made by the author to the collection of sarcophagi or coffins of the early Christians, removed from the Catacombs, and preserved in the museum of the Lateran Palace, where they were arranged by the late Padre Marchi for Pope Pius IX. There are more than twenty of these, sculptured with various designs—the Father and the Son, Adam and Eve and the Serpent, the Sacrifice of Abraham, Moses striking the Rock, Daniel and the Lions, and other Scripture themes. Amongst them also is Jonah and the "whale." ...

It may well have been a liquid that had an unfortunate side effect: it bleached Jonah's skin as white as a ghost. Perhaps the story of Jonah is, in reality, one of the earliest accounts on record of an alien abduction.

It will be seen that Jonah is being swallowed feet foremost, or possibly being ejected head first, by an enormous sea monster, having the chest and fore-legs of a horse, a long arching neck, with a mane at its base, near the shoulders, a head like nothing in nature, but having hair upon and beneath the cheeks, the hinder portion of the body being that of a serpent of prodigious length, undulating in several vertical curves. This sculpture appears to have been cut between the beginning and the middle of the third century, about A.D. 230, but it probably represents a tradition of far greater antiquity.

Almost certainly, we should not take the tales of the leviathan and Jonah and the whale literally—something that applies to much of the rest of the content of the Bible, particularly so the Old Testament. It is filled with all manner of bizarre tales, including those of a talking donkey and a talking snake. In all likelihood, the stories of both Jonah and the leviathan were based upon ancient encounters with sea serpent-type animals, the tales of which became more and more distorted as the fog of time ensured matters were exaggerated to greater and greater degrees.

Turning now to the strange and thought-provoking saga of the leviathan, *Britannica.com* says of the ancient creature: "*Leviathan*, Hebrew *Livyatan*, in

Jewish mythology, a primordial sea serpent. Its source is in prebiblical Mesopotamian myth, especially that of the sea monster in the Ugaritic myth of Baal. In the Old Testament, Leviathan appears in Psalms 74:14 as a multi-headed sea serpent that is killed by God and given as food to the Hebrews in the wilderness. In Isaiah 27:1, Leviathan is a serpent and a symbol of Israel's enemies, who will be slain by God. In Job 41, it is a sea monster and a symbol of God's power of creation."

In Matthew Henry's (1662–1714) *Commentary on the Whole Bible*, published in six volumes from 1706 to 1721, Henry offers the following description of the leviathan depicted in the book of Job:

> The description here given of the leviathan, a very large, strong, formidable fish, or water-animal, is designed yet further to convince Job of his own impotency, and of God's omnipotence, that he might be humbled for his folly in making so bold with him as he had done…. To convince Job of his own weakness he is here

A "leviathan" is a creature dating back to Mesopotamian mythology. It is a large sea serpent that also appears in the Bible's books of Psalms and Isaiah. The Bible's description is not detailed, so some have wondered if the creature in Job's tale is a fish, a whale, or perhaps a crocodilian.

challenged to subdue and tame this leviathan if he can, and make himself master of him, and, since he cannot do this, he must own himself utterly unable to stand before the great God. To convince Job of God's power and terrible majesty several particular instances are here given of the strength and terror of the leviathan, which is no more than what God has given him, nor more than he has under his check. The face of the leviathan is here described to be terrible, his scales close, his breath and neesings sparkling, his flesh firm, his strength and spirit, when he is attacked, insuperable, his motions turbulent, and disturbing to the waters, so that, upon the whole, he is a very terrible creature, and man is no match for him.... Whether this leviathan be a whale or a crocodile is a great dispute among the learned, which I will not undertake to determine; some of the particulars agree more easily to the one, others to the other; both are very strong and fierce, and the power of the Creator appears in them.

Henry continues:

The ingenious Sir Richard Blackmore, though he admits the more received opinion concerning the behemoth, that it must be meant of the elephant, yet agrees with the learned Bochart's notion of the leviathan, that it is the crocodile, which was so well known in the river of Egypt. I confess that that which inclines me rather to understand it of the whale is not only because it is much larger and a nobler animal, but because, in the history of the Creation, there is such an express notice taken of it as is not of any other species of animals whatsoever, by which it appears, not only that whales were well known in those parts in the time of Moses, who lived a little after Job, but that the creation of whales was generally looked upon as a most illustrious proof of the eternal power and godhead of the Creator; and we may conjecture that this was the reason (for otherwise it seems unaccountable) why Moses there so particularly mentions the creation of the whales, because God had so lately insisted upon the bulk and strength of that creature than of any other, as the proof of his power; and the leviathan is here spoken of as an inhabitant of the sea, which the crocodile is not; there in the great and wide sea, is that leviathan.

Henry explains further:

He shows how unable Job was to master the leviathan. 1. That he could not catch him, as a little fish, with angling. He had no bait wherewith to deceive him, no hook wherewith to catch him, no fish-line wherewith to draw him out of the water, nor a thorn to run through his gills, on which to carry him home. 2. That he could not make him his prisoner, nor force him to cry for quarter, or surrender himself at discretion. 3. That he could not entice him into a cage, and keep him there as a bird for the children to play with. There are creatures so little, so weak, as to be easily restrained thus, and triumphed over; but the leviathan is not one of these: he is made to be the terror, not the sport and diversion, of mankind. 4. That he could not have him served up to his table; he and his companions could not make a banquet of him; his flesh is too strong to be fit for food, and, if it were not, he is not easily caught. 5. That they could not enrich themselves with the spoil of him: Shall they part him among the merchants, the bones to one, the oil to another? If they can catch him, they will; but it is probable that the art of fishing for whales was not brought to perfection then, as it has been since."

And, finally:

6. That they could not destroy him, could not fill his head with fish-spears. He kept out of the reach of their instruments of slaughter, or, if they touched him, they could not touch him to the quick. 7. That it was to no purpose to attempt it: The hope of taking him is in vain. If men go about to seize him, so formidable is he that the very sight of him will appall them, and make a stout man ready to faint away: Shall not one be cast down even at the sight of him? and will not that deter the pursuers from their attempt? Job is told, at his peril, to lay his hand upon him, "Touch him if thou dare; remember the battle, how unable thou art to encounter such a force, and what is therefore likely to be the issue of the battle, and do no more, but desist from the attempt."

Still on the matter of strange creatures in ancient times, there is the following from the website of the Theoi Project, describing the legendary tale of the Hydra thus: "HYDRA LERNAIA (Lernaean Hydra) was a gigantic, nine-headed water-serpent, which haunted the swamps of Lerna. Herakles (Heracles) was sent to destroy her as one of his twelve labours, but for each of her heads that he decapitated, two more sprang forth. So with the help of Iolaos (Iolaus), he applied burning brands to the severed stumps, cauterizing the wounds and preventing the regeneration. In the battle he also crushed a giant crab beneath his heel which had come to assist the Hydra. The Hydra and the Crab were afterwards placed amongst the stars by Hera as the Constellations Hydra and Cancer."

Many may well find the saga of the Hydra to be fanciful in the extreme, perhaps even wholly unlikely. There is, however, a body of data that suggests the legend of the Hydra is based upon encounters with an all-too-real beast of the deep—or more than one of them. The almost certain answer to the Hydra controversy comes from Henry Lee, who, in the 1800s, spent a great deal of time immersed in the world of the sea serpent. Lee said, in his 1883 *Sea Monsters Unmasked* (which is now in the public domain):

> There can be little doubt that the octopus was the model from which the old poets and artists formed their ideas, and drew their pictures of the Lernean Hydra, whose heads grew again when cut off by Hercules; and also of the monster Scylla, who, with six heads and six long writhing necks, snatched men off the decks of passing ships and devoured them in the recesses of her gloomy cavern. Of the Hydra Diodorus relates that it had a hundred heads; Simonides says fifty; but the generally received opinion was that of Apollodorus, Hyginus, and others, that it had only nine.

> Apollodorus of Athens, son of Asclepiades, who wrote in stiff, quaint Greek about 120 B.C., gives in his "Bibliotheca" the following account of the many-headed monster. "This Hydra," he says, "nourished in the marshes of Lerne, went forth into the open country and destroyed the herds of the land. It had a huge body

The Hydra was a nine-headed sea serpent from Greek mythology. In one tale of the time, the hero Hercules kills the Lernean Hydra.

and nine heads, eight mortal, but the ninth immortal. Having mounted his chariot, which was driven by Iolaus, Hercules got to Lerne and stopped his horses. Finding the Hydra on a certain raised ground near the source of the Amymon, where its lair was, he made it come out by pelting it with burning missiles. He seized and stopped it, but having twisted itself round one of his feet, it struggled with him. He broke its head with his club: but that was useless; for when one head was broken two sprang up, and a huge crab helped the Hydra by biting the foot of Hercules. This he killed, and called Iolaus, who, setting on fire part of the adjoining forest, burned with torches the germs of the growing heads, and stopped their development. Having thus out-maneuvered the growing heads, he cut off the immortal head, buried it, and put a heavy stone upon it, beside the road going from Lerne to Eleonta, and having opened the Hydra, dipped his arrows in its gall."

If we wish to find in nature the counterpart of this Hydra, we must seek, firstly, for an animal with eight out-growths from its trunk, which it can develop afresh, or replace by new ones, in case of any or all of them being amputated or injured. We must also show that this animal, so strange in form and possessing such remarkable attributes, was well known in the locality where the legend was believed. We have it in the octopus, which abounded in the Mediterranean and Øgean seas, and whose eight prehensile arms, or tentacles, spring from its central body, the immortal head, and which, if lost or mutilated by misadventure, are capable of reproduction.

In a strange situation, then, the Hydra really did live. It just wasn't what the people of centuries ago thought it was.

It's intriguing to note that Henry Lee addressed yet another notable case of a water serpent from centuries ago, as his following words demonstrate:

Valerius Maximus, quoting Livy, describes the alarm into which, during the Punic wars, the Romans, under Attilius Regulus (who was afterwards so cruelly put to death by the Carthaginians), were thrown by an aquatic, though not marine, serpent which had its lair on the banks of the Bagrados, near Ithaca. It is said to have swallowed many of the soldiers, after crushing them in its folds, and to have kept the army from crossing the river, till at length, being invulnerable by ordinary weapons, it was destroyed by heavy stones hurled by balistas, catapults, and other military engines used in those days for casting heavy missiles, and battering the walls of fortified towns.

According to the historian, the annoyance caused by it to the army did not cease with its death, for the water was polluted with its gore, and the air with the noxious fumes from its corrupted carcass, to such a degree that the Romans were obliged to remove their camp. They, however secured the animal's skin and skull, which were preserved in a temple at Rome till the time of the Numantine war.

This combat has been described, to the same effect, by Florus as an incident known to everyone. Diodorus Siculus also tells of a great serpent, sixty feet long, which lived chiefly in the water, but landed at frequent intervals to devour the cattle in its neighbourhood. A party was collected to capture it; but their first attempt failed, and the monster killed twenty of them. It was afterwards taken in a strong net, carried alive to Alexandria, and presented to King Ptolemy II., the founder of the Alexandrian Library and Museum, who was a great collector of zoological and other curiosities. This snake was probably one of the great boas.

ANARCHY IN THE UNITED KINGDOM

Of the many and varied monstrous, supernatural beasts of Wales, certainly one of the most fear-inducing was the Gwrach-y-Rhibyn (Hag of the Mist), a water-based abomination. Notably, it is also referred to as the River Specter after claims that it lurks in Welsh rivers, ready to pounce upon the unwary and steal their souls. The exploits and nature of this nightmarish thing were expertly chronicled back in the nineteenth century by a man named Wirt Sikes. At the time, he was the American Consul for Wales. While the story of the Gwrach-y-Rhibyn is told in Sikes's 1880 book *British Goblins*, it is to Sikes's original notes that we turn our attention. They tell a story that is creepy, horrific, and unforgettable:

> A frightful figure among Welsh apparitions is the Gwrach-y-Rhibyn, whose crowning distinction is its prodigious ugliness. The feminine pronoun is generally used in speaking of this goblin, which unlike the majority of its kind, is supposed to be a female. A Welsh saying, regarding one of her sex who is the reverse of lovely, is, "Y mae mor salw a Gwrach-y-Rhibyn" (She is as ugly as the Gwrach-y-Rhibyn).

> The specter is a hideous being with disheveled hair, long black teeth, long, lank, withered arms, leathern wings, and a cadaver-

ous appearance. In the stillness of night it comes and flaps its wings against the window, uttering at the same time a blood-curdling howl, and calling by name on the person who is to die, in a lengthened dying tone, as thus: "Da-a-a-vy!" "De-i-i-o-o-o ba-a-a-ch!" The effect of its shriek or howl is indescribably terrific, and its sight blasting to the eyes of the beholder. It is always an omen of death, though its warning cry is heard under varying circumstances; sometimes it appears in the mist on the mountain side, or at cross-roads, or by a piece of water which it splashes with its hands.

The gender of apparitions is no doubt as a rule the neuter, but the Gwrach-y-Rhibyn defies all rules by being a female which at times sees fit to be a male. In its female character it has a trick of crying at intervals, in a most doleful tone, "Oh! oh! fy ngwr, fy ngwr!" (my husband! my husband!) But when it chooses to be a male, this cry is changed to "Fy ngwraig! fy ngwraig!" (my wife! my wife!) or "Fy mlentyn, fy mlentyn bach!" (my child, my little child!) There is a frightful story of a dissipated peasant who met this goblin on the road one night, and thought it was a living woman; he therefore made wicked and improper overtures to it, with the result of having his soul nearly frightened out of his body in the horror of discovering his mistake. As he emphatically exclaimed, "Och, Dduw! it was the Gwrach-y-Rhibyn, and not a woman at all."

The Gwrach-y-Rhibyn is a hag that inhabits rivers in Welsh tales.

The Gwrach-y-Rhibyn recently appeared, according to an account given me by a person who claimed to have seen it, at Llandaff. Surely, no more probable site for the appearance of a specter so ancient of lineage could be found, than that ancient cathedral city where some say was the earliest Christian fane in Great Britain, and which was certainly the seat of the earliest Christian bishopric.

My narrator was a respectable-looking man of the peasant-farmer class, whom I met in one of my walks near Cardiff, in the summer of 1878. "It was at Llandaff," he said to me, "on the fourteenth of last November, when I was on a visit to an old friend, that I saw and heard the Gwrach-y-Rhibyn. I was sleeping in my bed, and was woke at midnight by a frightful screeching and a shaking of my window. It was a loud and clear screech, and the shaking of the window was very plain, but it seemed to go by like the wind. I was not so much frightened, sir, as you may think; excited I was—that's the word—excited; and I jumped out of bed and rushed to the window and flung it open.

"Then I saw the Gwrach-y-Rhibyn, saw her plainly, sir, a horrible old woman with long red hair and a face like chalk, and great teeth like tusks, looking back over her shoulder at me as she went through the air with a long black gown trailing along the ground below her arms, for body I could make out none. She gave another unearthly screech while I looked at her; then I heard her flapping her wings against the window of a house just below the one I was in, and she vanished from my sight. But I kept on staring into the darkness, and as I am a living man, sir, I saw her go in at the door of the Cow and Snuffers Inn, and return no more. I watched the door of the inn a long time, but she did not come out.

"The next day, it's the honest truth I'm telling you, they told me the man who kept the Cow and Snuffers Inn was dead—had died in the night. His name was Llewellyn, sir—you can ask any one about him, at Llandaff—he had kept the inn there for seventy years, and his family before him for three hundred years, just at that very spot. It's not these new families that the Gwrach-y-Rhibyn ever troubles, sir, it's the old stock."

The close resemblance of this goblin to the Irish banshee (or benshi) will be at once perceived. The same superstition is found among other peoples of Celtic origin. Sir Walter Scott mentions it among the highlands of Scotland. It is not traced among other than Celtic peoples distinctly, but its association with the primeval mythology is doubtless to be found in the same direction with many other death-omens, to wit, the path of the wind-god Hermes.

The frightful ugliness of the Gwrach-y-Rhibyn is a consistent feature of the superstition, in both its forms; it recalls the Black Maiden who came to Caerleon and liberated Peredur: "Blacker were her face and her two hands than the blackest iron covered with pitch; and her hue was not more frightful than her form. High cheeks had she, and a face lengthened downwards, and a short nose with distended nostrils. And one eye was of a piercing mottled gray, and the other was as black as jet, deep-sunk in her head. And her teeth were long and yellow, more yellow were they than the flower of the broom. And her stomach rose from the breast-bone, higher than her chin. And her back was in the shape of a crook, and her legs were large and bony. And her figure was very thin and spare, except her feet and legs, which were of huge size." The Welsh word "gwrach" means a hag or witch, and it has been fancied that there is a connection between this word and the mythical Avagddu, whose wife the gwrach was.

SERPENTS, HUMAN SACRIFICE, AND SECRETS

The summer of 1969 was a strange period in the quest for the truth behind the legend of the Loch Ness Monster. It was a decidedly alternative period, too, given that information surfaced on a secret "dragon cult" operating in the vicinity of the huge lake. In early June, three American students paid a visit to Loch Ness. Their purpose was to visit Boleskine House, an old hunting lodge (which burned down in 2015) that had once been owned by one of the key players in the world of secret societies. We're talking about none other than Aleister Crowley (1875–1947), the famed English occultist and author.

While walking around a centuries-old cemetery near Boleskine House, they came across a strangely decorated piece of cloth—a tapestry, one might say. It was roughly four feet by five feet and was wrapped around a large sea-snail shell. It was covered in artwork of snakes and words that were soon shown to have been written in Turkish. One of the words translated as "serpent," which might have been an apt description for the beast of Loch Ness. Notably, Turkey has its own lake monster, which is said to dwell in the waters of Lake Van. But there was more to come: the tapestry found by the three students was adorned with images of lotus flowers. In ancient Chinese folklore, dragons had a particular taste for lotus flowers, and in lakes where dragons were said to reside, the people of China would leave such flowers on the shores as a means to appease the violent beasts.

Of the several other people who had the opportunity to see and examine the tapestry in June 1969 in the hours after it was found, one was an avid Nessie seeker named Frederick "Ted" Holiday. He couldn't fail to make a connection between the Loch Ness Monster and the dragon- and serpent-based imagery. On top of that, the matter of the lotus flowers led Holiday to conclude that this was evidence of some kind of clandestine "dragon cult" operating in the area. Holiday knew that Aleister Crowley was linked to all manner of secret societies, which provided another reason for Holiday to suspect the presence of a dragon cult in the area. As he began to dig even further into the story, Holiday uncovered rumors of alleged human sacrifice in the wooded areas surrounding Loch Ness as well as attempts by the secret group to "invoke" supernatural serpents from the dark waters of the loch.

In Chinese mythology, the dragon is often associated with the lotus flower (as well as chrysanthemums). Finding such imagery on a tapestry fragment near Loch Ness led Frederick Holiday into thinking there was a dragon cult associated with the lake monster.

The mysterious group in question, Holiday believed, was said to worship Tiamat, a terrifying Babylonian snake goddess or sea dragon who was revered as much as she was feared, chiefly because of her murderous ways. She mated with Abzu, the god of fresh water, to create a number of supernatural offspring, all of dragon- and serpent-like appearance. Among these were the dreaded Scorpion Men, hideous offspring of Tiamat that were, as their name suggests, a horrific combination of human and giant arachnid. So the legend goes, Abzu planned to secretly kill his children but was thwarted from doing so when they rose up and slayed him instead. Likewise, Tiamat was ultimately slaughtered— by the god of storms, the four-eyed giant known as Marduk.

Nonetheless, if one knew the ways of the ancients, one could still call upon the power and essence of the slain Tiamat as a means to achieve power, wealth, influence, and sex. Such rituals were definitively Faustian in nature, however, and the conjurer had to take great heed when summoning the spirit form of Tiamat, lest violent or even deadly forces be unleashed. It was highly possible, thought Holiday, that the monsters seen at Loch Ness were manifestations of Tiamat in some latter-day incarnation, having been specifically provoked to manifest by that aforementioned cult.

Nothing was ever conclusively proved, but the entire situation left a bad taste in Holiday's mouth, made him deeply worried for his own safety, and eventually convinced him that the legendary creature of Loch Ness was itself supernatural in nature.

Filey Brigg is a large, rocky peninsula that juts out from the coast of the Yorkshire, England, town of Filey. Local folklore suggests that the rocks are actually the remains of the bones of an ancient sea dragon. This is unlikely, to say the least, but the story may have at least a basis in reality. The story probably takes its inspiration from centuries-old sightings of giant monsters of the sea that called the crashing waters off Filey Brigg their home. One person who was able to attest to this was Wilkinson Herbert, a coast guard who, in February 1934, had a traumatic, terrifying encounter with just such a sea dragon at Filey Brigg. It was an appropriately dark, cloudy, and windy night when Herbert's life was turned upside down.

The first indication that something foul and supernatural was afoot came when Herbert heard the terrifying growling of what sounded like a dozen or more vicious hounds. The growling, however, was coming from something else entirely. As he looked out at the harsh, cold waves, Herbert saw, to his terror, a large beast, around thirty feet in length and equipped with a muscular, humped back and four legs that extended into flippers. For a heart-stopping instant, the bright, glowing eyes of the beast locked on to Herbert's eyes. Not surprisingly, he said, "It was a most gruesome and thrilling experience. I have seen big animals abroad but nothing like this."

Further up the same stretch of coastland is the county of Tyne and Wear. And in the vicinity of the county's South Shields is Marsden Bay, an area that is overflowing with rich tales of magic, mystery, witchcraft, and

Legend has it that Filey Brigg peninsula was formed from the bones of an ancient sea dragon.

supernatural, ghostly activity. Legend tells of a man named Jack Bates (aka "Jack the Blaster") who, with his wife, Jessie, moved to the area in 1782. Instead of setting up home in the village of Marsden, the Bates family decided to blast a sizeable amount of rock out of Marsden Bay and create for themselves a kind of grotto-style home.

It wasn't long before local smugglers saw Jack's cavelike environment as the ideal place to store their goods, which led Jack to become one of their number. It was a secret, working arrangement that existed until the year of Jack the Blaster's death in 1792. The caves were later extended to the point where they housed, rather astonishingly, a fifteen-room mansion. Today, the caves are home to the Marsden Grotto, one of the very few "cave pubs" in Europe.

Mike Hallowell is a local author and researcher who has uncovered evidence of a secret cult in the area that extends back centuries and engages in controversial and dangerous activities. It all began with the Viking invasion of the United Kingdom in the ninth century that brought with it the Vikings' beliefs in a violent, marauding sea monster known as the Shoney. Since the Shoney's hunting ground ranged from the coast of England to the waters of Scandinavia and the monster had a reputation for ferociousness, the Vikings did all they could to placate it. That primarily meant providing the beast with certain offerings—*human* offerings.

The process of deciding who would be the creature's victim was a grim one: the crews of the Viking ships would draw straws, and whoever drew the shortest straw would be doomed to a terrible fate. He would first be bound by hand and foot. Then, unable to move, he would have his throat violently slashed. After this, the body of the unfortunate soul would be tossed into the churning waters in the hope that the Shoney would be satisfied and refrain from attacking the Vikings' longships, as they were known. Sometimes, the bodies were never seen again. On other occasions, they washed up on the shore of Marsden, hideously mutilated and savagely torn to pieces.

Hallowell dug deeper into the enigma of Marsden's dragon cult and even contacted local police authorities to try to determine the truth of the matter—and of the murders.

Incredibly, this was not a practice strictly limited to the long-gone times when the Vikings roamed and pillaged. Mike Hallowell was able to determine that belief in the Shoney never actually died out. As a result, the last such sacrifice was rumored to have occurred in 1928. Hallowell's sources also told him that the grotto's caves regularly, and secretly, acted as morgues for the bodies of the dead that the Shoney tossed back onto the beach after each sacrifice.

The story becomes even more disturbing. As a dedicated researcher of the unknown, Hallowell dug deeper into the enigma of Marsden's dragon cult and even contacted local police authorities to try to determine the truth of the matter—and of the murders. It was at the height of his research that Hallowell received a number of anonymous phone calls, sternly and darkly warning him to keep away from Marsden and its tale of a "serpent sacrifice cult" and verbally threatening him as to what might happen if he didn't. To his credit, Hallowell pushed on, undeterred by the threats. And, although much of the data is circumstantial, Hallowell has made a strong case that such a cult continues its dark activities both in the Marsden area and possibly in other parts of the United Kingdom, too.

A BASILISK IN AFRICA

Anomalies researcher and writer Mike Dash pointed out on *Smithsonian* magazine's website on July 23, 2012: "Few creatures have struck more terror into more hearts for longer than the basilisk, a monster feared for centuries throughout Europe and North Africa. Like many ancient marvels, it was a bizarre hybrid: a crested snake that hatched from an egg laid by a rooster and incubated by a toad."

Tales of the basilisk really came to the fore in 79 C.E. in the pages of Pliny the Elder's *Natural History*. It states of the beast:

> It is produced in the province of Cyrene, being not more than twelve fingers in length. It has a white spot on the head, strongly resembling a sort of a diadem. When it hisses, all the other serpents fly from it: and it does not advance its body, like the others, by a succession of folds, but moves along upright and erect upon the middle. It destroys all shrubs, not only by its contact, but those even that it has breathed upon; it burns up all the grass, too, and breaks the stones, so tremendous is its noxious influence. It was formerly a general belief that if a man on horseback killed one of these animals with a spear, the poison would run up the weapon and kill, not only the rider, but the horse, as well. To this dreadful monster the effluvium of the weasel is fatal, a thing that has been tried with success, for kings have often desired to see its body when killed; so true is it that it has pleased Nature that there should be nothing without its antidote. The animal is thrown into the hole of the basilisk, which is easily known from the soil around it being infected. The weasel destroys the basilisk by its odor, but dies itself in this struggle of nature against its own self.

None other than Renaissance poly-math Leonardo da Vinci told a very similar story. He said that the monster "is found in the province of Cyrenaica and is not more than 12 fingers long. It has on its head a white spot after the fashion of a diadem. It scares all serpents with its whistling. It resembles a snake, but does not move by wriggling but from the center forwards to

In mythology, the horrifyingly ugly basilisk has taken a number of bizarre forms. This illustration is from a 1544 Swiss manuscript.

the right. It is said that one of these, being killed with a spear by one who was on horse-back, and its venom flowing on the spear, not only the man but the horse also died. It spoils the wheat and not only that which it touches, but where it breathes the grass dries and the stones are split."

Without doubt, the most notable account of the basilisk comes from the Polish city of Warsaw and dates from 1587. Midori Snyder, a novelist and student of mythology, says of this case that it revolved around "a terrifying encounter and eventual capture of a basilisk hiding in the cellar of a house who is suspected of bringing the plague." So the old story went:

> The 5-year-old daughter of a knife-smith named Machaeropaeus had disappeared in a mysterious way, together with another little girl. The wife of Machaeropaeus went looking for them, along with the nursemaid. When the nursemaid looked into the under-ground cellar of a house that had fallen into ruins 30 years earli-er, she observed the children lying motionless down there, without responding to the shouting of the two women. When the maid was too hoarse to shout anymore, she courageously went down the stairs to find out what had happened to the chil-dren. Before the eyes of her mistress, she sank to the floor beside them, and did not move. The wife of Machaeropaeus wisely did not follow her into the cellar, but ran back to spread the word about this strange and mysterious business. The rumor spread like wildfire throughout Warsaw. Many people thought the air felt unusually thick to breathe and suspected that a basilisk was hiding in the cellar.

HUMANOIDS OF THE WATER

You may wonder why this particular section of the book is devoted to the likes of Bigfoot, werewolf-type animals, humanoid frogs, and huge snakes. The answer is an intriguing one: they all have a profound affinity to water. Although deep waters are certainly not their constant realms of existence, they have all exhibited an astonishing ability to skillfully negotiate the waters of our world. For that reason alone, it's important we address this fascinating—and little-known—aspect of certain amazing monsters. Sasquatch: a skilled swimmer of lakes and rivers? Yes!

MERMAIDS AND MERMEN

The term "mermaid" is derived from two words. The first, "mere," is a Middle English word that translates as "sea." The second, "maid," refers to a girl or a woman. Ancient tales tell of mermaids who would sing in an enchanting and hypnotizing style while beckoning sailors to join them in the deep waters. The purpose was not quite as inviting as it might have seemed. In fact, the purpose was downright ruthless: to distract sailors from their work and cause their ships to run disastrously aground. It was death that the mermaids had on their minds. Other ancient tales tell of mermaids inadvertently squeezing the last breaths out of drowning men while attempting to rescue them. They are also said to particularly enjoy taking humans to their underwater lairs. In Hans Christian Andersen's story "The Little Mermaid," for example, it is said that mermaids often forget that humans cannot breathe underwater, while other legends suggest the sinister she-creatures deliberately drown men out of sheer venomous spite. They were, then, creatures perceived as sometimes friendly and other times downright deadly.

The fabled Sirens of Greek mythology are sometimes portrayed in folklore as being mermaid-like in nature and appearance. Related types of legendary creatures that fall into this category include water nymphs and selkies, animals that can allegedly transform themselves from seals into human beings and vice versa. Mermaids were noted in British folklore as being distinctly unlucky omens, occasionally foretelling disaster and sometimes even maliciously provoking it. As evidence of this, several variations on the ballad "Sir Patrick Spens" depict a mermaid speaking to the doomed ships. In some, she tells the crews they will never see land again, and in others, she claims they are near the shore, which the men are astute enough to know means that deep, malevolent deception is at work. The ballad is of Scottish origin and may refer to an actual event: namely, the bringing home of the Scottish queen, Margaret, Maid of Norway, across the North Sea in 1290. There is, however, some speculation that the ballad may actually relate to a voyage by the princess's mother, known as the Maid of Scotland, in 1281. Regardless of the specific

Mermaid myths date back to ancient Greek stories of the Sirens, who lured sailors to their deaths. While beautiful, mermaids were therefore feared for many centuries.

truth behind the ballad itself, its words are prime evidence of both the knowledge and the deep fear of mermaids that has existed in the British Isles for untold centuries.

One such account tells of a deadly mermaid inhabiting a small pool in the pleasant little village of Childs Ercall, England. In 1893, writer Robert Charles Hope quoted a local telling the notable story as follows in his book *The Legendary Lore of the Holy Wells of England*:

> There was a mermaid seen there once. It was a good while ago, before my time. I dare say it might be a hundred years ago. There were two men going to work early one morning, and they had got as far as the side of the pond in [a] field, and they saw something on the top of the water which scared them not a little. They thought it was going to take them straight off to the Old Lad himself! I can't say exactly what it was like, I wasn't there, you know; but it was a mermaid, the same as you read of in the papers.
>
> The fellows had almost run away at first, they were so frightened, but as soon as the mermaid had spoken to them, they thought no more of that. Her voice was so sweet and pleasant, that they fell in love with her there and then, both of them. Well, she told them there was a treasure hidden at the bottom of the pond— lumps of gold, and no one knows what. And she would give them as much as ever they liked if they would come to her in the water and take it out of her hands.
>
> So they went in, though it was almost up to their chins, and she dived into the water and brought up a lump of gold almost as big as a man s head. And the men were just going to take it, when one of them said: "Eh!" he said (and swore, you know), "if this isn't a bit of luck!" And, my word, if the mermaid didn't take it away from them again, and gave a scream, and dived down into the pond, and they saw no more of her, and got none of her gold. And nobody has ever seen her since then.

Commenting on the storyteller's tale, Hope added: "No doubt the story once ran that the oath which scared the uncanny creature involved the mention of the Holy Name."

Moving on, there is the story of Mermaid's Pool (also referred to as Blakemere Pool), which can be found at the Staffordshire, England, village of Thorncliffe on the Staffordshire Moorlands, which are dominated by forests, lakes, rolling hills, and crags. It's a story that dates back approximately one thousand years. Lisa Dowley is someone who has spent a great deal of time and effort pursuing the story and sorting fact from legend. She says:

The story transpires that this particular mermaid was once a maiden of fair beauty, and it came to pass—for reasons that are unclear—that she was persecuted, and accused of various crimes, by a gentleman named Joshua Linnet. It is not clear whether these accusations included being a witch, or whether he may have had his amorous advances rejected.

The said Mr. Linnet had this woman bound up and thrown into the bottomless Blakemere Pool. As she fought for her breath and life, the woman screamed vengeance on her accuser, Joshua Linnet, and that her spirit would haunt the pool from that moment hence, and swore that one day she would drag her accuser and executioner deep down beneath the dark depths of the Blakemere Pool to his own death.

Legend has it that one day many years ago, when the mere was being cleaned, a mermaid violently rose out of the water....

It is a recorded fact that three days later, Joshua Linnet was found face down, dead in the Blakemere Pool. When his body was dragged out and turned over by the locals, to their horror, what greeted them was that what was once his face, but was now nothing more than tattered shreds of skin, the injuries seemingly caused by sharp claws or talons.

Moving on, situated barely a stone's throw from the Shropshire, England, town of Newport and just over the border from rural Staffordshire, Aqualate Mere—at 1.5 kilometers long and 0.5 kilometers wide—is the largest natural lake in the Midlands, yet it is very shallow, extending down to little more than a uniform three feet. Legend has it that one day many years ago, when the mere was being cleaned, a mermaid violently rose out of the water—quite naturally scaring the living daylights out of the workmen—while simultaneously making shrieking, disturbing, and damning threats to utterly destroy the town of Newport if any attempt was ever made to empty Aqualate Mere of its precious waters. Very wisely, perhaps, the lake was not—and, to date, never has been—drained.

Sea serpent authority Henry Lee spoke of mermaids, too. One story in particular stood out for Lee, and in his 1883 work *Sea Fables Explained*, he recounted:

In the year 1797, Mr. Munro, schoolmaster of Thurso, affirmed that he had seen "a figure like a naked female, sitting on a rock projecting into the sea, at Sandside Head, in the parish of Reay. Its head was covered with long, thick, light-brown hair, flowing down on the shoulders. The forehead was round, the face plump, and the cheeks ruddy. The mouth and lips resembled those of a human being, and the eyes were blue. The arms, fingers, breast, and abdomen were as large as those of a full-grown female," and, altogether,

"That sea-nymph's form of pearly light,
Was whiter than the downy spray,
And round her bosom, heaving bright,
Her glossy yellow ringlets play."

"This creature," Mr. Munro himself said, "was apparently in the act of combing its hair with its fingers, which seemed to afford it pleasure, and it remained thus occupied during some minutes, when it dropped into the sea." The Dominie …

… saw the maiden there,
Just as the daylight faded,
Braiding her locks of gowden hair,
An' singing as she braided …

But he did not remark whether the fingers were webbed. On the whole, he infers that this was a marine animal of which he had a distinct and satisfactory view, and that the portion seen by him bore a narrow resemblance to the human form. But for the dangerous situation it had chosen, and its appearance among the waves, he would have supposed it to be a woman. Twelve years later, several persons observed near the same spot an animal which they also supposed to be a mermaid.

Again, Lee recounted the tale:

A very remarkable story of this kind is one related by Dr. Robert Hamilton … from his personal knowledge of some of the persons connected with the occurrence. In 1823 it was reported that some fishermen of Yell, one of the Shetland group, had captured a mermaid by its being entangled in their lines. The statement was that "the animal was about three feet long, the upper part of the body resembling the human, with protuberant mammae, like a woman; the face, forehead, and neck were short, and resembled those of a monkey; the arms, which were small, were kept folded across the breast; the fingers were distinct, not webbed; a few stiff, long bristles were on the top of the head, extending down to the shoulders, and these it could erect and depress at pleasure, something like a crest. The inferior part of the body was like a fish. The skin was smooth, and of a grey color. It offered no resistance, nor attempted to bite, but uttered a low, plaintive sound. The crew, six in number, took it within their boat, but, superstition getting the better of curiosity, they carefully disentangled it from the lines and a hook which had accidentally become fastened in its body, and returned it to its native element. It instantly dived, descending in a perpendicular direction."

Mr. Edmonston, the original narrator of this incident, was "a well-known and intelligent observer," says Dr. Hamilton, and in a communication made by him to the Professor of Natural History in the Edinburgh University gave the following additional particulars, which he had learned from the skipper and one of the crew of the boat: "They had the animal for three hours within the boat: the body was without scales or hair; it was of a silvery grey color above, and white below; it was like the human skin; no gills were observed, nor fins on the back or belly. The tail was like that of a dog-fish; the mammae were about as large as those of a woman; the mouth and lips were very distinct, and resembled the human. Not one of the six men dreamed of a doubt of its being a mermaid, and it could not be suggested that they were influenced by their fears, for the mermaid is not an object of terror to fishermen: it is rather a welcome guest, and danger is apprehended from its experiencing bad treatment."

Mr. Edmonston concludes by saying that "The usual resources of skepticism that the seals and other sea-animals appearing under certain circumstances, operating upon an excited imagination, and so producing ocular illusion, cannot avail here. It is quite impossible that six Shetland fishermen could commit such a mistake."

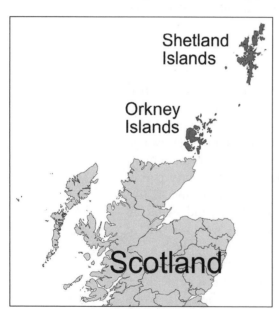

Only 158 miles apart, the Shetland Islands and Orkney Islands are located north of Scotland. The area has been known for sightings of unusual ocean creatures.

It's interesting to note that the Shetland Isles are only 158 miles from the Orkney Islands, where a strange affair was reported in the 1800s. It suggests nothing less than the ongoing presence of unusual and unidentified animals in the area. It dates from 1808 and the island of Stronsa, according to Lee, who writes:

According to the narrative, it was first seen entire, and measured by respectable individuals. It measured fifty-six feet in length, and twelve in circumference. The head was small, not being a foot long from the snout to the first vertebra; the neck was slender, extending to the length of fifteen feet. All the witnesses agree in assigning it blow-holes, though they differ as to the precise situation. On the shoulders something like a bristly mane commenced which extended to near the extremity of the tail. It had three pairs of fins or paws connected with the body; the anterior were the largest, measuring more than four feet in length, and their extremities were something like toes partially webbed. The skin was smooth and of a greyish colour; the eye was of the size of a seal's. When the decaying carcass was broken up by the waves, portions of it were secured (such as the skull, the upper bones of the swimming paws, &c.) by Mr. Laing, a neighbouring proprietor, and some of the vertebrae were preserved and deposited in the Royal University Museum, Edinburgh, and in the Museum of the Royal College of Surgeons, London. "An able paper," says Dr. Robert Hamilton, in his account of it, "on these latter fragments and on the wreck of the animal was read by the late Dr. Barclay to the Wernerian Society, and will be found in Vol. I. of its *Transactions*, to which we refer. We have supplied a wood-cut of the sketch … which was taken at the time, and which, from the many affidavits proffered by respectable individuals, as well as from other circumstances narrated, leaves no manner of doubt as to the existence of some such animal."

Now let us take a look at the male equivalents of mermaids: mermen. George Brisbane Scott Douglas (1856–1935) was the author of such acclaimed books as *Scottish Fairy and Folk Tales* and *New Border Tales*. He had a fascination for mysteries of the oceans, particularly so mermaids and the far-less-mentioned mer*men*. He said of mermen and mermaids that there were many strange tales of the creatures emanating from Scotland's Shetland Isles. "Beneath the depths of the ocean, according to these stories," Douglas wrote in *Scottish Fairy and Folk Tales*, an atmosphere exists adapted to the respiratory organs of certain beings, resembling in form the human race, possessed of surpassing beauty, of limited supernatural powers, and liable to the incident of death. They dwell in a wide territory of the globe, far below the region of fishes, over which the sea, like the cloudy canopy of our sky, loftily rolls, and they possess habitations constructed of the pearl and coral productions of the ocean. Having lungs not adapted to a watery medium but to the nature of atmospheric air, it would be impossible for them to pass through the volume of waters that intervenes between the submarine and supramarine world if it were not for the extraordinary power they inherit of entering the skin of some animal capable of existing in the sea, which they are enabled to occupy by a sort of demoniacal possession.

Douglas noted something that most people—having only a cursory knowledge of the merman/mermaid phenomenon—would likely be completely unware of. He acknowledged that although most people viewed such creatures as "of an animal human above the waist yet terminating below in the tail and fins of a fish," that was far from always being the case. He explained that the "most favorite form" was actually that of the "larger seal."

"Possessing an amphibious nature," he explained, "they are enabled not only to exist in the ocean, but to land on some rock, where they frequently lighten themselves of their sea-dress, resume their proper shape, and with much curiosity examine the nature of the upper world belonging to the human race. Unfortunately, however, each merman or merwoman possesses but one skin, enabling the individual to ascend the seas, and if, on visiting the abode of man, the garb be lost, the hapless being must unavoidably become an inhabitant of the earth."

Douglas was not only deeply familiar with mermen lore but collected a number of fascinating accounts of encounters with what appear to have been—rather incredibly—real half-man, half-fish-like entities. As one example of many, we have the following from Douglas, from the same book:

A story is told of a boat's crew who landed for the purpose of attacking the seals lying in the hollows of the crags at one of the stacks. The men stunned a number of the animals, and while they were in this state stripped them of their skins, with the fat attached to them. Leaving the carcases on the rock, the crew were about to set off for the shore of Papa Stour, when such a tremendous swell arose that every one flew quickly to the boat. All succeeded in entering it except one man, who had imprudently lingered behind. The crew were unwilling to leave a companion to perish on the skerries, but the surge increased so fast that after many unsuccessful attempts to bring the boat close in to the stack the unfortunate wright was left to his fate.

This statue on the coast of the Faroe Islands depicts a selkie, a being who can take the form of a seal. In some tales, they return to human form by taking off their seal skin as if it were a robe.

Douglas continued, detailing how things quickly developed in a strange and unforeseen fashion:

A stormy night came on, and the deserted Shetlander saw no prospect before him but that of perishing from cold and hunger, or of being washed into the sea by the breakers which threatened to dash over the rocks. At length he perceived many of the seals, who in their flight had escaped the attack of the boatmen, approach the skerry, disrobe themselves of their amphibious hides, and resume the shape of the sons and daughters of the ocean. Their first object was to assist in the recovery of their friends, who, having been stunned by clubs, had, while in that state, been deprived of their skins.

When the flayed animals had regained their sensibility, they assumed their proper form of mermen or merwomen, and began to lament in a mournful lay, wildly accompanied by the storm that was raging around, the loss of their sea-dress, which would prevent them from again enjoying their native azure atmosphere and coral mansions that lay below the deep waters of the Atlantic.

The chief lamentation of the mermen, said Douglas, was for one Ollavitinus, the son of Gioga, who,

having been stripped of his seal's skin, would be forever parted from his mates, and condemned to become an outcast inhabitant of the upper world. Their song was at length broken off by observing one of their enemies viewing, with shivering limbs and looks of comfortless despair, the wild waves that dashed over the stack. Gioga immediately conceived the idea of rendering subservient to the advantage of her son the perilous situation of the man. She addressed him with mildness, proposing to carry him safe on her back across the sea to Papa Stour, on condition of receiving the seal-skin of Ollavitinus.

A bargain was struck, added Douglas, and

Gioga clad herself in her amphibious garb; but the Shetlander, alarmed at the sight of the stormy main that he was to ride through, prudently begged leave of the matron, for his better preservation, that he might be allowed to cut a few holes in her shoulders and flanks, in order to procure, between the skin and the flesh, a better fastening for his hands and feet. The request being complied with, the man grasped the neck of the seal, and committing himself to her care, she landed him safely at Acres Gio in Papa Stour; from which place he immediately repaired to a skeo at Hamna Voe, where the skin was deposited, and honorably fulfilled his part of the contract by affording Gioga the means whereby her son could again revisit the ethereal space over which the sea spread its green mantle.

Finally, it is worth noting that the National Oceanic and Atmospheric Administration (NOAA) has felt the need to highlight tales of mermaids on its website—a site that is run by the U.S. government. Precisely why NOAA

You might be a little surprised to find stories about mermaids on the government site run by NOAA.

chose to address this controversial issue remains unknown. Maybe they know more than the rest of us do. NOAA tells us the following:

Mermaids—those half-human, half-fish sirens of the sea—are legendary sea creatures chronicled in maritime cultures since time immemorial. The ancient Greek epic poet Homer wrote of them in *The Odyssey*. In the ancient Far East, mermaids were the wives of powerful sea-dragons, and served as trusted messengers between their spouses and the emperors on land. The aboriginal people of Australia call mermaids *yawkyawks*—a name that may refer to their mesmerizing songs.

The belief in mermaids may have arisen at the very dawn of our species. Magical female figures first appear in cave paintings in the late Paleolithic (Stone Age) period some 30,000 years ago, when modern humans gained dominion over the land and, presumably, began to sail the seas. Half-human creatures, called chimeras, also abound in mythology—in addition to mermaids, there were wise centaurs, wild satyrs, and frightful minotaurs, to name but a few. But are mermaids real? No evidence of aquatic humanoids has ever been found. Why, then, do they occupy the collective unconscious of nearly all seafaring peoples? That's a question best left to historians, philosophers, and anthropologists.

And a question for seekers of monsters of the deep.

FREAKY FROG PEOPLE

One of the most bizarre of all encounters with strange and unknown animals occurred at Juminda Peninsula, Estonia, at some point in the late 1930s; the exact date is unclear. According to an investigation undertaken by acclaimed UFO expert Dr. Jacques Vallee, two witnesses encountered a small, humanoid creature, about three feet tall, with brown-green skin and distinct, froglike characteristics. Its eyes and mouth resembled slits, and it appeared to be not at all accustomed to walking on land; its awkward gait made that abundantly clear, particularly so when it caught sight of the pair and made good its escape. While it outran its pursuers, it did so in a very odd, near-drunk manner.

A similar affair occurred in the heart of woodland at Orland Park, Illinois, on September 24, 1951. The man who witnessed something both remarkable and disturbing was a steelworker named Harrison Bailey. As he walked through the park, Bailey was suddenly plagued by a burning sensation on his neck, which was accompanied by a sense of cramp in his neck, too. Sensing he was being watched, Bailey quickly swung around. He found himself confronted by a gray object of a large size he described as shaped like a "whirlwind."

Things then became decidedly weird: Bailey felt groggy and confused, almost as if he were in a dreamlike state. And then, nothing. His next memory was vague but revolved around being surrounded by a large group of eighteen-inch-high humanoids that resembled frogs. They asked bizarre questions such as where he was from and where he was going. All that Bailey could focus on was the fact that he felt somewhat paralyzed and unable to move properly. The unsettling feeling soon wore off, however, and Bailey was left to make his stumbling, slightly out-of-it way back home.

Despite having come out of the odd encounter unscathed, Bailey had a nagging feeling that there was more to the experience than he could consciously recall. Finally, he elected to do something about it and underwent regressive hypnosis. It proved to be beneficial, although it is quite another matter whether Bailey was pleased or relieved by what he learned after being placed in this altered state of mind.

In his hypnotic state, Bailey found himself back in the park, surrounded by those odd, diminutive things. He was able to build a much clearer image: the frogmen had slits for mouths; large, staring eyes; stripy, brown skin; and just three toes. All around the creatures were dozens of smaller, buglike things that raced wildly around the woodland floor. There then followed an amazing situation in which Bailey found himself in telepathic conversation with the frogmen, who informed him that humankind's warlike ways would be its downfall—and that they wanted Bailey to spread their warning. Bailey then found himself back in the woods and on a path back home.

Jacques Vallee—who is pictured here at right with fellow ufologist Dr. Allen Hynek—was known primarily for his UFO research. However, he did record some unusual stories about diminuitive, froglike people.

In many respects, Harrison Bailey's encounter sounds like a classic example of what has infamously become known as "alien abduction," except for one thing: the creatures that Bailey met with sound far more cryptozoological in nature than they do ufological.

Loveland is a city in southwestern Ohio that has a population of around twelve thousand. It was settled back in 1795. It's a small, picturesque town, filled with mountains of history, old buildings, and resident frog people. Yes, you did read that right. The controversy began in the summer of 1955—specifically in the month of July. It was around four o'clock in the morning, and all was black and shadowy. Robert Hunnicutt, a volunteer with the local Civil Defense unit, was driving on a road on the fringes of Loveland when he spotted something amazing and terrifying in equal measures: three or four (Hunnicutt wasn't sure) small, humanoid creatures standing under a bridge. Incredibly, they were described as being around three feet tall, walking on two legs, and with "lopsided chests, wide, lipless, froglike mouths, and wrinkles rather than hair."

A shocked Hunnicutt stopped and stared at the beasts for a few minutes, after which one of the frog things pointed a device—a weapon, or something else, Hunnicutt never knew—into the air, which gave off electric-blue flashes. Hunnicutt, at that point, wasted no time in getting out of the area as soon as possible. His destination: the headquarters of the Loveland Police, where he spoke to the chief of police, John Fritz. Evidently, the strange story was taken seriously, as Fritz had one of his armed deputies keep a vigil at the bridge to try to ascertain what Hunnicutt had seen.

Interestingly, Leonard Stringfield, a noted UFO researcher in Ohio at the time, looked into the affair. He uncovered something intriguing: "Despite my special affiliations with the Ground Observer Corps and the Air Defense Command, I was unable to get any details of official action from the Loveland Civil Defense Authority, from Frank Whitecotton, Coordinator for the Hamilton County GOC, or from the Loveland Chief of Police, John Fritz. However, I was able to learn from a member of the Loveland School Board that the incident had been investigated by the FBI."

The odd encounter was big news for a while but ultimately faded into obscurity; that is, until 1972, when a new report surfaced that, for the city's old-timers, instantly brought back memories of Robert Hunnicutt's face-to-face standoff with a group of monsters all those years earlier.

Mirroring the Hunnicutt affair, the area was in darkness when Ray Shockey's sighting took place. What is particularly notable is the fact that Shockey was a Loveland police officer on patrol at the time near the Little Miami River. As he drove past the river, Shockey spied what he at first believed was a dog, sitting at the side of the road. Given that it was a freezing, wintry, icy night, Shockey slowed down to see if the dog was okay. It quickly became apparent that the "dog" was something else entirely.

As Shockey's cruiser closed in, the four-foot-tall animal leapt up onto its hind limbs and stared directly at Shockey. This allowed the officer to see its strange, frog-like appearance. For a few minutes, the frogman and the officer stared at each other, after which the creature leapt over the guardrail and vanished into the heart of the shadowy river. Shockey raced back to headquarters and quickly prepared a report on his astonishing sighting, such was his conviction he had seen something truly out of this world. In the wake of the Shockey sighting, other accounts surfaced, all of a "frog-" or "lizard-like" nature.

Whatever the true nature of the frog people of Loveland, Ohio, their origins remain, even today, the mystery they were all those years ago, when the lives of two terrified men were forever changed.

> As Shockey's cruiser closed in, the four-foot-tall animal leapt up onto its hind limbs and stared directly at Shockey. This allowed the officer to see its strange, froglike appearance.

Finally, there is a very strange story of a giant, froglike animal that comes from none other than Loch Ness, Scotland! In the year 1880, one of the most spectacular and nerve-jangling of all Nessie encounters took place. The unlucky eyewitness—and that really is the only way we can describe him—was a man named Duncan MacDonald. It was his task to take a dip into Loch Ness at Johnnies Point and examine a ship that had sunk at the entrance to the Caledonian Canal at Fort Augustus. But MacDonald was confronted by something far stranger than a sunken ship. After being lowered to a depth of around thirty feet, he suddenly raced for the surface, practically screaming to his friends to haul him aboard the vessel.

It was several days before MacDonald could bring himself to confide in the rest of the crew what he had seen. It was nothing less than a froglike creature, around the size of a fully grown goat, perched on a rock shelf. The beady-eyed monster and the terrified diver locked eyes until MacDonald, having been momentarily paralyzed with fear, managed to swim for safety and reached the surface. Thankfully, the monster-sized frog—or whatever it was—did not pursue him. We'll return to other matters surrounding the legends of Loch Ness in later chapters.

A WOLFMAN OF THE WATERS

While the heading of this chapter may surprise you, it's a fact that within Scottish lore and legend, there are tales of what we can call wolfmen but the Scots call wulvers, which spend much of their time in deep waters. Krystin

Scott says of these often water-based wolfmen: "Wulvers are fond of fishing and are sometimes called the Fishing Werewolf. They can create fishing supplies out of resources that surround them, either stealing or making them by hand. They are frequently spotted fishing for their daily meal of Sillaks and Piltaks while perched upon a small rock known as a Wulver's Stane, which is located in a deepwater loch. Wulvers are patient creatures and can spend hours upon hours catching fish. Wulvers are also powerful swimmers and use their speed to catch fast-moving fish in the rivers and small lochs nearby."

In her 1933 book *Shetland Traditional Lore*, noted folklorist Jessie Margaret Saxby wrote: "The Wulver was a creature like a man with a wolf's head. He had short brown hair all over him. His home was a cave dug out of the side of a steep knowe, half-way up a hill. He didn't molest folk if folk didn't molest him. He was fond of fishing and had a small rock in the deep water which is known to this day as the 'Wulver's Stane.' There he would sit fishing sillaks and piltaks for hour after hour. He was reported to have frequently left a few fish on the windowsill of some poor body."

Unlike the traditional werewolf, the wulver was not a shapeshifter. Its semihuman, semiwolf appearance was natural and unchanging. One of the most fascinating, and certainly disturbing, accounts of a wulver came from Elliott O'Donnell. Shortly after the start of the twentieth century, O'Donnell interviewed a man named Andrew Warren, who told a startling story. O'Donnell carefully recorded every word that Warren had to say, as follows:

A wulver is not a werewolf but, rather, a half-man/half-wolf creature that does not shapeshift and spends much of its time in the water.

I was about fifteen years of age at the time and had for several years been residing with my grandfather, who was an elder in the Kirk [Church] of Scotland. He was much interested in geology, and literally filled the house with fossils from the pits and caves round where we dwelt. One morning he came home in a great state of excitement, and made me go with him to look at some ancient remains he had found at the bottom of a dried-up tarn [lake].

"Look!" he cried, bending down and pointing at them, "here is a human skeleton with a wolf's head. What do you make of it?" I told him I did not know, but supposed it must be some kind of monstrosity. "It's a werewolf," he rejoined, "that's what it is. A werewolf! This island was once overrun with satyrs and werewolves! Help me carry it to the house."

I did as he bid me, and we placed it on the table in the back kitchen. That evening I was left alone in the house, my grandfather and the other members of the household having gone to the kirk. For some time I amused myself reading, and then, fancying I heard a noise in the back premises, I went into the kitchen. There was no one about, and becoming convinced that it could only have been a rat that had disturbed me, I sat on the table alongside the alleged remains of the werewolf, and waited to see if the noises would recommence.

I was thus waiting in a listless sort of way, my back bent, my elbows on my knees, looking at the floor and thinking of nothing in particular, when there came a loud rat, tat, tat of knuckles on the window-pane. I immediately turned in the direction of the noise and encountered, to my alarm, a dark face looking in at me. At first dim and indistinct, it became more and more complete, until it developed into a very perfectly defined head of a wolf terminating in the neck of a human being.

Though greatly shocked, my first act was to look in every direction for a possible reflection—but in vain. There was no light either without or within, other than that from the setting sun— nothing that could in any way have produced an illusion. I looked at the face and marked each feature intently. It was unmistakably a wolf's face, the jaws slightly distended; the lips wreathed in a savage snarl; the teeth sharp and white; the eyes light green; the ears pointed. The expression of the face was diabolically malignant, and as it gazed straight at me my horror was as intense as my wonder. This it seemed to notice, for a look of savage exultation crept into its eyes, and it raised one hand—a slender hand, like that of a woman, though with prodigiously long and curved finger-nails—menacingly, as if about to dash in the window-pane.

Remembering what my grandfather had told me about evil spirits, I crossed myself; but as this had no effect, and I really feared the thing would get at me, I ran out of the kitchen and shut and locked the door, remaining in the hall till the family returned. My grandfather was much upset when I told him what had happened, and attributed my failure to make the spirit depart to my want of faith. Had he been there, he assured me, he would soon have got rid of it; but he nevertheless made me help him remove the bones from the kitchen, and we reinterred them in the very spot where we had found them, and where, for aught I know to the contrary, they still lie.

Dr. Karl Shuker, who has made a careful study of this particular case, says:

Quite aside from its highly sensational storyline, it is rather difficult to take seriously any account featuring someone (Warren's grandfather) who seriously believed that the Hebrides were "... once overrun with satyrs and werewolves"! By comparison, and despite his youthful age, Warren's own assumption that the skeleton was that of a deformed human would seem eminently more sensible—at least until the remainder of his account is read. Notwithstanding Warren's claim that his account was factual, however, the arrival of what was presumably another of the deceased wolf-headed entity's kind, seeking the return of the skeleton to its original resting place, draws upon a common theme in traditional folklore and legend.

THE DIDI

In 2007, cryptozoologist Richard Freeman traveled with a team of monster hunters to the country of Guyana at the northern coast of South America. Freeman and his crew were there to investigate reports of a Bigfoot-type creature known by locals as the Didi: a tall, hair-covered hominid that is much feared by those who live in the parts of Guyana where the animal-man lives. After the expedition was completed, I spoke with Freeman about his trek to South America. It turns out that Freeman uncovered accounts of not just the Didi but of several unknown water-based animals. Freeman told me:

In terms of the heat, it was the most difficult expedition I've ever been on. The temperature was well over one hundred degrees. And as we were mainly in the savannah, there was no shade at all. I actually got sunstroke once and passed out. It's difficult to describe how hot it really was; but at one point I couldn't take it anymore and I waded into a swamp full of mosquitoes and hid under a tree, just to get out the heat and sun. But in terms of what we uncovered, it was worth the heatstroke, the broken thumbs, and the infected feet that some of us got.

I asked him what sorts of evidence and accounts he uncovered, and an enthused and energized Freeman replied: "Well, we had gone out there with the intention of looking for the Didi that we were told lived in the savannah and the mountains of Guyana. And we were lucky enough to uncover information on them—and other stories on different creatures we didn't even know about. We'd heard in advance about giant snakes, giant ground sloths, and a couple of other things. But we were surprised and pleased to get much more, too."

Freeman continued: "One of the most interesting people we spoke with was a guy named Ernest. He was a former chief but had retired to run a fish farm. He had seen a weird creature that everyone who lived in the villages in the savannah called the 'red-faced pygmies.' Wherever we went, we heard stories about these creatures, and we met lots of witnesses to them, too. They all said the pygmies were about three to three and a half feet tall and had red faces. Ernest had met one when he was nineteen in the savannah, and it had grabbed his tobacco off him!"

There was far more to come, as Freeman made abundantly clear to me:

There are several pygmy tribes in African nations such as the Congo, Uganda, and Rwanda. This photo was taken in 1921 with a British visitor to demonstrate the short stature of the pygmy people.

> Another man, Kennard, said there was one these pygmies that haunted a certain stretch of the Savannah, and it would jump out and scare people—although, apparently, it never actually hurt anyone. They were described as having a weird grin on their faces; they walk erect and have brown skin, rather than fur. All the people we spoke with were adamant they were some type of small human, rather than an animal. Our guide, Damon Corrie, saw one once. He said he was in a tent one night and woke up to see one of these things looking down at him. And there are still sightings to this day in the savannah. I'd say they are probably a very primitive and very ancient tribe.

I then changed the direction: "What about the giant anacondas?"

Freeman had a fascinating reply:

> Well, Ernest had seen a very big anaconda about ten years ago, and that was around thirty feet long. This was actually the skin

of the snake, and apparently it had been shot by a British chap. From what we were told, if the story is true, then the snake was clearly transported back to England illegally. We were also told of huge anacondas, more than forty feet long, that were said to live in the caves at a place called Corona Falls and swam in the waters. The problem for us was that this was seventy miles or more from where we were; and with the savage heat and the river water being too low to travel by boat, this was one area we weren't able to get to in person.

Freeman told me of yet another strange animal that lived almost exclusively in the waters of the area:

This thing is called the Water Tiger. We spoke with several witnesses about this. One was an old man called Joseph who had seen a skin of the thing after it had been killed by hunters at some time in the 1970s. He said it was definitely a mammal and about ten feet long. It was white with black spots, and had a head still attached that was kind of like a tiger's head. He also said something very interesting: that the creature hunts in packs.

Someone else, a guy named Elmo, told us a similar story: that there is a "master water tiger," as he calls it. It sends the young ones out to hunt in the waters. Elmo is adamant they're not jaguars or giant otters, but are something very different. I wondered if it might be some sort of mustelid, but much, much bigger than known ones. And it's very aggressive, too. Ernest told us he was on a boat with his uncle once when something grabbed the boat, shook it violently, and they had to hang onto the overhanging tree branches to avoid getting thrown into the water. Ernest's uncle said it was a water tiger.

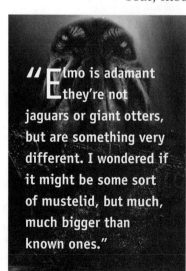

"Elmo is adamant they're not jaguars or giant otters, but are something very different. I wondered if it might be some sort of mustelid, but much, much bigger than known ones."

"And what about this hairy man-thing: the Didi?" I wanted to know.

Freeman had answers:

Well, before we went out there, we heard about this thing called the Didi, which was described as being enormous, covered in hair, and having large claws. This made me think it could actually have been some sort of surviving giant sloth. But when we got out there, everyone was adamant that the Didi is some sort of man, but covered in hair, and very similar to the Yeti or the Sasquatch. One story told to us dated from the 1940s, and was of a girl who got kidnapped by a Didi, lived with it, and apparently even had a half-breed child with it. Now, if that's true, that would imply the Didi is a hominid rather than an ape. The story was she eventually escaped on a hunter's canoe, and when the male Didi saw her leave, he supposedly ripped the half-breed child to pieces in a rage. We heard a couple of stories like this—of the Didi supposedly kidnapping people. But, I do think it's possible that some of the Didi stories could well be mistaken sightings of giant sloths that have become confused with the real Didi. So, the legends and stories might be based on two real creatures, rather than just one.

Then it was time to return to the creatures of the waters. Freeman had plenty more to say:

We also heard tales of dragons living up in the mountains; and although we didn't find the dragons, we did find a cave in the mountains where a burial had taken place and where there were a number of human skulls in an old pot. There was also a story from the 1950s we investigated of a group of cowboys who had tethered their horses near a lake one night and woke up to hear this loud breathing and the sounds of something big moving from the water—rivers and lagoons—towards the horses. Of course, they shot in the direction of whatever it was, and quickly untied the horses and left. But this area had dragon legends attached to it, too. But I wonder if some of these dragon tales might actually be mistaken sightings and legends of giant anacondas.

Without doubt, Guyana is a veritable lost world!

Lindsay Selby, who has done some expertise work in the field of cryptozoology, has also reported on unidentified animals in South America. As reported on the blog *Still on the Track*, she says:

There have been reports since the 1800s of living dinosaurs in Bolivia and other South American countries. At the end of the 19th century *Scientific American* recorded the following remarkable events: "The Brazilian Minister at La Paz, Bolivia, had remitted to the Minister of Foreign Affairs in Rio photographs of drawings of an extraordinary saurian killed on the Beni after receiving thirty-six balls. By order of the President of Bolivia the dried body, which had been preserved in Asuncion, was sent to La Paz." The "monster" was reported to be twelve meters long from snout to point of the tail, which

> "The 'monster' was reported to be twelve meters long from snout to point of the tail, which latter was flattened. Its head resemblance the head of a dog and its legs were short, ending with formidable claws."

latter was flattened. Its head resemblance the head of a dog and its legs were short, ending with formidable claws. The legs and abdomen sported a kind of scale armor, and all the back is protected by a still thicker and double cuirass, starting from behind the ears of the anterior head, and continuing to the tail. The neck is long, and the belly large and almost dragging on the ground.

BIGFOOT, A CREATURE OF THE WATER

So far, we have restricted our coverage of strange and monstrous creatures to massive amphibians, sea serpents, lake monsters, giant snakes, reptiles, and surviving dinosaurs. As for their lairs, they include caves, caverns, lagoons, and lakes. But how many people know that the world's most famous monster—Bigfoot, also known as Sasquatch—falls into the very same category? I would confidently judge that the answer is very few. Come with me now as we look at the secrets of Bigfoot's world of the watery depths. We'll begin with the largely unknown issue of the Bigfoot creatures being skilled swimmers that, as the evidence will soon show, spend a lot of time deep in the water.

Between the nights of December 26 and 29, 1980, multiple extraordinary events of the UFO kind occurred within Rendlesham Forest, Suffolk, England. These events involved military personnel from the nearby Royal Air Force stations of Bentwaters and Woodbridge. Since then, countless U.S. Air Force personnel who were stationed in the area at the time have spoken out regarding their knowledge of a small, triangular-shaped object that was seen maneuvering in the forest.

Others described seeing in the dark woods almost ghostly, extraterrestrial types of beings of short size and with eerie, feline-like eyes. Strange and unknown lights were seen dancing around the night skies, circling both the forest and the twin military facilities. There were stories that the amazing movements of the UFOs were caught on radar. There was even hushed talk that the military personnel involved in the incident were silenced by ominous Men in Black-style characters.

As for the official story, many attempts have been made to suggest that the beam from a local lighthouse—situated at nearby Orford Ness—was the cause of all the fuss. Here is where we come to something decidedly strange and intriguing. It has nothing to do with the lighthouse *per se* but everything to do with the twelfth-century town of Orford itself. Wondering what I mean by that? Well, read on.

First, here is a bit of important background data on Orford Castle, near which an "amphibian man" was seen and captured. According to the website *Castles.nl*:

> Orford Castle was a royal castle built by King Henry II of England, between 1165 and 1173, because he wanted to re-establish royal influence across the region. Before that time the area had been under control by the Bigod family who resided in nearby Framlingham Castle. Hugh Bigod had been one of a group of dissenting barons during the Anarchy in the reign of King Stephen. Henry had initially confiscated Framlingham Castle from Hugh, but had returned it in 1165.
>
> In 1174 Henry crushed the Bigods when they revolted again and ordered the permanent confiscation of Framlingham Castle. During the revolt Orford Castle was heavily garrisoned with 20 knights. Henry died in 1189 and although the political

A little-known fact is that Bigfoot is actually a creature that spends a great deal of time in the water, even swimming deep into the murkiness of a bog, swamp, or river.

importance of Orford Castle diminished, the port of Orford grew in importance. By the start of the 13th century, royal authority over Suffolk firmly established, it handled even more trade than the more famous port of nearby Ipswich. In 1216 Orford Castle was taken by the invading Prince Louis of France (later to become King Louis VIII of France).

John Fitz-Robert became the governor of the royal castle under the young King Henry III of England, followed by Hubert de Burgh. Under King Edward I governorship of Orford Castle was given to the De Valoines family, and it passed by marriage to Robert de Ufford, the 1st Earl of Suffolk, who was granted it in perpetuity by Edward III in 1336. No longer a royal castle, Orford was passed on through the Willoughby, Stanhope and Devereux families.

It is truly ironic that many of those who are skeptical of the Rendlesham Forest UFO case of December 1980 are so very often keen to suggest that the airmen who were involved merely mistook the illumination from the nearby Orford Lighthouse for something more exotic. Why? Well, Orford itself is a veritable hotbed of weirdness. That has been the case not just for the last few years or even since the events at Rendlesham occurred. Rather, Orford has been what the late John Keel would have termed a "window area" for no less than centuries.

Consider—as just one example of several—the following account of the single-named Ralph, a monk and an abbot of Coggeshall, Essex, England. Recorded way back in the year 1200 in *Chronicon Anglicanum*, Ralph describes the remarkable capture in the area of a definitive wild man of the woods:

> In the time of King Henry II, when Bartholomew de Glanville was in charge of the castle at Orford, it happened that some fishermen fishing in the sea there caught in their nets a Wildman. He was naked and was like a man in all his members, covered with hair and with a long shaggy beard. He eagerly ate whatever was brought to him, but if it was raw he pressed it between his hands until all the juice was expelled.

> He would not talk, even when tortured and hung up by his feet. Brought into church, he showed no sign of reverence or belief. He sought his bed at sunset and always remained there until sunrise. He was allowed to go into the sea, strongly guarded with three lines of nets, but he dived under the nets and came up again and again. Eventually he came back of his own free will. But later on he escaped and was never seen again.

Or, maybe, the beastman—or, far more likely, given the large passage of time, one of its offspring—*was* seen again, albeit hundreds of years further down the line. At some point during the summer of 1968, one Morris Allen—who grew up in the vicinity of Orford—was walking along the coast near the town of Orford itself when, in the distance, he saw someone squatting on the sand and leaning over something.

As he got closer, Allen said, he could see that the man was dressed in what looked like an animal skin and was savagely tearing into the flesh of a dead rabbit. The man was dirt-encrusted, with long, tangled hair, and had wild, staring eyes. Allen could only watch with a mixture of fascination and horror. Suddenly, the man held his head aloft and quickly glared in Allen's direction, as if he had picked up his scent. The wild man quickly scooped up the rabbit, bounded off into the grass, and was forever lost from sight. For a highly traumatized Morris Allen, it was an event destined never to be forgotten.

Perhaps the wild man of Orford lives on, taunting and tantalizing people with the occasional sighting of its bestial form. It can now be said, with a high degree of accuracy, that in the "weird stakes," there is far more to Orford than just its infamous lighthouse.

Max Westenhofer was a German pathologist who, in the early 1940s, made a comment that was as controversial as it was thought-provoking: "The postulation of an aquatic mode of life during an early stage of human evolution is a tenable hypothesis, for which further inquiry may produce additional supporting evidence." Almost two decades later, a marine biologist named Alister Hardy added that very ancient "primitive ape stock" may have been forced—by competing predators and circumstances—"to feed on the sea shores and to hunt for food, shell fish, sea urchins, etc., in the shallows of the coast. I suppose that they were forced into the water just as we have seen happen in so many other groups of terrestrial animals."

While it is obvious that lakes, oceans, and rivers are not the natural habitats of Bigfoot, there is a large body of data available showing that, unlike many apes and monkeys, Bigfoot is quite an adept swimmer and a creature for whom water is far from being an alien environment.

The North American Wood Ape Conservancy reports on its website: "Swimming must be examined alongside the terrestrial gait of the wood ape since it appears to be an important means of locomotion throughout the range of this species in North America, especially on the west coast. Circumstantial evidence, such as reports of the presence of wood apes on small islands off the

Marine biologist Alister Hardy speculated that one species of ancient hominid might have adapted to living along the seashores, feeding off fish and crustaceans.

coast of British Columbia, has suggested they swim. Observations of wood apes actually swimming have confirmed this."

Lisa Shiel, who has had personal interactions with Bigfoot, has uncovered an example of Bigfoot in the water from the nineteenth century. She outlines the story: "In the 1830s, reports emerged from the area around Fish Lake, Indiana, of a four-foot-tall 'wild child' loitering in the vicinity—and swimming in the lake."

Shiel continues: "In another incident that took place in September 1967, a fisherman casting his net on the delta of the Nooksack River in Washington State felt something tug on his net. A moment later something began dragging his net upstream. When he shined his flashlight at the thief, he saw a hairy hominid in the river hauling in the net."

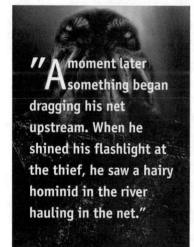

"A moment later something began dragging his net upstream. When he shined his flashlight at the thief, he saw a hairy hominid in the river hauling in the net."

A third case comes from the people who run the website *Today in Bigfoot History!* They state: "William Drexler's campsite overlooked Phantom Ship Island in Oregon. He had just finished his sausage and egg breakfast and was smoking his morning pipe, just looking out over Crater Lake. That is when he noticed something moving on Phantom Ship Island."

Phantom Ship Island is a small, craggy island on Crater Lake that takes its name from its "ghost ship"-like appearance, which is particularly noticeable when the mist hovers low and thick. The story continues: "Drexler got out his binoculars. It took him a minute or two before he was able to get a good bead on the moving figure. What Drexler saw was a brownish gray Bigfoot, obviously soaking wet, stretching out on some rocks near the water's edge. The creature was luxuriated. Drexler watched the creature for awhile lounge in the sun. Then after a bit the Bigfoot climbed to the other side of the island and Drexler lost sight of it."

One of the most fascinating examples originated near Ketchikan, Alaska, at some point around the turn of the 1960s. It was a story provided to longtime Bigfoot authority and investigator John Green. The story had a bit of a "friend of a friend" aspect to it, but that makes it no less fascinating. It revolved around a young boy named Errol, who, on one particular night, was out fishing with his father when his flashlight illuminated something terrifying standing in the water: a large, humanoid creature, but one that was clearly not human, staring intently at him.

Not surprisingly, the boy screamed at the top of his lungs and fled for his life. A posse of men came running just in time to illuminate the dark waters with their flashlights. They saw to their astonishment the huge beast dive into the water and start swimming "like a frog" before vanishing from view, plunging ever deeper into the depths. In moments, it was gone—demonstrating its skills as a powerful and fast swimmer.

Rupert Matthews, the author of *Bigfoot*, reports: "In July 1965 a Sasquatch was seen swimming some distance away from the shore of Princess Royal Island, British Columbia. The fisherman who saw it realized with no little apprehension that it was actually swimming for his boat, so he started up his outboard motor and sped off. At this point four more Sasquatch appeared on a nearby beach and watched him."

There have been sightings of swimming Bigfoot in Texas, too. Rob Riggs has studied reports of the creatures in and around the Big Thicket area of the Lone Star State and has recorded some of them in his book *In the Big Thicket: On the Trail of the Wild Man*. He tells of one particularly notable case of a watery Sasquatch, seen by a man named John: "John's family home is on the edge of the Trinity River swamps near Dayton. One night he heard a disturbance

Cryptozoologist and author Rupert Matthews related a story in his book *Bigfoot* about a swimming Bigfoot spotted near Princess Royal Island in Canada.

on the porch where he kept a pen of rabbits. He investigated just in time to see a large, dark form make off with rabbit in hand. John impulsively followed in hot pursuit, staying close enough to hear the rabbit squeal continuously."

John was able to close in on the creature to a point where he witnessed something amazing occur, as Riggs reveals: "Standing on the high bank in the moonlight he watched dumb-struck as what looked like a huge ape-like animal swam to the other side of the river, easily negotiating the strong current, and never letting go of the rabbit."

In March 2007, the "Goldie E." family told of swimming Bigfoot around Trinidad, California. Rather bizarrely, the creatures were reportedly seen swimming alongside sea lions as they negotiated the waters from Trinidad Head Rock to Flat Iron Rock. The biting, cold waters apparently affected the Bigfoot not a bit.

Constructed in the early part of the nineteenth century, England's historic Shropshire Union Canal, or the "Shroppie" as it is known affectionately by those who regularly travel its extensive and winding waters, is some sixty-seven miles in length and extends from Ellesmere Port near the city of Liverpool right down to Autherley Junction at Wolverhampton in the Midlands. The southern end of the old canal, which was originally known as the Birmingham and Liverpool Junction Canal, was the last of the great British narrow boat canals to be built and is a testament to the masterful engineering of Thomas Telford. Deep cuttings and massive embankments are the veritable hallmarks of the canal, and they paint a picture that is as eerie as it is picturesque.

The Shropshire Union Canal is quite possibly Britain's most haunted waterway, as the local folk who know the lore of the canal are well aware. At the city of Chester's old Northgate, for example, and where the canal was dug into part of the town's old moat, a ghostly Roman centurion can be seen—when circumstances are said to be right, that is—still guarding the ancient entrance to the city. Then there is the "shrieking specter" of Belton Cutting, which is a veritable wailing, Banshee-style monstrosity that strikes cold, stark fear into the hearts of those who have the misfortune to cross its terrible path.

From the site of the former lockkeeper's cottage at Burgedin, on the nearby Montgomery Canal, come intriguing reports of the ghostly, ethereal figure of an early Welsh princess named Eira. And bringing matters relatively more up to date, there is the spectral American Air Force pilot whose aircraft crashed near the canal at Little Onn, at Church Eaton, Staffordshire, during World War II. There is also the "helpful resident ghost" of Tyrley Middle Lock at Market Drayton, which has allegedly been seen opening and closing the lock gates for those novice, holidaying boaters who, from time to time, negotiate the waters of the long canal. But by far the most infamous ghostly resident of the Shropshire Union Canal is a truly diabolical entity that has become known as the Man-Monkey.

It was within the packed pages of Charlotte Sophia Burne's book of 1883, *Shropshire Folklore*, that the unholy antics of the creature—which some perceive to be the closest thing that Britain may have to the North American Bigfoot and the Himalayan Yeti—were first unleashed upon an unsuspecting general public. According to Burne:

> A very weird story of an encounter with an animal ghost arose of late years within my knowledge. On the 21st of January 1879, a labouring man was employed to take a cart of luggage from Ranton in Staffordshire to Woodcock, beyond Newport in Shropshire, for the ease of a party of visitors who were going from one house to another. He was late in coming back; his horse was tired, and could only crawl along at a foot's pace, so that it was ten o'clock at night when he arrived at the place where the highroad crosses the Birmingham and Liverpool canal.

It was then, Burne faithfully recorded, that the man received what was undoubtedly the most terrifying shock of his entire life: "Just before he reached

The Shropshire Union Canal in England is said to be haunted by ghosts, banshees, and an apelike human.

the canal bridge, a strange black creature with great white eyes sprang out of the plantation by the roadside and alighted on his horse's back. He tried to push it off with his whip, but to his horror the whip went through the thing, and he dropped it on the ground in fright."

Needless to say, Burne added: "The poor, tired horse broke into a canter, and rushed onwards at full speed with the ghost still clinging to its back. How the creature at length vanished, the man hardly knew." But the story was far from over, Burne learned: "He told his tale in the village of Woodseaves, a mile further on, and so effectively frightened the hearers that one man actually stayed with friends there all night, rather than cross the terrible bridge which lay between him and his home."

By the time the unnamed laborer reached the village of Woodseaves, the poor fellow was in a state of "excessive terror" and promptly retired to his bed for several days, "so much was he prostrated by his fright." Burne also recorded that, on the following day, another individual traveled back to the sinister bridge and spied the man's whip, still lying at the very place where it had fallen to the ground after the nightmarish and bizarre encounter.

Dark tales of the crazed beast and its infernal nighttime activities began to spread like absolute wildfire throughout the little villages and hamlets of the area, as Burne quickly learned and recorded thus in her book: "The adventure, as was natural, was much talked of in the neighbourhood, and, of course, with all sorts of variations." Most regrettably, Burne failed to elaborate on the particular nature of these "variations" and gossip.

At any rate, the local constabulary had heard all about the nature and exploits of the hairy demon and knew exactly what was afoot, as Burne carefully chronicled: "Some days later the man's master was surprised by a visit from a policeman, who came to request him to give information of his having been stopped and robbed on the Big Bridge on the night of the 21st January."

The "master," who, apparently, was very much amused by this development in the escalating and seemingly mutating story, carefully explained to the visiting policeman that this was completely untrue and that, in reality, it was his employee who had reported a strange encounter at the "Big Bridge" but that there was most definitely no robbery involved at all. Interestingly, when the real details of what had occurred were related to the policeman, he was seemingly completely nonplussed, came to the realization that no actual crime had been committed at all, and merely replied in a distinctly matter-of-fact fashion: "Oh, was that all, sir? Oh, I know what that was. That was the Man-Monkey, sir, as does come again at that bridge ever since the man was drowned in the cut."

Charlotte Burne also revealed that she personally had the opportunity to speak with the man's employer, but, also to our cost today, she did not expand upon the specific nature of the conversation within the pages of *Shropshire Folklore*. Nevertheless, Burne did describe the master as being a "Mr. B_____ of L_____d." And although the man's name remains unknown to us (and probably always will remain so), "L_____d" might well be a reference to the ancient, nearby Staffordshire city of Lichfield.

So what, precisely, was the strange, hairy critter that was seen wildly roaming the distinctly darkened corners of the Shropshire Union Canal by moonlight on that winter's night way back in January 1879? Was it truly some form of Bigfoot or Yeti-like entity? Could it potentially have been an exotic escapee of the simian kind, perhaps one that originated with a private zoo somewhere in the area or a traveling menagerie of the type that were popular back then? Did it have wholly supernatural origins rather than physical ones? Or was it something else entirely? The questions are many. The answers are few. But there is more on the matter of the Man-Monkey.

Elliott O'Donnell was a prestigious author who penned dozens of titles on the world of the paranormal; he died in 1965 at the age of ninety-three. In his 1912 book *Werewolves*, O'Donnell said: "It is an old belief that the souls of cataleptic and epileptic people, during the body's unconsciousness, adjourned temporarily to animals, and it is therefore only in keeping with such a view to suggest that on the deaths of such people their spirits take permanently the form of animals."

This, O'Donnell said, accounted for the fact that the places where such people died "are often haunted by semi and wholly animal types of phantasm."

Dr. David Clarke, a folklorist, notes that the story of the Man-Monkey identifies it "as a human revenant who returns to haunt a bridge in animal form. The manner of its appearance, in the form of 'a strange black creature with great white eyes' and the fear it created by its actions leaping on the back of the horse, resonates with contemporary accounts of ghostly activity elsewhere."

So what, precisely, was the strange, hairy critter that was seen wildly roaming the distinctly darkened corners of the Shropshire Union Canal by moonlight...?

The human dead returned in animal form was not the only theory suggested for the presence of the Man-Monkey, however. A rumor quickly circulated in the area that a gorilla had escaped from a traveling menagerie that had recently visited the nearby town of Newport. While it's not entirely impossible that such a creature could have briefly survived in the cold wilds of Staffordshire, it should be noted that the "circus escapee" theory is one that is trotted out on numerous occasions—and all across the world—to try to rationalize reports similar to that of the Man-Monkey. In nearly all cases, no evidence of any such escapee is found.

There is clearly something supernatural about the Man-Monkey, since sightings of the always-solitary beast have continued to be reported into the twenty-first century. And they are almost identical in nature: the location is usually Bridge 39, the monster leaps out of the trees and terrifies the unwary, and it displays qualities and characteristics that are part flesh and blood and part spectral. Whatever the true nature of Ranton's resident hairy monster-man, it shows no signs of leaving its tree-covered haunt anytime soon. Should you, one day, find yourself in the vicinity of Ranton, take great care if you are forced to cross Bridge 39. The Man-Monkey may be waiting in the wooded wings, ready to strike at a moment's notice.

The remarkable (and related) tale of Paul Bell is, for me at least, a highly memorable one. Bell said that he was a keen fisherman and told me how in July and August 1976, he had spent several Saturdays out at the canal with his rods, reels, and bait, soaking in the intense heat of what was without doubt an absolutely scalding hot couple of months. I seriously doubt that anyone who is old enough to remember the summer of '76 will ever quite forget those truly extraordinary temperatures that briefly and memorably plunged the entire nation into utterly scalding chaos. But it was something far stranger than the occasional extreme nature of the British weather that Bell had fixed on his mind.

He told me how, on one particular Saturday afternoon, he was sitting near the water's edge—very near to where the events of 1879 occurred—on a small, wooden stool that he always carried with him when he was "literally frozen solid" by the sight of "what at first I thought was a big log floating down the cut, about sixty or seventy feet away," he said. According to Bell, however, it was no log; it was something else entirely. As it got closer, Bell was both astonished and horrified to see a large "dark brown and black coloured" eel or snakelike creature—possibly ten feet in length or a little bit more—moving slowly in the water, with its head—which "looked like a black sheep"—flicking rapidly from side to side.

Although he had an old Polaroid camera with him, Bell said he never even thought to take a photograph. Instead, he merely stared in awe and shock as the animal cruised leisurely and blissfully past him before finally vanishing out of sight. Bell stressed that the creature apparently did not see him ("or if it did, it never attacked me"), and it did not appear to exhibit any outright hostile tendencies.

While traveling near Shropshire Union Canal, Paul Bell happened to see the Man-Monkey peering at him from the bushes very near to where the creature was seen back in 1879.

I had heard such accounts on several previous occasions—namely, of giant eels roaming British waterways, particularly those of the West Midlands—so Paul Bell's story was not that unusual to me, even though it involved what was without doubt an unknown animal of truly impressive proportions. What elevated it to a far stranger level was the fact that Bell claimed, quite matter-of-factly, that the following Saturday, he was fishing in practically the same spot when he "got the feeling I was being watched" and saw something equally monstrous, yet manifestly different in nature and appearance. That's right: the Man-Monkey.

Peering across the width of the canal, Bell was both horrified and petrified to see a dark, hairy face staring intently at him out of the thick, green bushes. The head of the animal was unmistakably human-like "but crossed with a monkey," said Bell, who added: "As soon as it saw me looking at it, up it went and ran right into the trees and I lost it." He went on: "That was it; a second or two was all at the most. But as it got up and ran I knew it was a big monkey. There's nothing else it could have been. But what flummoxed me more than seeing it, though, was what was it doing there?"

At this stage, many might be inclined to ask: Is it just too much to accept when someone claims to have seen not just one but *two* strange animals in the exact same area? Maybe, for some, but I will later reveal that sightings of hairy beastmen and water-based monsters in the same area are curiously prevalent in Britain. Furthermore, there's an intriguing theory as to why this should be so, which I will discuss in due course. Until then, on with the sightings.

According to Scottish legend, the kelpie, or water horse, is a wholly supernatural creature that haunts the rivers, bridges, and lochs of ancient Scotland and has the uncanny ability to shapeshift. The most common form that the kelpie takes is that of a horse—hence the name. It stands by the water's edge, tempting any passing and weary traveler to mount it and thereby continue their journey. That, however, is always the fatal downfall of the traveler, as invariably, the beast is then said to rear violently and charge headlong into the depths of the river or loch and thus drown its terrified rider in the process.

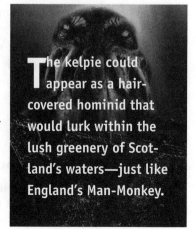

The kelpie could appear as a hair-covered hominid that would lurk within the lush greenery of Scotland's waters—just like England's Man-Monkey.

Notably, the kelpie was also said to be able to transform itself into both a beautiful maiden or mermaid and into a large, hairy man that would hide in the vegetation of Scottish waterways and leap out and attack the unwary, not unlike the Man-Monkey of the Shropshire Union Canal.

With the above said, the kelpie may simply be a denizen of the world of folklore and nothing else at all. But the parallels between the Scottish legends and the events

Could it be that the large, eel-like beast seen by fisherman Paul Bell in the hot summer of 1976 was in reality a kelpie-style shapeshifter...?

at Bridge 39 in January 1879 are undeniably remarkable. The kelpie could appear as a hair-covered hominid that would lurk within the lush greenery of Scotland's waters—just like England's Man-Monkey. The kelpie would reportedly violently attack passersby. And the kelpie was said to be a much-feared killer of human beings, as the Man-Monkey may well have been.

On this latter point, you will recall that the police in the vicinity of Bridge 39 had specifically associated the sightings of the Man-Monkey at Woodseaves in 1879 with the then recent death of a man who had unfortunately "drowned in the cut." The several parallels with the world of the kelpie are, without doubt, truly uncanny. It goes without saying that none of this proves kelpies exist, either in the world of the normal or in that of the paranormal. It does, however, strongly suggest a belief in, and an outright acceptance of, kelpie-like entities in rural Shropshire and Staffordshire by elements of the British Police Force, no less, in the latter part of the nineteenth century—which is, without doubt, a revelation of a pretty extraordinary magnitude.

It also suggests that if the latter-day Man-Monkey reports are genuine (and I see no reason to dispute them or their attendant sources, having personally interviewed many of them), then far from being merely a harmless relic of centuries-old Scottish folklore, the kelpie is still among us, still thriving, and still up to its infernal, and sometimes deadly, activities.

And another thought while we are discussing things of a kelpie nature. Could it be that the large, eel-like beast seen by fisherman Paul Bell in the hot summer of 1976 was in reality a kelpie-style shapeshifter that, one week after his initial encounter, assumed for the same startled witness the form of the diabolical Man-Monkey? Given that ancient Scottish legend and folklore suggests the kelpie can shapeshift from water horse to hairy beastman and vice versa, ad infinitum, this would certainly seem to suggest such an incredible possibility. If that was the case, Bell can most definitely count his lucky stars that he did not pay for the encounter with both his soul and his life.

SECRET CAVES AND SHADOWY CAVERNS

Now let us see how Bigfoot comes into play in relation to these monsters of the deep. It is a little-known fact that there exist numerous reports of the creatures living deep underground: in caves, caverns, and tunnels. In that sense, Bigfoot is truly a beast of the underworld and an animal well placed in the pages of this book. The Solomon Islands, located near Paupa New Guinea, were named by a Spanish adventurer, one Alvaro de Mendana. He has gone down in history as the first European (so far as is known) to have visited the islands, in 1568. And there are more than a few of those islands—more than nine hundred of them, in fact, of widely varying degrees of size. Although no European visited the islands prior to the sixteenth century, archaeological digging has demonstrated that primitive humans inhabited at least some of them as far back as 29000 B.C.E. There are also good indications that before Europeans made their way to the Solomon Islands, the people regularly practiced cannibalism and were a violent and wild bunch. The islands are also noted for something else besides a long and winding history: the presence of beasts that sound suspiciously Bigfoot-like.

We have a man named Marius Boirayon to thank for uncovering most of the currently available data on these marauding and not always particularly friendly creatures. A skilled engineer and helicopter pilot, Boirayon has unearthed witness accounts that describe creatures very much like Bigfoot: most of them are around ten feet in height and have flaming-red eyes, hair that is a cross between brown and a deep red, and apelike faces—most, but not all of them.

Boirayon has made another parallel between the beasts of the Solomon Islands and the United States' Bigfoot: just as there appears to be more than one kind of beastman in the United States—the monster of the Pacific Northwest is manifestly different from the Skunk Ape of Florida—the same can be said about the Solomon Islands.

Boirayon's findings suggest that there could be as many as three varieties of hairy hominids on the Solomon Islands. One of them is a smallish creature that is far more like a hairy wild man of old English lore than it is a cryptid ape. The second resembles the traditional Bigfoot. The third sounds like something akin to the gigantic Nyalmo of the Himalayas in the sense that it is described as a massive creature that typically reaches heights of fifteen and maybe even twenty feet, despite how admittedly unlikely such a scenario sounds.

The Bigfoot of the Solomon Islands is hardly what one would call friendly: downright hostile would be a far better way of wording it. Kidnapping and eating the locals seem to be among the creatures' favorite pastimes. As just one example of many, Boirayon uncovered the traumatic and terrifying story of Mango, a woman who was abducted from her village home by one of the creatures and held prisoner by it for around a quarter of a century before she was finally able to escape. To the horror of her family and old friends, when Mango returned, she was not the person she once was: living with the hideous beast for so long had driven her utterly insane.

The Solomon Islands is a nation consisting of some nine hundred islands northeast of Australia and east of Papua New Guinea. One might not expect a Man-Monkey creature to live in this tropical land, but there have, indeed, been reports of hairy ape-men there.

Notably, while held by the wild thing, Mango allegedly gave birth to its equally hideous-looking child. Given that it is genetically impossible for humans and apes to interbreed, the likelihood is that the monsters of the Solomon Islands are not so monstrous after all but are some form of ancient offshoot of the human race.

That the tropical jungles of the Solomon Islands could accommodate—and even conceivably hide—creatures up to around nine or ten feet tall is not at all unlikely. It's difficult, however, to imagine that towering monsters of fifteen to twenty feet in height could remain hidden. There is, however, an intriguing theory to explain the reason why such immense things can't be tracked down, caught, or killed. It's a theory that is chiefly focused around the island of Guadalcanal, the location of the 1942–1943 Battle of Guadalcanal, which saw Allied forces fighting the Japanese during World War II.

The people of Guadalcanal talk of long-standing legends of a vast underground world, far below their island, that is only accessible if one knows where the secret entrance points can be found. So extensive are these massive caves, caverns, and underground realms that thousands of the violent and giant beasts are rumored to inhabit their darkest corners. Much of the lore points in the direction of Guadalcanal's mountains, where the tunnels and caves are said to begin, which are rumored to run so deep that one might be forgiven for thinking one had entered the nightmarish realm of hell itself. It's not impossible that the descriptions of the massive sizes of the creatures are down to folkloric exaggeration and that, in reality, we should be looking at beasts of a far more manageable eight or nine feet tall. As for the cave rumors, there are more than a few cases of Bigfoot reportedly being a dweller of the wild and rarely explored underground.

Lest you think that these reports and stories might solely be the domains of "friend of a friend" tales and impossible-to-prove myths, it is well worth taking note of the story of a man named Ezekiel Alebua, told for the record. He was none other than the third prime minister of the Solomon Islands—a position he held from December 1986 to March 1989.

When he was a child, Alebua was taken by his father to a large cavern on the east side of Guadalcanal, where his father pointed out something incredible: huge, humanoid skeletons, somewhere in the order of fifteen feet long, scattered on the cave floor. How, exactly, Alebua's father knew of the cave and its eerie, long-dead inhabitants remains a mystery. Similar tales of massive, apelike animals and deep, labyrinthine tunnels can be found on a number of other islands that comprise the Solomon Islands, including Malaita, Choiseul, and Santa Isabel.

In the latter part of the nineteenth century, a British adventurer and explorer named Hugh Nevill was told of a race of creatures that were part human and part ape but were, by the time Nevill heard the story, dead and gone—somewhere in the vicinity of five human generations earlier. They resided in the southeast corner of Sri Lanka and, before their assumed extinction, were constantly at war with another race of hairy humanoids known as the Nittaewo. Both types of creatures were fairly small, around four to five feet in height. They shared a liking for living in deep, natural caves and caverns and had a love of fresh, raw meat. They were not totally savage, however, as is evidenced by their apparent use of primitive stone tools.

It was not their constant warring with each other that wiped out the Nittaewo and their unnamed furry foes, however. It was man. Reportedly, the last of the Nittaewos were killed in a violent confrontation at a cave in the Kattaragama Hills.

The beautiful valley of Nant Gwynant in Wales harbors a dark secret: a frightening humanoid creature lives there in what is called the Cave of Owen Lawgoch.

A similar story was told to an explorer named Frederick Lewis, also suggesting the Nittaewos were long gone. This account came from one Dissan Hamy, whose grandfather reportedly helped build a huge bonfire at the mouth of the cave as a means to kill the creatures by smoke inhalation.

Oliver Lewis, a key and integral player at the Centre for Fortean Zoology, has investigated a fascinating old legend pertaining to what can only be termed a definitive Welsh Bigfoot. He reveals that villagers in Nant Gwynant—a picturesque valley situated in Snowdonia, Gwynedd, North Wales—have for many a century told, in hushed tones, a turbulent and nightmarish story of how a dark and mysterious cave in the old valley—the Cave of Owen Lawgoch—came to be known as the abode of "the hairy man."

Lewis's word has shown that long, long ago, villagers and shepherds in the area of Nant Gwynant were plagued by a silent and stealthy thief who would break into their homesteads under the protective covers of shadow and darkness on a disturbingly regular basis. Those same villagers and shepherds would awaken to find that their goats and cows had been inexplicably milked, much-needed food was stolen, and a number of sheep were taken during the night, never to be seen again, their unfortunate fates surely sealed. The carnage and thievery, says Lewis, "went on for some years and every time anyone laid a trap for the thief it never took the bait and the finger of popular suspicion passed from ne'er-do-well to ne'er-do-well, with each suspect's guilt eventually being disproved."

So, what—allegedly, at least—was the true nature of the nightmarish beast said to have been roaming the densely treed, ancient valley? According to North Wales-based legend, it was a creature of undeniably primitive proportions and terrifying appearance that seemed intent on tormenting the people of the picturesque area whenever and however possible. As Lewis notes:

"One day a shepherd was returning from the mountains later than usual and spotted something strange; a huge, burly naked man covered from head to toe in thick red fur was resting on a neighboring hill. The shepherd suspected that this out of place and strangely hirsute giant might be the thief that was plaguing the village, so the shepherd snuck past the man without being detected and ran back to the village as soon as he was out of sight."

The story continued that when the shepherd in question breathlessly reached the heart of Nant Gwynant, he persuaded all of the available men of the village to join him in a quest to, once and for all, rid the area of the creature that had elected to descend upon it and its people. Evidently, and unfortunately, not much thought went into this particular exercise.

It basically involved little more than the hysterical posse charging up the green hill and toward the wild man with crude, homemade weapons in hand while simultaneously screaming at him at the top of their lungs. Not surprisingly, alerting the hairy man-thing to their presence was hardly the cleverest move that the group could have made. The mighty beast shot away—on all fours, interestingly enough—and, as Lewis noted, in a fashion that suggested "the skill and precision of a deer."

A close and careful watch of the hill and its immediate surroundings was made from that day onward in the event the beastman might return to once again wreak diabolical havoc upon Nant Gwynant and its frayed populace. It was, without doubt, a most wise decision. Barely a few days passed before the menacing entity returned to both feed voraciously and spread fear and chaos across the immediate land.

This time, however, the villagers took a new and novel approach to tackling their quarry. The plan was to let loose a pack of vicious hounds upon the British Bigfoot-type animal in the hope that the dogs would succeed where the men had overwhelmingly failed. Unfortunately, this action proved utterly fruitless, too. As soon as the creature caught wind of the scent of the hounds, the hairy thing was gone, once again bounding away in almost graceful fashion as it made its successful escape, easily leaving the snarling dogs far, far behind.

Lewis reveals that a distinctly alternative plan of action was then put into place: "One man came up with the idea of consulting a magician. The magician told the villagers to find a red-haired greyhound without a single hair of a different color and this would be able to catch the man. After much searching and bartering with local towns and villages the people of Nant Gwynant found a dog that fitted the bill and proudly took him home. When the villagers next saw the hairy man they were ready with the red greyhound and it was set loose to catch the hairy man. The hairy man escaped again by leaping down a small cliff."

As soon as the creature caught wind of the scent of the hounds, the hairy thing was gone, once again bounding away in almost graceful fashion as it made its successful escape....

Were the people of Nant Gwynant cursed to forever have the marauding thing in their midst? No. If the men, the dogs, and even the supernatural powers of a renowned and mysterious purveyor of ancient magic had failed to put paid to the monster-man and its terrible actions, then, quite clearly, another approach was needed. It fell upon one of the women of the village to come up with a plan of attack to rid the area of the terrifying beast. Lewis demonstrates what happened next:

> One woman was so angered by her frequent losses she decided to stay up every night and hide herself in the front room of her farmhouse to wait for when the hairy man decided to pay a visit. Sure enough after a few weeks the hairy man paid a visit to the wrong

house and the lady was waiting with a hatchet. She remained hidden until the man had squeezed his bulky frame halfway through the window before she struck the hairy man with her hatchet. The unexpected blow cleaved off the hairy man's hand in one blow and he recoiled back out of the window before the woman could smite him with a further whack. The brave woman dashed out of her door, hatchet in hand ready to finish the man off but by the time she had gotten outside he had fled.

The wretched terror that had descended upon Nant Gwynant had finally reached its end, much to the overwhelming relief of the entire neighborhood, as Lewis reveals: "When the village awoke the next day and the men learned what had happened they followed the trail of blood the hairy man had left behind to a cave beneath a local waterfall. As the big hairy man was never seen again it was assumed by the villagers that he had died in the cave, so the cave was named 'the cave of the hairy man.'"

Chinese characters on a cliffside in Hubei Province, China, translate as "Wild Man Cave," home of the Yeren.

Next to the legendary, fire-breathing dragon, it's China's most famous monsters, the Yeren, huge, unidentified apes, that almost certainly—in terms of its close proximity—have connections to the Abominable Snowman of the Himalayas and the various, similarly large animals said to roam the huge mountains, such as the Nyalmo. While the Yeren have been seen in a number of areas of China, one area more than any other is a hotbed for sightings: Hubei, a province in central China. It's a vast place dominated by numerous mountains—including the Daba Mountains and the Wudang Mountains—and the Jianghang Plain. Hubei is also a province through which flows the massive, nearly four-thousand-mile-long Yangtze River.

It's specifically the western portion of Hubei in which the Yeren have been spotted. The area is noted for its dense forest and treacherous mountains. As for what the Yeren are, that is the big question. At the top of the list is *Gigantopithecus*, a massive ape, presumed extinct, that dwelled in China hundreds of thousands of years ago—and perhaps is not quite so extinct after all. Coming in at a close second is some form of huge, and unacknowledged, kind of orangutan.

Interestingly, just like Bigfoot in the United States, the Yeren come in a variety of colors. Its hair has been described as red, brown, and even—on a few occasions—black. As for its height, while most reports describe creatures as ranging from the average height of an adult human male to about eight feet, there are a number of cases involving colossal mountain monsters in excess of ten feet. Despite their imposing appearance, however, the Yeren are said to be relatively placid, quiet creatures that shun humankind.

Sightings of the Yeren cannot be blamed on hype born out of the fascination for Bigfoot. This is made abundantly clear by the fact that reports of these immense animals have been reported for centuries. A translated seventeenth-century document from Hubei notes: "In the remote mountains of Fangxian County, there are rock caves, in which live hairy men as tall as three meters. They often come down to hunt dogs and chickens in the villages. They fight with whoever resists."

Of course, the final comment, about the creatures being prone to violence, suggests that if, one day, you are confronted by a Yeren, you should not assume it's as docile as many cryptozoologists claim it to be! Also, the reference to the Yeren's hunting dogs adds weight to the notion that dogs and Bigfoot are hardly on friendly terms—as we have seen previously.

The evidence for the existence of the Yeren in more recent years is equally impressive. In 1940, it's said that the body of a dead Yeren turned up in Gansu. Female and over six feet in height, it was examined by a biologist named Wang Tselin of Chicago. Interestingly, Tselin was unable to figure out if the beast was some form of ape, a primitive human, or something that was an odd combination of both. In Tselin's own words:

Around September or October, we were travelling from Baoji to Tianshui via Jiangluo City; our car was between Jiangluo City and Niangniang Plain when we suddenly heard gunshots ahead of us. When the car reached the crowd that surrounded the gunman, all of us got down to satisfy our curiosity. We could see that the "wildman" was already shot dead and laid on the roadside.

The body was still supple and the stature very tall, approximately 2 metres. The whole body was covered with a coat of thick greyish-red hair which was very dense. Since it was lying face-down, the more inquisitive of the passengers turned the body over to have a better look. It turned out to be a mother with a large pair of breasts, the nipples being very red as if it had recently given birth. The hair on the face was shorter. The face was narrow with deep-set eyes, while the cheek bones and lips jutted out. The scalp hair was roughly one *chi* [one foot] long and untidy. The appearance was very similar to the plaster model of a female Peking Man. However, its hair seemed to be longer and thicker than that of the ape-man model. It was ugly because of the protruding lips.

According to the locals, there were two of them, probably one male and the other female. They had been in that area for over a month. The "wildmen" had great strength, frequently stood erect and were very tall. They were brisk in walking and could move as rapidly uphill as on the plain. As such, ordinary folks could not catch up with them. They did not have a language and could only howl.

In its haste to escape the approaching jeep, the red-haired creature raced up a slope but lost its footing and tumbled onto the road, landing right in front of the shocked group.

Moving on to May 1976, there is a fascinating story of a number of government personnel based at Hubei who, as they drove along a stretch of road dominated by thick woods in the predawn hours, came face-to-face with a Yeren.

In its haste to escape the approaching jeep, the red-haired creature raced up a slope but lost its footing and tumbled onto the road, landing right in front of the shocked group. Reportedly, the animal did not rear up onto its legs but took a crouching stance—perhaps intending to intimidate the group by provoking fear that it was about to lunge at them. Fortunately, that did not happen. Instead, the beast raced off yet again—after one of the men hurled a stone in its direction. Although the creature had the undeniable physical traits of an ape, its eyes were described as being eerily human-like, displaying intelligence and inquisitiveness.

As sightings of the creatures continued to be reported in the 1970s and then into the 1980s, the Chinese Academy of Sciences got in on the act and established an ambitious program to try to resolve the mystery of the Yeren once and for all. It was no easy task, and no hard, undeniable evidence ever surfaced. That's not to say there was a shortage of credible witness testimony, however: the reports poured in.

One such witness said to the academy of their encounter with a Yeren:

He was about seven feet tall, with shoulders wider than a man's, a sloping forehead, deep-set eyes and a bulbous nose with slightly upturned nostrils. He had sunken cheeks, ears like a man's but bigger, and round eyes, and also bigger than a man's. His jaw jutted out and he had protruding lips. His front teeth were as broad as a horse's. His eyes were black. His hair was dark brown, more than a foot long and hung loosely over his shoulders. His whole face, except for the nose and ears, was covered with short hairs. His arms hung below his knees. He had big hands with fingers about six inches long and thumbs only slightly separated from the fingers. He didn't have a tail, and the hair on his body was short. He had thick thighs, shorter than the lower part of his leg. He walked upright with his legs apart. His feet were each about 12 inches long and half that broad in front and narrow behind, with splayed toes. He was a male. That much I saw clearly.

Moving on to the 1990s, as monster authority Brad Steiger has noted: "In October 1994, the Chinese government established the Committee for the Search for Strange and Rare Creatures, including among its members specialists in vertebrate paleontology and paleoanthropology. A loose consensus among interested members from the Chinese Academy of Sciences maintains that the Yeren are some species of unknown primates."

Today, the search for the Yeren continues in China in much the same way that Bigfoot is sought in the United States and the Yowie in Australia.

One of the most thought-provoking theories for Bigfoot's overwhelming elusiveness suggests that the creatures spend a great deal of time living in natural caves and caverns as well as old, abandoned mines. In the early 1900s, a number of stories surfaced in the Oregon press that, upon careful reflection, might offer a degree of support for this intriguing theory that Bigfoot is a creature of the underground. The reports are made all the more significant because they reference in excess of a decade of sightings of large, hairy creatures, all in a specific vicinity where underground digging was known to be widespread.

In 1900, a Curry County, Oregon, newspaper reported on an amazing story: "The Sixes mining district in Curry County has for the past 30 years glorified in the exclusive possession of a 'kangaroo man.' Recently while Wm.

The elaborate system of caves in Oregon is home to magnificent formations such as Miller's Chapel (pictured). The caves (and abandoned mines) in the state are also an ideal home for cryptid humanoids.

Page and Johnnie McCulloch, who are mining there, went out hunting McCulloch saw the strange animal-man come down a stream to drink. In calling Page's attention to the strange being it became frightened, and with cat-like agility, which has always been a leading characteristic, with a few bounds was out of sight."

Despite having been given the extremely odd nickname of the "kangaroo man," the newspaper's description of the beast is actually quite Bigfoot-like, as the following extract from the article clearly demonstrates:

> The appearance of this animal is almost enough to terrorize the rugged mountainsides themselves. He is described as having the appearance of a man—a very good looking man—is nine feet in height with low forehead, hair hanging down near his eyes, and his body covered with a prolific growth of hair which nature has provided for his protection. Its hands reach almost to the ground and when its tracks were measured its feet were found to be 18 inches in length with five well formed toes. Whether this is a devil, some strange animal or a wild man is what Messrs. Page and McCulloch would like to know.

Four years later, in 1904, the creature—or a similar one of its kind—was again plaguing the mine-filled area. The press enthusiastically reported on the latest development:

At repeated intervals during the past ten years thrilling stories have come from the rugged Sixes mining district in Coos County, Oregon, near Myrtle Point, regarding a wild man or a queer and terrible monster which walks erect and which has been seen by scores of miners and prospectors.

The appearance again of the "Wild Man" of the Sixes has thrown some of the miners into a state of excitement and fear. A report says the wild man has been seen three times since the 10th of last month.

The first appearance occurred on "Thompson Flat." Wm. Ward and a young man by the name of Burlison were sitting by the fire of their cabin one night when they heard something walking around the cabin which resembled a man walking and when it came to the corner of the cabin it took hold of the corner and gave the building a vigorous shake and kept up a frightful noise all the time—the same that has so many times warned the venturesome miners of the approach of the hairy man and caused them to flee in abject fear.

Mr. Ward walked to the cabin door and could see the monster plainly as it walked away, and took a shot at it with his rifle, but the bullet went wide of its mark. The last appearance of the animal was at the Harrison cabin only a few days ago. Mr. Ward was at the Harrison cabin this time and again figures in the excitement.

About five o'clock in the morning the wild man gave the door of the cabin a vigorous shaking which aroused Ward and one of the Harrison boys who took their guns and started in to do the intruder. Ward fired at the man and he answered by sending a four-pound rock at Ward's head but his aim was a little too high. He then disappeared into the brush.

Many of the miners avow that the "wild man" is a reality. They have seen him and know whereof they speak. They say he is something after the fashion of a gorilla and unlike anything else that has ever been known; and not only that but he can throw rocks with wonderful force and accuracy. He is about seven feet high, has broad hands and feet and his body is covered by a prolific growth of hair. In short, he looks like the very devil.

Maybe, in light of all of the above, our quest to learn the truth of Bigfoot should shift from the woods, the forests, and the mountains to somewhere else entirely: the mysterious, dark underworld beneath our feet.

In a 1908 edition of the *Alaska-Yukon Magazine*, there appeared a fascinating story from one Frank E. Howard. It was an article that told of an incident that occurred during the summer months just a few years previously. The location was a mountainous region on Alaska's Malaspina Glacier, where Howard was prospecting. As he negotiated the perilous glacier, Howard had a disastrous fall into a deep crevasse. Fortunately, Howard was not injured, but there was a problem: there was no way for him to climb out the same way he had fallen in. He had just one option, therefore: he had to follow the crevasse, hoping it would lead downhill and to a point where he could finally leave the crevasse and make his way down the glacier. Thankfully, it did exactly that. Howard told the magazine:

> I arose and started down the slope with the idea of reaching the water and following along its margin while the tide was low, in search of some crevasse leading out into the open bay. I was sure the great cavern was crevassed to the surface at some point beyond.
>
> As I kept going ahead I noticed a gradual increase of light, and in a few more steps, I stood in a broad wall of blue light that came

Frank Howard fell into a crevasse while prospecting near Malaspina Glacier. Stuck inside the deep, blue, ice walls, he spied the hulking form of what appeared to be a massively large human.

down from above and, looking up, I saw there was no clear opening to the surface. But objects were now revealed some distance around.

Then an object rose slowly out of the glimmer and took form—a spectral thing, with giant form, and lifelike movement. The object rose erect, a goliath in the shape of a man. Then, watching me with a slantwise glance, it walked obliquely from me, until its form faded in the gloom of the cavern.

It's Howard's final words that suggest strongly that the mighty creature was a Bigfoot: "With its shaggy light-colored fur and huge size, the creature in some ways resembled a bear with bluish gray fur, but that it had a roughly human form, and at all times walked erect."

Ed Ferrell, author of the book *Strange Stories of Alaska and the Yukon*, says of the story: "There is no further record of Frank Howard. Yet his account is consistent with other reports of Bigfoot or Sasquatch."

Raincoast Sasquatch author J. Robert Alley comments: "It seems plausible that this event may have happened in some form or another, as described…. At any rate it is an intriguing tale, if not simply a good yarn, and Ferrell's summation of the creature described as 'consistent with sasquatch' seems quite appropriate."

It should not come as a surprise to learn that the vast wildernesses, thick forests, and massive mountain ranges of Russia are home to Bigfoot-type beasts. They are known to the local folk as Almasty. For some researchers, the creatures are unknown apes. For others, they are nothing less than still surviving pockets of Neanderthals. Both scenarios are amazing in terms of their potential implications. But whatever the true identity of the Almasty, there's very little doubt that it exists. The sheer number of witness reports makes that very clear. The Almasty is a creature that has a long history attached to it, a fact that adds to the likelihood of it being a genuine animal of very ancient proportions.

What is very possibly the earliest report on record of the giant, hairy Almasty came from one Hans Schiltenberger. In the 1400s, Schiltenberger was taken prisoner by Turkish forces and was, as David Hatcher-Childress notes, placed "in the retinue of a Mongol prince named Egidi."

It transpires that upon his return to Europe in 1427, he began writing a book about his experiences with the Turks. The book surfaced in 1430 and is notable for its reference to strange and savage creatures that Schiltenberger was told of, which were said to live high in the Tien Shan Mountains of Mongolia, bordering Russia. Schiltenberger's translated words state:

The inhabitants say that beyond the mountains is the beginning of a wasteland which lies at the edge of the earth. No one can

The Tien Shan Mountains in Central Asia is a remote part of the world where there are few people, an ideal spot to house unknown creatures.

survive there because the desert is populated by so many snakes and tigers. In the mountains themselves live wild people, who have nothing in common with other human beings. A pelt covers the entire body of these creatures. Only the hands and face are free of hair. They run around in the hills like animals and eat foliage and grass and whatever else they can find. The lord of the territory made Egidi a present of a couple of forest people, a man and a woman. They had been caught in the wilderness, together with three untamed horses the size of asses and all sorts of other animals which are not found in German lands and which I cannot put a name to.

Evidently, the creatures still exist: in August 2005, a Ukranian newspaper, *Situation*, described a recent encounter with no less than an entire group of Almasty on the Demedzhi Plateau in the Crimea. The newspaper reported:

Ivan S., 21, and his group of 12 tourists were spending their second day camped on the plateau. The kids went to sleep early, while the adults stayed up a while. "The night was very bright with a full moon," reported Crimean ufologist Anton A. Anfalov. "Ivan's assistant, Sasha and several of the men left the campsite to use the bathroom and when they returned, they looked terrified and trembled with fear. It was then everyone heard a frightful growl near the camp."

Suddenly, the group was confronted by a pack of huge, approximately eight-foot-tall, "naked, hairy men." The newspaper quoted Sasha:

"There were three creatures. And they were about six meters away from us. The hairy humanoids were 2 to 2.5 meters in height. Their true height was hard to estimate because they were all crouched down and balancing themselves on their fists, like large apes. All three were growling at us. Their faces were very hairy, almost without wrinkles, and their eyes were not shiny at all. Their heads were set or positioned very low, as if they had no necks. On their backs they had something like humps on their spine. The creatures were very aggressive. Everyone was scared and the beasts' growls awoke the children who became hysterical."

Situation had more to say: "The standoff lasted for about 45 minutes. Finally, the creatures turned and bounded away with strange ape-like bouncing leaps. The campers spent a sleepless night around their fire. In the morning Ivan and the others searched the ground around their camp, but due to a dense layer of fallen leaves the creatures didn't leave any distinct prints."

Moving on to 2009, in April of that year, Russian newspaper *Pravda* revealed—in an article titled "Russian Scientists Use Google Maps to Find Yeti"—that there had been more than twenty sightings of Almasty by hunters in the forests of Kemerovo. Not only that, there were reports of strange, large footprints having been discovered in the depths of nearby caves: "Scientists

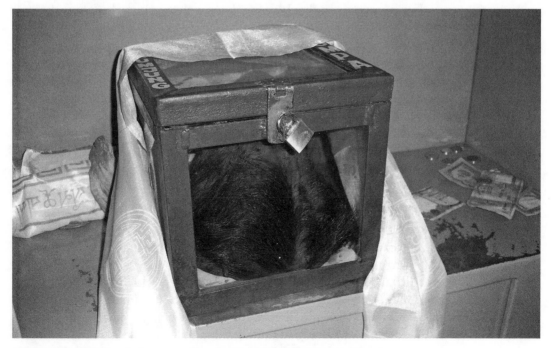

This purported Yeti scalp is preserved at the Khumjong Monastery in Nepal.

found two identical yeti footprints. One of them was left on the rock and it dates back 5,000 years ago, and the other footprint which was left not long ago was found at the bottom of the cave."

Pravda spoke with one of the unnamed scientists, who said: "They are absolutely identical. Five thousand years ago yetis settled down in this cave and now their descendants are still living here. The conditions in the cave are suitable for yeti. The cave defends them from rains, snow and wind. There is also a lake in the middle of the cave where yetis can find clean water."

The newspaper added: "Unfortunately, the scientists did not manage to see yetis that time. They say their snowmobiles were too noisy and yetis had to hide somewhere in the forests. However, the scientists say they managed to reach their main goal—they got the proof that yetis are living there. A new expedition to the site will be arranged this summer."

But that was not all, as *Pravda* made very clear: "Members of the Kosmopoisk association have returned from an expedition to Russia's Kirov Region where they searched for a Bigfoot that allegedly lived in that region. Kosmopoisk leader Vadim Chernobrov says the expedition has discovered a den occupied by a mysterious giant and an underground passage dug obviously not by a human."

Ivan Konovalov was a forest warden who, for thirty years, worked in the Kirov Region. He told of his 1985 encounter with an Almasty:

> It was snowing on the day when I was walking along the fir wood and suddenly heard snap of twigs. I turned around and saw an awesome creature covered with dark hair that was much taller than me. It smelt strongly. The beast leant against a pine tree and started bending it down to the ground.
>
> The tree was rather thick, but it cracked under the creature's burden. Then the creature started breaking the tree against the knee. Its hands were as thick and long as its legs. Quite of a sudden, the creature felt something and turned its 'face' to me. I saw two black eyes and the impression at the bottom of the eyes deeply impressed me. I still remember the look of the eyes. Then the creature flung the tree and quickly left. But I stood thunderstruck and could not move a finger.

"DREADED WILD MEN Strike Fear into Indian Children" was the eye-catching title of an article that jumped out of the pages of the March 3, 1934, edition of the *Lethbridge Herald* newspaper, which covered Alberta, Canada. The story was a fascinating one, given that it focused on the often-reported possibility that the Bigfoot creatures are able to remain out of harm's way and detection by living in underground realms such as ancient caverns and incredibly deep cave systems.

The article began by stating that Native American children in the vicinity of Harrison Mills, British Columbia, had been warned to stay close to "their mothers' apron strings, for the fearsome 'Sasquatch' had returned to spread terror through peace-loving Chehalis tribes."

It was noted that although reports of the much-feared creatures were all the rage in the area some three decades earlier, this was the first time since around 1914 that they had been seen "on the prowl" in the area. It appeared that the first of the recent encounters came from a man named Frank Dan.

The *Lethbridge Herald* captivated its readers with the details of the uncanny event: "Investigating the persistent barking of his dog at night, Dan came face to face with a hairy giant who, according to Dan, was tall and muscular, prowling in the nude. He was covered in black hair from head to foot except for a small space around the eyes. Dan ran breathlessly into his house and secured the door. Peeking through the window, he saw the giant stride leisurely into the nearby bush and disappear."

The writer of the article noted something very interesting: "The Indians say the Sasquatch dwell in caves and subterranean caverns on the borders of lakes in the mountain vastnesses [sic]. Many strange tales are told of the appearances of the elusive people."

Despite the unsettling nature of the story, the newspaper finished on a humorous note, whether deliberate or not: "A Chehalis woman related that, when her husband was returning from the hunt with a score or more of ducks he had shot, a Sasquatch stepped out of the bush and took the ducks from him—except one, which the giant stuffed into the shirt of the frightened Indian."

Selfish, it would appear, Bigfoot is not!

Situated in Southeast Asia and Oceania, Indonesia is made up of a huge number of islands—literally thousands. One of those islands is Flores, more than five thousand square miles in area and with a population of close to two million. Its wild animal population is notable and includes the deadly Komodo dragon and the Flores giant rat. The island may be home to something far stranger, too.

The Nage people of Flores tell of a somewhat human-like ape called the Ebu gogo. The Ebu gogo was covered in hair and had distinct apelike qualities but walked upright like a human. At barely three feet tall, they were hardly on a par with Bigfoot, but that does not take away the fact that, for the Nage people, the creatures generated a great deal of folklore and history.

The Nage people of Flores tell of a somewhat human-like ape called the Ebu gogo. The Ebu gogo was covered in hair and had distinct apelike qualities but walked upright like a human.

According to the legend, the presence of the animals was first noted when a tribe of people set up a village in an area known as Ua at some point in the 1700s. All of the Ebu gogo on Flores lived deep inside an extensive network of caves somewhere in the central part of the island, which extended in length to almost a mile. Reportedly, the colony ran to around four dozen creatures. It wasn't long before curiosity got the better of the Ebu gogo, and they began making regular visits to the village perimeter, watching the people from a safe distance.

Over time, the Ebu gogo gained more confidence and, finally, were invited to partake in a village feast. By all accounts, they ate and drank heartily, hence the name given to them by the villagers, which translates as "ancestor who eats everything."

As a demonstration that the Ebu gogo were something more than mere unknown apes, they loved to dance, had their own fairly complex language, and could even mimic—to an eerie degree—the words of the Nage people. Whether they actually understood the words they mimicked is very much a matter for debate.

It wasn't long, however, before matters began to deteriorate and tensions grew. Not content with the large banquets that the Nage invited the Ebu gogos to attend, the greedy creatures began raiding the farms of the villagers, grabbing crops and killing animals for food. According to legend, two children of the village were seized by the Ebu gogo and taken to the caves, where the ape-men demanded the children show them how to make fire. Fortunately, the terrified children managed to escape, fleeing back to the safety of the village.

For the folk of Ua, enough was, by now, enough. They decided that the Ebu gogo had to be exterminated one way or another. They came up with a plan: The village elders invited the creatures to a massive feast, at which the Ebu gogo were encouraged to drink as much powerful wine as they could. The ever-hungry beasts didn't need telling twice, and they were soon stuffed and drunk. At the end of the night, the beasts staggered back to the caves and fell into deep, alcohol-induced sleeps.

Then, when the Ebu gogo were down for the count, the villagers hauled a huge amount of palm fiber to the cave, set it alight, and asphyxiated the creatures as they slept. Reportedly, however, two of the Ebu gogo—a male and a female—were seen fleeing into the woods, which suggests the possibility that they didn't become extinct after all.

There is a very intriguing footnote to the story of the Ebu gogo of Flores. In 2003, at a cave called Liang Bua in western Flores, the skeletal remains of a number of creatures dubbed "hobbits" were found. Examinations of the bones showed they were approximately three feet, three inches tall and humanoid. They were given the official title of *Homo floresiensis*.

The 2003 discovery, which became the subject of a 2004 paper in the journal *Nature*, might also have been the impetus for the tales of the mysterious ape called Orang Pendek. In a specially prepared report, cryptozoologist Richard Freeman tells the story and reveals his interpretation of the Orang Pendek angle:

An artist's rendition of what the Orang Pendek looks like based on witness descriptions. Also shown is a comparison between an average human's height and that of the creature.

> Some theorize that the Orang-pendek may be a small hominian. As far back as the 1940s William Charles Osman Hill, primatologist, zoologist, and anatomist, postulated that Orang-pendek might have a possible connection to the fossils of *Homo erectus*. Along with the Nittaewo of Sri Lanka, he believed that they might be a dwarf island form of *Homo erectus*. Island dwarfism occurs when a species colonizes an island smaller than the landmass from whence it came. With fewer resources the species' descendants evolve into a smaller species.

The notion of a tiny island hominian was proven in a spectacular manner in 2004. Australian paleontologist Mike Morwood was excavating the Liang Bua cave in the west of Flores when he made a remarkable discovery, an adult skull of a human-like creature, but of tiny proportions. Further excavations uncovered more of the skeleton and a number of other individuals. Most incredibly of all, the remains were not fossilized. Their constitution was likened to wet tissue paper. The bones had to be allowed to dry before they could be excavated. Besides the creatures were tools, weapons, and evidence of fire use.

The creatures were named *Homo floresiensis* and in life would have stood only one meter tall. Despite having a smaller cranial capacity than a chimpanzee, it seems that *Homo floresiensis* was highly intelligent. Not only did it use fire and stone tools, it seems to have hunted pygmy stegodont elephants and giant rodents with which it shared its island home.

Some tried to discredit the find as nothing more than microcephalic examples of modern man. This theory is quite absurd as the skull of *Homo floresiensis* are rounded and not elongate or proportionately tiny in the way microcephalics invariably are.

Neither could microcephalics produce the tools that the remains were found alongside. Finally, the idea of a number of microcephalics, a rare condition as it is, all being found in the same cave is patently absurd.

In general, life expectancy for individuals with microcephaly is reduced and the prognosis for normal brain function is poor. The prognosis varies depending on the presence of associated abnormalities.

Recent work seems to suggest that *Homo floresiensis* is even more incredible than we first thought. It now seems that, rather than being a descendent of *Homo erectus* as originally postulated, but outside of the genus Homo and more closely related to the African Australopithecus. The last known Australopithecus, *Australopithecus africanus*, died out 1.9 million years ago.

It seems that the Liang Bua population of *Homo floresiensis* was killed during the eruption of a volcano around 12,000 years ago. But anthropologist Gregory Forth and others have suggested that *Homo floresiensis* survived in other parts of Flores until recently and may have been the genesis of the Ebu gogo legends.

Indeed, the Ebu gogo is said to survive in the deep jungles of Flores even today. The legend of the Ebu gogo's destruction by fire may be a distorted retelling of real events. Around 1830 a volcano known as Ebu Lobo erupted, spewing lava for a distance of 4km. The date matches fairly well with the date that the Ebu gogo were supposedly destroyed. Could the localized eruption have killed off a late surviving population of *Homo floresiensis* or have forced them away from the area, leading to the folktale?

It seems quite possible that *Homo floresiensis* and the Ebu gogo are one and the same as are the other Flores creatures known under different names. It is also perfectly possible that *Homo floresiensis* is still alive and well on Flores and on other Indonesian islands.

When it was first discovered, many people made the link between *Homo floresiensis* and the Orang-pendek. Debbie Martyr told me of stories from Sumatra of a race of tiny hairy people. They used tools and fire and lived only in the very deep jungle. But here is the catch, the native people knew them to be totally distinct from the Orang-pendek.

These little people were smaller than Orang-pendek and though hairy, they were much less ape-like. Unlike Orang-pendek they fashioned tools, used fires and lived in small tribes. Orang-pendek has no use of fire. It may use sticks as weapons but—as far as we know—it does not seem to fashion tools. Furthermore, it is solitary.

Homo floresiensis and Orang-pendek do not match up well. The latter is larger, more primitive, and more solidly built. All of the tracks I have seen of the Orang-pendek show an offset big toe, a feature indicative of an ape. All the eyewitness descriptions seem to be recalling an upright ape and not a hominian.

Of relevance to the matter of primitive hominids in the United Kingdom is the story of the noted Devon folklorist and acclaimed writer Theo Brown. The author of such titles as *Devon Ghosts* and *Family Holidays around Dartmoor*, Brown collected a number of potentially related stories, including one chilling recollection by a friend of hers who had been walking alone at dusk near the Neolithic earthworks at the top of Lustleigh Cleave, which sits on the extreme east side of Dartmoor, England, in the Wrey Valley.

A partial skeleton of a *Homo floresiensis* is on display at the Natural History Museum in London, England.

Lustleigh Cleave is an extraordinarily strange place at the best of times, a valley where an inordinate number of unexplained incidents and anomalous phenomena seem to take place on an amazingly regular basis. Moreover, the remains of prehistoric stone huts can be seen in the vicinity, and an ancient burial monument, Datuidoc's Stone—which is estimated to have originated at some point around 550 to 600 C.E.—stands, to this very day, pretty much as it did all those thousands of years ago.

Jon Downes says of the weirdness that dominates the area: "I have got reports of sightings of a ghostly Tudor hunting party, of mysterious lights in the sky, and even the apparitions of a pair of Roman Centurions at Lustleigh Cleave."

But, adds Downes, getting to the most important aspect of the story, "Theo Brown's friend saw, clearly, a family of 'cave men,' either naked and covered in hair or wrapped in the shaggy pelts of some wild animal, shambling around the stone circle at the top of the cleave."

Whether a person believes in Bigfoot, is highly skeptical, or has an open and undecided mind, the fact is that just about everyone is familiar with the

In Rudyard Kipling's *The Jungle Book,* Mowgli is a boy raised by wolves in the Indian jungles; a "Mowgli" is sometimes used now as a generic word for a wild man.

word "Bigfoot." But there's a possibility that, had circumstances not dictated otherwise, the legendary hairy giant of the woods might have become known by a very different name: Mowgli. It's a term that was briefly in use in the earlier part of the twentieth century before it was eclipsed first by Sasquatch and then, from 1958 onward, Bigfoot.

Almost certainly, the name Mowgli was lifted from *The Jungle Book*, Rudyard Kipling's collection of stories, published in 1894, that told of the adventures of a young, feral boy named Mowgli in the wooded wilds of central India.

We see evidence of the word "Mowgli" in a number of newspaper accounts that surfaced in the first decade of the twentieth century. We will begin with the *Van Wert Daily Bulletin*, an Ohio-based publication that, on October 28, 1905, ran an article by the title of "British Columbia Mowglis: Tribe of Wild Men Roaming Woods and Frightening People." The article stated:

James Johnson, a rancher living near Cornox, seven miles from Cumberland, B.C. [British Columbia, Canada], reports several Mowglis, or wild men, who have been seen in that neighborhood by ranchers, says a Nanaimo (B.C.) correspondent of the San Francisco Call. Johnson asserts that they were performing what seemed to be a sort of "sun dance" on the sand. One of them caught a glimpse of Johnson, who was viewing the proceedings from behind a big log. The Mowglis disappeared as if by magic into a big cave.

Thomas Kincaid, a rancher living near French creek, while bicycling from Cumberland, also reports seeing a Mowgli, whom he describes as a powerfully built man, more than six feet in height and covered with long black hair. The wild man upon seeing Kincaid uttered a shriek and disappeared into the woods.

Upon arriving home Kincaid wrote Government Agent Bray of Nanaimo, inquiring if it would be lawful to shoot the Mowgli, as he was terrorizing that vicinity. The government agent replied that there was no law permitting such an act.

It is reported that on a recent hunting expedition up the Quailicum river an Indian saw a Mowgli and, mistaking him for a bear, shot at and wounded him. During the past month no less than eleven persons coming to Nanaimo from Cumberland have seen the wild men. Parties have been organized and every effort is being made to capture the Mowglis.

It's intriguing to note that, as was the case in more than a few early reports of unknown apes in the United States, the Mowglis were tied to the presence in the area of a "big cave." Further proof, perhaps, of their predilection for a life spent largely under the surface of the planet.

Less than one year later, the *Yukon World* published a story of the Mowglis. The date was August 1906, and the feature was titled "Alberni Has a Wild Man Vancouver Island Mowgli Said to Be No Myth—Seen by a Prospector Recently." The newspaper recorded:

The famous Vancouver island mowgli is no myth. A prospector is now in Vancouver who says he saw the wild man at Alberni a few days ago. He will not allow his name to be used, asserting that he [was] "not looking for notoriety." He says: "A few days ago myself and another prospector dropped right onto the wild man on the shores of Horn Lake, Alberni. The mowgli was clothed in sunshine and a smile except that his body was covered with a growth of hair much like the salmon berry-eating bears that infest the region. The wild man ran with astonishing agility as soon as he saw us. We found the wickieup in which he had been sheltering and also many traces of where he had been gathering roots along the lake bank for sustenance. That wild man is no figment of the imagination. You can take my word for that."

As fascinating as both newspaper accounts were, the term "Mowgli" was never embraced in the style, and certainly not to the scale, that "Bigfoot" was decades later. Perhaps we should be thankful: "Bigfoot" is far more evocative and descriptive than "Mowgli."

As this chapter and the one preceding it demonstrate, just like our lake monsters and our giant snakes, Bigfoot too has an affinity to water, caves, and caverns. Truly, Bigfoot is a monster of the deep, even though many might not realize it.

REPTILIANS AND ALIEN INFLUENCES

There can be few people with an interest in the field of cryptozoology who have not heard of the so-called Reptilians. Seven- to eight-foot-tall creatures, they are just about the closest thing one can imagine to the famous monster of the waters in the 1954 movie Creature from the Black Lagoon. *Many researchers of this phenomenon assume these creatures are extraterrestrials from faraway galaxies. That may not be the case, though. There are few sightings of these creatures on land. They are only occasionally seen aboard UFOs. When they are seen, it is often in underground locations. It's entirely possible, then, that the natural domains of the Reptilians are subsurface realms filled with water. Such a thing is not at all impossible: marine reptiles, as they are officially known, are reptiles that, over millions of years, have evolved to such an extent that they spend most of their time in the water. That may very well be the case for the Reptilians, too. Keeping that in mind, let's see what we know about these dangerous creatures.*

A REPTILIAN FROM THE STARS

Within the realms of ufology, the paranormal, the folkloric, and conspiracy theorizing, there is quite possibly no phenomenon guaranteed to provoke more controversy, debate, and unbridled paranoia than that concerning the Reptilians. Diabolical, ominous, shapeshifting entities from faraway star systems and twilight dimensions beyond our own, the reptilians are cold-hearted, ruthless entities that have played formative roles in the development and manipulation of human history, folklore, mythology, and culture. They are the secret rulers of the planet, exerting powerful, Machiavellian influence over each and every one of us.

Seven to twelve feet tall, green-skinned, scaled, and monstrous, the Reptilians are the real masters of the world. Using their shapeshifting skills, they have infiltrated and enslaved government, industry, society, royalty, and even the world of Hollywood. In fact, just about no one is free of the terrifying presence and wrath of the dreaded Reptilians.

They are creatures whose existence and presence in our world has nurtured legends of dragons, aliens, and demons. Even the biblical story of the talking snake that tempted Adam and Eve to eat from the Tree of Knowledge in the Garden of Eden can be traced back to Reptilian presence and control.

The Reptilians are the masterminds behind alien abductions. They greedily feast upon the thousands of people who, every year, vanish without trace. They surround us at all times, disguised and camouflaged, using and abusing us as the mood or need takes them. They can even count Queen Elizabeth II and Prince Charles among their vile, flesh-eating and blood-drinking numbers. And their mightiest of all figures secretly inhabit vast, underground caverns that exist far below our surface world.

Quetzalcoatl is illustrated here in the pages of the sixteenth-century Codex Telleriano-Remensis. Here, the Aztec god takes a human form, though he is often depicted as a feathered serpent, which is what his name means.

So we are told by the conspiracy minded, at least.

Perhaps the most famous of all the Reptilians was Quetzalcoatl. He was a god of Mesoamerican lore—Mesoamerican meaning central to the cultures and people of Mexico, Belize, Nicaragua, Costa Rica, El Salvador, Guatemala, and Honduras. According to predominantly Aztec legend, Quetzalcoatl was a highly advanced entity with near-magical skills and possessed of highly advanced sciences who tried to bring civilization, technology, and a new world to the Mesoamericans. His name translates as "feathered serpent," hence the potential connection to the controversy surrounding the so-called Reptilians of UFO lore.

Nicoletta Maestri says of Quetzalcoatl that he is "represented in many different ways according to different epochs and Mesoamerican cultures. He is both represented in his non-human form, as a feathered serpent, with plumage along its body and around the head, as well as in his human form, especially among the Aztecs and in Colonial codices. In his human aspect, he is often depicted in dark color with a red beak, symbol of Ehecatl, the wind god, and with a cut shell as a pendant, symbol of Venus. In many images he is depicted wearing a plumed headdress and holding a plumed shield."

So far as can currently be determined, the worship of this enigmatic deity began at some point between 100 B.C.E. and 100 C.E. It should be noted, however, that devotion to serpent-like gods in Mesoamerica in general began much earlier. Evidence of such worship can be found in Tabasco, Mexico, and is estimated to have dated back to at least 900 B.C.E., when it was embraced by the Olmec people.

As evidence of the influence that serpent gods had over Mesoamericans, one need only take a look at the Temple of the Feathered Serpent, which is situated at Teotihuacan, about thirty miles outside of Mexico City, and was constructed around 100 B.C.E. Classic imagery of feathery serpents, or war serpents, adorns the huge step-pyramid, as it is known, which is also termed the Temple of Quetzalcoatl, even though it predates widespread worship of Quetzalcoatl. Such was the reverence with which the people viewed their serpent god, human sacrifice to whom was both widespread and commonplace.

Interpretations on what or who Quetzalcoatl was are as many as they are varied.

Within Mormon lore, James Edward Talmage recounts in his 1899 work *"The Book of Mormon": An Account of Its Origin, with Evidences of Its Genuineness and Authenticity*: "The story of the life of the Mexican divinity, Quetzalcoatl, closely resembles that of the Savior; so closely, indeed, that we can come to no other conclusion than that Quetzalcoatl and Christ are the same being. But the history of the former has been handed down to us through an impure Lamanitish source, which has sadly disfigured and perverted the original incidents and teachings of the Savior's life and ministry."

Karl Andreas Taube is an archaeologist who has studied the stories of Quetzalcoatl and states that, in his opinion, the god symbolized fertility. He says: "It is possible that the alternating serpent heads, Quetzalcoatl and the War Serpent, refer to dual aspects of rulership, the feathered serpent with fertility and the interior affairs of the state, and the War Serpent with military conquest and empire."

David Carrasco, a noted historian, has suggested Quetzalcoatl is a deity that represents culture and civiliza-

And now we come to the most controversial theory of all: that Quetzalcoatl was an ancient astronaut who was determined to bring culture and science to what he perceived as a decidedly primitive body of people.

tion. And now we come to the most controversial theory of all: that Quetzal-coatl was an ancient astronaut who was determined to bring culture and science to what he perceived as a decidedly primitive body of people.

On this matter, it is intriguing to note that throughout Mesoamerica, Quetzalcoatl was associated with the planet Venus. Alberto Mendo, in his paper "Quetzalcoatl: Beyond the Feathered Serpent," notes that "the date of birth of Quetzalcoatl and the day when Venus reappears on the same position in the eastern horizon once every eight years" is the same. Author Vicky Anderson, in her article "Goddess, the Divine Feminine," says: "To the ancient Maya and the Aztecs, the god Xolotl was the evening star and his brother Quetzalcoatl was the morning star. The Maya and the Aztecs prophecy that, one day, the god Quetzalcoatl will return to the Earth from Venus."

John Major Jenkins offers the opinion that "the Toltec pantheon that represented the Zenith Cosmology was Quetzalcoatl, whose earliest astronomical association is with the Pleiades.... The Pleiades were known as the serpent's rattle, and the flight of the Pleiades into alignment with the zenith sun evoked the image of a flying serpent."

That Quetzalcoatl was so inextricably tied to the heavens above makes it relatively easy to understand why suggestions have been made that he was an extraterrestrial entity. Quetzalcoatl researcher Rick Popko has a scenario for the nature of the legend that is definitively extraterrestrial-themed but in a different way. He offers the following:

> The theory I have is that Q was actually a very large UFO. As the craft entered Earth's atmosphere, it broke into flames and began its long descent, flaming, smoking and spiraling out of control. If this thing was multiple football fields in size, from the ground, it could very well look like a flaming serpent head, and the spiral smoke trails could be interpreted as feathers. Of course a ship of this size is going to make a big impact when it crashes and probably take out a lot of innocent people in the process. Keep in mind most of these people have probably never seen anything like this in their lives, let alone watch it crash into their society and kill a bunch of people. Heck if I were there at the time, I'd probably bow down to it as my god as well.

A writer on the website *Arcturi* notes: "Ancient Aliens have been suspected to have helped create many wonders we see today including the massive Temples found through Central America and the Yucatan Peninsula. Like other great American civilizations, Reptilians have been an integral part in the Aztec civilization which cultivated a belief system around the alien we now know as the Reptilians."

Writer Paul Dale Roberts, in his article "In Search of Quetzalcoatl," says of the Quetzalcoatl saga:

> What is also interesting is that there is a reptilian influence.... The reptilian influence is saturated throughout Egypt, East Asia, India and the list goes on and on.
>
> I believe the reptilian influence represents ancient astronauts that resembled reptiles. The reptile influence can even be found in our own bible as it was the serpent that influenced Eve to bite from the forbidden fruit. Could it be that ancient astronauts back long ago were living amongst our advanced cultures like the Phoenicians, Egyptians and bringing their knowledge of science, math and astronomy to cultures like the Olmecs, Toltecs and Mayans?

Finally—and notably for our purposes—as a writer for the website *Myths and Legends* notes, this legendary Reptilian had a connection to water, particularly the seas:

> Quetzalcoatl's departure from his people was the work of his old enemy, Tezcatlipoca, who wanted people to make bloodier sacrifices than the flowers, jade, and butterflies they offered to Quetzalcoatl. Tezcatlipoca tricked Quetzalcoatl by getting him drunk and then holding up a mirror that showed Tezcatlipoca's cruel face. Believing that he was looking at his own imperfect image, Quetzalcoatl decided to leave the world and threw himself onto a funeral pyre. As his body burned, birds flew forth from the flames, and his heart went up into the heavens to become Venus, the morning and evening star. Another version of the myth says that Quetzalcoatl sailed east into the sea on a raft of serpents. Many Aztecs believed that he would come back to his people one day after a period of 52 years. In the early 1500s, the Spanish conqueror Hernán Cortés took advantage of this belief by encouraging the people of Mexico to view him as the return of the hero-god Quetzalcoatl.

The Aztecs mistook Spanish conquistador Hernán Cortés for the god Quetzalcoatl upon returning from his overseas voyage.

REPTILIANS ON THE LOOSE

*R*eptiles *Magazine* writes on the topic of "herps," or the reptiles and amphibians studied by herpetologists: "It's two parts hydrogen and one part oxygen. This amazing liquid known as water makes up approximately two-thirds of the weight of an average amphibian or reptile, and it's essential for their physical well-being. Not only do internal body processes, such as cell and organ functions, require this precious liquid, but external body processes, such as shedding, are also reliant upon water to function properly. In the case of some herps, such as frogs and salamanders, the absence of water in the physical environment leads to a quick demise. Others, such as desert reptiles, do not seem quite as demanding; however, they also require this vital substance."

Presumably this applies to Reptilians, too—those humanoid–reptoid creatures that reportedly lurk near swamps, rivers, lakes, and seas worldwide. Some have even suggested the British royal family includes dangerous and deadly shapeshifting creatures. Are their majesties in reality hideous, giant-sized Reptilians, resembling the fictional beast portrayed in the 1954 movie *Creature from the Black Lagoon*? Certainly, it's a scenario that many conspiracy theorists adhere to. And, it must be said, there is a large body of data pertaining to these allegedly human, flesh-eating, blood-drinking monstrosities. But before we get to the matter of Queen Elizabeth II and the rest of the royals, let's first take a look at some classic accounts of Reptilians encountered over the course of the last six decades.

Theories have abounded for some time that the members of the British royal family are actually Reptilians in human guise.

One highly strange encounter with what can only be described as a definitive Reptilian monster occurred on the night of Saturday, November 8, 1958. The unlucky soul who had the misfortune to fall foul of the unearthly beast was Charles Wetzel, who at the time was driving his green, two-door Buick Super along North Main Street in Riverside, California, near the Santa Ana River. As Wetzel reached a stretch of the road that had flooded, the radio of his car began to crackle loudly and in a highly distorted fashion. With the water levels high and Wetzel trying to figure out what was wrong with the radio, he slowed down to make sure he wouldn't drive off the side of the road. Soon, he would find that there were far worse things than a flooded road and a wonky radio.

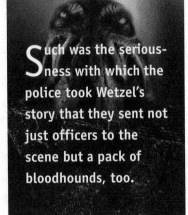

Such was the seriousness with which the police took Wetzel's story that they sent not just officers to the scene but a pack of bloodhounds, too.

As Wetzel continued to slowly negotiate the road, he was shocked to the core by the sight of an extraordinary creature that surfaced from the shadows and, in brazen fashion, stood in the middle of the road, preventing Wetzel from going any further. He could only sit and stare, in a combination of fear and awe, as he tried to comprehend the thing that stood before him.

Humanoid in shape and in excess of six feet in height, it had a large, round head described as being "pumpkin"-like; glowing eyes; a prominent mouth that had beak-like qualities to it; and scaly skin that resembled leaves. Strangest of all, the legs of the beast did not extend from beneath its torso but from its sides. Actually, that may not have been so strange after all: lizards and other reptiles are built in precisely that fashion. Add to that a pair of long, muscular arms, and you have a definitive monster.

What began as a bone-chilling standoff quickly mutated into something else entirely. The reptile-man issued a loud, high-pitched noise that was part scream and part gurgle, after which it suddenly charged at Wetzel's Buick. He could only sit, paralyzed with fear, as the scaly thing raced toward the hood of the vehicle, then lunged and violently clawed the windshield.

Although it was good fortune that Wetzel happened to have a rifle with him, by his own admission, he was fearful about using it—but not because it might injure or kill the animal-man. Wetzel's big concern was that if he fired through the windshield and failed to kill it, the shattered glass would allow the monster to reach inside and haul him out of the car, presumably to tear him to pieces. With his body flooded with adrenaline, Wetzel took the only option he felt was available to him: he floored the accelerator, spun the wheels, and shot away. In doing so, he ran the beast down, which was evident by the fact that Wetzel felt the car go over its large body.

While some might consider a story like this to be nothing more than a hoax, it probably was not. The rationale for this is that Wetzel quickly reported the affair to the local police, who launched an investigation. It's most unlikely that a hoaxer would run the risk of being charged with wasting police time or for filing a bogus report. Such was the seriousness with which the police took Wetzel's story that they sent not just officers to the scene but a pack of bloodhounds, too. The monster, whatever it was, was never found, dead or alive. There was, however, evidence that corroborated Wetzel's amazing experience: vicious-looking claw marks on the windshield and on the underside of the Buick. They were calling cards that Wetzel preferred to try to forget about.

In 1972, the people of Thetis Lake in British Columbia, Canada, found themselves thrust into a saga of monstrous proportions—as in literally monstrous proportions. On August 19, two young men, Robin Flewellyn and Gordon Pile, encountered a scaly, humanoid monster that looked like the deadly, fictional beast of the 1954 Universal movie *Creature from the Black Lagoon.* Rather odd for something that seemed Reptilian in nature, the monster was silver in color. And the pair didn't just encounter the thing; they were chased by it, too. Fortunately, despite its clear attempts to try to injure or kill them, the friends managed to avoid its deadly clutches and headed for the nearest police station. Such was the state of fear into which Flewellyn and Pile had been plunged that the police considered their story to be a true one.

It was a story bolstered by the fact that four days later, the monster was seen again at Thetis Lake, this time roaming around the opposite side of the lake. The witnesses were Michael Gold and Russell Van Nice, who confirmed the silver color of the creature, the scaly skin, and that it appeared to have a spike or spikes protruding from the top of its head.

One day later, the story was big news: it was covered in the pages of the *Victoria Times* along with a graphic drawing of the monster of Thetis Lake. Interest and concern were growing. Perhaps in an effort to lay the matter to rest and ensure that concern didn't erupt into full-blown hysteria, the police maintained quickly that they had solved the affair. What the witnesses had seen, the police assured the media and the local population, was nothing stranger than an escaped pet tegu lizard. Cryptozoologist Dr. Karl Shuker made an important comment on this most unlikely scenario: "Native to South America, tegus can grow up to four feet long, but are not bipedal or humanoid in shape, do not have crests, are not silver in color, have typical five-toed, lizard-like feet as opposed to three-toed flippers, do not have a fish-like mouth, but do have a very long, noticeable tail (unlike the Thetis Lake monster)."

Shuker added: "Not surprisingly, given the considerable morphological discrepancies noted above, investigators of this case do not share the police's enthusiasm for accepting a tegu as the Thetis Lake monster's identity."

In the summer of 1988, a terrifying creature began haunting the woods and little towns of Lee County, South Carolina, specifically the Scape

Ore Swamp area. It quickly became known as Lizard Man for its alleged green and scaly body. A bipedal lizard roaming the neighborhood? Maybe, yes. It all began—publicly if not chronologically—when on July 14, 1988, the Waye family phoned the Lee County sheriff's office and made a strange and disturbing claim. Something wild and animalistic had attacked their 1985 Ford. It looked as if something large, powerful, and deeply savage had viciously clawed, and maybe even bitten into, the body of the vehicle, particularly the hood. Somewhat baffled, the deputies responded to the call.

Sure enough, the Wayes were right on target: their vehicle was battered and bruised in the extreme. In addition, there were footprints across the muddy area. It was clearly time to bring in Sheriff Liston Truesdale. There was a strong probability that the prints were those of a fox. Larger prints, also found, were suspected of being those of a bear—although some observers suggested they had human qualities.

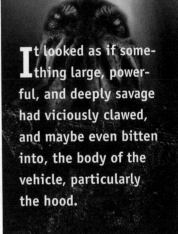

It looked as if something large, powerful, and deeply savage had viciously clawed, and maybe even bitten into, the body of the vehicle, particularly the hood.

In such a close-knit neighborhood, it didn't take long before news got around, and numerous locals turned up to see what all the fuss was about. It's notable that Sheriff Truesdale told Bigfoot investigator Lyle Blackburn, who wrote the definitive book on the affair—titled, of course, *Lizard Man:* "While we were there looking over this situation, we learned that people in the Browntown community had been seeing a strange creature about seven feet tall with red eyes. Some of them described it as green, but some of them as brown. They thought it might be responsible for what happened."

A mystery and a monster were unleashed.

The publicity afforded the Waye incident prompted someone who ultimately became the key player in the matter to come forward. His name was Chris Davis, at the time seventeen years of age. Chris's father, Tommy, had seen the sensationalized coverage given by the media to the attack on the Waye family's vehicle and contacted Sheriff Truesdale. Specifically, Tommy took his son to tell the police what he had told him. It was quite a story.

Back in 1988, Chris was working at a local McDonald's. On the night of June 29—roughly two weeks before the Waye affair exploded—Chris was on the late shift, which meant he didn't finish work until after two o'clock in the morning. His journey home ensured that he had to take a road across a heavily forested part of the swamp, where that morning he had a blowout. Chris pulled up at a crossroads and, helped by the bright moonlight, changed the tire. As he finished the job and put the tools back into the trunk, Chris saw something looming out of the trees. Large, humanlike in shape, and possessing two glowing, red eyes and three fingers on each hand, it was something horrific. Chris panicked, jumped in his vehicle, and sped off. Based on what Chris had to say next, that was a very wise move:

> I looked back and saw something running across the field towards me. It was about 25 yards away and I saw red eyes glowing. I ran into the car and as I locked it, the thing grabbed the door handle. I could see him from the neck down—the three big fingers, long black nails and green rough skin. It was strong and angry. I looked in my mirror and saw a blur of green running. I could see his toes and then he jumped on the roof of my car. I thought I heard a grunt and then I could see his fingers through the front windshield, where they curled around on the roof. I sped up and swerved to shake the creature off.

The reports didn't end there.

Sheriff Truesdale received more and more reports, to the extent that an *X-Files*-style dossier was compiled. This dossier included the fascinating account of Johnny Blythers, who, on July 31, 1990, described for the sheriff's department the events of the previous night:

> Last night about 10:30 P.M., we were coming home from the Browntown section of Lee County. It was me, my mother (Bertha Mae Blythers), [and] two sisters…. I started talking about the time we passed the flowing well in Scape Ore Swamp. I said they ain't no such thing as a Lizard Man. If there was, somebody would be seeing it or caught it.
>
> We got up about a mile or mile and a half past the butter bean shed, about 50 feet from the dirt road by those two signs; my mother was driving the car.
>
> It was on the right side; it came out of the bushes. It jumped out in the road. My mother swerved to miss it, and mashed the brakes and sped up. It jumped out of the bushes like he was going to jump on the car. When my mother mashed the brakes, it looked like it wanted to get in the car.

Johnny's mother, Bertha Mae, gave her own statement on that terrifying drive through the spooky swamp:

> This past Monday night I went to my mother's house in Browntown to pick up my son. We went to McDonald's on Highway 15 near Bishopville to get something to eat. We left there about 20 minutes after 10:00 P.M., was headed home and came through Browntown and Scape Ore Swamp….
>
> We passed the bridge and was down the road near a mile. I was looking straight ahead going about 25 miles per hour, and I saw

this big brown thing. It jumped up at the window. I quickly sped up and went on the other side of the road to keep him from dragging my 11-year-old girl out of the car. I didn't see with my lights directly on it. It nearly scared me to death.

Then there was the statement of Tamacia Blythers, Bertha Mae's daughter: "Tall—taller than the car, brown looking, a big chest, had big eyes, had two arms. Don't know how his face looked, first seen his eyes. Never seen nothing like it before. I didn't see a tail. Mother says if she hadn't whipped over he would have hit her car or jumped on it. Mother said she was so scared her body light and she held her heart all the way home."

In addition, Lyle Blackburn has uncovered other reports of the beast dating from 1986 to well into the 2000s. Two of the key players in this saga are now dead: Johnny Blythers and Chris Davis, the former in a car accident in 1999 and the latter from a shotgun blast, the result of a drug deal gone bad, almost a decade to the day after Blythers's death.

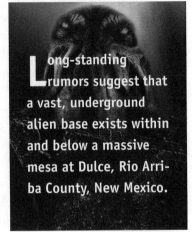

Long-standing rumors suggest that a vast, underground alien base exists within and below a massive mesa at Dulce, Rio Arriba County, New Mexico.

As for the legendary Lizard Man: what, exactly, was it? Certainly, the name provoked imagery of a malevolent, scaly, green monster. But let's not forget that there were references to the beast having a brown color. This leads us to Lyle Blackburn's conclusions. To his credit, Blackburn undertook a personal, on-site investigation with his colleague, Cindy Lee, and studied all the evidence in unbiased fashion. Blackburn noted that, despite the undeniably memorable name, the various descriptions of the beast as being brown in color simply did not accord with anything of a Reptilian nature.

Blackburn suggested that if a Bigfoot dwelled in watery bottomlands, where it might become "covered in algae-rich mud or moss, this could explain its green, wet-like appearance. It doesn't explain the three fingers, but greenish mud which has dried and cracked could certainly give a scaly appearance."

It's a good theory, and it's a far more likely scenario than that of a huge, bipedal lizard roaming around the swamps of South Carolina.

Long-standing rumors suggest that a vast, underground alien base exists within and below a massive mesa at Dulce, Rio Arriba County, New Mexico. Interestingly, we can prove there has been a wealth of weird activity in the area. For example, the FBI has officially declassified a large file on cattle mutilations in and around Dulce, spanning the mid- to late 1970s. Also, on December 10, 1967, the Atomic Energy Commission (AEC) detonated a twenty-nine-kiloton-yield nuclear device 4,240 feet below ground in an attempt to provoke the release and production of natural gas. Thus was born Gasbuggy, a program of an overall project known as Operation Plowshare, which, ostensibly, was designed to explore the peaceful uses of atomic energy. Notably, the location of the Gasbuggy test, which covered an area of 640 acres, was New Mexico's Carson National Forest, which just happens to be situated only twelve miles from the town of Dulce. Today, people are forbidden from digging underground in that area, which is very interesting in view of the underground base allegations.

Within conspiracy-based research circles, it has been suggested that the nuclear detonation had a very different goal: to destroy the aforementioned alien base and wipe out the deadly, hostile extraterrestrials. Certainly, it's a strange and foreboding story. There are no shortages of accounts suggesting that such a base existed (and may still exist) in which freakish monsters were being created by the alien entities. As one example of many, we have the following comments that came later from someone we might justifiably call a ufological whistleblower: Edward Snowden.

> U.S. Energy Secretary John Herrington named the Lawrence Berkeley Laboratory and New Mexico's Los Alamos National Laboratory to house advanced genetic research centers as part of a project to decipher the human genome. The genome holds the genetically coded instructions that guide the transformation of a single cell, a fertilized egg, into a biological organism.

> "The Human Genome Project may well have the greatest direct impact on humanity of any scientific initiative before us today," said David Shirley, Director of the Berkeley Laboratory. Covertly, this research has been going on for years at the Dulce bio-genetics labs. Level 6 is hauntingly known by employees as "Nightmare Hall." It holds the genetic labs at Dulce. Reports from workers who have seen bizarre experimentation are as follows:

> "I have seen multi-legged 'humans' that look like half-human/half-octopus. Also reptilian-humans, and furry creatures that have hands like humans and cries like a baby, it mimics human words. Also, huge mixtures of lizard-humans in cages. There are fish, seals, birds and mice that can barely be considered those species. There are several cages (and vats) of winged-humanoids, grotesque bat-like creatures, but 3 1/2 to 7 feet tall. Gargoyle-like beings and Draco-Reptoids.

> "Level 7 is worse, row after row of thousands of humans and human mixtures in cold storage. Here too are embryo storage vats of humanoids in various stages of development. I frequently encountered humans in cages, usually dazed or drugged, but sometimes they cried and begged for help. We were told they were hopelessly insane, and involved in high risk drug tests to

cure insanity. We were told to never try to speak to them at all. At the beginning we believed that story. Finally in 1978 a small group of workers discovered the truth."

This brings us to the most controversial claim of all, which revolves around the British royal family. There's no doubt that when it comes to conspiracy theories, one controversial claim beats just about all the rest. It's the assertion that the British royal family are nothing less than deadly, bloodthirsty, shapeshifting monsters with incredible power and influence. "Bloodthirsty" is an apt word to use, since the royals are said to quaff human blood just about as enthusiastically as the rest of the British population likes to knock back pints of beer at the local pub. Here's where controversial exceeds controversial.

Welcome to the world of the Reptilians—eight-foot-tall, interdimensional monsters that masquerade as people. At least, that's how the story goes. There's one person to thank (if that's the correct term to use!) for bringing this strange and enduring claim to light. His name is David Icke. Once a well-known goalkeeper for the English soccer team Coventry City, Icke is today a leading light in the shadowy domains where the conspiracy-minded and the paranoid hang out. His books include *The Biggest Secret* and *The David Icke Guide to the Global Conspiracy.*

Are the likes of Queen Elizabeth II, her husband Prince Philip (the Duke of Edinburgh), and heir to the throne Prince Charles really monsters that are either (a) an ancient species that originated right here on Earth or (b) extraterrestrials from a faraway world? We'll start with the first theory. According to those who adhere to it, the royal family is at the top of the pile when it comes to the matter of who owns the planet.

Forget presidents and prime ministers. The real, secret forces that control and manipulate our world are said to be the Babylonian Brotherhood, an ancient race of dangerous shapeshifters that were responsible for legends like that of Quetzalcoatl—whose name means "feathered serpent" and who was a significant, deity-like force in Mesoamerica that first surfaced around 100 B.C.E. The entity is said to have brought sci-

Reptilians are otherworldly creatures, perhaps from another dimension, who have the ability to disguise themselves as human beings.

ence, farming, and culture to that area. Given the apparent hatred of the Reptilians for humans, Quetzalcoatl's actions were probably self-serving instead of generous, designed to keep people in their place and under his firm and cold-hearted control.

It's intriguing to note that almost three thousand years ago, the ancient people of Mexico had other serpent-based gods, which helps nurture the idea that yesterday's Reptilian gods are still among us and are just about as widespread now as they were then. Today, however, their influence is not just in Mesoamerica but all across the world and even in the domain of politics. That's right: it's not just the British royal family who are said to be monsters.

Leading Reptilians (according to the likes of David Icke) include former U.S. president Bill Clinton, former U.S. secretary of state Hillary Clinton, former U.S. secretary of state Henry Kissinger, and former U.S. president George W. Bush. Reptilians in entertainment include the late Hollywood legend Bob Hope.

One of those who helped to bring this matter to the attention of the conspiracy-obsessed—and, in quick time, to the media and popular culture—was a Californian woman named Arizona Wilder. She claims to have been mind-controlled and manipulated by the world's most infamous secret society, the dreaded Illuminati. Wilder's claims get even, ahem, wilder as she claims to have witnessed diabolical human sacrifice at the hands of the Rockefellers, the Rothschilds, members of the Bush family, and at least one pope. As for Queen Elizabeth II, read on.

Certainly, Arizona Wilder's most graphic and controversial claim is that she witnessed the queen partake in human sacrifices and saw her eat the flesh and drink the blood of her unfortunate human victims. On one occasion, says Wilder, Queen Elizabeth was so fired up that she practically tore out a poor soul's throat, drinking it down as it spewed forth. According to Wilder, in her Reptilian form, the queen has skin that is a pale, sickly color. Her face, meanwhile, changes into something that closely resembles a beak.

Adding more to this story is Wilder's claim that, back in 1981, she met with Lady Diana Spencer, soon to become Diana, Princess of Wales. According to Wilder, the princess-to-be was forced to take part in a ritual of ancient and secret proportions that involved the queen, Prince Philip, and Prince Charles and his lover and now wife, Camilla Parker Bowles. Placed into a drugged state, Diana was told that there was one reason, and one reason only, for her marriage to Charles: to ensure that the royal/Reptilian bloodline continued. When Diana was tragically killed in Paris, France, in 1997—an incident still shrouded in mystery and intrigue years later—Icke weaved her untimely death into his Reptilian scenario.

Conspiracy theorists who fully believed the Reptilian scenario practically foamed at the mouth when Mohamed Al-Fayed—the father of Dodi Fayed, who was Diana's boyfriend at the time of her death and who died with her in the terrible car crash that took three lives—referred to Camilla Parker Bowles as Prince Charles's "crocodile wife." Then, when Fayed labeled the entire royal family the "Dracula family," it only added to the idea that the royals were drinkers of human blood. Were Fayed and Al-Fayed, in a less than subtle fashion, trying to warn people of the growing, Reptilian threat in their midst?

Today, the so-called Reptilian agenda terrifies, intrigues, and entertains countless people. The phenomenon clearly isn't going away anytime soon. Are the numerous people who make up the British royal family shapeshifting reptiles with origins that date back millennia? Is the entire issue nothing but the likes of fabrication, lies, pranks, and jokes? Or does it hazily lie somewhere in between? It depends on whom you ask—as is the case with practically all conspiracy theories of a highly bizarre nature. Moreover, there is another aspect to this saga to consider, which focuses on the matter of so-called alien abductions, as we'll now see.

It was on June 24, 1947, that the so-called modern era of ufology began with pilot Kenneth Arnold's encounter with a squadron of flying saucers over the Cascade Mountains in Washington State. For the most part, however, it wasn't until the early years of the 1950s that people began reporting encounters with alleged alien entities. That was the period in which, all across the United States, reports came pouring in of encounters with what became known as the Space Brothers. They were reported as being incredibly human-looking and sporting heads of long, blond hair. Typically, they would warn witnesses of the perils of atomic war and express concerns about our violent, warlike ways.

As the 1960s began, reports started to surface of so-called alien abductions, and these increased greatly in the 1970s and even into the 1980s and 1990s. In the 1980s, there was another development in the matter of human–alien interaction, revolving around the aforementioned Reptilians. Not content with ruling the planet—under the shapeshifted guise of world leaders and royalty—the Reptilians have also surfaced prominently in the issue of alien abductions.

Stories told by abductees related to Reptilians are as controversial as the nonabductee stories concerning the British royal family. The reasons are very different, however. For the most part, the Reptilians are present during abductions aboard alleged alien spacecraft that involve women, and they're not looking for DNA, cells, or blood. It's sex that these appearance-changing stud muffins are after. And, apparently, more than a few women have been very satisfied by the experiences. One of them is Pamela Stonebrooke, a writer and jazz-music performer who makes no bones about the fact that, from her

> Today, the so-called Reptilian agenda terrifies, intrigues, and entertains countless people. The phenomenon clearly isn't going away anytime soon.

perspective, getting "examined" aboard a UFO by something that appears half human and half crocodile is not a bad thing. Not everyone agrees, however.

Many people who have experienced sex at the hands of the Reptilians are, quite understandably, reluctant to go public with their experiences, at least not with their full names. One such person is "Audrey," a thirty-eight-year-old woman who claims seven very close encounters with male Reptilians between 2001 and 2007. A resident of Sedona, Arizona—a place renowned for a wide range of paranormal phenomena—Audrey was first abducted by what she later recalled, in somewhat of a drugged, hypnotized state, was a group of military personnel in black fatigues late one night on the edge of town.

As she drove home after visiting a friend in Flagstaff, Audrey caught sight of a black van following her, which loomed out of the shadows and ran her off the road. The next thing she remembered was being manhandled into that same van. After that, it was lights out. She later woke up to find herself strapped to a table in a brightly lit, circular room. In front of her were three men in black fatigues. As Audrey strained to sit up, she watched in terror as all three men suddenly shimmered, as if caught in something akin to a heat haze. In no more than six or seven seconds they were replaced by a trio of approximately eight-foot-tall, green-colored monsters that looked like Godzilla's younger and smaller brothers.

Audrey states that the aliens moved toward the table, unstrapped her, and, one by one, had sex with her. She was somewhat embarrassed to admit that the encounter was exciting, if fraught. She was, however, unable to shake

off the taboo of what she described as having sex with animals—if that's what they really were. According to Audrey, all of the other experiences occurred in her own home—again, late at night—and sex was the only thing that happened.

Perhaps the most disturbing encounter was the fourth one, in which two men dressed in black suits, white shirts, and red ties, with near-identical, slicked-back hair, materialized in her bedroom as she lay in bed, listening to music on her iPod. As with the previous encounter, the men transformed into what she said looked like giant lizards. Once again, Audrey had a swinging time, but again, she was eaten up by guilt, as she was on every subsequent occasion.

The Reptilians, according to at least one witness, looked as if they could be related to Godzilla, the star of numerous Japanese monster movies.

There was, however, one unforeseen side effect of all this. For around almost a year after the final encounter occurred, whenever a man would look or stare at her, Audrey would have shivers go up and down her spine. She was fearful of the possibility that they, too, were Reptilian shapeshifters that could take on human form. If a man looked at her for more than a second or two in a bar or restaurant, she would get the chills. If, while walking around Sedona, a man gave her a friendly nod, she thought it meant he was a Reptilian. Realizing that she was plunging close to a state of mental illness, Audrey eventually pulled herself back from the brink of complete and utter paranoia and moved on with her life. So, apparently, did the Reptilians.

It should be noted that there are numerous such reports both on and off the record that display uncannily similar aspects. This has led even some quite conservative alien-abduction researchers to take the matter of shapeshifting sex very seriously. And there is one final thing about the matter worth pondering: If these stories are not the result of wild fantasies and erotic dreams, then perhaps there really is an alien, Reptilian agenda on our planet. It's one thing to talk about sex with scaly extraterrestrials who have forked tongues and thrashing tails and use women for sex. It's quite another, however, to suggest they're running the planet. Unless, of course, you have encountered the Reptilians yourself. Sometimes, truth really is stranger than fiction.

> And there is one final thing about the matter worth pondering: If these stories are not the result of wild fantasies and erotic dreams, then perhaps there really is an alien, Reptilian agenda on our planet.

We'll close the matter of the Reptilians with the words of Pamela Stonebrooke, who prepared the following for free, public consumption to reveal her connection to the Reptilian phenomenon in all of its stark reality. Here is the statement prepared by Stonebrooke in 1998:

> I'm writing this in response to the news item that appeared in a recent issue of the *New York Post* about my forthcoming book, *Experiencer: A Jazz Singer's True Account of Extraterrestrial Contact*. Since the article unfortunately conveyed the impression that the book would be sensationalistic, it seems appropriate that I share some thoughts with you, and set the record straight about the book I am writing. I know that the *New York Post* piece seriously misrepresented the true nature of the book.
>
> The book is multi-faceted, and treats the abduction phenomenon, in all of its complexity, with the sensitivity, respect and seriousness it deserves, presenting not only my own experiences, but those of other experiencers as well. I'll be examining and exploring my contact experiences in light of their transformative aspects, recognizing that the phenomenon is, and can be, an

incredible catalyst for expanded self-awareness. Interaction with extraterrestrial intelligence has many aspects, of course, but the transformational aspect is fundamental to me.

The book will tell about my reptilian encounters, a subject that very few women are prepared to go public with or speak openly about. I praise the courage of the few that already have—and endured public ridicule as a result. Reptilians are not a politically correct species in the UFO community, and to admit to having sex with one—much less enjoying it—is beyond the pale as far as the more conservative members of that community are concerned. But I know from my extensive reading and research, and from talking personally to dozens of other women (and men), that I am not unique in reporting this kind of experience. I am the first to admit that this is a vastly complex subject, a kind of hall of mirrors, where dimensional realities are constantly shifting and changing. Certainly, the reptilians use sex to control people in various ways. They have the ability to shapeshift and to control the mind of the experiencer, as well as to give tremendous pleasure through their mental powers. I have wrestled with all of these implications and the various levels of meaning and possibilities represented by my encounter experiences. I will say, however, as I have said before, that I feel a deep respect for the reptilian entity with whom I interacted, and a profound connection with this being.

In a past life regression I did recently, I went to a very remote period in earth's history (perhaps hundreds of thousands of years ago), and saw myself as one of a brotherhood of reptilian warriors facing a catastrophic event in which we perished together (it was possibly nuclear in nature, since I saw a red cloud and felt tremendous heat). I believe that on one level, I may be meeting these entities again, perhaps fellow warriors from the past warning us of an impending, self-inflicted doom—or perhaps they are different aspects of myself. I don't really know; I'm just trying to unravel this puzzle like everyone else.

Following my initial Art Bell interview, I received hundreds of letters and e-mails, many from people describing similar encounters to mine. I know that there are people out there who are suffering in isolation and silence, thinking they are going crazy. I have been able to give some of these people strength and courage, so that they can move through their fear and come out the other side, empowered and still able to celebrate life as the incredible adventure that it truly is. I know that when I was processing my Grey experiences, if it had not been for people like John Mack, Budd Hopkins, Kim Carlsberg, Whitley Strieber, John Carpenter, and other researchers and experiencers who have been courageous enough to come forward, putting their lives and reputations on the line, I would have stayed in fear a lot longer, cowering in a corner, my self-esteem and identity shattered. Thanks to them and to the wonderful members of my support group, I am still standing, intact and whole.

I believe that the alien abduction experience is profoundly linked to the momentous shift in consciousness that is occurring as we enter the new millennium. We are witnesses to and participants in the most fantastic era in human history. And contrary to the mood of pessimism from some individuals regarding the way mainstream media treats the UFO phenomenon, and the trepidation that is felt regarding its ultimate impact on the human race, I am unashamedly a "Positive." Everywhere I turn, I find much greater public acceptance of the alien abduction/UFO phenomenon, and active curiosity from enormous numbers of people. I am also encouraged by the fact that many more experiencers are coming forward, no longer hiding behind the cloak of anonymity. I believe that within ten years the reality of alien abduction will be accepted as a fact by the majority of people on this planet, and ridicule of the subject by the media or anyone else will be regarded as naive and irresponsible.

I think the problem that exists between ufology and the media stems from the fact that the UFO community has been so sadly wounded in the past fifty years by rejection and ridicule that it has been somewhat demoralized as a movement. It has been a long, uphill battle, with many martyrs shedding their blood along the way, but I believe that we are winning the battle for public acceptance and are closer than ever before to solving the mystery of the alien presence itself. I am looking forward to appearing on major TV talk shows, and to bringing the message directly to the public about this phenomenon. This is a subject that must—and will—be taken seriously, even, eventually, by the likes of Leno and Letterman. I was amazed, I might add, by the number of editors in the New York publishing community who are "believers," and I predict that within the next few years, UFO and abduction books will routinely top the bestseller lists as the public hungers to learn more about what our encounters mean, and their implications for the human race.

If my book is successful, everyone in the UFO community will benefit. The floodgates are about to open, and when they do, all experiencers, UFO investigators, writers and researchers will find wider acceptance for their work. The days and years ahead are going to be full of challenges and opportunities, but we need to change ourselves in order to change the world. We need to work together harmoniously with mutual understanding and respect.

I want to thank everyone who is willing to cut me some slack with regard to the article in the *New York Post*. I'm sure it won't be the last test of my strength or your discernment. Please keep those stones in hand until you read my book. I am confident that if and when you do, you will be able to recommend it to experiencers and non-experiencers alike. I would also like to thank everyone in the UFO community who has assisted me on my journey to awareness these past five years.

So far, Stonebrooke's book has not surfaced. Hopefully, one day, it will, and we will have a greater understanding of the Reptilian phenomenon.

THEORIES

When it comes to the matter of trying to determine what the many and varied monsters of our oceans, lakes, and rivers really are, there is one person—more than any other—who did exactly that. A noted crypto-zoologist named Bernard Heuvelmans. Astutely aware that witness testimony was the most important part of creature-seeking, Heuvelmans created a list of the most frequently seen mysterious beasts. Heuvelmans' approach is still in place to this day. Monster-seeker Jonathan Downes, as you will soon see, has also come up with a categorization process for strange beasts—a process that is very different from that of Heuvelmans but no less fascinating. As a result of the damage we are presently and constantly doing to our planet, there is also a category for animals that have become monsters due to widespread pollution.

HEUVELMANS' CREATURE CATEGORIZATION

Henry Lee was the nineteenth-century expert on sea serpents, as we have seen. As far as the twentieth century is concerned, there is no doubt regarding to whom the crown was passed. It was one Bernard Heuvelmans, whose 1968 book *In the Wake of the Sea-Serpents* is the defining work on the subject. Cryptozoological legend Loren Coleman—who, with Patrick Huyghe, wrote *The Field Guide to Lake Monsters, Sea Serpents, and Other Mysterious Denizens of the Deep*—wrote of his fellow creature enthusiast, who died in 2001:

Belgian-Dutch scientist and explorer Bernard Heuvelmans (1916–2001) is considered to be one of the founders of the field of cryptozoology.

Heuvelmans was born in Le Havre on October 10, 1916, of a Dutch mother and a Belgian father in exile, and was raised as a "native of Belgium." Heuvelmans found he had a love of natural history from an early age, keeping all kinds of animals, especially monkeys. At school, he shocked his Jesuit teachers by his unholy interest in evolution and jazz. His interest in unknown animals was first piqued as a youngster by his reading of science-fiction adventures such as Jules Verne's *Twenty Thousand Leagues Under the Sea* and Sir Arthur Conan Doyle's *The Lost World*. He never forgot these initial passions.

Coleman continued:

Heuvelmans began to gather material about yet-to-be-discovered animals in what he would later refer as his growing "dossiers" on them. From 1948 on, Heuvelmans exhaustively sought evidence in scientific and literary sources. Within five years he had amassed so much material that he was ready to write a large book. That book turned out to be *Sur la piste des betes ignorees*, published in 1955, and better known in its English translation three years later as *On the Track of Unknown Animals*. Almost five decades later, the book remains in print, with more than one million copies sold in various translations and editions, including one in 1995, with a large updated introduction. The book's impact was enormous.

Coleman is 100 percent correct: *On the Track of Unknown Animals* and the later work *In the Wake of the Sea-Serpents* became classics of the literature and important research tools for creature seekers everywhere.

Of particular importance is Heuvelmans's theory—based upon 358 sightings—that more than one kind of animal fall into the sea serpent category. Heuvelmans's list of creatures is an important one, as it not only describes the physical appearances of the animals but also reveals which kinds of creatures are most often seen—at least, at the time that Heuvelmans compiled his list. He began with what he termed the "long-necked" type, for which Heuvelmans had forty-eight reports. This particular group, he added, had necks that ranged from long to "very long" and other qualities such as a "median hump on the back" or "a pair of horns on the head." As for the color of the creatures, they were typically mottled.

Second on Heuvelmans's list was the "merhorse." It had, said Heuvelmans, a "long floating mane," huge eyes, a long neck, and whiskers on the face. For this entry, Heuvelmans had studied no fewer than thirty-seven cases. The third entry was focused on the "many-humped" animal. As the name suggests, the creature had a "string of dorsal humps of virtually equal size." Its neck, which featured white stripes, was not overly large. Now we move on to the "many finned" beast of the deep. These creatures had "several triangular fins looking like a huge crest." They also had a jagged crest on the spine and "prominent" eyes. Then there was the "super otter." Heuvelmans described it as having "a slender medium-length neck" and a "long tapering tail." The color was beige or grey, according to the thirteen sightings that Heuvelmans had in his files.

The "super eel" played an important role in Heuvelmans's work, and even today, reports of massive eels continue to grow. Twelve reports that Heuvelmans had on file allowed him to make a good image of the animals. They had a long neck, which formed "an extension of the head." The tail was "long [and] tapering." The creature "leaps out of the water and falls back with a splash," Heuvelmans told his readers.

The "marine saurian" was very much like a crocodile, albeit seen in an "oceanic habitat." Then there was the "father-of-all-the-turtles." Yes, we're talking about massive turtles. Finally, Heuvelmans introduced his followers to "yellow belly," a beast that was yellow with black stripes. He said of his list, "It is not surprising that the types based on a few not very detailed sightings have few determining characteristics. It follows that the least well-defined types may include several different species, not necessarily related to one another."

Working in the wake of Bernard Heuvelmans—pun intended—is Michael A. Woodley, whom I interviewed on his work in this amazing field of sea serpents. I asked Woodley, the author of *In the Wake of Bernard Heuvelmans*, what led him to immerse himself in the world of ocean monsters. He told me: "My earliest scientific interest was in marine biology. Most people who get into sea life at the age of ten start off interested in the obvious animals—sharks and whales—but I found the Cnidaria—jellyfish, sea anenomies, hydras—to be especially fascinating due mostly to their complex life cycles. To me they were so alien compared to other forms of marine life, and I felt them thusly to be especially worthy of study."

Woodley continued:

My first exposure to cryptozoology came when I found a well-illustrated book on sea monsters in the library of my primary school. I vividly remember reading about the McCleary encounter of 1962 in which he claimed to be the lone survivor of a sea monster attack that allegedly resulted in the loss of four of his friends whilst diving off the Florida coast; the story was gruesomely illustrated as I recall. It was this that got me thinking about the possibilities of large and maybe even dangerous, unaccounted-for animals lurking in the world's oceans. It also triggered in me a lifelong dislike of the sea.

I suppose then that it was a fascination with both the unknown and the unusual that really roped me into cryptozoology, although I will admit that my interest has always been heavily skewed towards dracontology, the study of sea serpents. My first exposure to Heuvelmans came much later on, when I read of his work in an essay on sea serpents by the mystery-writing couple, Janet and Colin Bord. It featured in a general text on anomalistics and introduced me to the basics of Heuvelmans's classification scheme. I seem to recall that it came as a surprise to me that a qualified zoologist would actually write in a scientific manner about a topic such as sea serpents.

It wasn't until quite some years after this that I got around to seeing a copy of *In the Wake of the Sea-Serpents*. My copy arrived in the summer of 2006, fully six weeks after I had put in an order for it on Amazon. I had actually forgotten all about the order, so its unexpected appearance came as a very pleasant surprise. I quickly absorbed the book's content and set about formulating my own ideas. It wasn't long before I decided that they needed to be written down, and that's when I started on the book.

I asked Woodley: "How do you compare Heuvelmans's importance and relevance to cryptozoology in the past with the cryptozoological field of today?" He replied:

This is a question that will probably get you as many different answers as there are cryptozoologists; my particular take on it is that ultimately, cryptozoologists generally align with one of two camps on the issue. There are many cryptozoologists who believe that the field needs to come out from under Heuvelmans's shadow, so to speak; that it effectively needs a fresh start as they feel that Heuvelmans's influence ultimately had a detrimental influence on efforts to garner mainstream credibility for the field. I tend to label those who hold this view as the "new" cryptozoologists; they recognize Heuvelmans's historical significance as effective founder and chief popularizer of the field, but basically regard him in much the same way that the majority of modern psychiatrists might regard Freud—as an ultimately misguided visionary.

On the other hand, there are those, like myself, who perceive Heuvelmans's fundamental interdisciplinary vision of cryptozoology and the methods he developed for the evaluation and analysis of non-autoptic evidences as being still central to contemporary cryptozoology. Those who maintain this position could be labeled as "Heuvelmansian" cryptozoologists, I would personally describe myself as a "neo-Heuvelmansian," as whilst I maintain that Heuvelmans's theories and methods are still relevant to contemporary cryptozoology, I recognize their limitations and have attempted to improve on them.

On the matter of Woodley's book, I wondered what prompted him to decide to write on the controversial subject of sea serpents. He said in return:

Since Heuvelmans penned *In the Wake of the Sea-Serpents*, there has been very little progress made in really advancing his thinking on the issue of marine cryptid identity hypotheses. The Coleman-Huyghe classification model [named for Loren Coleman and Patrick Huyghe], for all its numerous merits, was ultimately an attempt at lumping and splitting, within Heuvelmans's original categories, albeit one that was extremely original. There is of course the model of Bruce Champagne, which is especially interesting because it attempts to quantitatively score the evidence associated with marine cryptid encounters. In addition, and perhaps most significantly, it also looks at ecological and ethological correlates associated with the sightings and their locations, which he uses in the building of more heuristic "multifactor" marine cryptid identities. The problem with the Champagne model is its unfortunate lack of visibility within cryptozoological circles; only specialists in the field ever seem to have heard of it.

> // There are many cryptozoologists who believe that the field needs to come out from under Heuvelmans's shadow, so to speak; that it effectively needs a fresh start...."

There existed, in my opinion, an opportunity for a book that would attempt to take Heuvelmans's theories to the "next level" (to use the cliché); i.e., one which would examine the veracity of Heuvelmans's identity hypotheses simply as they stood at the time of his death, from the perspective of contemporary advances in zoology, ecology, and evolutionary biology. It was especially in regards to the latter two that I felt the most new light could be shed on his theories, as I believe ecological inference and evolutionary narratives to be the most useful tools in evaluating the contemporary plausibility of Heuvelmans's identity hypotheses and in creating a framework with which viable alternatives to his proposed identities could be proposed to account for the sightings "clusters" from which he made his initial deductions.

I do not believe that Heuvelmans got it completely right, and there is certainly scope for new identity theories to be added to any potential future classification scheme in the vein of Coleman, Huyghe, and Champagne; however, the creation of new categories was not the main purpose of the book. It was primarily an attempt at dealing with Heuvelmans's theories on his own terms, so to speak.

This prompted me to wonder how Woodley felt about Heuvelmans's conclusions and theories. How were they similar to Woodley's own theories, and how did they differ? Woodley's answer was an intriguing one: "It is obvious that Heuvelmans's invocation of multiple identity hypotheses was an improvement over [Antoon Cornelis] Oudemans's single hypothesized *Megophius megophius*, which was basically an attempt to condense all the factors associated with alleged sightings of unknown large marine animals into one massively oversimplified identity." He continued:

> In criticizing Heuvelmans it is easy to point out the obvious errors—for example, there is his claim for the existence of armored archaeocetes, which turned out to be due to the presence of turtle shell fragments found intermingled with basilosaur fossils, or there was his belief that the allometric scaling between leptocephalus and adult eels holds true for leptocephalus at 6 feet (unfortunately it doesn't—the adult forms are only marginally larger than the larval forms). However, in raising these criticisms it is necessary to remember that Heuvelmans was writing in an era when these suppositions were considered at least plausible.

> A more valid point for criticism concerning Heuvelmans's identity hypotheses concerns the fact that he could theoretically have done much more with his data in terms of quantitative correlative analysis both between and within groups of sightings and with respect to broader ecological patterns. As I mentioned previously, I consider myself to be a neo-Heuvelmansian, which means that I believe Heuvelmans's methods for evaluating non-autoptic evidence sources, coupled with professional fieldwork,

to be the essential bread and butter of cryptozoology. This is not to say that I don't embrace new ways of evaluating the evidence, and indeed I believe that cryptozoology can only benefit from this kind of thinking—this being the basis of the book.

A nuanced treatment of the differences between Heuvelmans's identity theories and my own revisions would take to long to present here (plus it would negate the need to buy the book!), but let's suffice it to say that there probably aren't any Cretaceous period reptiles swimming around in the oceans, there may be a rather large marine cousin of the centipede lurking in the depths, and super-otters may well actually be otters!

Moving away from the subject in general but to the specific issue of Woodley's own book on sea serpents, I put this to him: "How do you hope the book will be received?"

His answer: "I know that there will be much scope for disagreement, particularly between myself and the new cryptozoologists who might not see the contemporary relevance of Heuvelmans's identity hypotheses to the field, or who may even question the scientific legitimacy of such speculation. It is actually my fondest wish that the contents of this book be debated as it is through reasoned debate that new perspectives can be gleaned and progress can be made."

"What has been the reaction thus far?" I asked.

Woodley said: "[Dr.] Charles Paxton [a statistical ecologist and an expert on the Loch Ness Monster controversy] and I have exchanged e-mails concerning the text; he is of the opinion that whilst they are certainly fun to generate, cryptid classification schemes are essentially nonscientific; a point which I readily cede on the grounds that such hypothesizing can have no true scientific value in the absence of a criterion for falsification—something which I hope to address statistically in a paper that is currently in preparation."

Asked how long he had been working on the book, Woodley stated:

I started on the long-necked seal chapter back in April of 2007, during my final semester at Columbia Uni-

Heuvelmans' theories about sea serpents have at times been criticized by those who found errors in his research. His hypothesis about armored archaeocetes, for example, was disproved as a result of a site contaminated by turtle shell fragments.

versity. It was my intention at the time to have it published as a short book; however, there were no takers initially. I then approached Jonathan Downes of the Centre for Fortean Zoology, and he suggested that it be incorporated into the *2008 Yearbook*. This was how things stayed until January of this year when I suggested to him that we create a book incorporating reviews and reevaluations of all of Heuvelmans's proposed marine cryptid identity hypotheses. He agreed that this was a good idea, and to compensate for the sudden absence of the long-necked seal article from the yearbook, I agreed to write an article on the Mongolian Death Worm, in which I would utilize the "plausibility method" to reevaluate the current identity hypotheses for this cryptid.

In the conclusion of the book, I mention that I am contemplating a follow-up work, in which I will hopefully get around to dealing with the issue of rationally expanding Heuvelmans's identity taxonomy for marine cryptids. However, I feel that before this can be attempted, a variety of issues need to be addressed. For example, there is the matter of being able to scientifically falsify cryptid hypotheses, the key to which may be found in the patterns of cumulative species description and will, as was mentioned previously, constitute the basis of a published statistical treatment of the subject. There is also the issue of the use of binomial nomenclature in cryptozoology. Heuvelmans was very liberal in ascribing binomial names to his putative species, and the new cryptozoologists tend to rule these out as *nomina nuda*. However, what is seldom discussed is Heuvelmans's reasoning behind ascribing to cryptids binomial names in the first place.

In a 1982 essay, Heuvelmans critiqued the 1958 decision of the International Congress for Zoology to reject the "parataxa" concept, which was first proposed by [Raymond C.] Moore and [P. C.] Sylvester-Bradley as a means of classifying inconclusive fossilized remains, animal tracks, and body fossils (imprints), a revised form of which has been subsequently accepted as "ichnotaxa." Heuvelmans suggested that in essence, binomial names in cryptozoology could be rationalized on the basis of their being parataxanomic, as cryptids tend only to be known through anecdote or through other inconclusive evidences (photographs, footprints, etc.). The utility of Heuvelmans's parataxa concept as a means of generating taxonomic "place-holder" names with which cryptids can be formally recognized upon discovery needs, I feel, to be firmly established within cryptozoology.

A Global Template for Monsters

How is it that so many people are fascinated by reports of lake monsters, sea serpents, Cthulhu-like beasts, mermaids, and more? Jonathan Downes, of the Centre for Fortean Zoology, believes he has found at least a partial answer to this question. Downes is keen to stress that his theory does not explain every aspect of the overall "mystery animal" controversy, just that it could explain a good portion of it. With that said, I will now hand you over to Downes, who says:

> Researchers Albert Budden and Paul Devereux have both written extensively about "energies" which can have certain effects on the human mind. Devereux suggests consciousness-affecting energy can originate via natural radioactivity and electro-magnetic fields. His books list numerous examples of anomalous experiences he believes have occurred after an encounter with these energies. Budden contends that modern electro-magnetic pollution as well as natural electro-magnetism can have a radical and often deleterious effect on people. None of this is completely proven, but between them they are building a persuasive case for the earth's natural energies playing a part as being at least the stimulus for "paranormal" experiences. But here's the important question in relation to the above: why should so many of these experiences result in the manifestation of creatures of a definitive cryptozoological nature? I have more than a few ideas when it comes to answering that particular question:

> What I saw at Bolam, England, in January 2003 [a Bigfoot-type creature] was a very real phenomenon. Whether it had any objective reality outside of my own experience, I'm not sure. But there were several of us who saw this thing at once; or, largely the same thing. I'm fairly convinced that what I saw was a parapsychological phenomenon, rather than a flesh and blood one.

> What I believe is a theory that [zoologist and cryptozoologist] Richard Freeman and I came up with. Actually, he came up with it first. Richard noticed that wherever he went on an expedition, the same types of mystery animal were being reported. As just one of many examples, he was in Thailand in 2000 and came back telling me that, as well as the Naga—this giant, water-based and cave-based snake he was looking for, and which is analogous to the western dragon, and perhaps lake monsters as

well—there were sightings of a Bigfoot-type of hairy beast, a large and mysterious golden cat, and a large winged thing called the Garuda [a bird man from Indo-Chinese legend that is akin to the Japanese Tengu], very much like the Owlman of Cornwall. Everywhere you go, there is what Richard calls a "global template" for monsters. Richard and I have looked into this very deeply, and you basically have got the same types of paranormal mystery animals reported all over the world, and in nearly each and every culture. There are the big, hairy, ape-like creatures. You have the little, hairy, ape-like creatures. You have phantom black dogs, phantom big cats, dragons and lake monsters, and you have the large flying things. So, we were looking for a unifying theory behind all this.

And it's now that we come to the heart of that unifying theory: Richard and I have concluded that you have to go back to when the human race was a couple of thousand small, hairy creatures walking around on the plains of East Africa. And every man, woman, and child on the planet is descended from these same little, hairy creatures. And, at that time, there would have been a lot of things that would have scared the hell out of them, and which they would have been in mortal danger from, such as large, wild hunting dogs, and big cats of that era. They may even have been in dire danger from their own relatives, such as the smaller, stronger, hairy men, and the larger, and now-extinct, primitive giant apes. They would have also been in danger from crocodiles, alligators—huge ones, perhaps—and possibly very large birds, too, which the fossil record shows did exist; *very* large. All of these things would have provoked a "fight or flight" response in our ancestors. And all of these types of creature are present in today's world as mystery animals.

As this sign near a transmitter pole warns, electromagnetic pollution can be dangerous to humans. Some have even speculated it might "reboot" our brains if we get too much exposure.

Richard and I believe the memories of these creatures, and our ancestors' experiences with them, and fear of them, have become hardwired into our subconscious as a kind of fossil memory. And when I say "our," I mean everyone. It's in all of us, whether we know it or not. And under certain circumstances, something can make your brain reboot to that primitive state, and perhaps create images of those primitive creatures our ancestors lived in fear of. This is, we believe, in much the same way as when your computer reboots it first goes back to its most primitive state, no matter how many programs you might be running when it crashes and needs to reboot. We think that when this happens to the human brain, you can experience one of those archetypal, primal fears, in the form of a dragon, a big cat, a black dog, and even the large hairy man-beast.

A fascinating theory, certainly, but what might make the human brain reboot in this fashion? The human brain is, basically, an incredibly sophisticated computer. And one of the things that makes computers reboot from time to time is an electrical power surge. I think it's very interesting that in places where the British Bigfoot has been seen, such as at Bolam Lake—and where lake monsters are seen, too—we had an enormous amount of electrical equipment fail on us. This was equipment that was tested in Devon before we left, and even on the day before I had my encounter, and it all worked perfectly—until we got to the lake. The idea of power failures in such situations goes back to John Keel, et al, and is very well known.

We also found there were strange magnetic anomalies at the lake, too. And when we got back to CFZ headquarters in Devon, England, we found there were veins of magnetic iron ore underneath that very part of the country. And we're wondering if these weird magnetic anomalies, caused by perfectly natural phenomena, can affect, or interfere with, the human brain, and cause it to reboot to that most primitive stage, and those very primitive, fossil memories—as Richard and I call them—of all these various types of archetypal creatures in cryptozoology, and you can experience one of these great primal fears. In my case, at Bolam, it was in the form of a large ape-like animal.

Getting back to the issue of rebooting monsters, I'm careful to point out the following: we admit it's not a theory that can explain everything, because some of the world's man-beasts, such as the Yeti and Orang-Pendek, *are* flesh and blood. Some of the Bigfoot sightings are; some aren't. The same goes for some monsters seen in lakes and rivers. And what I can also tell you is that what I saw at Bolam had a great effect on my cerebral cortex. Endorphins are the pleasure chemicals released during sex. There are two substances which mimic the production of endorphins. They are chocolate and opiates, both of which I have abused in my time. And I know the effect that drugs can have on the central nervous system. And, after whatever it was I saw in Bolam in 2003, my body was immediately flooded with endorphins. That is a sign, to me, that something was playing around with my cerebral cortex.

As for the other people at Bolam who saw the same thing I saw, well, maybe we can externalize these images—like a Tulpa, a creature created by the imagination and externalized by the human mind. Or, quite possibly, the expectation of us all potentially seeing a British Bigfoot at Bolam made us all hardwire the very same image when we were all rebooted.

With Downes's words taken into consideration, we may examine further cases that seem to fall into this category. A similar theory has been postulated by North Carolina-based researcher Micah Hanks, author of the groundbreaking book *Magic, Mysticism and the Molecule*. His words, provided very generously to me, follow:

Another theory regarding Bigfoot and other such cryptid apes is that their ability to disappear and stay hidden is connected somehow to UFOs and alien technology.

From time to time there are reports that fall under the "Bigfoot" category that, to put it simply, present a lot of disturbing problems for eyewitnesses. While these "high strangeness" reports (an expression that had become innate to the study of odd occurrences tucked within the realms of Forteana) are seldom in the minority, they are often overlooked by the greater cryptozoology community for a number of reasons.

Primarily, this has to do with the fact that the study of creatures like "Bigfoot," by virtue of the designated title *cryptozoology* (the study of hidden animals), approaches this mystery from the perspective that these entities, whatever they may *really* be, are in fact some form of biological entity that closely resembles humankind.

To wit, if indeed the Sasquatch myth is anything more than a myth, the best avenue, and thus the most widely accepted approach to their study, seems to be afforded us in their treatment as flesh-and-blood entities. However, when peering a bit deeper into the mystery, these "beings" may boast a number of curious elements that beg further consideration … and may similarly warrant different modes of thought applied to understanding their overall meaning.

Chief among the kinds of "mysteries" I allude to here are the cases of "disappearing" Bigfoot creatures which, again, will most often tend to be dismissed by the serious Sasquatch researcher. Indeed, there are a small minority in the collected witness accounts that not only involve the appearance of creatures like Bigfoot, but also apparent metaphysical abilities some have ascribed to them in terms of being able to simply "vanish" into thin air.

On a personal note, I should mention here no less than two stories along these lines that I've been told over the years…. While one seems like it may have been told to me under less-than-reliable circumstances, on at least one occasion while visiting a Bigfoot conference in Newcomerstown, Ohio, I was nonetheless told in strictest confidence by one of the presenters about his own encounter with "Chewbacca" on a dark country road in Pennsylvania back during the mid-1990s. It was right around dusk, and as he watched the animal strolling along the roadway between two corn fields, illuminated in the headlights of his vehicle, the thing very suddenly vanished, leaving no trace of the creature he had observed! For rather obvious reasons, the presenter in question had felt it might be in good taste to omit this aspect of the story from his presentation.

This illustrates, again, the general treatment toward the high-strangeness angle associated with the annals of Sasquatchery. Indeed, while there may be a plethora of reports that seem to involve odd goings-on ranging from the disappearances described above, to Bigfoot creatures seen wearing clothing—and even Sasquatch encounters that occur in conjunction with flying saucers—these things seem *so outrageous* within the cultural context we have ascribed to the Bigfoot beast (that of a relic hominid and possible missing link, or similar species that has evolved parallel to our own) that we simply cannot accept them.

But asking one of those *really difficult questions*, I think we must consider something else that is troubling about the mystery surrounding Bigfoot: while these "animals" appear to be quite physical and consisting of flesh and blood like you or I, they have a curious preponderance in terms of there elusiveness. That is, even if a small population of the creatures were all that existed worldwide, shouldn't we have just a bit more hard evidence supporting their existence?

To be fair, many would argue that such evidence *does* exist, in fact, and that the real problem involves the various avenues that are not being reached in terms of bringing compelling evidence to the forefront of the scientific mainstream. However, the apparent lack of what we might at least call a "smoking gun" could again point to the notion that there could be more to the elusiveness these creatures have such an apparent mastery of.

> "One working premise I've considered has to do with the possibility that Bigfoot creatures, while physical to some degree, may actually represent some aspect of *humanity*."

One working premise I've considered has to do with the possibility that Bigfoot creatures, while physical to some degree, may actually represent some aspect of *humanity*. This sounds very strange, and difficult to accept, no doubt. But bear with me for a moment: while they obviously aren't "human" like you or I, the thought has crossed my mind nonetheless that Bigfoot creatures could potentially by semi-physical entities, or representative of some kind of consciousness, but which for some reason are perceived in a variety of capacities by most humans which entails tapping into a sort of archetypal substructure within our own consciousness. In other words, certain strange phenomena witnessed at various times may appear as "monsters" similar to humans, simply because whatever the consciousness/intelligence behind those encounters may actually be exists beyond the realm of that which is entirely perceptible to humans, at least in a conventional sense.

While other alternatives exist in terms of the "disappearing" Bigfoot reports (such as active camouflaging abilities, etc.), it is still worthy of consideration, when taking into account those serious high-strangeness reports, whether there could possibly be an ongoing interaction humanity is having with *something*, and that while Sasquatch may appear to us as one piece of that puzzle, they also seem to be, in this context at least, something which is only one aspect of a much larger mystery: an enigma spanning the various realms of human consciousness and perceptibility.

Perhaps the words of Downes and Hanks go some significant way to explain how, and why, all of our lake monsters, sea serpents, and other water-based monsters are all so frustratingly elusive. They may not be all that they seem to be.

MODERN-DAY MONSTERS AND ENVIRONMENTAL POLLUTION

There's little doubt that some of the strangest mysteries concerning monsters of the deep are related to what I term modern-day monsters. These cases involve unidentified creatures that have surfaced out of nowhere—quite literally. We are talking about animals that somehow appear not to have existed, or been seen, prior to the turn of the twenty-first century. How could such a thing be? Well, the answer to that question is as controversial as the creatures themselves. Sightings of Ogopogo date back several centuries. Encounters with the creature of Loch Ness and the River Ness in Scotland were chronicled more than a millennium ago. The beasts you are about to learn about now are definitively Johnny-Come-Lately monsters. And there is a very good reason for that, as will soon become apparent. We'll begin with the marauding creature known as Bownessie.

A resident of Lake Windermere, England, Bownessie was 100 percent unknown prior to 2006. In terms of the publicity, however, it has done a great job of catching up. As for Lake Windermere itself, according to the *Encyclopaedia Britannica Online*: "The lake is 10.5 miles (17 km) long and 1 mile (1.6 km) wide and has an area of 6 square miles (16 square km). It lies in two basins separated by a group of islands opposite the town of Bowness on the eastern shore and is drained by the River Leven. Part of Lake District National Park, Windermere is a popular tourist center with facilities for yachting and steamers operating in the summer."

> A resident of Lake Windermere, England, Bownessie was 100 percent unknown prior to 2006. In terms of the publicity, however, it has done a great job of catching up.

As the above data demonstrates, Lake Windermere is much smaller than Loch Ness; nonetheless, that has not stopped a mysterious creature from appearing in its depths, which extend to 219 feet at the deepest. Now, with that all said, let us take a look at the saga of Bownessie and how and why it has become a monster of the modern era.

The first person to have encountered Bownessie was a journalist named Steve Burnip, who saw the creature in 2006. He said of his close encounter of the monstrous type: "I saw a straight line of broken water with three humps. It was about twenty feet long and it went in a straight line up the lake. I nudged my wife and watched open-mouthed as it gradually faded from sight. The water was not choppy, so I know it wasn't the wind, and I know what the wake from motorboats looks like and it wasn't that either."

Thus, a monster was born. Or, at the very least, unveiled and unleashed.

Then, in February 2007, Linden Adams was confronted by the sight of an unidentified animal that, it was estimated, was somewhere around fifteen feet in length. It should be noted that there are no known animals in the lakes and rivers of the United Kingdom of such an extraordinary size. Such was Adams's amazement regarding what he and his wife encountered that he created a website to ensure that every sighting could be logged and studied. Also in 2007, this time late at night, the crew members of a six-ton yacht were rocked—quite literally—when something large slammed into their craft. It was never identified.

Two years later, in 2009, a Mr. Noblett was hit by a large wave on the lake. At the time, Noblett was swimming in Lake Windermere, something that may not have been a wise thing to do given the fact that there was an unidentified thing swimming around the lake. Possibly, Bownessie was attracted by the water that had been disturbed by Noblett's swimming and decided to see what was afoot. Thankfully, Noblett neither incurred Bownessie's wrath nor became a meal for the monster.

Lake Windermere in Cumbria, England, is yet another home for a Nessie-like creature; this one has come to be called Brownessie and was first spotted in 2006.

In 2011, Tom Pickles saw Bownessie as he kayaked across the lake. The animal he saw was, to quote the man himself, "a giant dark brown snake with humps measuring three car lengths." Its skin seemed to resemble that of a seal, but, Pickles explained, its form was "completely abnormal." A woman with Pickles, named Sarah Harrington, concurred and said that the thing in the water was "like an enormous snake."

> There was talk of the animal having been a sturgeon, which can grow to immense sizes. It is, however, unlikely that such a huge fish ... could be lurking in English rivers and not be found until 2015.

There was yet another profound sighting in 2011. It was reported by Brian and June Arton of Hovingham, North Yorkshire, England. Mr. Arton told the media: "We'd just checked into our hotel room at around 4:00 P.M. when I opened the veranda doors and saw something about three hundred yards away in the middle of the lake. I joked to my wife: 'There's the Loch Ness monster' as it had humps, but I thought it had to be a pontoon or a very strange shaped buoy. It wasn't until we saw the *Westmorland Gazette* the next day that we realized that it could have been a sighting of 'Bownessie.'"

That case was followed by a retired priest, one Colin Honour, who, along with his wife, Christine, also had a brief view of something large in Lake Windermere. He shared the details with a journalist from the *Westmorland Gazette* newspaper, whose story provided the amazing and disturbing facts. Colin Honour said it was November 17, 2012, when he and Christine had a brief encounter. He said: "It was a very calm and clear day. We were looking at the Lake and my wife spotted something in the water. She thought it was a log at first but then it moved. There were no boats around and we could see three definite humps in the water—it must have been about five or six meters in length. We didn't do anything with the photographs we took at the time because we felt they weren't terribly conclusive, but in the light of the recent article, perhaps they'll provide further evidence of Bownessie."

Matt Benefield, a petrophysicist (someone who studies chemical and physical rock properties), had his sighting at the north end of the lake on January 12, 2014. He remembered very well how things went down: "It was a really calm day and the water was very still. There was nobody out in the water, it was very quiet. When I was looking back through the photos, one caught my eye. I wouldn't normally think anything of it, but it was the two ripples in the water that got me thinking there was possibly something strange in the Lake."

Finally, we have the story of Ellie Williams, who worked for *Autographer Magazine* in London, England. It's most fortunate indeed that Williams was a professional photographer, as her words demonstrate: "My brief time at Windermere was to try to create a video through time lapsed photographs showing the seasonal changes over a day. I put the camera in place at around 7:00 A.M.

and collected it again around 3:00 P.M. When I downloaded the pictures to my phone I thought, great, I have caught some wildlife—I thought it was a swan. However, when I download the image onto my laptop I could tell it definitely wasn't a swan—it was far too big. I was shocked but also very excited by the find. I checked the pictures taken on either side of the lake and can say it was definitely not the result of a prank because I would have captured those responsible on film. It certainly is very interesting."

Now let's address another very recent case from the United Kingdom.

It was a warm, sunny day in June 2015 when a large animal was encountered by a pair of amazed and frightened fishermen on the River Nene, which is located in the Fens region of Cambridge, England. They quickly shared the details of the sighting with the BBC—such was the pair's concern for what was lurking in the waters of England. One of them said: "I enjoy going out on my boat. One day we were on our boat going up towards Whittlesey and the boat suddenly juddered as if there was something large in the water. My friend and myself looked at each other and I looked down to see what we had hit. I saw the most extraordinary thing. I saw the biggest fish I have ever seen in my life. I like boating and I like wildlife, but I had never seen a fish like this before. It was absolutely huge—it was over six foot long. It was swimming alongside us and our boat had struck it, and it was as if it was showing us the side of itself where the propeller had hit it and we could see the white flesh. My friend saw it and exclaimed 'Blimey is that a dolphin?' It was so big. We're going to go out again this year and see if we can see it."

There was talk of the animal having been a sturgeon, which can grow to immense sizes. It is, however, unlikely that such a huge fish (which can grow to a length of eighteen feet) could be lurking in English rivers and not be found until 2015. Although the two men did not secure a definitive explanation for what they had seen, it's important to note that another witness came forward named Michelle Cooper. She too was so amazed by what she had seen that she decided to contact *Cambridge News*. It turns out that Cooper's confrontation occurred in 2014, but she had stayed steadfastly silent until the story of the two fishermen surfaced a year later. She recalled what happened all too well:

> I told people about it last year and they just took the mickey but now that these anglers have seen it too I know what they mean by being terrified. I am five-foot-four-inches tall and it was bigger than me. The water was crystal clear and I had a good look at it. I didn't see any white like the fishermen. I saw dark brown and when I researched what it could be, I found it looked exactly like the giant eels you get in America. I was really shaken up by it. It was terrifying but I don't think it would hurt anyone. It seems to just stay low down on the riverbed. It was so big it did create a

wave and knocked my boat. I've seen pike and catfish and it definitely wasn't that. I went for my camera to get a picture of it but it moved too fast and was gone before I could get a shot.

Now we come to a truly amazing, Minnesota-based case of incredible proportions, which revolves around nothing less than a hideous, bloated, huge frog.

The state of Minnesota is famously referred to as the "Land of 10,000 Lakes." Why might that be? Because it is home to no fewer than an incredible *11,842* lakes. Yes, you read that right. One of those inviting bodies of water, Lake Itasca, reportedly has something incredible hiding in its waters—something that you would be very wise to avoid. That "something" was never seen—at least, as far as we know—prior to 2013. That, of course, eerily mirrors what we know from the United Kingdom—that there seems to be something strange going on, something that is causing unidentified, large animals to suddenly appear out of the blue. Like Windermere Lake in England, Minnesota's Lake Itasca is not a particularly large body of water. In fact, its depth is less than forty feet, and it has a square mileage of approximately two miles. But for such a small location, it is home to something abominable that is also massive.

Don is a fisherman who contacted me after reading an online article I wrote several years ago on lesser-known monsters. A resident of Clearwater County, Minnesota, he had a traumatic experience in March 2013, one that he will likely never forget. Very much the same might be said for Don's German shepherd dog, Ben, who also had the misfortune to come face-to-face with the vile thing. In this case, they encountered no long-necked beast, no creature with a huge, humped back or powerful tail. What they encountered was an enormous frog. As Don told me, the water on that fateful day was calm and tranquil until they noticed a sudden disturbance near the shore. Don was puzzled; Ben was excited. Don put Ben on his leash and headed to the site of all the commotion. Man and man's best friend were about to find themselves plunged into a nightmarish situation.

Don said that as the pair got close, an immense frog came crawling out of the shallow waters. This frog was—wait for it— around four feet in length. A true monster, to be sure. The creature eyed the pair in creepy fashion, just as Don and Ben did to the mighty amphibian. It quickly vanished into the waters of Lake Itasca, leaving man

Mutations in frogs, like this milk frog, may be the result of environmental pollution. Amphibians, which depend on clean water, are especially vulnerable.

and dog astounded and more than a bit scared. Don has returned to Lake Itasca on many occasions since, but he has yet to see the massive frog again.

It should be noted that there is a precedent for accounts of huge and monstrous frogs, as Dr. Karl Shuker notes:

> On 31 December 1945, an article penned by Harvard University herpetologist Arthur Loveridge was published in the zoological journal *Copeia*, concerning an attack some months earlier upon an askari (native policeman) at Tapili, Niangara, in what was then the Belgian Congo (later renamed Zaire, and now called the Democratic Republic of Congo). Loveridge's source of information concerning this incident was a Mr C. Caseleyr, then Administrator of the Niangara Territory. The askari had come to Caseleyr to inform him that while walking by a pool earlier that evening, he had been bitten on one of his legs by what proved to be a very large frog—he'd lunged out at his attacker with a large club that he was carrying and had killed it outright. And as conclusive proof of his statement, the askari had brought with him the frog's body to show it to Caseleyr.

Now we come to what it might be that is causing all of these huge animals—Bownessie, the giant frog of Lake Itasca, and the monster fish of England's waters—to suddenly surface when they were never reported prior to the late 1990s and early 2000s. It all revolves around environmental pollution. A writer for *Science Direct* states:

> Environmental pollution is one of the most serious problems facing humanity and other life forms on our planet today. Environmental pollution is defined as "the contamination of the physical and biological components of the earth/atmosphere system to such an extent that normal environmental processes are adversely affected." Pollutants can be naturally occurring substances or energies, but they are considered contaminants when in excess of natural levels. Any use of natural resources at a rate higher than nature's capacity to restore itself can result in pollution of air, water, and land.

Ken Gerhard is an extremely well-respected cryptozoologist who very likely has solved the riddle of these overgrown things. He says:

> If you remember, back in 1995 there was an incredibly large number of deformed frogs that were found in a pond in southwest Minnesota. It made big, national news. It was kind of looked at as a sign of the times: there was so much pollution that man's impact on the environment was causing these really bizarre frog

mutations, where they would have extra limbs, missing limbs, weird eyes, and things like that. So, it has occurred to me over the past couple of years that, perhaps, we're looking at something very similar here in Texas. It is likely that one or more combinations of chemicals, biological, and physical factors are responsible for causing the malformations.

I most assuredly did recall the Minnesota mutations. The U.S. government's U.S. Geological Survey (USGS), an agency of the Department of the Interior, was particularly perturbed about what was happening. The USGS said: "Malformed frogs first became the topic of national news in August 1995 when students at a middle school in southern Minnesota discovered one-half of all the frogs they caught in a nearby pond were malformed. Since then, malformed frogs have been reported throughout Minnesota and elsewhere in the United States and Canada. Malformations included missing limbs, missing digits, extra limbs, partial limbs, skin webbing, malformed jaws, and missing or extra eyes."

Finally, there is further data in hand suggesting that our pollutants are creating monsters.

In other words, there was evidence that normal creatures *were being changed*, and changed in bizarre ways. The USGS had far more to say on all of this:

> Pesticides are known to cause malformation or death of frogs when present in sufficient concentrations. Studies in Canada show a relation between the percentage of malformed frogs and pesticide use. Methoprene, an insecticide widely used to control mosquitoes, also has been suspected as having caused malformations…. Endocrine disruptors also are being studied to determine if they are responsible for some of the frog malformations in Minnesota. Endocrine disruptors are natural and human-made chemicals that interfere with or mimic natural hormones that control development, growth, and behavior of organisms. The number of endocrine disruptors is unknown; only during the last decade has screening of chemicals begun to evaluate endocrine-disrupting activity.

The USGS came to its unsettling conclusion: "It is likely that one or more combinations of chemicals, biological, and physical factors are responsible for causing the malformations in Minnesota frogs. Chemical combinations may be mixtures of natural and human-made organic chemicals, each of which is harmless on its own but toxic when combined. The number of possible combinations of chemicals, biological, and physical factors is enormous, which may explain why finding the causes for frog malformations has been a difficult task."

Could such "combinations of chemicals, biological, and physical factors" have led to the spawning of a monstrous frog? The chances are high: after all, Lake Itasca is in Minnesota, the very state where so much mutation of the frog population occurred. Is pollution causing a birthing of monsters? Almost certainly, yes. Let's take a look at further data that suggests this is indeed what is happening.

It has been suggested that both Bownessie and the large creature reported to the BBC in 2015 might be giant eels. If so, how did such generally small creatures grow to such immense proportions? Richard Freeman, the zoological director of Britain's Centre for Fortean Zoology (CFZ), points out: "Common eels swim out to the Sargasso Sea to breed then die. The baby eels follow scent trails back to their ancestral fresh waters homes and the cycle begins again. Sometimes, however, a mutation occurs and the eel is sterile. These stay in fresh water and keep on growing. Known as eunuch eels, no-one knows how old they get or how big."

Jonathan Downes, who runs the CFZ, shares something interesting and thought-provoking: "In February 2004 two Canadian tourists came upon a 25-foot eel floating in the shallows of Loch Ness. At first they thought it was dead but when it began to move they beat a hasty retreat."

Roland Watson, who penned a must-have book, *The Water Horses of Loch Ness*, has said: "It is well known that Loch Ness is teeming with eels. No one knows accurately how many eels inhabit the loch because of their behavior. This is because eels are classed as benthic or 'bottom feeders' in that they tend to live on or close to the surface of a sea or lake bottom."

As for how those eels may have grown so large, Downes has his own theory. It's one that has been endorsed by more than a few monster hunters on both sides of the pond: "One theory suggests that these rare, naturally occurring, mutations may now be on the increase due to pollution," he says. "PCBs [polychlorinated biphenyls] have long been implicated in causing sterility in fish. Could they be causing the birth of much larger eunuch eels in the deep lakes of Scotland?"

Downes said to creature seeker Hayley Stevens: "European eels are not supposed to get bigger than 4 feet but there is (or was) a 5 foot plus one in Blackpool Tower Aquarium [England], of all places. I think that once or twice in a generation in a large body of water like Windermere or Loch Ness, a specimen of eight-to-twelve feet could be living."

They just might. And not just in the likes of Loch Ness, Scotland, but in Lake Windermere, England, too.

Finally, there is further data in hand suggesting that our pollutants are creating monsters. We need to return to our good friend Ken Gerhard, who has pursued lake monsters, werewolves, Bigfoot, and the chupacabra. As for the latter beast, Gerhard has spent many a year pursuing what have become known as the "Texas chupacabras." They are hairless canids that look like huge rats but are actually coyotes. The lack of hair is not due to down-to-earth mange, however. Rather, it's clear that these animals are developing in hairless states. There are other anomalies, too: the creatures have strange "pouches" on their back limbs. They have huge overbites. On occasion, they will run on their hind legs in a strange, awkward, bouncing fashion. They hunt in the day and do not appear to be intimidated or frightened by the presence of people. This brings us to how and why regular coyotes are quickly turning into something else. Gerhard proposes an answer:

> Many of these Texas chupacabras have been reported in areas in and around coal-burning power plants. Coal-burning power plants release massive amounts of toxins, including something called sulfur dioxide, which—in laboratory tests—has been proven to be a mutagen. This is a toxin that can get into an animal's blood make-up and actually cause their cells to mutate. Maybe, as a result of the pollution, the immune systems of these animals have been weakened to the point where, when they do contract the mange mites, their resulting symptoms are much more extreme than anything we've encountered before. This may be why they become *completely* hairless so fast, and why they look so sickly. It might also explain the physical changes, like the forelimb lengths, the overbites, and the pouches.

That the state of Texas is home to around twenty coal-burning plants is notable. As for sulfur dioxide (also known as SO_2), in 2005 the National Center for Biotechnology Information noted that when mice were exposed to sulfur dioxide in lab tests, the outcome was catastrophic: "The results indicate that inhalation exposure to SO_2 damages the DNA of multiple organs in addition to the lung, and suggests that this damage could result in mutation, cancer, and other diseases related to DNA damage."

What all the data in this chapter demonstrates is that we, the human race, are the ones creating the monsters of the twenty-first century, albeit inadvertently rather than deliberately. As the outrageous and unfortunate increase in the polluting of the planet continues at its current dangerous and terrifying pace, we are sure to see the emerging of even more monsters of the deep for multiple generations to come.

FURTHER READING

"1925—Russia's Caucasus Pamir Range, the Vanch Mountains." 2014. *Bigfoot Encounters*. Accessed April 16, 2020. http://www.bigfootencounters.com/sbs/vanch.htm.

Absher, J. R. "327-Pound Gator Gar May Smash Record." *Outdoor Life*, February 17, 2011. https://www.outdoorlife.com/blogs/newshound/2011/02/327-pound-gator-gar-may-smash-record/.

Adomnan of Iona. *Life of St. Columba*. London: Penguin Classics, 1995.

"Alberni Has a Wild Man Vancouver Island Mowgli Said to Be No Myth—Seen by a Prospector Recently." *Yukon World*, August 1906.

"Aleister Crowley." *Thelamapedia*, April 2, 2011. http://www.thelemapedia.org/index.php/Aleister_Crowley.

Allen, Joseph. 2002. "The White God Quetzalcoatl." *NEPHI Project*. Accessed March 3, 2019. https://www.nephiproject.com/white_god_quetzalcoatl.htm.

Alley, J. Robert. *Raincoast Sasquatch*. Surrey, BC, Canada: Hancock House Publishers, 2003.

Amanda. "The Gwrach y Rhibyn." *Vampires.com*, July 11, 2010. http://www.vampires.com/the-gwrach-y-rhibyn/.

"Analysis of the Tim Dinsdale Film." 2009. *Legend of Nessie*. Accessed June 22, 2019. http://www.nessie.co.uk/htm/the_evidence/analysis.html.

Andrews, Roy Chapman. "Mongolian Death Worm: the Gobi Desert's Killer Cryptid." *Down the Chupacabra Hole*, April 1, 2019. https://downthechupacabrahole.com/tag/roy-chapman-andrews/.

Arment, Chad. *Boss Snakes: Stories and Sightings of Great Snakes in North America*. Greenville, OH: Coachwhip Publications, 2015.

Astonishing Legends. 2019. "The Soay Island Sea Monster." *Astonishing Legends*, March 18, 2017. https://www.astonishinglegends.com/astonishing-legends/2017/3/18/the-soay-island-sea-monster.

Australian Museum. "Megalania Prisca." *AustralianMuseum.net.au*, November 14, 2018. https://australianmuseum.net.au/learn/australia-over-time/extinct-animals/megalania-prisca/.

Baumann, Elwood D. *The Loch Ness Monster*. New York: Franklin Watts, 1972.

Bayanov, Dmitri. *In the Footsteps of the Russian Snowman*. Surrey, BC, Canada: Hancock House Publishers, 2004.

Beach Combing. "*Did You Hear the One about Nessie, the Sceptic and the Water Horse?*" Strange History, February 2, 2014. http://www.strangehistory.net/2014/02/02/15035/.

Belekurov, Shaun. "Is the Loch Ness Monster a Shapeshifter?" *Paranormal Underground*, July 2010.

Benedict, Adam. "Cryptid Profile: The Father of All Turtles." *Pine Barren Institute*, August 18, 2018. https://pinebarrensinstitute.com/cryptids/2018/8/18/cryptid-profile-the-father-of-all-turtles.

Bill. "The Legendary Kraken." *Ancient Origins*, March 26, 2013. http://www.ancient-origins.net/myths-legends-europe/legendary-kraken-00267.

Black, John. "The Story of Jonah." *Ancient Origins*, February 16, 2013. http://www.ancient-origins.net/myths-legends/story-jonah-00160.

Blackburn, Lyle. *Lizard Man: The True Story of the Bishopville Monster*. San Antonio, TX: Anomalist Books, 2013.

Boirayon, Marius. 2012. "The Giants of the Solomon Islands and Their Hidden UFO Bases." *The Watcher Files*. Accessed June 2, 2019. http://www.thewatcherfiles.com/giants/solomon-giants.htm.

———. *Solomon Island Mysteries*. Kempton, IL: Adventures Unlimited Press, 2010.

Bord, Janet & Colin Bord. *Alien Animals*. London: Panther Books, 1985.

———. *Bigfoot Casebook*. Enumclaw, WA: Pine Winds Press, 2006.

"British Columbia Mowglis: Tribe of Wild Men Roaming Woods and Frightening People." *Van Wert Daily Bulletin*, October 28, 1905.

Brown, Raymond. "Mystery Monster Fish in Cambridgeshire River Terrifies Anglers." *Cambridge News*, June 19, 2015. http://www.cambridge-news.co.uk/Mystery-monster-fish-Cambridgeshire-river/story-26729586-detail/story.html.

———. "'Terrifying Mystery Monster Lurking in Cambridgeshire River Now Sighted Twice Could Be Giant Eel." *Cambridge News*, June 25, 2015. http://www.cambridge-news.co.uk/Mystery-monster-lurking-Cambridgeshire-river/story-26766152-detail/story.html.

Bryner, Jeanna. "What's the Differences between Alligators and Crocodiles?" *Live Science*, Septmber 15, 2012. https://www.livescience.com/32144-whats-the-difference-between-alligators-and-crocodiles.html.

Campbell, Elizabeth. *The Search for Morag*. Letchworth,England: Garden City Press, 1972.

Campbell, J. F. *Popular Tales of the West Highlands*, Volume 1. Edinburgh, Scotland: Birlinn, 1999.

Capps, Chris. "The Elephant Men of Narrabeen Lake." *Unexplainable.net*. Accessed August 12, 2019. http://www.unexplainable.net/simply-unexplainable/the-elephant-men-of-nar.php.

Carlyle, Alexander. *An Ode on the Popular Superstitions of the Highlands of Scotland*. London: British Library, 2011.

Carmichael, Alexander. *Popular Tales of the Western Highlands*. Edinburgh, Scotland: Edmonston & Douglas, 1860.

Caro, G. B. "Boleskine House, The Home of the Wickedest Man in the World." *Murder Is Everywhere*, July 19, 2013. http://murderiseverywhere.blogspot.com/2013/07/boleskin-house-home-of-wickedest-man-in.html.

Carrasco, David. *Quetzalcoatl and the Irony of Empire: Myths and Prophecies in the Aztec Tradition*. Boulder, CO: University Press of Colorado, 2001.

"Chase Gorilla to Mountains." *Gettysburg Times*, January 28, 1921.

Childress, David Hatcher. *Bigfoot Nation: The History of Sasquatch in America*. Kempton, IL: Adventures Unlimited Press, 2018.

———. *Yetis, Sasquatch & Hairy Giants*. Kempton, IL: Adventures Unlimited Press, 2010.

Chorvinsky, Mark. "'Champ of Lake Champlain." *Strangemag.com*. Accessed May 12, 2019. http://www.strangemag.com/champ.html.

———. "The Lake Storjson Monster." *Strangemag.com*. Accessed July 28, 2019. http://www.strangemag.com/lakestorsjonmonster.html.

Churton, Tobias. *Aleister Crowley, the Beast in Berlin*. Rochester, VT: Inner Traditions, 2014.

Coleman, Loren. *Bigfoot! The True Story of Apes in America*. New York: Paraview-Pocket Books, 2003.

———. "Lake Winnipegosis Monster Sighting." *Cryptomundo*, August 19, 2006. http://cryptomundo.com/cryptozoo-news/winnipegogo/.

———. *Tom Slick and the Search for the Yeti*. London: Faber & Faber, 1989.

———. "Was Arthur Grant's Nessie Encounter Fact or Fiction?" *Cryptomundo*, November 19, 2011. http://cryptomundo.com/cryptozoo-news/grant-ln/.

———. "The Water Horse Land Sightings at Loch Ness." *Cryptonews*, December 22, 2007. http://www.cryptozoonews.com/ness-land/.

Coleman, Loren, and Jerome Clark. *Cryptozoology A to Z*. New York: Simon & Schuster, 1999.

Coleman, Loren, and Patrick Huyghe. *The Field Guide to Bigfoot and Other Mystery Primates*. San Antonio, TX: Anomalist Books, 2006.

———. *The Field Guide to Lake Monsters, Sea Serpents, and Other Mystery Denizens of the Deep*. New York: Penguin Group, Inc., 2003.

Cope, Tabitca. "Paddler—Lake Creature, Submarine or Rish?" *Cryptozoo-oscity*, November 24, 2009. http://cryptozoo-oscity.blogspot.com/2009/11/paddler-lake-creature-submarine-or-fish.html.

———. "Wally the Wallow Lake Creature." *Cryptozoo-oscity*, October 6, 2009. http://cryptozoo-oscity.blogspot.com/2009/10/wally-wallowa-lake-creature.html.

Cornelius, J. Edward. *Aleister Crowley and the Ouija Board*. Port Townsend, WA: Feral House, 2005.

Cornell, James. *The Monster of Loch Ness*. New York: Scholastic Book Services, 1977.

Costello, Peter. *In Search of Lake Monsters*. San Antonio, TX: Anomalist Books, 2015.

Courage, Katherine Harmon. "Could an Octopus Really Be Terrorizing Oklahoma's Lakes?" *Octopus Chronicles*, December 19, 2013. http://blogs.scientificamerican .com/octopus-chronicles/could-an-octopus-really-be-terrorizing-oklahomae28099 s-lakes/.

Darwin, Charles. *The Variation of Animals and Plants under Domestication*. New York: D. Appleton & Co., 1883.

Dash, Mike. "On the Trail of the Warsaw Basilisk." *Smithsonian Magazine*, July 23, 2012. http://www.smithsonianmag.com/history/on-the-trail-of-the-warsaw-basi lisk-5691840/?no-ist.

Dieckhoff, Henry Cyril. *Mythological Beings in Gaelic Folklore*. Inverness, Scotland: Gaelic Society of Inverness, 1918.

Dinsdale, Angus. *The Man Who Filmed Nessie: Tim Dinsdale and the Enigma of Loch Ness*. Surrey, Canada: Hancock House Publishers, 2013.

Dinsdale, Tim. Letter to F. W. Holiday, April 1974.

———. *The Leviathans*. Armonk, NY: Futura Publications, 1976.

———. *The Story of the Loch Ness Monster*. London: Target, 1977.

Downes, Corinna. "Where Do We Go from Here? Is It Down to the Lake I Fear?" *Still on the Track*, September 21, 2009. http://forteanzoology.blogspot.com/2009/09/ corinna-downes-where-do-we-go-from.html.

Downes, Jonathan. *Monster of the Mere*. Woolsery, England: CFZ Press, 2002.

Downes, Jonathan, and Nigel Wright. *The Rising of the Moon*. Bangor, Northern Ireland: Xiphos Books, 2005.

Dr. Beachcombing. "Marco Polo Meets a Dragon?" *Strange History*, May 30, 2011. http://www.strangehistory.net/2011/05/30/marco-polo-meets-a-dragon/.

Drinnon, Dale A. "Storsjoodjuret in Lake Storsjon." *Frontiers of Zoology*, May 12, 2013. http://frontiersofzoology.blogspot.com/2013/05/storsjoodjuret-in-lake-storsjon.html.

Dunning, Brian. "Ollgoi-Khorkhoi: The Mongolian Death Worm." *Skeptoid*, January 3, 2013. https://skeptoid.com/episodes/4344.

Emery, David. "Alligators in the Sewers." *Live About*, July 5, 2015. https://www.live-about.com/alligators-in-the-sewers-3298849.

"Expeditions: Loch Morar." 2015. *The Centre for Fortean Zoology*. Accessed August 3, 2019. http://www.cfz.org.uk/expeditions/morag/morag.htm.

Fleming, Maureen, and Virginia King. *The Loch Ness Monster Mystery*. Hawthorn, Australia: Mimosa Publications Ltd., 1995.

Freeman, Richard. "Debbie Martyr." *Fortean Times*, April 2004.

———. *Dragons: More Than a Myth?* Woolsery, England: CFZ Press, 2005.

———. "On the Trail of the Orang Pendek, Sumatra's Mystery Ape." *The Guardian*, September 8, 2011. http://www.theguardian.com/science/blog/2011/sep/08/orang-pendek-sumatra-mystery-ape.

———. *Orang-Pendek: Sumatra's Forgotten Ape*. Woolsery, England: CFZ Press, 2011.

———. "Welsh Dragons." *The Spooky Isles*, July 25, 2014. http://www.spookyisles .com/2014/07/welsh-dragons-everything-you-need-to-know/.

"FW Holiday and the Loch Ness terror." 2015. *All about Heaven.* Accessed July 11, 2019. http://www.allaboutheaven.org/observations/8707/221/f-w-holiday-and-the-loch-ness-terror-010851.

Gaal, Arlene. *In Search of Ogopogo.* British Columbia, Canada: Hancock House Publishers, 2001.

Gaia. "What is Astral Projection?" *Gaia.com,* June 26, 2018. https://www.gaia.com/article/what-is-astral-projection.

Gerhard, Ken. *A Menagerie of Mysterious Beasts.* Woodbury, MN: Llewellyn Publications, 2016.

Gerhard, Ken, and Nick Redfern. *Monsters of Texas.* Woolsery, England: CFZ Press, 2010.

Gibbons, William J. *Mokele-Mbembe: Mystery Beast of the Congo Basin.* Greenville, OH: Coachwhip Publications, 2010.

Gordon, Seton. *A Highland Year.* London: Eyre & Spottiswoode, 1944.

Gould, Charles. *Dragons, Unicorns, and Sea Serpents.* Mineola, NY: Dover Publications, 2002.

Gould, Rupert T. *The Loch Ness Monster.* Secaucus, NJ: Citadel Press, 1976.

Green, John. *On the Track of the Sasquatch.* New York: Ballantine Books, 1973.

———. *Sasquatch: The Apes Among Us.* Victoria, BC, Canada: Cheam Publishing, 1978.

Guest, E. A. "The Other Paradigm." *Fate,* April 2005.

"Hairy Wild Man Sought in Swamp." *Oshkosh Northwestern,* April 15, 1938.

Hallowell, Michael J. *The House That Jack Built.* Stroud, England: Amberley Publishing, 2008.

Hardiman, James. *The History of the Town and County of the Town of Galway from the Earliest Period to the Present Time.* Dublin: W. Folds & Sons, 1820.

Henderson, William T. *Notes on the Folk-Lore of the Northern Counties of England and the Borders.* Lenox, MA: HardPress Publishing, 2012.

Heuvelmans, Bernard. *In the Wake of the Sea-Serpents.* New York: Hill & Wang. 1968.

———. *On the Track of Unknown Animals.* London: Routledge, 1995.

Holiday, F. W. *The Dragon and the Disc.* New York: W.W. Norton, 1973.

———. "Exorcism and UFO Landing at Loch Ness." *Flying Saucer Review,* September-October 1973.

———. *The Great Orm of Loch Ness.* New York W.W. Norton, 1969.

Holiday, Ted. *The Goblin Universe.* Woodbury, MN: Llewelyn Publications, 1986.

"Humboldt County, Trinidad, California Sasquatches Swimming Offshore." *Bigfoot Encounters,* winter 2007. http://www.bigfootencounters.com/stories/trinidadCA07.htm.

Johnson, Ben. 2015. "The Kelpie." *Historic UK.* Accessed February 13, 2019. http://www.historic-uk.com/CultureUK/The-Kelpie/.

———. "The Mermaids of the Peak District." *Historic UK.* Accessed February 13, 2019. http://www.historic-uk.com/CultureUK/The-Mermaids-of-the-Peak-District/.

Johnstone, Christian Isobel. *Clan-Albin: A National Tale. Volume I.* Edinburgh, Scotland: John Moir, 1815.

Jones, Josh. "Aleister Crowley: *The Wickedest Man in the World* Documents the Life of the Bizarre Occultist, Poet & Mountaineer." *Open Culture*, March 20, 2014. http://www.openculture.com/2014/03/aleister-crowley-the-wickedest-man-in-the-world.html.

Justice, Aaron. "Megalania Prisca: Dragon of the Australian Outback." *The Cryptozoologist*, May 31, 2012. http://thecryptozoologist.webs.com/apps/blog/show/15615981-megalania-prisca-dragon-of-the-a0ustralian-outback.

Keating, Kevin. "Did Navy Use Fish Story as Cloak? Pend Oreille Paddler Said to Be Subs." *The Spokesman-Review*, November 15, 1996. http://m.spokesman.com/stories/1996/nov/15/did-navy-use-fish-story-as-cloak-pend-oreille/.

Kirk, John. *In the Domain of Lake Monsters*. Toronto, Canada: Key Porter Books, 1998.

Krystek, Lee. "The Monstrous Sea Serpent of Gloucester." *The Museum of Unnatural History*. Accessed June 20, 2019. http://www.unmuseum.org/glserpent.htm.

Lee, Henry. *Sea Monsters Unmasked*. London: Forgotten Books, 2017.

Lewis, Chad, and Noah Voss. *Pepie: The Lake Monster of the Mississippi River*. Eau Claire, WI: On the Road Publications, 2014.

"Loch Morar Monster Morag Sightings Uncovered." *BBC.com*, February 25, 2013. http://www.bbc.com/news/uk-scotland-highlands-islands-21574832.

"London Underground Ghosts—British Museum Station." *Ghost-Story.co.uk*. Accessed August 2, 2019. http://www.ghost-story.co.uk/stories/londonundergoundghostsbritishmuseumstation.html.

Lowe, Keith, *Tunnel Vision*. London: MTV Books, 2001.

Macinlay, James M. *Folklore of Scottish Lochs and Springs*. Whitefish, MT: Kessinger Publishing, 2004.

Mackal, Roy P. *A Living Dinosaur?: In Search of Mokele-Mbembe*. Boston, MA: Brill Academic. 1987.

———. *The Monsters of Loch Ness*. Chicago, IL: Swallow Press, 1980.

Maestri, Nicoletta. "Quetzalcoatl—Pan-Mesoamerican Deity." *ThoughtCo.com*, April 3, 2019. https://www.thoughtco.com/quetzalcoatl-feathered-serpent-god-169342.

Marsden, William. *The History of Sumatra*. London: Thomas Payne & Son, 1874.

McGrath, Andy. "Bownessie; Dragon of the North." *The National Cryptid Society*, April 6, 2018. https://nationalcryptidsociety.org/2018/04/06/bownessie-dragon-of-the-north/.

Meredith, Dennis L. *Search at Loch Ness*. New York: Quadrangle, 1977.

Merrill, Randy. "Mapinguari: Legendary Man-Eating Cryptid of the Amazon Rainforest." *The Demon Hunter's Compenium*, June 29, 2013. http://demonhunterscompendium.blogspot.com/2013/06/mapinguari-legendary-man-eating-cryptid.html.

Michaels, Denver. "The Oklahoma Octopus." *DenverMichaels.net* (blog), May 2, 2018. https://www.denvermichaels.net/the-oklahoma-octopus/.

"Monstrous Mystery in the Lake District as Bownessie Makes a Splash." *Yorkshire Post*, September 6, 2009. https://www.yorkshirepost.co.uk/news/analysis/monstrous-mystery-in-the-lake-district-as-bownessie-makes-a-splash-1-2298225.

Moore, Jim. 2014. "Alister Hardy's Original 'Aquatic Ape Theory.'" *Aquaticape.org*. Accessed June 28, 2019. http://www.aquaticape.org/hardy.html.

———. "The Wyvern of Wonderland." *Hypnogoria*, February 27, 2015. http://hypno goria.blogspot.com/2015/02/folklore-on-friday-wyvern-of-wonderland.html.

Muralikrishna, Iyyanki V., and Valli Manickam. 2017. "Environmental Pollution. *Science Direct*. Accessed May 14, 2019. https://www.sciencedirect.com/topics/earth-and-planetary-sciences/environmental-pollution.

"Mysterious Jungle Races of Sumatra." *Singapore Free Press and Mercantile Advertiser*, July 19, 1932.

Naish, Darren. "The Loch Ness Monster Seen on Land." *Science Blogs*, October 2, 2009. http://scienceblogs.com/tetrapodzoology/2009/10/02/loch-ness-monster-on-land/.

———. "Photos of the Loch Ness Monster, Revisited." *Scientific American*, July 10, 2013. http://blogs.scientificamerican.com/tetrapod-zoology/photos-of-the-loch-ness-monster-revisited/.

———. "The Soay Island Sea Monster of 1959." *Scientific American*, March 16, 2017. https://blogs.scientificamerican.com/tetrapod-zoology/the-soay-island-sea-mon ster-of-1959/.

Napier, John. *Bigfoot: The Yeti and Sasquatch in Myth and Reality*. New York: E. P. Dutton, 1973.

National Ocean Service. 2019. "Are Mermaids Real?" *National Ocean Service*. Accessed February 20, 2019. https://oceanservice.noaa.gov/facts/mermaids.html.

National Ocean Service. "What Is the Bloop?" *National Ocean Service*. Accessed February 20, 2019. https://oceanservice.noaa.gov/facts/bloop.html.

National Oceanic and Atmospheric Administration. "Icequakes (Bloop)." *PMEL Acoustics Program*. Accessed March 11, 2019. https://www.pmel.noaa.gov/acoustics/sounds/bloop.html.

Nicholson, Andrew. "In Search of Australia's Monster Reptiles." *Weird Australia*, March 16, 2014. https://weirdaustralia.com/2014/03/16/in-search-of-australias-monster-reptiles/.

Nielson, Larry. "The Legend of Pepie." *Pepie.net*. Accessed June 3, 2019. http://pepie.net/.

NOAA Fisheries. "African Coelacanth." *NOAA Fisheries*. Accessed October 4, 2019. https://www.fisheries.noaa.gov/species/african-coelacanth.

Omand, Donald. *Experiences of a Present Day Exorcist*. London: William Kimber, 1970.

"Operation Deepscan." *Legend of Nessie*. Accessed September 21, 2019. http://www.nessie.co.uk/htm/searching_for_nessie/deepscan.html.

Parkinson, Daniel. "The Linton Worm." *Mysterious Britain*. Accessed March 15, 2019. http://www.mysteriousbritain.co.uk/scotland/roxburghshire/legends/the-linton-worm.html.

Plambeck, Steve. "A Beast with Two Backs—The Gray Photo Deconstructed." *The Loch Ness Giant Salamander*, August 28, 2012. http://thelochnessgiantsalaman der.blogspot.com/2012/08/a-beast-with-two-backs-gray-photo.html.

Quinn, Owen. "Paranormal Ponderings: Australian Giant Lizards." *Following the Nerd*, May 11, 2013. http://www.followingthenerd.com/ftn_news/paranormal-ponder ings-australian-giant-lizards/.

Radford, Benjamin. "Mokele-Mbembe: The Search for a Living Dinosaur." *Live Science*, August 13, 2013. http://www.livescience.com/38871-mokele-mbembe.html.

Radford, Benjamin. "Mongolian Death Worm: Elusive Legend of the Gobi Desert." *Live Science*, June 21, 2014. https://www.livescience.com/46450-mongolian-death-worm.html.

Ranelagh, John. *The Agency: The Rise and Decline of the CIA.* New York: Simon & Schuster, 1986.

Redfern, Nick. "A 30th Anniversary of Monstrous Terror." *Mysterious Universe*, December 3, 2018. https://mysteriousuniverse.org/2018/12/a-30th-anniversary-of-monstrous-terror/.

————. *The Bigfoot Book: The Encyclopedia of Sasquatch, Yeti, and Cryptid Primates.* Detroit, MI: Visible Ink Press, 2015.

————. "The Camel-Horse of Loch Ness." *Mysterious Universe*, June 16, 2015. http://mysteriousuniverse.org/2015/06/the-camel-horse-of-loch-ness/.

————. "The Great Eel of Birmingham." *There's Something in the Woods*, April 18, 2008. http://monsterusa.blogspot.com/2008/04/great-eel-of-birmingham.html.

————. Interview with Jonathan Downes, June 2, 2005.

————. Interview with Jonathan Downes, March 26, 2012.

————. Interview with Ken Gerhard, July 14, 2014.

————. Interview with Ronan Coghlan, March 18, 2012.

————. Interview with Timothy Green Beckley, September 21, 2010.

————. *Man-Monkey: In Search of the British Bigfoot.* Woolsery, England: CFZ Press, 2007.

————. "More on Teggie: The Bala Lake Monster(s)." *Mysterious Universe*, September 6, 2016. https://mysteriousuniverse.org/2017/09/more-on-teggie-the-bala-lake-monsters/.

————. "Sea Serpents & Heuvelmans: Author Interviewed." *There's Something in the Woods*, May 27, 2008. https://monsterusa.blogspot.com/2008/05/sea-serpents-heuvelmans-author.html.

————. "Teggie, the Terror of the Lake." *There's Something in the Woods*, April 22, 2015. https://mysteriousuniverse.org/2015/04/teggie-the-terror-of-the-lake/.

Rife, Philip. *Bigfoot Across America.* Bloomington, IN: iUniverse, 2000.

Roberts, Paul Dale. "In Search of Quetzalcoatl." *Unexplained-Mysteries.com*, February 26, 2009. http://www.unexplained-mysteries.com/column.php?id=147918.

Ronanus, Ego. "One Eyed Monster." *The Cenre for Fortean Zoology*, June 9, 2014. http://cfz-usa.blogspot.com/2014/06/one-eyed-monster.html.

Sanidopoulos, John. "Saint Columba and the Loch Ness Monster." *Mystagogy*, November 12, 2010. http://www.johnsanidopoulos.com/2010/11/saint-columba-and-loch-ness-monster.html.

Saxby, Jessie Margaret Edmonston. *Shetland Traditional Lore.* New York: Scribner, 1890.

Shiels, Tony "Doc." *Monstrum, A Wizard's Tale.* Woolsery, England: CFZ Press, 2011.

Shuker, Karl P. N. "Does the Loch Ness Monster Have a Split Personality? Revealing Nessie's Strangest Identities." *Karl Shuker* (blog), July 16, 2013. http://karlshuker.blogspot.com/2013/07/does-loch-ness-monster-have-split.html.

———. *Dragons in Zoology, Cryptozoology, and Culture*. Greenville, OH: Coachwhip Publications, 2013.

———. "A Giant Dog-Fanged Mystery Frog from the Congo." *Karl Shuker* (blog), September 11, 2015. http://karlshuker.blogspot.com/2015/09/a-giant-dog-fanged-mystery-frog-from.html.

———. *Mirabilis: A Carnival of Cryptozoology and Unnatural History*. San Antonio, TX: Anomalist Books, 2013.

———. "Wulvers and Wolfen and Werewolves, Oh My!—Tales of the Uninvited." *Karl Shuker* (blog), July 28, 2012. http://karlshuker.blogspot.com/2012/07/wulvers-and-wolfen-and-werewolves-oh-my.html.

Simpson, Jacqueline. *British Dragons*. London: B. T. Batsford, 1980.

Smithsonian Ocean. 2019 "Giant Squid." *Smithsonian Ocean*. Accessed March 15, 2019. https://ocean.si.edu/ocean-life/invertebrates/giant-squid.

Speed, Barbara. "Yes, They Really Have Found Alligators in the New York Sewer System." *CityMetric*, August 12, 2014. http://www.citymetric.com/yes-they-really-have-found-alligators-new-york-sewer-system-102.

Steadman, Ian. "The Bloop Mystery Has Been Solved: It Was Never a Giant Sea Monster." *Wired*, November 29, 2012. http://www.wired.co.uk/news/archive/2012-11/29/bloop-mystery-not-solved-sort-of.

Steiger, Brad. *Real Monsters, Gruesome Critters, and Beasts from the Darkside*. Detroit, MI: Visible Ink Press, 2011.

Stevens, Hayley. "Revisiting Bownessie." *Hayley Is a Ghost*, June 18, 2011. https://hayleyisaghost.co.uk/revisiting-bownessie/.

Stewart, W. Grant. *The Popular Superstitions and Festive Amusements of the Highlanders of Scotland*. London: Aylott & Jones, 1851.

"Stokes Alligator, Alabama—the largest alligator ever recorded." *Our Planet*. Accessed October 5, 2019. https://ourplnt.com/largest-alligator-ever-measured/largest-alligator-2014-stokes-alligator-alabama-river/#axzz67p7zefQV.

"A Strange Fish in Loch Ness." *Inverness Courier*, October 8, 1868.

Strickler, Lon. "The Thetis Lake Monster Legend." *Phantoms & Monsters*, February 6, 2010. http://www.phantomsandmonsters.com/2010/02/thetis-lake-monster-legend.html.

Swancer, Brent. "Carnivorous Cryptid Plants of the World." *Mysterious Universe*, May 13, 2014. http://mysteriousuniverse.org/2014/05/carnivorous-cryptid-plants-of-the-world/.

"Swimming Bigfoot 1948, Upper Crater Lake, Wyoming: Bigfoot Sunning on Phantom Ship Island." *Today in Bigfoot History*, December 1, 2014. https://bigfoothistory.wordpress.com/tag/swimming-bigfoot/.

Thomson, David. *The People of the Sea*. Edinburgh, Scotland: Canongate Classic, 1996.

Thorner, W. E. "The Torness Trows—An Eyewitness Account." *OrkneyJar*. Accessed September 23, 2019. http://www.orkneyjar.com/folklore/trows/hoytrow.htm.

"Tiamat: Lady of Primeval Chaos, the Great Mother of the Gods of Babylon." *Gateway to Babylon*. Accessed April 28, 2019. http://www.gatewaystobabylon.com/gods/ladies/ladytiamat.html.

Tonnies, Mac. *The Cryptoterrestials*. San Antonio, TX: Anomalist Books, 2010.

Treat, Wesley, Heather Shade, and Rob Riggs. *Weird Texas*. New York: Sterling Publishing Co., 2005.

"A True Account of Alien Abduction." *UFO Casebook*. Accessed February 17, 2019. http://www.ufocasebook.com/trueaccountofalienabduction.html.

Tyson, Donald. *The Dream World of H.P. Lovecraft*. Woodbury, MN: Llewellyn Publications, 2010.

U. S. Geological Survey. "Malformed Frogs in Minnesota: An Update." *U.S. Geological Survey*, May 2001. http://pubs.usgs.gov/fs/fs-043-01/.

"Uncanny Happenings at Manor of Boleskine." *Empire News*, November 12, 1933.

Warms, John. *Strange Creatures Seldom Seen*. Greenville, OH: Coachwhip Publications, 2015.

Watson, Roland. "New Theory on the Hugh Gray Photograph." *Loch Ness Monster* (blog), September 5, 2012. http://lochnessmystery.blogspot.com/2012/09/new-theory-on-hugh-gray-photograph.html.

———. "The Hugh Gray Photograph Revisited." *Loch Ness Monster* (blog), June 26, 2011. http://lochnessmystery.blogspot.com/2011/06/hugh-gray-photograph-revisited_26.html.

———. "Tim Dinsdale, Nessie and the Paranormal." *Loch Ness Monster* (blog), September 18, 2012. http://lochnessmystery.blogspot.com/2012/09/tim-dinsdale-nessie-and-paranormal.html.

———. *The Water Horses of Loch Ness*. Roland H. Watson, 2011.

Wayman, Erin. "Did Bigfoot Really Exist? How Gigantopithecus Became Exitinct." *Smithsonian Magazine*, January 9, 2012. http://www.smithsonianmag.com/science-nature/did-bigfoot-really-exist-how-gigantopithecus-became-extinct-16649201/.

"The Web of Fear." *BBC*. Accessed May 28, 2019. http://www.bbc.co.uk/doctorwho/classic/episodeguide/weboffear/.

Weeks, Linton. "The Elegant Secrets of Flying Snakes." *NPR*, March 7, 2014. http://www.npr.org/sections/theprotojournalist/2014/03/07/286833436/the-elegant-secrets-of-flying-snakes.

"What Does a Bunyip Look Like?" *Centre for Fortean Zoology Australia*, April 2, 2012. http://www.cfzaustralia.com/2012/04/what-does-bunyip-look-like.html.

Whyte, Constance. *More Than a Legend, The Story of the Loch Ness Monster*. London: Hamish Hamilton, 1961.

Witchell, Nicholas. *The Loch Ness Story*. London: Corgi Books, 1982.

Zarzynski, Joseph W. *Monster Wrecks of Loch Ness and Lake Champlain*. Wilton, NY: M-Z Information, 1986.

INDEX

Note: (ill.) indicates photos and illustrations.

Molde, Norway, 181, 182
Mongolia monsters, 291–92
Moon, Mary, 92
Moore, Raymond C., 330
Morag, 71, 81–83
Morgan, John, 156
Morgawr, 67–68, 147
Morwood, Mike, 297
Moses, 233
Mowgli, 300 (ill.), 300–301
M'Quhae, Peter, 14–17
Mullins, Chris, 126, 135
Munn, A., 28
Munro, Mr., 250–51
Murray, Alexander, 35

N

Naga, 172, 331
Naish, Darren, 137–38
Nant Gwynant, Snowdonia, Gwynedd, North Wales, 281 (ill.), 282–84
Narrabeen, Australia, 162
National Ocean Service (NOS), 42
National Oceanic and Atmospheric Administration (NOAA), 42–43, 255–56
Neakok, Nathaniel, 121–22
Nessies. *See* Loch Ness monsters (Nessies)
Nevill, Hugh, 281
New Mexico monsters, 114–16, 313–14
New York monsters, 87–89, 88 (ill.), 89 (ill.), 213–14, 215 (ill.)
Newfoundland monsters, 28–30, 29 (ill.), 34–35
Newport, England, 275
Nganaoa, 32
Nicholson, Andrew, 161
Nicholson, Edward, 110
"Night Gaunts," 39–40
Nile River, 151
Nittaewos, 281–82
Noblett, Mr., 338

Nooksack River, Washington, 270
North Carolina monsters, 167–68
northern pike, 141–44, 142 (ill.)
Norway monsters, 12–14, 23–24, 27, 78, 174–76, 180, 181, 181 (ill.)
Nova Scotia monsters, 12
nsanga, 103
Nugent, Rory, 104
Nyalmo, 279

O

ocean creatures
    Cthulhu, 37–45, 41 (ill.), 43 (ill.)
    giant squid, 27–35, 29 (ill.), 31 (ill.), 33 (ill.)
    Kraken, 20–27, 21 (ill.), 25 (ill.)
    nineteenth-century sea serpents, 1–35, 3 (ill.), 5 (ill.), 11 (ill.), 13 (ill.), 15 (ill.), 18 (ill.)
    octopus attacks, 35–37, 36 (ill.)
O'Connell, Thomas, 86
O'Connor, Thomas, 30
octopus attacks, 35–37, 36 (ill.)
O'Donnell, Elliott, 260, 274–75
O'Faodhagain, Eoin, 70–71
O'Flaherty, Roderic, 215–16
Ogopogo, 92–94, 93 (ill.)
Ohio monsters, 258–59
Okanagan Lake, British Columbia, 92–94
Oklahoma monsters, 44–45
Ollavitinus, 255
Olsen, G. A., 90
Olsson, Martin, 176
O'Malley, Irwin J., 169–70
Omand, Donald, 76–80
One Eye, 208–9
Operation Deepscan, 65
Orang Pendek, 297 (ill.), 297–99

Oregon monsters, 36, 90–91, 122–23, 270, 287–89
Orford Ness, England, 266–68
Orkney Islands, 252 (ill.), 253–55
Orland Park, Illinois, 257–58
Örvar-Oddr, 20–21, 21 (ill.)
Osman Hill, William Charles, 297
Ostersund, Sweden, 176
Oudemans, Antoon Cornelis, 328
Owen, Richard, 16–17, 158, 159
Owlman of Cornwall, 332

P

Pacific Marine Environmental Laboratory (PMEL), 43–44
Page, Wm., 288
Panama monsters, 209–10
Park, W. J., 96
Parker Bowles, Camilla, 316, 317
Pauline, 7–8
Paxton, Charles, 329
Pearce, Gill, 146
Peek, W. P., 201
Pepie, 94 (ill.), 94–95
Pfleng, Rudolph, 163–64
Phantom Ship Island, Oregon, 270
Philip, Prince, 315, 316
Philippines monsters, 149–50
Phillips, B. W. B., 162
Phillips, David Atlee, 211–12
Pickles, Tom, 339
Picot, Theophilus, 34
pike, northern, 141–44, 142 (ill.)
Pile, Gordon, 310
Pius IX, Pope, 231
Plambeck, Steve, 60, 192–94
Plantin, Andreas, 178
Pleasence, Donald, 220
plesiosaurs, 54–57, 55 (ill.)